Proof Theory and Logic Programming

This book develops a modern perspective on logic programming by viewing computation as proof search, whereby program execution is seen as the search for proof. It reveals how programs can be naturally and declaratively expressed as logical formulas and their execution as a systematic search for proofs within classical, intuitionistic, and linear logics. It employs sequent calculus as the essential tool for analyzing the operational reading of logic programs. It introduces and applies advanced techniques such as focused proofs to expose the underlying mechanisms of goal-directed search and backchaining. A key feature is its in-depth coverage of higher-order quantification and its implications for logic programming. Beyond theory, the book explores practical applications, including encoding security protocols, specifying operational semantics, and static analysis of Horn clauses, demonstrating the versatility and power of this proof-theoretic approach.

DALE MILLER is Director of Research at Inria Saclay-Île-de-France. He has been a professor at the University of Pennsylvania, Pennsylvania State University, and the École Polytechnique in France. He served as Editor-in-Chief of the *ACM Transactions on Computational Logic* and has received an ERC Advanced Investigators Grant, the LICS Test-of-Time Award (twice), and the Dov Gabbay Prize for Logic and Foundations. He is an ACM Fellow.

"Starting from a mathematically simple framework, Gentzen's sequent calculus, Miller's book reveals proof theory as the foundation and organizing principle for understanding a range of logics – from classical and intuitionistic logic to linear logic. From the start, Miller considers a wide range of choices that we make when formulating a logic with a particular emphasis on structural properties such as weakening and contraction. More importantly, Miller carefully reveals organizing principles such as focusing and polarization that lead us to understand proof search as computation. This book summarizes and synthesizes decades of research by one of the field's pioneers. Miller takes the reader on a rigorous, yet accessible journey starting from fundamental proof-theoretic principles to proof search and logic programming. The book is a joy to read and a valuable resource for anyone interested in the intersection of logic, computation, and language design."

– *Brigitte Pientka, McGill University*

"Miller's book represents a long-awaited authoritative source on the proof-theoretic account of logic programming. It is ideal for students, educators, and researchers seeking to understand logic programming from a principled standpoint. Miller develops this account via the theoretical lens of sequent calculus, carefully illustrating how the choice of logic and search strategy affects operational properties of computation and structural properties of proofs. The material is interleaved with examples and exercises, providing a first-of-its-kind resource for learners on subjects such as focused proof systems, linear logic programming, and higher-order logic programming. The book concludes with two case studies, showcasing how a logic programming language incorporating the book's earlier developments can be used for modeling communication protocols and operational semantics."

– *Chris Martens, Northeastern University*

Proof Theory and Logic Programming
Computation as Proof Search

DALE MILLER
Inria Saclay-Île-de-France

Shaftesbury Road, Cambridge CB2 8EA, United Kingdom

One Liberty Plaza, 20th Floor, New York, NY 10006, USA

477 Williamstown Road, Port Melbourne, VIC 3207, Australia

314–321, 3rd Floor, Plot 3, Splendor Forum, Jasola District Centre, New Delhi – 110025, India

103 Penang Road, #05–06/07, Visioncrest Commercial, Singapore 238467

Cambridge University Press is part of Cambridge University Press & Assessment, a department of the University of Cambridge.

We share the University's mission to contribute to society through the pursuit of education, learning and research at the highest international levels of excellence.

www.cambridge.org
Information on this title: www.cambridge.org/9781009561297
DOI: 10.1017/9781009561280

© Dale Miller 2026

This publication is in copyright. Subject to statutory exception and to the provisions of relevant collective licensing agreements, no reproduction of any part may take place without the written permission of Cambridge University Press & Assessment.

When citing this work, please include a reference to the DOI 10.1017/9781009561280

First published 2026

Cover image: © Nadia Miller

A catalogue record for this publication is available from the British Library

A Cataloging-in-Publication data record for this book is available from the Library of Congress

ISBN 978-1-009-56129-7 Hardback

Cambridge University Press & Assessment has no responsibility for the persistence or accuracy of URLs for external or third-party internet websites referred to in this publication and does not guarantee that any content on such websites is, or will remain, accurate or appropriate.

For EU product safety concerns, contact us at Calle de José Abascal, 56, 1°, 28003 Madrid, Spain, or email eugpsr@cambridge.org

To the memory of my mother

Contents

Preface		*page* xi
1	**Introduction**	1
1.1	A Spectrum of Logics	1
1.2	Logic and the Specification of Computations	3
1.3	Proof Search and Logic Programming	4
1.4	Designing Logic Programming Languages	5
1.5	Why Use Logic to Write Programs?	6
1.6	The Structure of This Book	7
1.7	Bibliographic Notes	7
2	**Terms, Formulas, and Sequents**	9
2.1	Untyped λ-Terms	9
2.2	Types	12
2.3	Signatures and Typed Terms	13
2.4	Formulas	14
2.5	Sequents	17
2.6	Bibliographic Notes	18
3	**Sequent Calculus Proof Rules**	20
3.1	Sequent Calculus and Proof Search	20
3.2	Inference Rules	23
3.3	Additive and Multiplicative Inference Rules	26
3.4	Sequent Calculus Proofs	29
3.5	Permutations of Inference Rules	30
3.6	Focused and Unfocused Proof Systems	31
3.7	Cut-Elimination and Its Consequences	32
3.8	Bibliographic Notes	36

4	**Classical and Intuitionistic Logics**	37
4.1	Classical and Intuitionistic Inference Rules	38
4.2	The Identity Rules and Their Elimination	44
4.3	Cut Elimination and Its Consequences	49
4.4	Derivable and Admissible Rules	53
4.5	Negation, False, and Minimal Logic	55
4.6	Choices to Consider during the Search for Proofs	57
4.7	Bibliographic Notes	59
5	**Two Abstract Logic Programming Languages**	61
5.1	Goal-Directed Proof Search	61
5.2	Horn Clauses	63
5.3	Hereditary Harrop Formulas	68
5.4	Backchaining as Focused Rule Application	72
5.5	Completeness of Focused Proofs	75
5.6	A Canonical Kripke Model	87
5.7	Synthetic Inference Rules	90
5.8	Disjunctive and Existential Goals	93
5.9	Examples of *fohc* Logic Programs	95
5.10	Dynamics of Proof Search for *fohc*	97
5.11	Examples of *fohh* Logic Programs	98
5.12	Dynamics of Proof Search for *fohh*	101
5.13	Limitations to *fohc* and *fohh* Logic Programs	101
5.14	Bibliographic Notes	104
6	**Linear Logic**	107
6.1	Reflections on the Structural Inference Rules	108
6.2	*LK* vs *LJ*: An Origin Story for Linear Logic	110
6.3	Sequent Calculus Proof Systems for Linear Logic	112
6.4	Introducing Zones into Sequents	122
6.5	Embedding *fohh* into Linear Logic	127
6.6	A Model of Resource Consumption	129
6.7	Multiple-Conclusion Uniform Proofs	133
6.8	Conservativity Results	137
6.9	Generalizing Synthetic Inference Rules	138
6.10	Bibliographic Notes	140
7	**Formal Properties of Linear Logic Focused Proofs**	143
7.1	Generalized Paths and Introduction Phases	144

7.2	Admissibility of the General Initial Rule	148
7.3	Cut Rules and Cut Elimination	149
7.4	The Focused Proof System Is Sound and Complete	160
7.5	Bibliographic Notes	169

8	**Linear Logic Programming**	**172**
8.1	Encoding Multisets as Formulas	172
8.2	A Syntax for Lolli Programs	173
8.3	Permuting a List	174
8.4	Multiset Rewriting on the Left	176
8.5	Context Management in a Theorem Prover	178
8.6	Multiset Rewriting on the Right	181
8.7	Specification of Sequent Calculus Proof Systems	182
8.8	Bibliographic Notes	185

9	**Higher-Order Quantification**	**187**
9.1	Introduction	187
9.2	Higher-Order Quantification	189
9.3	Near-Focused Proofs	191
9.4	The Proof Theory of Higher-Order Quantification	199
9.5	Examples Using Quantification of Type o	201
9.6	Higher-Order Programming	202
9.7	Proving That Reverse Is Symmetric	206
9.8	Exploiting the Hiding of Specification Details	208
9.9	Synthetic Rules and Higher-Order Logic	211
9.10	Bibliographic Notes	213

10	**Specifying Computations Using Multisets**	**216**
10.1	Numerals as Multisets	216
10.2	Letters and Words	218
10.3	Encoding Finite Automata	219
10.4	Properties about Finite Automata	223
10.5	Encoding Pushdown Automata	226
10.6	Bibliographic Notes	227

11	**Collection Analysis for Horn Clauses**	**229**
11.1	Introduction	229
11.2	The Undercurrents	230
11.3	Abstraction and Substitution in Proof Theory	231
11.4	Multiset Approximations	233

11.5	Formalizing the Method	237
11.6	Set Approximations	237
11.7	Automation of Analysis	240
11.8	List Approximations	242
11.9	Bibliographic Notes	244

12 Encoding Security Protocols — 245
12.1	Communicating Processes	245
12.2	Specifying Communication Protocols	249
12.3	Protocols as Theories in Linear Logic	254
12.4	Abstracting Internal States	256
12.5	Agents as Nested Implications	257
12.6	Bibliographic Notes	260

13 Formalizing Operational Semantics — 261
13.1	Three Frameworks for Operational Semantics	261
13.2	The Abstract Syntax of Programs-as-Terms	263
13.3	Big-Step Semantics: Call-by-Value Evaluation	265
13.4	Small-Step Semantics: π-Calculus Transitions	265
13.5	Binary Clauses	268
13.6	Linear Logic	273
13.7	Bibliographic Notes	278

Solutions to Selected Exercises — 280
References — 296
Index — 314

Preface

This book develops the proof theory of classical, intuitionistic, and linear logics, and demonstrates its application to the design and usage of logic programming languages. We establish a proof-theoretic foundation using Gentzen's sequent calculus for logic programming languages based on first-order and higher-order classical, intuitionistic, and linear logics. This approach provides the basis for the well-known languages Prolog (employing first-order Horn clauses in classical logic) and λProlog (utilizing higher-order hereditary Harrop formulas in intuitionistic logic), as well as the linear logic programming languages Lolli and Forum. As we will illustrate, these increasingly expressive logic programming languages enable the logic programming paradigm to capture essential aspects of modular programming, higher-order programming, abstract data-types, state encapsulation, and concurrency.

The book develops three primary themes.

1. **Proof search:** The sequent calculus offers a natural framework for formalizing logic programming and elucidating the operational interpretation of logic formulas as programs through their impact on the construction of proofs. A two-stage proof construction method, based on *goal-reduction* and *backchaining*, will be formalized using the concepts of *uniform proofs* and *focused proofs*.
2. **Proof theory:** We present sequent calculus proof systems for classical, intuitionistic, and linear logics, which include first-order and higher-order quantification. The completeness of *focused proofs* is established by providing a direct proof of a cut-elimination theorem for these proofs.
3. **Logic programming:** The book offers numerous examples of logic programs that leverage higher-order quantification and linear logic. We will

demonstrate how the theory of focused proofs can be employed to directly reason about such programs.

This book assumes a basic understanding of the syntactic properties of first-order logic and the (simply typed) λ-calculus as a prerequisite. While prior experience with formal proof representations (such as natural deduction and sequent calculus) is not required, it would be beneficial. We will occasionally include examples of logic programs, presented using the syntactic conventions of λProlog, to illustrate proof-theoretic concepts. Although familiarity with Prolog or λProlog may aid in understanding these examples, readers without such prior knowledge should still be able to follow them, as λProlog program elements correspond directly to formulas within the logics being discussed.

The first part of this book, concluding with Chapter 9, details how the sequent calculus can both design and analyze logic programming languages based on classical, intuitionistic, and linear logics. Readers primarily interested in the design and application aspects of logic programming can safely bypass Section 5.5 and Chapter 7, which present the formal proofs of the key properties of focused proofs. The second part of the book, starting with Chapter 10, explores various applications of logic programming. The chapters within this second part are independent of each other, allowing readers unfamiliar with the application area covered in one chapter to skip it without affecting their comprehension of the other chapters.

Many chapters include exercises designed to clarify and expand upon the ideas presented in the main text. Exercises marked with (‡) have partial or complete solutions provided at the end of this book.

Given the expansive nature of *computational logic* and *logic programming*, it is important to highlight certain topics that are not covered in this book. One such topic is the Curry–Howard correspondence (the "proofs-as-programs" paradigm). Relating computation to proof search offers an entirely different dimension to the role of logic and proof in computation offered by the Curry–Howard correspondence. Readers interested in this correspondence and its role as a foundation for functional programming may still find much of the underlying proof theory presented here relevant, especially in its extensions to linear logic. Furthermore, the logic programming paradigm discussed here can specify type checking, type inference, and the operational semantics of functional programs. Other currently popular themes in the logic programming community, such as *negation-as-failure*, *answer-set programming*, *stable models*, and *constraint programming*, are also not explored in this text.

Preface

This book is a synthesis of decades of research conducted by the author, his collaborators, and many others. Earlier versions of parts of this book have been used in graduate-level (M2) courses in Paris, Copenhagen, Venice, Bertinoro, and Pisa. I extend my gratitude to the many students who engaged with this material, as well as to Arunava Gantait, Gopalan Nadathur, and Aarrya Saraf for their valuable feedback on earlier drafts. I also thank my daughter, Nadia Miller, for her cover artwork.

Chapter 1

Introduction

There are many ways to define computation and to reason about it. Pioneering work by Church, Turing, Gödel, Curry, and others demonstrated that several formal specifications, such as the λ-calculus, Turing machines, and recursive equations, all describe the same set of computable functions. Similarly, numerous programming languages (e.g., LISP, C, Pascal, and Ada) have been invented, all theoretically capable of implementing this set of functions.

Given logic's foundational role in mathematics and philosophy, it is intriguing to consider adding a computing framework that uses logical expressions as programs to this rich landscape. The logic programming paradigm emerges from directly addressing questions like: How can logic be used directly as a programming language? What level of expressiveness can such languages achieve? What advantages arise from basing program syntax and semantics on established logical techniques and concepts?

We will delve deeper into these questions in Chapter 2. Before exploring how various logics can serve as a foundation for logic-based programming, the remainder of this introduction will organize some of these logics and their associated proof concepts into the framework used throughout this book.

1.1 A Spectrum of Logics

The syntax for terms and formulas will be given in Chapter 2 using the framework provided by Church [1940] in his Simple Theory of Types: In particular, both terms *and* formulas are simply typed λ-terms, and the equality of terms and formulas is identified with the equality of such λ-terms (i.e., by the equations of α, β, and η conversion). Terms that have a particular primitive type – the Greek letter omicron o (following Church [1940]) – are classified as formulas. The symbols ∧, ∨, and ⊃ are written in infix to denote conjunction, disjunction, and implication. Negation is written as the prefix operator ¬.

In this book, logics are classified along two principal axes. The first axis involves the universal ∀ and existential ∃ quantifiers. A logic without quantifiers is a *propositional logic*. A logic with quantifiers is a *quantificational logic*. Quantifiers in this book will bind *typed variables* (again following Church [1940]). A logic in which the type of a quantified variable is limited to primitive and non-propositional types is *first-order*. A *higher-order* logic allows quantification at all types, including propositional and functional types.

The second axis consists of the following three logics.

1. *Classical logic* is a logic of truth values. For example, propositional formulas are either true or false depending on the truth value of the propositional variables it contains. Such a truth value can be computed using truth tables. For example, the formulas $p \vee \neg p$ and $((p \supset q) \supset p) \supset p$ are true no matter what truth value is given to p and q.
2. *Intuitionistic logic* can be seen as a logic based on a constructive approach to proof. For example, a proof that the formula $\exists x.B(x)$ is a theorem must contain a specific term, say t, and a proof that $B(t)$ is a theorem. Similarly, a proof that $B_1 \vee B_2$ is a theorem contains a specific value of $i \in \{1, 2\}$ and a proof of B_i. For this reason, the formula $p \vee \neg p$ may not be a theorem since, without more information about p, we might not be able to provide a proof of either p or $\neg p$. If p is a statement such as $3 = 4$, then we can prove $p \vee \neg p$ since we can presumably prove $\neg (3 = 4)$. However, if we know nothing about p, we cannot prove either of these disjuncts.
3. *Linear logic*, introduced by Girard [1987], can be seen as a logic of resources. For example, having one occurrence of p can be different from having two occurrences, as in $p \wedge p$. As such, it is possible to model vending machines (e.g., two 50-cent coins yield one coffee), Petri nets, and process calculi.

Gentzen [1935] introduced the *sequent calculus* as a technical device to represent proofs in both classical and intuitionistic logics. The sequent calculus also provides an ideal setting for describing proofs for linear logic. As a result, we adopt the sequent calculus here and stress the modular and straightforward way it can be used to describe provability in these three logics. Our approach here does not attempt to merge classical, intuitionistic, and linear logics into one logic: Instead, we view these logics as having different but closely related proof systems. In fact, the proof systems will be so closely related that results in one of these logics can often be lifted with slight modifications to provide results in another logic.

1.2 Logic and the Specification of Computations

Logic can be applied to the specification of computation in a few ways. We give an overview of these roles for logic to identify the particular niche that is our focus in this book.

In the specification of computation, logic is generally used in one of two approaches. In the *computation-as-model* approach, computations are encoded as mathematical structures containing such items as nodes, transitions, and states. Logic is used externally to make statements *about* those structures. That is, computations are used as models for logical formulas. Intensional operators, such as the triples of Hoare logic or the modals of temporal and dynamic logics, are often employed to express propositions about state changes. This use of logic to represent and reason about computation is the most broadly successful use of logic specifications with computation.

The *computation-as-deduction* approach uses pieces of logic's syntax (such as formulas, terms, types, and proofs) as elements of the specified computation. In this more rarefied setting, there are two different approaches to how computation is modeled.

The *proof-normalization* approach views the state of a computation as a proof term and the process of computing as normalization (known variously as β-reduction or cut-elimination). Functional programming can be explained using proof-normalization as its theoretical basis (following Martin-Löf [1982], for example). Proof normalization has been used to justify the design of new functional programming languages: See, for example, Abramsky [1993].

The *proof-search* approach views the state of a computation as a sequent (a structured collection of formulas) and the process of computing as the process of searching for a proof of a sequent: The changes that take place in sequents capture the dynamics of computation. This perspective on computation is the subject of this book.

Both of these programming paradigms based on deduction must accommodate nondeterminism in their computational mechanisms. When functional programming languages are designed based on proof normalization, explicit control of the order in which redexes are rewritten is usually described using either the *call-by-value* or *call-by-name* evaluation order. When logic programming languages, such as Prolog and λProlog, are designed based on proof search, elements of nondeterminism are often removed by imposing depth-first search and backtracking.

The separation of proof normalization from proof search given above is informal and suggestive. Such a division helps point out different sets of concerns represented by these two broad approaches. For example, proof normalization focuses on describing rewritings and their confluence, while proof search focuses on the nondeterminism and the reverse reading of inference rules. New advances in computational logic and proof theory might allow us to merge or reorganize this classification.

1.3 Proof Search and Logic Programming

The earliest theoretical framework for logic programming was not an analysis of proof but rather of resolution *refutation* (see, for example, Robinson [1965]) and, in particular, SLD resolution. This choice of foundations for logic programming was unfortunate for at least the following reasons.

1. Resolution is used to *refute*: That is, it attempts to derive a contradiction. This choice is counterintuitive since logic programming seems to be about *proving* a goal formula from a collection of other formulas (the logic program).
2. Most refutation systems work with formulas that are in conjunctive normal form and Skolem normal form. Unfortunately, classical logic is the only logic we wish to study for which restricting to such normal forms is possible. Furthermore, these normal forms are not preserved when higher-order predicate variables are substituted with expressions containing quantifiers and connectives.
3. A key inference step in resolution is the computation of *most general unifiers*. In many ways, unification is really an *implementation* of the interplay between quantification and equality. It seems more natural to understand that interplay before attempting to implement it. In this book, the implementation technique of unification plays no central role.

It is thus appealing to find a different approach to describing logic programming that is cast in terms of proving and in which normal forms and unification are not required. The sequent calculus provides just such a setting. Furthermore, removing unification from the abstract notion of proof search has a couple of benefits. First, it allows interplay between universal and existential quantifiers to be explored without forcing the use of *Skolem functions*. Second, using *most general unifiers* within resolution means that it cannot handle those situations where most general unifiers do not exist (which can happen when attempting to unify simply typed λ-terms).

1.4 Designing Logic Programming Languages

An early concern in the development of Prolog focused on how best to control search within a Prolog interpreter. For example, Kowalski [1979] proposed the equation

$$\text{Algorithm} = \text{Logic} + \text{Control},$$

which makes the important point that there is a gap between logic (here, first-order Horn clause specifications) and algorithms. For example, the naive Horn clause specification of the Fibonacci series can yield both an exponential-time algorithm and a linear time algorithm depending on whether a top-down (goal-directed) or a bottom-up (program-directed) proof search is employed. Clearly, the programmer must be able to have some control over which of these algorithms ultimately arises from this single logic specification. Various non-logical features have also been added to Prolog – such as the cut ! and negation-as-failure – to allow for some explicit control of search.[1]

Given that the logical foundation of Prolog is rather weak (see the discussion in Section 5.12), the design of new logic programming languages has made several additional extensions to logic, yielding an equation more like the following.

$$\begin{aligned}
\text{Programming} = \text{Logic} &+ \text{Control} + \text{Input/Output} \\
&+ \text{Higher-order programming} \\
&+ \text{Data abstractions} \\
&+ \text{Modules} \\
&+ \text{Concurrency} + \ldots.
\end{aligned}$$

---

[1] We shall make no further mention of Prolog's cut (!) operator in this book: In fact, both the name "cut" and the "!" symbol will have entirely different meanings here.

Such extensions are generally made in an *ad hoc* fashion, and logic, which was the motivation and the intriguing starting point for a language like Prolog, was moved from center stage. With such an approach to designing a programming language, the features added to address, say, higher-order programming can interact in complex ways with features added to address, say, modules. Describing such interaction of features can greatly complicate a programming language's design, implementation, and semantic specification.

An interesting project to pursue is to see how one might satisfy the equation

$$\text{Programming} = \text{Logic}.$$

If this equation is at all possible, then one will probably need to rethink what is meant by "Programming" and by "Logic." In this book, "Programming" will generally be understood as high-level specifications of computations: Building efficient and low-level programs will not be addressed. This book also explores reinterpreting "Logic" by moving from first-order classical logic and Horn clauses to intuitionistic and linear logics, possibly employing higher-order quantification. Goal-directed control will be built into the proof systems we ultimately employ. Chapters 10 through 13 provide several extended examples in which specifying computation exploits these richer logics.

1.5 Why Use Logic to Write Programs?

Several benefits arise from writing programs as logic formulas and viewing computation as the construction of proofs. We list several here.

1. Logical formulas have various operations that generally satisfy valuable properties. For example, applying substitutions to formulas or replacing a subformula with an equivalence subformula is logically meaningful; we can also expect such operations to yield meaning-preserving transformations on programs.
2. There are generally multiple ways to describe central concepts in logic. For example, the set of theorems can usually be described as both the set of all provable formulas and all true formulas (based on some suitable model theory). Also, provability might be characterized in strikingly different ways: via, for example, sequent calculus proofs, natural deduction, resolution refutations, and tableaux. Thus, different execution models for logic programs might be deployed while preserving the original meaning of programs.

3. Proof theory generally comes with various kinds of abstractions, and a suitably designed logic programming language can harness these. For example, higher-order intuitionistic logic can provide logic programs with abstract data types, as well as modular and higher-order programming. Furthermore, one such abstraction will not have undefined interactions with other abstractions.
4. The logics we consider here have universally accepted descriptions. Thus, logic programs can be meaningful many years in the future even if no particular compiler or interpreter used to execute them today is available in that future time.

Such benefits from using logic as a programming language are striking and worthy of additional exploration.

1.6 The Structure of This Book

This book is divided into two parts.

The first part, comprising Chapters 1–9, presents the proof-theoretic foundations and designs of various logic programming languages based on classical, intuitionistic, and linear logics over first-order and higher-order quantification. Ultimately, all our logic programming languages (including first-order Horn clauses and higher-order hereditary Harrop formulas) will be seen as sitting inside higher-order linear logic. The chapters in this part build on previous chapters. These chapters should be read in the order presented. On first reading, one might skip the proofs of various metatheory results (such as are found in Section 5.5 and Chapter 7).

The second part, Chapters 10–13, offers applications of the logic programming languages described in the first part. These chapters can be read in any order since they do not significantly build on each other.

1.7 Bibliographic Notes

The *Stanford Encyclopedia of Philosophy* has good overview articles on proof theory by Rathjen and Sieg [2020], the development of proof theory by von Plato [2018], intuitionistic logic by Moschovakis [2024], linear logic by Di Cosmo and Miller [2019], and Church's Simple Theory of Types by Benzmüller and Andrews [2019].

For more about the use of resolution and SLD resolution to describe logic programming based on Horn clauses in first-order classical logic, see the early papers by Apt and Emden [1982] and Emden and Kowalski [1976], as well as textbooks by Gallier [1986] and Lloyd [1987]. The author has written about the influences that logic programming and proof theory have had on each other in Miller [2021] as well as a survey in Miller [2022b] of some of the uses of proof theory as a foundation for logic programming.

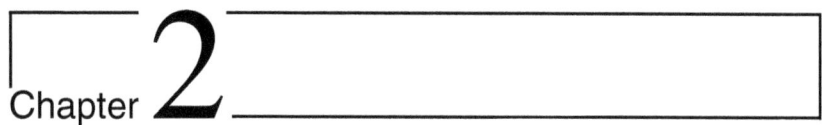
Chapter 2

Terms, Formulas, and Sequents

This book covers topics in both first-order and higher-order logic. Only first-order quantification is used in Chapters 3 through 8, although higher-order quantification will be used in most of the remaining chapters. This chapter provides the basic syntactic definitions and operations for higher-order quantification and higher-order substitutions: The first-order variants of quantification and substitution can be seen as a natural restriction on the general setting.

In his seminal paper, Church [1940] introduced the *Simple Theory of Types*. This higher-order version of classical logic relies on the simply typed λ-calculus for its syntactic structure. Since Church's goal was to establish a logical foundation for mathematics, he incorporated the mathematically motivated axioms of choice, extensionality, and infinity into his system. Removing these axioms yields the *Elementary Theory of Types*, a term introduced in Andrews [1974]. We will use this latter system as the template to formulate first- and higher-order quantification within classical, intuitionistic, and linear logics.

2.1 Untyped λ-Terms

Throughout this book, we will primarily use simply typed λ-terms. However, we will briefly consider the untyped λ-calculus first, as it shares the same equality theory with simply typed terms.

We begin by assuming that there is a fixed and denumerably infinite set of *tokens* (or identifiers). This section will use "token" and "variable"

9

interchangeably. Later, when we discuss different ways to declare types and binding scopes for tokens, we will distinguish between tokens used as variables and those used as constants.

There are three ways to build λ-terms:

1. As mentioned above, tokens, acting as variables, are λ-terms.
2. Given two terms, say M and N, their *application* is (MN). Application is the infix juxtaposition operation and it associates to the left.
3. Given a term M and a token x, the *abstraction* of x over M is $(\lambda x.M)$. Here, the token x is a bound variable with scope M. We often drop the outermost parentheses to improve readability.

We assume familiarity with the concepts of free and bound occurrences of variables in λ-terms. Two terms are considered α-*convertible* if they differ only in the names of their bound variables. We identify two terms when they are α-convertible. A subexpression of the form $(\lambda x.M)N$ is a β-*redex* and a subexpression of the form $(\lambda x.(Mx))$, where x has no free occurrence in M, is an η-*redex*. Replacing an occurrence of the β-redex $((\lambda x.M)N)$ with the capture-avoiding substitution of N for x in M, also written as $M[N/x]$, is called β-*reduction*. The converse relation is called β-*expansion*. A term M is β-*convertible* to a term N if there is a sequence (including the empty sequence) of β-reductions and β-expansions steps that rewrites M to N. Replacing an occurrence of an η-redex $(\lambda x.(Mx))$ with M is called η-*reduction*. The converse relation is called η-*expansion*. A term M is η-*convertible* to a term N if there is a sequence (including the empty sequence) of η-reductions and η-expansions steps that rewrites M to N. A term M is $\beta\eta$-*convertible* to N if there is a sequence of β-conversion and η-conversion steps that carries M to N. When we use the terms β-*conversion* and $\beta\eta$-*conversion*, we always assume the availability of α-conversion as well.

A term is β-*normal* if it does not contain a β-redex. Stated in a positive way, a term is β-normal if it has the form $\lambda x_1. \cdots \lambda x_n.(h t_1 \cdots t_m)$ where $n, m \geq 0$ and where $h, x_1, \ldots, x_n$ are tokens, and the terms $t_1, \ldots, t_m$ are all in β-normal form. In this case, we call the list $x_1, \ldots, x_n$ the *binder*, the token h the *head*, and the list $t_1, \ldots, t_m$ the *arguments* of the term.

Let θ be the list of pairs $\langle x_1, t_1 \rangle, \ldots, \langle x_n, t_n \rangle$, where, for all $i = 1, \ldots, n$, x_i is a variable and t_i is a λ-term. Occasionally, we will treat such a θ as a *substitution*: In particular, if s is a term (or formula), then the *application of the substitution θ to the term s*, written using the postfix notation $s\theta$, denotes the β-normal form of $[\lambda x_1. \cdots \lambda x_n.s]t_1 \cdots t_n$.

2.1 Untyped λ-Terms

Exercise 2.1. (‡) *Not all λ-terms are β-convertible to a β-normal term. Of the following terms, determine which is not β-convertible to a β-normal term and which are. In the latter case, compute that normal form.*

1. $((\lambda x.y)(\lambda x.x))$
2. $((\lambda x.x)(\lambda x.x))$
3. $((\lambda x.(xx))(\lambda x.x))$
4. $((\lambda x.(xx))(\lambda x.(xx)))$
5. $((\lambda x.((xx)x))(\lambda x.((xx)x)))$
6. $((\lambda x.y)((\lambda x.(xx))(\lambda x.(xx))))$

Exercise 2.2. Church numerals *are the following sequence of closed λ-terms:*

$$(\lambda f.\lambda x.x) \quad (\lambda f.\lambda x.(fx)) \quad (\lambda f.\lambda x.(f(fx))) \quad (\lambda f.\lambda x.(f(f(fx)))) \quad \ldots$$

These terms can encode the natural numbers $0, 1, 2, 3, \ldots$. The two λ-terms

$$S = \lambda N.\lambda M.\lambda f.\lambda x.((Nf)(Mf\,x)) \text{ and } P = \lambda N.\lambda M.\lambda f.\lambda x.((N(Mf))\,x)$$

can compute the sum (using S) and product (using P) of two Church numerals. Check this claim by computing the β-normal forms of the following two λ-terms, which encode $2 + 3$ and 2×3.

$$((S\,(\lambda f.\lambda x.(f(fx))))\,(\lambda f.\lambda x.(f(f(fx)))))$$

$$((P\,(\lambda f.\lambda x.(f(fx))))\,(\lambda f.\lambda x.(f(f(fx)))))$$

Exercise 2.3. (‡) *Computing β-normal forms can cause the size of terms to grow quickly. For example, consider the following sequence of λ-terms.*

$$E_0 = (((\lambda g.\lambda e.e) \quad (\lambda e.\lambda f.(e(ef)))) \quad (\lambda f.\lambda x.(f(fx))))$$
$$E_1 = (((\lambda g.\lambda e.(ge)) \quad (\lambda e.\lambda f.(e(ef)))) \quad (\lambda f.\lambda x.(f(fx))))$$
$$E_2 = (((\lambda g.\lambda e.(g(ge))) \quad (\lambda e.\lambda f.(e(ef)))) \quad (\lambda f.\lambda x.(f(fx))))$$
$$E_3 = (((\lambda g.\lambda e.(g(g(ge)))) \quad (\lambda e.\lambda f.(e(ef)))) \quad (\lambda f.\lambda x.(f(fx))))$$

In general, the term E_n is the Church numeral encoding n applied twice to the encoding of 2. The β-normal form of E_0 encodes 2 while E_1 reduces to the encoding of 4. What number is encoded by the β-normal form of E_n?

The above two exercises demonstrate the computational capabilities of λ-terms. This observation forms the basis for many functional programming languages that rely on the λ-terms for computation. Although the dynamics of β-reduction is important for us here, we will employ those dynamics in a more straightforward fashion: In particular, β-reduction will usually be used to instantiate quantified expressions.

> **Exercise 2.4.** (‡) *Is there an expression N such that $(\lambda x.w)[N/w]$ is equal to $\lambda y.y$ (modulo α-conversion, of course)? Phrased slightly differently, is there an expression N such that $((\lambda w.\lambda x.w)N)$ has $(\lambda y.y)$ as a β-normal form? The expression N may or may not have free occurrences of variables.*

Curry [1942] showed that mixing untyped λ-terms with logical connectives can lead to an inconsistent logic. One way to avoid such an inconsistency is to apply a typing discipline to the λ-terms. We next introduce the types used in the Simple Theory of Types, the logic introduced in Church [1940] and which underlies much of what follows in this book.

> **Exercise 2.5.** (‡) *To illustrate the paradox in Curry [1942], we first set Y to $\lambda f.(\lambda x.f(x\ x))\ (\lambda x.f(x\ x))$. Show that if g is any untyped λ-term, then $(Y\ g)$ β-converts to $(g\ (Y\ g))$. Thus, any expression g will have a fixed point $(Y\ g)$. Let B be the term $\lambda x.x \supset \mathsf{f}$, which is one way to write negation ("implies false"). Clearly, negation should not have a fixed point! By considering the expression $Y(\lambda x.x \supset \mathsf{f})$, show how to derive an inconsistency.*

2.2 Types

Let S be a fixed, nonempty set of tokens. The tokens in S will be used as *primitive types* (also called *sorts*). The set of *types* is the smallest set of expressions that contains the primitive types and is closed under the construction of *arrow types*, denoted by the binary, infix symbol $\to$. The Greek letters τ and σ are used as syntactic variables ranging over types. The type constructor $\to$ associates to the right: read $\tau_1 \to \tau_2 \to \tau_3$ as $\tau_1 \to (\tau_2 \to \tau_3)$.

These types are called *simple types*. Such type expressions do not contain binders or variables; in particular, type polymorphism is not supported in the underlying logic (although it appears in several examples we give in subsequent chapters). These types are used as *syntactic types* to separate expressions of different *syntactic categories*. For example, in Section 13.2, the syntax of the π-calculus is encoded using two primitive types n (for names) and p (for process). The type $n \to p$ is a syntactic type denoting an abstraction of a name over a process. This type does not denote all functions from names to processes. Of course, every abstraction of type $n \to p$ does indeed represent a function from names to processes: For example, if $M : n \to p$ and N is a name, then the β-normal form of (MN) is a process (the result of substituting N for the abstracted variable of M). However, there are functions from names to processes that do not correspond to an actual syntactic expression of type $n \to p$: For example, the function that maps a particular name, say a, to the process expression P_1 and all other names to a different process P_2 is not encoded in the syntax as an expression of type $n \to p$.

Let τ be the type $\tau_1 \to \cdots \to \tau_n \to \tau_0$ where $\tau_0 \in \mathcal{S}$ and $n \geq 0$. The types $\tau_1, \ldots, \tau_n$ are the *argument types of* τ while the type τ_0 is the *target type of* τ. If $n = 0$, then τ is τ_0, and the list of argument types is empty. The *order* of a type τ is defined as follows: If τ is primitive, then τ has order 0; otherwise, the order of τ is one greater than the maximum order of its argument types. As a recursive definition, the order of a type, written $\text{ord}(\tau)$, is defined as follows.

$$\text{ord}(\tau) = 0 \quad \text{provided } \tau \in \mathcal{S}$$
$$\text{ord}(\tau_1 \to \tau_2) = \max(\text{ord}(\tau_1) + 1, \text{ord}(\tau_2)).$$

Note that τ has order 0 or 1 if and only if all the argument types of τ are primitive types.

2.3 Signatures and Typed Terms

Signatures are used to formally *declare* that specific tokens are assigned a certain type. In particular, a *signature (over S)* is a set Σ (possibly empty) of pairs, written as $x : \tau$, where τ is a type and x is a token. We require signatures to be *determinate* in the sense that for every token x, if $x : \tau$ and $x : \sigma$ are members of Σ then τ and σ are the same type expression.

A signature Σ is said to have order n if every type associated with a token in Σ has an order less than or equal to n. Thus, Σ is a *first-order signature* if whenever $h : \tau$ is a member of Σ, $\text{ord}(\tau) \leq 1$.

A *typing judgment*, $\Sigma \Vdash t : \tau$, relates a signature Σ, a λ-term t, and a type τ. We consider the variables in Σ as being bound over such a judgment. Common inference rules for determining such typing rules are the following.

$$\frac{\Sigma, x_1 : \tau_1, \ldots, x_n : \tau_n \Vdash t : \tau_0}{\Sigma \Vdash \lambda x_1 \ldots \lambda x_n . t : \tau_1 \to \cdots \to \tau_n \to \tau_0}$$

$$\frac{\Sigma \Vdash t_1 : \sigma_1 \quad \cdots \quad \Sigma \Vdash t_n : \sigma_n \quad h : \sigma_1 \to \cdots \to \sigma_n \to \tau_0 \in \Sigma}{\Sigma \Vdash (h\ t_1\ \cdots\ t_n) : \tau_0}$$

Both rules are restricted so that $\tau_o \in \mathcal{S}$ and $n \geq 0$. Also, the variables $x_1, \ldots, x_n$ are assumed to not occur in Σ.

Figure 2.1 Typing judgment for Σ-terms of type τ.

$$\frac{}{\Sigma, x : \tau \Vdash x : \tau} \qquad \frac{\Sigma \Vdash t : \sigma \to \tau \quad \Sigma \Vdash s : \sigma}{\Sigma \Vdash (t\ s) : \tau} \qquad \frac{\Sigma, x : \tau \Vdash M : \sigma}{\Sigma \Vdash (\lambda x..M) : \tau \to \sigma}.$$

The last inference rule assumes that the bound variable x does not occur in Σ. These three typing rules can be used with terms not in β-normal form. However, we restrict the typing judgment in this book so that only β-normal formulas are given types. Thus, we adopt the inference rules in Figure 2.1 as the official rules for this judgment.

When the judgment $\Sigma \Vdash t : \tau$ is provable, we say that t is a *Σ-term of type τ*. Note that if a term is given a type, then that term is β-normal. Furthermore, any term given a type is also said to be in *$\beta\eta$-long normal form*. This normal form can be arrived at by first computing the β-normal form and then applying some η-expansion steps. For example, if $i \in \mathcal{S}$, then the judgment $\Sigma \Vdash \lambda x.x : (i \to i) \to i \to i$ is not provable, but the judgment

$$\Sigma \Vdash \lambda x.\lambda y.xy : (i \to i) \to i \to i,$$

based on the η-expanded version of the term $\lambda x.x$, is provable.

Exercise 2.6. (‡) *Fix the set of sorts S and the signature Σ over S. Prove that if there are* primitive *types τ and τ' such that $\Sigma \Vdash t : \tau$ and $\Sigma \Vdash t : \tau'$, then $\tau = \tau'$. Show that this statement is not true if we allow τ and τ' to be non-primitive.*

2.4 Formulas

Most descriptions of predicate logic first present *terms* and then present *formulas* as a separate structure incorporating terms. Following Church [1940],

2.4 Formulas

we instead define *formulas* as terms of the particular type o (the Greek letter omicron).

When defining the formulas of a given logic (e.g., first-order classical logic), we first fix the declaration of the *logical constants*. That signature, which we denote as Σ_{-1} (the signature of the foundations), attributes to various tokens types with target type o.

These logical constants are divided into two groups: propositional constants and quantifiers. The *propositional constants* are given types that only use the primitive type o and have order 0 or 1. For example, in Chapter 4, when we introduce the formulas of classical and intuitionistic first-order logics, the following signature is used to declare the propositional connectives used in those formulas.

$$\{\mathsf{t} : o,\ \mathsf{f} : o,\ \wedge : o \to o \to o,\ \vee : o \to o \to o,\ \supset : o \to o \to o\}.$$

The binary symbols $\wedge$, $\vee$, and $\supset$ are written as infix operators. For example, the λ-term $((\wedge\ P)\ Q)$ is written in the more common form $(P \wedge Q)$. Also, $\wedge$ and $\vee$ associates to the left, $\supset$ associating to the right, and $\wedge$ has higher priority than $\vee$, which has higher priority than $\supset$.

There are two classes of *quantifiers* we consider in this book, namely, $\forall_\tau$, for universal quantification for type τ, and $\exists_\tau$, for existential quantification for type τ. Both $\forall_\tau$ and $\exists_\tau$ are assigned the type $(\tau \to o) \to o$. In principle, there are countably infinitely many such quantifiers, one for each type τ. The expressions $\forall_\tau(\lambda x.B)$ and $\exists_\tau(\lambda x.B)$ are abbreviated as $\forall_\tau x.B$ and $\exists_\tau x.B$, respectively, or as simply $\forall x.B$ and $\exists x.B$ if the value of the type subscript is not important or can easily be inferred from context. Note that the binding mechanism used in quantification is really the binding mechanism in the λ-calculus.

After fixing the set of logical constants, we generally fix the non-logical symbols by declaring another signature Σ_0. Let $c : \tau_1 \to \cdots \to \tau_n \to \tau_0 \in \Sigma_0$, where τ_0 is a primitive type and $n \geq 0$. If τ_0 is o, then c is a *predicate symbol of arity n*. If $\tau_0 \in \mathcal{S}\backslash\{o\}$ (i.e., τ_0 is not o), then c is a *function symbol of arity n*. A $\Sigma_{-1} \cup \Sigma_0$-term of type o is also called a $\Sigma_{-1} \cup \Sigma_0$-*formula*, or more usually either a Σ_0-*formula* (since Σ_{-1} is usually fixed) or just a *formula* (if Σ_0 is understood).

A logic is *propositional* if its only logical connectives are propositional connectives (i.e., it involves no quantifiers). A logic is *first-order* if the only quantifiers allowed in its formulas are contained in the set

$$\{\forall_\tau : (\tau \to o) \to o \mid \tau \in \mathcal{S}\backslash\{o\}\} \cup \{\exists_\tau : (\tau \to o) \to o \mid \tau \in \mathcal{S}\backslash\{o\}\}.$$

The types in this signature are of order 2. The restriction on the type of quantifiers, namely $\tau \in \mathcal{S}\setminus\{o\}$, implies that in a first-order formula, the only quantification is over primitive (and non-formula) types. A logic that provides no restriction on the types used in quantification is a *higher-order logic*: We consider such a logic starting in Chapter 9.

Assume that Σ_{-1} declares logical connectives for a first-order logic and that Σ_0 is a first-order signature. Let τ be a primitive type different from o. A first-order term t of type τ is either a token of type τ or it is of the form $(f\ t_1 \ldots t_n)$ where f is a function symbol of type $\tau_1 \to \cdots \to \tau_n \to \tau$ and, for $i = 1, \ldots, n$, t_i is a term of type τ_i. In the latter case, f is the head, and $t_1, \ldots, t_n$ are the arguments of this term. Similarly, a first-order formula has either a logical symbol at its head, in which case it is said to be *non-atomic*, or it has a non-logical symbol at its head, in which case it is *atomic*.

As mentioned above, formulas in both classical and intuitionistic first-order logics make use of the same set of logical connectives, namely, $\wedge$ (conjunction), $\vee$ (disjunction), $\supset$ (implication), t (truth), f (false), $\forall_\tau$ (universal quantification over type τ), and $\exists_\tau$ (existential quantification over type τ). The negation of B, sometimes written as $\neg B$, is an abbreviation for the formula $B \supset f$.

Similarly to the way $\text{ord}(\tau)$ counts the nesting of $\to$ to the left of $\to$ in type τ (see Section 2.2), the function $\text{order}(B)$ counts the nestings of $\supset$ to the left of $\supset$ in the formula B. This *clausal order* function is defined using the following recursion for classical and intuitionistic logic formulas.

$$\text{order}(A) = 0 \quad \text{provided } A \text{ is atomic, t, or f}$$
$$\text{order}(B_1 \wedge B_2) = \max(\text{order}(B_1), \text{order}(B_2))$$
$$\text{order}(B_1 \vee B_2) = \max(\text{order}(B_1), \text{order}(B_2))$$
$$\text{order}(B_1 \supset B_2) = \max(\text{order}(B_1) + 1, \text{order}(B_2))$$
$$\text{order}(\forall x.B) = \text{order}(B)$$
$$\text{order}(\exists x.B) = \text{order}(B)$$

Note that $\text{order}(\neg B) = \text{order}(B) + 1$. The clausal order of a finite set or multiset of formulas is the maximum clausal order of any formula in that set or multiset.

The *polarity of a subformula occurrence* within a formula is defined as follows. If a subformula C of B occurs to the left of an even number of occurrences of implications in B, then C is a *positive* subformula occurrence of B. On the other hand, if a subformula C occurs to the left of an odd number of occurrences of implication in a formula B, then C is a *negative* subformula occurrence of B. More formally:

1. B is a positive subformula occurrence of B.
2. If C is a positive subformula occurrence of B then C is a positive subformula occurrence in $B \wedge B'$, $B' \wedge B$, $B \vee B'$, $B' \vee B$, $B' \supset B$, $\forall_\tau x.B$, and $\exists_\tau x.B$; C is also a negative subformula occurrence in $B \supset B'$.
3. If C is a negative subformula occurrence of B then C is a negative subformula occurrence in $B \wedge B'$, $B' \wedge B$, $B \vee B'$, $B' \vee B$, $B' \supset B$, $\forall_\tau x.B$, and $\exists_\tau x.B$; C is also a positive subformula occurrence in $B \supset B'$.

Of course, if B contains no occurrences of implications, then all subformula occurrences in B are positive occurrences.

2.5 Sequents

Proof and provability are generally described for a collection of formulas instead of a single, isolated formula. For example, a typical way to describe the provability of the implication $B \supset C$ is to pose the hypothetical judgment involving two formulas: if B then C. Gentzen [1935] introduced *sequents* as one way to organize the multiple formulas involved in stating a provable statement. In their simplest form, sequents are a pair written $\Gamma \vdash \Delta$, of the two collections of formulas Γ and Δ. When sequents are used in classical and intuitionistic logics, the claim that the sequent $\Gamma \vdash \Delta$ is provable amounts to the claim that one of the formulas in Δ is provable from the assumptions occurring in Γ. Section 3.1 will give more intuition about sequents and logical reasoning.

Within this book, sequents will vary somewhat in structure: We outline some of that variability here.

The collections of formulas within sequents will be either lists, multisets, or sets (although almost always, they will be multisets). Sequents can also be *one-sided* or *two-sided*. One-sided sequents are usually written as $\vdash \Delta$, and two-sided sequents are usually written as $\Gamma \vdash \Delta$. Here, Γ and Δ are one of the three kinds of collections of formulas mentioned above. In the two-sided sequent $\Gamma \vdash \Delta$, we say that Γ is this sequent's *left-hand side* and that Δ is its *right-hand side*. Sometimes, we divide left-hand and right-hand contexts into two zones separated by a semicolon; for example, $\Gamma; \Gamma \vdash \Delta; \Delta'$ and $\vdash \Delta; \Delta'$.

The formulas in a sequent are typed, and the signatures that declare the types of the tokens in those formulas must be specified. As in Section 2.4, we generally assume that once we pick a particular logic (classical, intuitionistic, or linear), we have fixed the signature Σ_{-1}. Furthermore, a set of non-logical constants Σ_0 will often be fixed. Finally, Gentzen's rules for the treatment of quantifiers involve the introduction of *eigenvariables*: These variables may appear free in the formulas of some sequents. To properly declare those variables and their types, we prefix a sequent with a signature: for example, $\Sigma :: \vdash \Delta$ and $\Sigma :: \Gamma \vdash \Delta$. In all these cases, a formula that appears in Δ or Γ must be given type o using the union of the three signatures Σ_{-1}, Σ_0, and Σ.

We note some issues concerning matching expressions with schematic variables. For example, let B denote a formula and let Γ and Γ' denote collections of formulas. Consider what it means to match the expressions B, Γ' and Γ', Γ'' to a given collection, which we assume contains $n \geq 0$ occurrences of formulas.

1. If the given collection is a list, then B, Γ' matches if the list is nonempty and B is the first formula, and Γ' is the remaining list. The expression Γ', Γ'' matches if Γ' is some prefix and Γ'' is the remaining suffix of that list: There are $n + 1$ possible matches.
2. If the given collection is a multiset, then B, Γ' matches if the multiset is nonempty and B is a formula in the multiset and Γ' is the multiset resulting from deleting one occurrence of B. The expression Γ', Γ'' matches if the multiset union of Γ' and Γ'' is Γ: There can be as many as 2^n possible matches since each member of Γ can be placed in either Γ' or Γ''.
3. If the given collection is a set, then B, Γ' matches if the set is nonempty and B is a formula in the set, and Γ' is either the given set or the set resulting from removing B from the set. The expression Γ', Γ'' matches if the set union of Γ' and Γ'' is Γ: There can be as many as 3^n possible matches since each member of Γ can be placed in either Γ' or Γ'' or in both.

2.6 Bibliographic Notes

Church's approach to specifying terms and formulas in the Simple Theory of Types is a popular choice in the construction of modern theorem prover systems: For example, it is used in the HOL family of provers (see Gordon [2000]) as well as in Isabelle (see Paulson [1994]), Abella (see Baelde

2.6 BIBLIOGRAPHIC NOTES 19

et al. [2014]), and the logic programming language λProlog (see Miller and Nadathur [2012]). The textbooks by Andrews [1986] and Farmer [2023] treat this logic in detail.

For a comprehensive treatment of the untyped λ-calculus, see Barendregt [1984], and of the typed λ-calculus, see Krivine [1990] and Barendregt et al. [2013]. The use of untyped λ-terms here is similar to the so-called Curry-style of typed λ-terms: Bound variables are not assumed globally to have types but are provided a type when they are initially bound. This approach to typing contrasts with that used by Church, where variables have types independent of whether or not they are bound. For more about these different approaches to types in the λ-calculus, see Pfenning [2008].

Richer types than the simple types introduced in this chapter are useful within logical formulas and logic programming. For example, the programming language λProlog has a form of polymorphic typing (see Nadathur and Pfenning [1992], Caires and Monteiro [1994], Appel and Felty [2004], and Miller and Nadathur [2012]). The Elf logic programming language (based on the LF logical framework of Harper et al. [1993]) uses dependently typed λ-terms (see Pfenning [1989] and Pfenning and Schürmann [1999]).

This book's approach to the sequent calculus differs from Gentzen [1935] in three ways.

1. In terms of notation, Gentzen used the symbol $\longrightarrow$ to separate the left side from the right side instead of the $\vdash$ symbol. We prefer to reserve $\longrightarrow$ for specifications of computation where it is often used to denote rewriting or the evolution of computations (see, for example, Chapter 12).
2. Gentzen used lists to encode the left and right sides of sequents. We will almost exclusively use multisets instead. Hence, no order between formulas is maintained in the contexts in our sequents.
3. Gentzen introduced the important concept of *eigenvariables* into his proof structures along with certain global conditions needed to keep their use sound. Here, we view eigenvariables as locally bound over sequents (see Section 3.2.3).

The perspective that (natural deduction) proofs correspond to (dependently) typed λ-terms and that β-reductions correspond to (functional) computation is part of the well-known *Curry–Howard correspondence* approach to modeling computation (see Sørensen and Urzyczyn [2006]). This approach to computation is not used in this book: Instead, we model computation as the search for (cut-free) proofs.

Chapter 3

Sequent Calculus Proof Rules

A familiar form of formal proof, often attributed to Frege and Hilbert, accepts specific formulas as *axioms* (e.g., $(p \supset (q \supset p))$ and $(((p \supset q \supset r) \supset (p \supset q) \supset (p \supset r)))$ and certain *inference rules* (e.g., from p and $(p \supset q)$ conclude q). A formal *Frege proof* is a list of formulas such that every formula occurrence in that list is either an axiom or the result of applying an inference rule to previous formulas in the list. Such proof structures are simple structures, and axioms and inference rules can be picked in such a way as to provide a proof system for classical logic or intuitionistic logic. While Frege proofs are easy to check for correctness, they are challenging to use as the basis of automated proof search algorithms. Figure 3.1 provides an example of a Frege proof. As we shall see shortly, sequent calculus proofs provide a much more structured approach to formal proofs. We will use sequent calculus proofs to provide abstract execution models for the logic programming paradigm.

3.1 Sequent Calculus and Proof Search

The sequent calculus makes at least two significant departures from Frege proofs. First, while inference rules are applied to formulas in Frege proofs, they are applied to sequents—a more complex structure—in the sequent calculus. Second, no axioms are used within the sequent calculus proof systems we study here: The burden of proof falls entirely on inference rules over sequents.

In Section 2.5, we presented sequents as formal, syntactic structures containing one or more collections of formulas. Before formally presenting

3.1 SEQUENT CALCULUS AND PROOF SEARCH

Three axiom schemas for propositional classical logic.

$(Ax1)$ $X \supset Y \supset X$
$(Ax2)$ $((X \supset (Y \supset Z)) \supset ((X \supset Y) \supset (X \supset Z))))$
$(Ax3)$ $(((X \supset f) \supset f) \supset X))$

One inference rule: The rule of *modus ponens* which allows us to conclude B if $A \supset B$ and A have already been proved.

These axioms and inference rules ensure the principle of *ex falso quodlibet*: From false, any formula follows. The following list of formulas is a Frege proof of the formula $(f \supset w)$: Here, w can be any formula of propositional classical logic.

(1) $((w \supset f) \supset f) \supset w$ by $(Ax3)$
(2) $(((w \supset f) \supset f) \supset w) \supset (f \supset (((w \supset f) \supset f) \supset w))$ by $(Ax1)$
(3) $f \supset (((w \supset f) \supset f) \supset w)$ by $mp\ (1), (2)$
(4) $(f \supset (((w \supset f) \supset f) \supset w)) \supset$
         $((f \supset ((w \supset f) \supset f)) \supset (f \supset w))$ by $(Ax2)$
(5) $(f \supset ((w \supset f) \supset f)) \supset (f \supset w)$ by $mp\ (3), (4)$
(6) $f \supset ((w \supset f) \supset f)$ by $(Ax1)$
(7) $f \supset w$ by $mp\ (6), (5)$

Figure 3.1 An example of a Frege proof (taken from Hughes [2006]).

inference rules using sequents in Section 3.2, we provide an informal reading of two-sided sequents in which the right-hand side is a collection containing exactly one occurrence of a formula. Consider, for example, attempting to prove that for every natural number n, the product $n(n+1)$ is even. An informal proof of this fact can be organized as follows. To prove this is true for all natural numbers, pick some arbitrary number, say, m. Now, m is either even or odd. If m is even, then the product $m(m+1)$ is even. If m is odd, then $m+1$ is even, and, again, the produce $m(m+1)$ is even. Hence, in either case, this product is even.

A first step in formalizing this proof is to identify (and name) three lemmas about natural numbers that this argument accepts as previously proved.

L_1 $\forall n.(\text{even } n) \vee (\text{odd } n)$
L_2 $\forall n.(\text{odd } n) \supset (\text{even } (s\ n))$
L_3 $\forall n.\forall m.\forall p.((\text{even } n) \vee (\text{even } m)) \supset (\text{times } n\ m\ p) \supset (\text{even } p)$

For these lemmas to be proper formulas as defined in the Chapter 2, we must assume that the set of sorts S contains a primitive type, say, nat and that the signature of non-logical constants Σ_0 must contain the following declarations:

     z : nat, s : nat $\to$ nat,
     $even$: nat $\to o$, odd : nat $\to o$, $times$: nat $\to$ nat $\to$ nat $\to o$

We assume that natural numbers are encoded as $\{z, (s\ z), (s\ (s\ z)), \ldots\}$, and that the predicate (times n m p) hold precisely when p is the product $n \times m$. Imagine that we now take a blank sheet of paper and write at the top the three lemmas which we accept as assumptions and write at the bottom of that sheet the formula $\forall n.\forall p.$(times n $(s\ n)$ p) $\supset$ (even p). Our task is to fill in the gap between the assumptions at the top and the conclusion at the bottom. A sequent is essentially a representation of the status of that sheet of paper: In this case, that sequent (named T_1) is

$$T_1 \qquad \cdot\,; L_1, L_2, L_3 \vdash \forall n.\forall p.(\text{times } n\ (s\ n)\ p) \supset (\text{even } p).$$

The prefix, which is just the dot $\cdot$, is meant to show that there are no eigenvariables bound over this particular sequent. One way to make progress on finishing a proof of this sequent is to take a new sheet of paper on which we write the assumptions L_1, L_2, L_3 and (times n $(s\ n)$ p) at the top and write the conclusion (even p) at the bottom of that sheet. Thus, we now have an additional assumption that p is the product $n(n + 1)$ and the different conclusion (even p). This new state in the construction of a formal proof is represented by the sequent

$$T_2 \qquad n, p; L_1, L_2, L_3, (\text{times } n\ (s\ n)\ p) \vdash (\text{even } p).$$

Note that the variables n and p are bound over this sequent. The next step in building our proof uses lemma L_1 to add the assumption (even n) $\vee$ (odd n). That is, our sheet of paper now has five formulas at the top, and it is encoded as the sequent

$$T_3 \qquad n, p; L_1, L_2, L_3, (\text{times } n\ (s\ n)\ p), (\text{even } n) \vee (\text{odd } n) \vdash (\text{even } p).$$

The case analysis induced by the disjunctive assumption leads the proof to have two subproofs. That is, the current sheet of paper can be replaced by two sheets that are identical, except that one of those sheets replaces that disjunction with (even n), and the other sheet replaces it with (odd n). These two sheets are encoded as the following two sequents.

$$T_4 \qquad n, p; L_1, L_2, L_3, (\text{times } n\ (s\ n)\ p), (\text{even } n) \quad \vdash (\text{even } p),$$
$$T_5 \qquad n, p; L_1, L_2, L_3, (\text{times } n\ (s\ n)\ p), (\text{odd } n) \quad \vdash (\text{even } p).$$

One way to represent the status of the proof's development is to organize these sequents into the tree

$$\dfrac{\dfrac{\dfrac{T_4 \quad T_5}{T_3}}{T_2}}{T_1}.$$

To complete the formal description of this proof, we need to label each horizontal line by the name of an inference rule. For example, the uppermost horizontal line is justified by the "rule of cases" (also called the $\vee L$ rule in Chapter 4). As this tree shows, the process of proving sequent T_1 has reduced it to attempting to prove the two sequents T_4 and T_5.

This proof can be completed by appealing to lemma L_3 to justify sequent T_4 and appealing to lemmas L_2 and L_3 to justify sequent T_5.

Our subsequent study of sequent calculus proofs will not be limited to capturing natural or human-readable proofs. Instead, we focus on low-level aspects of proof that will ultimately make it possible to automate proof search for some fragments of logic. The analysis of sequent calculus proofs by Gentzen also allows for the more general (albeit less intuitive) *multiple-conclusion sequent*. Thus, while the comma on the left can be viewed as a conjunction, the comma on the right can be viewed as a disjunction. For example, the sequent $x, y : B_1, B_2, B_3 \vdash C_1, C_2$ can be viewed as semantically related to the formula $\forall x. \forall y. [(B_1 \wedge B_2 \wedge B_3) \supset (C_1 \vee C_2)]$.

3.2 Inference Rules

An inference rule in a sequent calculus proof system has a single sequent as its conclusion and zero or more sequents as its premises. There are three main categories of inference rules used in sequent calculi we study here: the *structural rules*, the *identity rules*, and the *introduction rules*. We examine each class separately below.

3.2.1 Structural Rules

There are three standard structural rules, called *exchange*, *contraction*, and *weakening*, and they are presented in Figure 3.2 in both left- and right-side versions. All these structural rules can be used with contexts that are list structures. The exchange rules, xL and xR, allow exchanging two adjacent elements. These structural rules are not used when contexts are multisets or sets. The contraction rules, cL and cR, can be used on lists and multisets to replace two occurrences of the same formula with one occurrence: These structural rules are not used when contexts are sets. The weakening rules, wL and wR, can insert a formula into a context. If used with a list, these rules insert the new formula occurrence only at the end of the context. If contexts

$$\dfrac{\Sigma :: \Gamma, B, C, \Gamma' \vdash \Delta}{\Sigma :: \Gamma, C, B, \Gamma' \vdash \Delta}\ xL \qquad \dfrac{\Sigma :: \Gamma \vdash \Delta, B, C, \Delta'}{\Sigma :: \Gamma \vdash \Delta, C, B, \Delta'}\ xR$$

$$\dfrac{\Sigma :: \Gamma, B, B \vdash \Delta}{\Sigma :: \Gamma, B \vdash \Delta}\ cL \qquad \dfrac{\Sigma :: \Gamma \vdash \Delta, B, B}{\Sigma :: \Gamma \vdash \Delta, B}\ cR$$

$$\dfrac{\Sigma :: \Gamma \vdash \Delta}{\Sigma :: \Gamma, B \vdash \Delta}\ wL \qquad \dfrac{\Sigma :: \Gamma \vdash \Delta}{\Sigma :: \Gamma \vdash \Delta, B}\ wR$$

Figure 3.2 Structural rules.

$$\dfrac{}{\Sigma :: B \vdash B}\ \textit{init} \qquad \dfrac{\Sigma :: \Gamma \vdash \Delta, B \quad \Sigma :: B, \Gamma' \vdash \Delta'}{\Sigma :: \Gamma, \Gamma' \vdash \Delta, \Delta'}\ \textit{cut}$$

Figure 3.3 The two identity rules: Initial and cut.

are sets, the only structural rules that make sense to specify are the weakening rules.

In this book, we shall never use the exchange rules, and contexts will almost always be multisets. We shall only use the weakening and contraction rules in our proof systems. If we have a set of formulas that we wish to place into a sequent, we shall always coerce that set into the multiset where every set element occurs exactly once.

> **Exercise 3.1.** Let Δ' be a permutation of the list Δ. Show that a sequence of xR rules can derive the sequent $\Sigma :: \Gamma \vdash \Delta$ from the sequent $\Sigma :: \Gamma \vdash \Delta'$.

3.2.2 Identity Rules

The identity rules consist of the *initial* and *cut* rules, examples of which are displayed in Figure 3.3. Both rules contain repeated schema variable occurrences: In the initial rule, the variable B is repeated in the conclusion, and in the cut rule, the variable B is repeated in the premises. Checking if an application of one of these rules is correct requires comparing the identity of two formula occurrences. Although the structural rules address the structure of the contexts used in forming sequents, the identity rules address the meaning of the sequent symbol $\vdash$. In particular, these two rules state that $\vdash$ is reflexive and transitive. In Section 4.2, we illustrate that, in a certain sense, these two rules describe dual aspects of $\vdash$.

3.2 INFERENCE RULES

In some textbooks, an inference rule with zero premises is called an *axiom*. We shall reserve that term for a *formula* that is accepted as the starting point of some forms of proofs (e.g., the Frege proofs described in Section 3.1). Since sequents are not formulas, we call the leaves of sequent calculus proof trees *initial sequents*.

3.2.3 Introduction Rules

An inference rule in the final group of rules introduces one occurrence of a logical connective into the conclusion of the inference rule. In two-sided sequent systems, a logical connective is introduced on the left and right by different and small collections of inference rules. Here, the term "a small collection" means a collection of 0, 1, or 2 rules. (In the informal reading of sequents provided in Section 3.1, a left-introduction rule describes how to reason *from* a logical connective while the right-introduction rule describes how to reason *to* a logical connective.) If sequents are one-sided, the left-introduction rules for a connective are usually replaced by the right-introduction rules for that connective's De Morgan dual. Thus, one-sided systems are usually limited to those logics where all connectives have De Morgan duals. The only one-sided sequent calculus proof system in this book is a proof system for linear logic that appears in Chapter 6.

Figure 3.4 presents a few examples of introduction rules for some logical connectives. That figure provides two left-introduction rules and one right-introduction rule for conjunction. In contrast, both implication and universal

$$\frac{\Sigma :: B, \Gamma \vdash \Delta}{\Sigma :: B \wedge C, \Gamma \vdash \Delta} \wedge L \qquad \frac{\Sigma :: C, \Gamma \vdash \Delta}{\Sigma :: B \wedge C, \Gamma \vdash \Delta} \wedge L$$

$$\frac{\Sigma :: \Gamma \vdash \Delta, B \quad \Sigma :: \Gamma \vdash \Delta, C}{\Sigma :: \Gamma \vdash \Delta, B \wedge C} \wedge R \qquad \frac{}{\Sigma :: \Gamma \vdash \Delta, t} tR$$

$$\frac{\Sigma :: \Gamma_1 \vdash \Delta_1, B \quad \Sigma :: C, \Gamma_2 \vdash \Delta_2}{\Sigma :: B \supset C, \Gamma_1, \Gamma_2 \vdash \Delta_1, \Delta_2} \supset L \qquad \frac{\Sigma :: B, \Gamma \vdash \Delta, C}{\Sigma :: \Gamma \vdash \Delta, B \supset C} \supset R$$

$$\frac{\Sigma \Vdash t : \tau \quad \Sigma :: \Gamma, B[t/x] \vdash \Delta}{\Sigma :: \Gamma, \forall_\tau x.B \vdash \Delta} \forall L \qquad \frac{\Sigma, y : \tau \ : \ \Gamma \vdash \Delta, B[y/x]}{\Sigma :: \Gamma \vdash \Delta, \forall_\tau x.B} \forall R$$

Figure 3.4 Examples of left- and right-introduction rules.

quantification are given one left- and one right-introduction rule. There is one right-introduction rule and zero left-introduction rules for t.

The rules in Figure 3.4 also illustrate the role that the signature Σ plays in specifying the quantifier introduction rules. In particular, introducing the universal quantifier $\forall$ on the left uses the signature and the judgment $\Sigma \Vdash t : \tau$ to determine the range of suitable substitution terms t. On the other hand, the right-introduction rule for $\forall$ changes the signature from $\Sigma \cup \{y : \tau\}$ above the line to Σ below the line. Note that if we think of signatures as lists of distinct typed variables, we must maintain that the variable y is not free in any formula in the rule's conclusion. By viewing quantifiers as bindings in formulas and signatures as binders for sequents, the inference rule $\forall R$ essentially allows for the *mobility* of a binder: Reading this inference rule from premise to conclusion, the binder for y *moves* from a sequent-level binding to the formula level binding for x. At no point is the binder replaced with a free variable. Of course, this movement of the binder is only allowed if no occurrences of the bound variable above the line are unbound below the line. Thus, all occurrences of y in the upper sequent must appear in the displayed occurrence of $B[y/x]$. Following Gentzen [1935], such sequent-level bound variables are called *eigenvariables*. Note that since we identify all binding structures that differ by only an alphabetic change of variables, the $\forall R$ rule could also be written as

$$\frac{\Sigma, x : \tau \;::\; \Gamma \vdash \Delta, B}{\Sigma \;::\; \Gamma \vdash \Delta, \forall_\tau x.B} \;\forall R.$$

In this form, the mobility of the binder for x is more apparent.

The premise $\Sigma \Vdash t:\tau$ for the $\forall L$ rule should be written as $\Sigma_{-1} \cup \Sigma_0 \cup \Sigma \Vdash t:\tau$ where Σ_{-1} and Σ_0 are the signatures for the logical and non-logical constants, respectively. Since both these signatures are global for any particular proof, we write this condition with only one signature for convenience. Also, one has the choice to either include this typing judgment as a part of the proof (hence, the proof of the typing judgment is a subproof of a proof of the conclusion to this rule) or as a side condition, namely, the requirement that that premise is provable (in this case, the proof of that side condition is not incorporated into the sequent proof).

3.3 Additive and Multiplicative Inference Rules

When an inference rule has two premises, there are two natural ways to relate the contexts in the two premises with the context in the conclusion. Such an

3.3 ADDITIVE AND MULTIPLICATIVE INFERENCE RULES

inference rule is *multiplicative* if contexts in the premises are merged to form the context in the conclusion. The cut rule in Figure 3.3 and the ⊃L rule in Figure 3.4 are examples of *multiplicative* rules. A rule is *additive* if the contexts in the premises are the same as the context in the conclusion. The ∧R rule in Figure 3.4 is additive. An additive version of the cut inference rule can be written as

$$\frac{\Sigma :: \Gamma \vdash \Delta, B \quad \Sigma :: B, \Gamma \vdash \Delta}{\Sigma :: \Gamma \vdash \Delta}.$$

The use of the terms multiplicative and additive will be addressed when the *exponentials* of linear logic are presented in Section 6.3.3 (see Exercise 6.3).

The following is a more general definition of these terms, which can be applied to all inference rules in this book. Given an inference rule, we classify an occurrence of a formula in its concluding sequent as either a *subject occurrence* or a *context occurrence*. In an introduction rule, the subject occurrence is the single formula occurrence introduced by that rule. In the initial rule, both the formula occurrences required by that rule are the subject occurrences. Finally, if the rule is a cut rule, then no formula occurrence in the conclusion is a subject occurrence. A context occurrence is any occurrence of a formula in the conclusion that is not a subject occurrence.

An inference rule is *additive* if every occurrence of a context formula in the concluding sequent has an occurrence in *every* premise sequents. An inference rule is *multiplicative* if every occurrence of a context formula in the concluding sequent has an occurrence in *exactly one* premise sequent. In both cases, these occurrences in the conclusion and the premises are always on the same side of their respective sequents. This characterization of additive and multiplicative rules can be applied to rules that do not have two premises. For example, the tR rule in Figure 3.4 is additive and is not multiplicative. However, the introduction rule

$$\overline{\Sigma :: \cdot \vdash t}$$

is additive and multiplicative since the conditions on context formulas are vacuously true. (We shall sometimes use · to mark an empty part of a sequent.)

The following two introduction rules for conjunction are multiplicative rules.

$$\frac{\Sigma :: B, C, \Gamma \vdash \Delta}{\Sigma :: B \wedge C, \Gamma \vdash \Delta} \wedge L^m \qquad \frac{\Sigma :: \Gamma_1 \vdash \Delta_1, B \quad \Sigma :: \Gamma_2 \vdash \Delta_2, C}{\Sigma :: \Gamma_1, \Gamma_2 \vdash \Delta_1, \Delta_2, B \wedge C} \wedge R^m.$$

Exercise 3.2. (‡) *Show that if the structural rules of weakening and contraction are available, then the rules $\wedge R$ and $\wedge L$ (from Figure 3.4) can be derived from $\wedge R^m$ and $\wedge L^m$, and conversely.*

This exercise illustrates that the structural rules allow an additive rule to account for a multiplicative rule and vice versa. The following collection of inference rules suggests another connection between these concepts.

$$\dfrac{\dfrac{\overline{\Sigma :: B \vdash B}\ \text{init} \quad \overline{\Sigma :: B \vdash B}\ \text{init}}{\Sigma :: B \vdash B \wedge B}\wedge R \quad \dfrac{\Sigma :: \Gamma, B, B \vdash \Delta}{\Sigma :: \Gamma, B \wedge B \vdash \Delta}\wedge L^m}{\Sigma :: \Gamma, B \vdash \Delta}\ \text{cut.}$$

Thus, if we adopt $\wedge L^m$ and $\wedge R$ as the left- and right-introduction rules for conjunction, we can infer the cL rule. Similarly, if we adopt $\wedge L$ and $\wedge R^m$ as the left- and right-introduction rules for conjunction, we can infer the following instance of wL rule.

$$\dfrac{\dfrac{\overline{\Sigma :: B \vdash B}\ \text{init} \quad \overline{\Sigma :: C \vdash C}\ \text{init}}{\Sigma :: B, C \vdash B \wedge C}\wedge R^m \quad \dfrac{\Sigma :: \Gamma, B \vdash \Delta}{\Sigma :: \Gamma, B \wedge C \vdash \Delta}\wedge L}{\Sigma :: \Gamma, B, C \vdash \Delta}\ \text{cut.}$$

Since we do not wish for the structural rules to enter our proof systems without *explicitly* adding them, we must choose carefully how we pair left- and right-introduction rules. Gentzen's original sequent calculus (and the ones we adopt for classical and intuitionistic logics in Chapter 4) pairs $\wedge L$ with $\wedge R$. When we turn to linear logic in Chapter 6, we will allow for two conjunctions, written as & and $\otimes$, where the right-introduction rule for & is additive and the right-introduction rule for $\otimes$ is multiplicative. The left-introduction rule for & will be similar to $\wedge L$ and for $\otimes$ will be similar to $\wedge L^m$.

Naive implementations of additive and multiplicative inference rules have contrasting costs depending on whether we are building proofs (starting with premises) or searching for proofs (starting with the conclusion). Additive rules are expensive to build since we must check the equality of contexts (and contexts can be thousands of possibly large formulas), but cheap to search for since the premises only require sharing pointers to the conclusion's contexts. Conversely, multiplicative rules are cheap to use in the proof building sense since we only need to combine pointers to the context of the premises, but expensive to do in the proof search setting since there can be an exponential number of possible context splittings for generating the premises.

3.4 Sequent Calculus Proofs

Building on the definitions of formulas and sequents in Chapter 2 and the introduction of inference rules in Section 3.2, we formally define *sequent calculus proofs*.

Assume that we have picked a particular style of sequent (e.g., one-sided or two-sided) and let **S** be a sequent. A *derivation for* **S** is a tree of inference rules such that the root is labeled with **S**. We also assume that every occurrence of an inference rule in a derivation is such that its conclusion is either the root sequent (also called the *endsequent*) or is the premise of another occurrence of an inference rule in that tree. This derivation is a *proof of* **S** if every sequent labeling leaves of the derivation is the conclusion of an inference rule with zero premises (rules such as *init* in Figure 3.3 or tR in Figure 3.4). Thus, a derivation can denote a *partial proof* since it may have leaves not justified by some inference rule. When we display derivation trees, leaves with no line drawn over them are considered open or incomplete. If a line is drawn over them, then that sequent is justified by an inference rule with no premises.

By a *proof system*, we mean a collection of inference rules, such as those described in Section 3.2. Let $\mathcal{X}$ be such a set of rules for two-sided sequents. We write $\Sigma :: \Gamma \vdash_{\mathcal{X}} \Delta$ to denote that the sequent $\Sigma :: \Gamma \vdash \Delta$ has a proof in $\mathcal{X}$. Shorthand notations are used: $\Gamma \vdash_{\mathcal{X}} \Delta$ omits the empty Σ, and $\vdash_{\mathcal{X}} \Delta$ also omits the empty Γ. The same conventions apply for proof systems using one-sided sequents except that we do not write the left-hand context (keeping just the signature). Although the $\vdash$ symbol (without a subscript) indicates a sequent, it will occasionally be used as the proposition that the same sequent is provable in a proof system that can be inferred from context. The reader should always be able to disambiguate between these two senses of the $\vdash$ symbol.

> **Exercise 3.3.** *Consider a (trivial) sequent calculus proof system containing just the cut and initial inference rules (see Figure 3.3). Describe what can be proved using just those two rules. Show that every provable sequent can be proved without the cut rule.*

3.5 Permutations of Inference Rules

Sequent calculus inference rules can often be permuted over each other. For example, consider the following three introduction rules.

$$\frac{\Sigma :: \Gamma_1 \vdash \Delta_1, B \quad \Sigma :: C, \Gamma_2 \vdash \Delta_2}{\Sigma :: B \supset C, \Gamma_1, \Gamma_2 \vdash \Delta_1, \Delta_2} \supset L \qquad \frac{\Sigma :: B, \Gamma \vdash \Delta, C}{\Sigma :: \Gamma \vdash \Delta, B \supset C} \supset R$$

$$\frac{\Sigma :: B, \Gamma \vdash \Delta \quad \Sigma :: C, \Gamma \vdash \Delta}{\Sigma :: B \vee C, \Gamma \vdash \Delta} \vee L$$

Here, the left- and right-hand contexts are assumed to be multisets. In the first derivation in Figure 3.5, the right-introduction rule for implication is below the left-introduction rule of a disjunction. The second derivation in that figure has the same root and leaf sequents but the introduction rules are switched. Note that the second derivation uses two occurrences of $\supset R$ while the first proof uses only one occurrence of that rule.

Sometimes inference rules can be permuted if additional structural rules are employed. For example, consider the first derivation in Figure 3.6. It is possible to switch the order of the two introduction rules it contains, but this requires introducing some weakenings and a contraction, as is witnessed by the second derivation in that figure. If these additional structural rules are not permitted in a given proof system (as we shall see is the case in intuitionistic logic), then the original two inference rules cannot be permuted.

Understanding when inference rules permute over each other makes it possible to improve the effectiveness of searching for proofs. Consider again the derivations in Figure 3.5. Imagine attempting to find a proof of the sequent $\Sigma :: \Gamma, p \vee q \vdash r \supset s, \Delta$ following the development of the first derivation in that figure: Namely, we first do an $\supset R$ rule followed by the $\vee L$ rule. Additionally,

$$\frac{\dfrac{\Sigma :: \Gamma, p, r \vdash s, \Delta \quad \Sigma :: \Gamma, q, r \vdash s, \Delta}{\Sigma :: \Gamma, p \vee q, r \vdash s, \Delta} \vee L}{\Sigma :: \Gamma, p \vee q \vdash r \supset s, \Delta} \supset R$$

$$\frac{\dfrac{\Sigma :: \Gamma, p, r \vdash s, \Delta}{\Sigma :: \Gamma, p \vdash r \supset s, \Delta} \supset R \quad \dfrac{\Sigma :: \Gamma, q, r \vdash s, \Delta}{\Sigma :: \Gamma, q \vdash r \supset s, \Delta} \supset R}{\Sigma :: \Gamma, p \vee q \vdash r \supset s, \Delta} \vee L$$

Figure 3.5 Two derivations that differ in the order of two inference rules.

$$\cfrac{\cfrac{\Sigma :: \Gamma_1, r \vdash \Delta_1, p \qquad \Sigma :: \Gamma_2, q \vdash \Delta_2, s}{\Sigma :: \Gamma_1, \Gamma_2, p \supset q, r \vdash \Delta_1, \Delta_2, s} \supset L}{\Sigma :: \Gamma_1, \Gamma_2, p \supset q \vdash \Delta_1, \Delta_2, r \supset s} \supset R$$

$$\cfrac{\cfrac{\cfrac{\Sigma :: \Gamma_1, r \vdash \Delta_1, p}{\Sigma :: \Gamma_1, r \vdash \Delta_1, p, s} wR}{\Sigma :: \Gamma_1 \vdash \Delta_1, p, r \supset s} \supset R \qquad \cfrac{\cfrac{\Sigma :: \Gamma_2, q \vdash \Delta_2, s}{\Sigma :: \Gamma_2, q, r \vdash \Delta_2, s} wL}{\Sigma :: \Gamma_2, q \vdash \Delta_2, r \supset s} \supset R}{\cfrac{\Sigma :: \Gamma_1, \Gamma_2, p \supset q \vdash \Delta_1, \Delta_2, r \supset s, r \supset s}{\Sigma :: \Gamma_1, \Gamma_2, p \supset q \vdash \Delta_1, \Delta_2, r \supset s} cR} \supset L$$

Figure 3.6 Two derivations that illustrate the permutation of inference rules supported by structural rules.

assume that there is, in fact, no proof of the left premise $\Sigma :: \Gamma, p, r \vdash s, \Delta$ (e.g., an exhaustive search fails to find a proof of this sequent). If we employ a naive proof search strategy, we might make another attempt to find a proof of the endsequent by switching the application of the $\vee L$ and the $\supset R$ rules. As it is clear from the second derivation, this other order of rule applications leads to an attempt to prove the same left premise for which we already know no proof exists. This second attempt at proving this endsequent does not need to be made.

An inference rule asserts that whenever its premises are provable, its conclusion is provable. The converse – that is, if the conclusion is provable, then all the premises are provable – does not always hold. If this converse does hold for an inference rule, we say that that rule is *invertible*. From the point of view of searching for a proof, whenever invertible introduction rules are available to prove a given sequent, they can be applied in any order and without considering any other order of applying them. One way to show that an inference rule is invertible is to show that for every pair of inference rules for which the rule in question appears above another inference rule, the order of that pair of rules can be switched.

3.6 Focused and Unfocused Proof Systems

The sequent calculus proof systems described in this chapter and used in Chapter 4 are not well suited to support the computation-as-proof-search paradigm. Consider, for example, the following situation. Let Γ be a multiset containing 1,000 non-atomic formulas and let A be an atomic formula.

Attempting to find a proof of the sequent $\Gamma, B_1 \vee B_2, C_1 \wedge C_2 \vdash A$ by using an introduction rule requires selecting which of the 1,002 occurrences of non-atomic formulas will get its top-level connective introduced. Of course, the premises that result from applying that rule will likely have about 1,000 non-atomic formulas on their left-hand side. For example,

$$\cfrac{\cfrac{\Gamma, B_1, C_1, C_2 \vdash A}{\Gamma, B_1, C_1 \wedge C_2 \vdash A} \wedge L^m \quad \cfrac{\Gamma, B_2, C_1, C_2 \vdash A}{\Gamma, B_2, C_1 \wedge C_2 \vdash A} \wedge L^m}{\Gamma, B_1 \vee B_2, C_1 \wedge C_2 \vdash A} \vee L.$$

is one of about a million choices. Also, the choice to do the $\vee L$ below the $\wedge L^m$ is a choice that is *not important* since permuting the $\wedge L^m$ below $\vee L$ will yield the same premises.

As we shall see in Chapter 5, there are occasions when it is possible to organize sequent proofs into two alternating phases. One of these phases is the *goal-reduction phase* in which only right-introduction rules are attempted when trying to prove a sequent with a non-atomic right-hand side. The other phase is the *backchaining phase* where *focused* applications of left-introduction rules are attempted. This two-phased description of proof construction was first formalized using the technical notion of *uniform proofs* described in Miller et al. [1987, 1991]. Soon after Girard introduced linear logic in [1987], Andreoli [1992] designed a similar, two-phase structure for proofs in linear logic. Since his proof system was based on linear logic, Andreoli's proof system was able to move from using phases based on the left vs right distinction central to the notion of uniform proof to using phases based on the more foundational *invertible* vs *non-invertible* distinction of inference rules (see Section 4.3.4).

We sometimes refer to Gentzen-style sequent calculus proof systems as *unfocused*. We will eventually introduce explicitly *focused* proof systems in Section 5.4: All such proof systems will employ the down-arrow symbol $\Downarrow$ to designate the focus of a sequent. In particular, we use sequents of the form $\Sigma :: \Gamma \Downarrow D \vdash A$ in Section 5.4 and $\Sigma :: \Psi; \Delta \Downarrow D \vdash \Gamma; \Upsilon$ in Section 6.7. In both of these sequents, the formula occurrence D is the *focus* of that sequent.

3.7 Cut-Elimination and Its Consequences

In the construction of proofs in mathematics, discovering useful lemmas is a key activity. Consider again the example from Section 3.1 where we considered

3.7 CUT-ELIMINATION AND ITS CONSEQUENCES

proving that the product $n(n + 1)$ is even for all natural numbers n. The part of the proof of this theorem illustrated was straightforward since we employed the three lemmas L_1, L_2, and L_3. Of course, these three lemmas needed to be discovered and proved. The cut inference rule in Figure 3.3 formally allows lemmas to be proved and used in a proof. For example, assume that L_1, L_2, and L_3 have sequent calculus proofs Ξ_1, Ξ_2, and Ξ_3, respectively.[1] The following derivation injects those lemmas into the proof of our original theorem, $(\forall n. \forall p.(\text{times } n \ (s \ n) \ p) \supset (\text{even } p))$, which we abbreviate as the formula G.

$$
\cfrac{
  \Xi_1 \atop \cdot ::\cdot \vdash L_1
  \quad
  \cfrac{
    \Xi_2 \atop \cdot ::\cdot \vdash L_2
    \quad
    \cfrac{
      \Xi_3 \atop \cdot ::\cdot \vdash L_3
      \quad
      \vdots \atop \cdot :: L_1, L_2, L_3 \vdash G
    }{\cdot :: L_1, L_2 \vdash G} \ cut
  }{\cdot :: L_1 \vdash G} \ cut
}{\cdot ::\cdot \vdash G} \ cut
$$

Thus, these instances of the cut rule allow us to move from searching for a proof of G to searching for a proof of G using L_1, L_2, and L_3.

For all of the sequent calculus proof systems we consider in this book, the *cut-elimination theorem* holds: That is, a sequent has a proof if and only if it has a *cut-free proof* (a proof with no occurrences of the cut rule). In subsequent chapters, we shall prove two cut-elimination theorems: Section 5.5 provides one for intuitionistic logic, and Chapter 7 presents one for linear logic. This important theorem has several consequences, some of which we describe below.

The consistency of a logic is usually a simple consequence of cut-elimination. For example, if a formula B and its negation $B \supset f$ are provable, then the sequents $\cdot \vdash B$ and $\cdot \vdash B \supset f$ are provable. Since the rule for introducing implication on the right is invertible (as we shall see in Section 4.3.4), it must be the case that the sequent $B \vdash f$ is provable. Applying the cut inference rule to proofs of the two sequents $\cdot \vdash B$ and $B \vdash f$ yields a proof of $\cdot \vdash f$. By the cut-elimination theorem, however, the sequent $\cdot \vdash f$ has a proof without cuts. Thus, the last inference rule of this proof must be either an introduction rule or a structural rule. Generally, there is no introduction rule for f on the right. Also, the structural rules will not yield a provable sequent either. Thus, there can be no cut-free proof of $\cdot \vdash f$: Hence, a formula and its negation cannot both be provable.

---

[1] These three lemmas can be proved in a proof system that formalizes the induction rule. In this book, we shall not present such proof systems.

The success of proving the cut-elimination theorem also signals that certain aspects of the logic's proof system were well designed. For example, logical connectives generally have left- and right-introduction rules when using two-sided sequents. If we think of a sequent as describing a sheet of paper with the assumptions listed at the top of the page and the conclusion at the bottom, then the left- and right-introduction rules yield two *senses* to how connectives are used within a proof. In particular, the left-introduction rules describe how we argue *from* formulas, while the right-introduction rules describe how we argue *to* formulas. For example, the $\supset$R rule in Figure 3.4 describes how one uses hypothetical reasoning to prove the formula $B \supset C$ while the $\supset$L rule shows that we use $B \supset C$ as an assumption by attempting a proof of B and by attempting the original sequent again, but this time with the additional assumption C added to the set of hypotheses. Of course, if we consider the model-theoretic semantics of the connectives, they usually have only one *sense*: For example, $B \wedge C$ is true if and only if B and C are true. The cut-elimination theorem implies that the two senses attributed to a logical connective work together to define one logical connective. We return to this aspect of cut elimination in Sections 4.2 and 5.6.

When formulas do not involve higher-order quantification, a formula occurring in a sequent in a cut-free proof is always a subformula of some formula of the endsequent. This invariant is the so-called *subformula property* of cut-free proofs. When searching for a proof, one needs only to choose how to rearrange subformulas of the endsequent: Of course, instantiations of a quantified formula must also be considered to be subformulas of that quantified formula. In the first-order setting, all proper subformulas of a given formula have fewer occurrences of logical connectives. Thus, having proofs restricted to arrangements of subformulas is an interesting and powerful restriction. In contrast, cut elimination in the higher-order setting does not guarantee the subformula property since instantiating a predicate variable can result in formulas with more occurrences of logical connectives than the formula into which the predicate variables were instantiated. This aspect of higher-order logic is illustrated in Section 9.1.

Note that the Frege proof of $f \supset w$ in Figure 3.1 does not satisfy the subformula property: In particular, none of the formulas appearing in that list of formulas is a subformula of $f \supset w$ except for the conclusion of that proof.

3.7 CUT-ELIMINATION AND ITS CONSEQUENCES

When one attempts to use the sequent calculus to formalize proofs of mathematically interesting theorems, one discovers that the cut rule is one of the most frequently used inference rules. Eliminating cuts in such proofs would yield huge, low-level proofs where all lemmas are "in-lined" and reproved at every instance of their use. Cut-free proofs can thus be huge objects. For example, suppose one uses the number of sequents in a proof to measure its size. In some cases, cut-free proofs are hyperexponentially bigger than proofs allowing cut (see Exercise 2.3 for a similarly explosive growth). Thus, sequents with proofs of relatively small size can have cut-free proofs that require more inference rules than the number of sub-atomic particles in the universe. If a cut-free proof is actually computed and stored in some computer memory, the theorem that that proof proves is likely to be *mathematically uninteresting*. This observation does not disturb us here since we are interested in cut-free proofs as tools for describing *computation*. Cut-free proofs are neither illuminating nor readable; instead, they are structures more akin to the classic notion of Turing machine configurations. They provide a low-level and detailed computation trace.

Encoding a computation as a cut-free proof can be superior to encoding it via Turing machine configurations since there are several profound ways to reason with actual proof structures. For example, assume that we have a cut-free proof of the two-sided sequent $\mathcal{P} \vdash G$ for some logic, say, $\mathcal{X}$. As we shall see, in many approaches to proof search, it is natural to identify the left-hand context $\mathcal{P}$ with a (logic) program and G as the goal or query to be established. A cut-free proof of such a sequent is then a trace establishing this goal from this program. Now assume that we can prove $\mathcal{P}' \vdash^+ \mathcal{P}$ where $\mathcal{P}'$ is some other logic program and $\vdash^+$ is provability in $\mathcal{X}^+$, which is some strengthening of $\mathcal{X}$ in which, say, induction principles are added (as well as cut). If the stronger logic satisfies cut elimination, $\mathcal{P}' \vdash G$ has a cut-free proof in the stronger logic $\mathcal{X}^+$. If things have been organized well, it can then become a simple matter to see that cut-free proofs of such sequents do not make use of the stronger proof principles and, hence, $\mathcal{P}' \vdash G$ has a cut-free proof in $\mathcal{X}$. Thus, using cut-elimination, we have been able to move from a *formal* proof about programs $\mathcal{P}$ and $\mathcal{P}'$ immediately to the conclusion that whatever goals can be established for $\mathcal{P}$ can be established for $\mathcal{P}'$. The ability to do such direct, logically principled reasoning about programs and computations is a valuable feature of the proof search paradigm.

3.8 Bibliographic Notes

In this chapter, we have presented a broad overview of sequent calculus proof systems. Chapter 4 contains proof systems for classical and intuitionistic logics, and Chapter 6 contains proof systems for linear logic.

Kleene [1952] presents a detailed analysis of the permutability of inference rules for classical and intuitionistic sequent calculus proof systems.

Statman [1978] showed that there exists a sequence $H_0, H_1, H_2, \ldots$ of theorems of first-order classical logic such that the size of H_n and the size of a sequent calculus proof (with cut) of H_n are linear in n, while the size of the shortest cut-free proof of H_n is *hyperexponential* in n. Here, the *hyperexponential function* can be defined as $h(0) = 1$ and $h(n+1) = 2^{h(n)}$.

The main proof systems presented in this book will have a cut-elimination theorem. We shall prove the cut-elimination theorem for these proof systems using the nonstandard technique of proving them for focused instead of unfocused proof systems. Several good references exists for the more standard approach of proving the cut-elimination theorem of unfocused proof systems. The original proof in Gentzen [1935] is a good place to read about proving this result for classical and intuitionistic logics. The textbooks by Gallier [1986], Girard et al. [1989], Negri and von Plato [2001], and Bimbó [2015] provide more modern presentations. Still more novel and metalevel approaches to proving cut-elimination can be found in Pfenning [2000], Miller and Pimentel [2004], and Miller and Pimentel [2013].

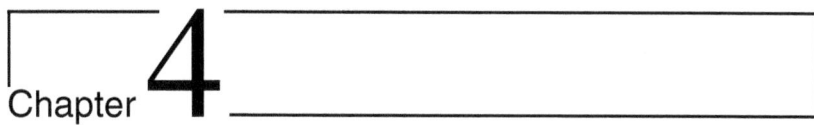
Chapter 4

Classical and Intuitionistic Logics

Classical and intuitionistic logics provide the foundation to many logic-based computational tools, such as interactive and automatic theorem provers, logic programs, model checkers, and programming language type systems. There are several ways to describe the difference between these two logics, including the following.

1. Intuitionistic logic results from admitting only those proofs that can be seen as providing *constructive evidence* of what is proved. Classical logic admits these proofs and others that need not be constructive. For example, classical logic admits the axiom of the *excluded middle* as a proof principle, even though there might not be a constructive way to tell whether a formula or its negation holds.
2. The semantics of intuitionistic logic can be based on *possible world semantics* or *Kripke models* (see Kripke [1965] and Troelstra and van Dalen [1988]). In such models, standard classical models are called *worlds*. These worlds are arranged in a tree structure. A path in such a tree represents a possible evolution of truth in those worlds. In such models, an implication is true in a given world if it is true in all worlds to which it evolves.

Gentzen provided an entirely different characterization of the differences between classical and intuitionistic logic that involved the role of structural inference rules within the sequent calculus. This characterization plays an essential role in this book. A careful reading of Gentzen's characterization will help us motivate the introduction of linear logic in Chapter 6.

This chapter presents sequent calculus proof systems for classical and intuitionistic logics that are small variations of the *LK* and *LJ* proof systems in Gentzen [1935]. After presenting some basic properties of those proof systems, we highlight some issues that arise when systematically searching for proofs in those proof systems.

> **Exercise 4.1.**(‡) *Prove that there are irrational numbers, a and b, such that a^b is rational. An easy, non-constructive proof starts with the observation that $\sqrt{2}^{\sqrt{2}}$ is either rational or irrational (an instance of the excluded middle). Complete that proof. Can you provide a constructive proof of this statement?*

4.1 Classical and Intuitionistic Inference Rules

Both intuitionistic and classical logics will use the same connectives: In particular, the signature of logical connectives, Σ_{-1}, for both of these logics is

$$\{f : o, t : o, \wedge : o \to o \to o, \vee : o \to o \to o, \supset : o \to o \to o\} \cup$$
$$\{\forall_\tau : (\tau \to o) \to o, \exists_\tau : (\tau \to o) \to o \mid \tau \in \mathcal{S}\backslash\{o\}\}$$

Here, the set of primitive types S is assumed to be fixed and to contain the type o. This signature is a first-order signature over the sorts $\mathcal{S}\backslash\{o\}$ (see Section 2.3). If we use $\{o\}$ for S, then this signature does not contain any quantifiers and is, therefore, the signature for a propositional logic.

Our proof systems for provability in classical and intuitionistic logics use sequents of the form $\Sigma :: \Gamma \vdash \Delta$, where both Γ and Δ are multisets of Σ-formulas. The introduction, identity, and structural rules for this proof system are given in Figures 4.1, 4.2, and 4.3, respectively. Of the four inference rules with two premises, $\supset$L and *cut* are multiplicative, while $\wedge$R and $\vee$L are additive.

The left- and right-introduction rules for t and f can be derived from the binary connective for which they are the unit. In particular, the $\wedge$R has two premises for the binary connective. The n-ary generalization of the $\wedge$R will have n premises. Since t is the unit for $\wedge$, we can interpret it as the 0-ary conjunction. Thus, the tR rule has zero premises. Furthermore, the n-ary version of the $\wedge$L rule has n instances, one for each of its n conjuncts. Thus, there is no

4.1 Classical and Intuitionistic Inference Rules

$$\frac{\Sigma :: B, \Gamma \vdash \Delta}{\Sigma :: B \wedge C, \Gamma \vdash \Delta} \wedge L \qquad \frac{\Sigma :: C, \Gamma \vdash \Delta}{\Sigma :: B \wedge C, \Gamma \vdash \Delta} \wedge L \qquad \frac{}{\Sigma :: \Gamma \vdash \Delta, t} \, tR$$

$$\frac{\Sigma :: B, \Gamma \vdash \Delta \quad \Sigma :: C, \Gamma \vdash \Delta}{\Sigma :: B \vee C, \Gamma \vdash \Delta} \vee L \qquad \frac{\Sigma :: \Gamma \vdash \Delta, B \quad \Sigma :: \Gamma \vdash \Delta, C}{\Sigma :: \Gamma \vdash \Delta, B \wedge C} \wedge R$$

$$\frac{}{\Sigma :: \Gamma, f \vdash \Delta} \, fL \qquad \frac{\Sigma :: \Gamma \vdash \Delta, B}{\Sigma :: \Gamma \vdash \Delta, B \vee C} \vee R \qquad \frac{\Sigma :: \Gamma \vdash \Delta, C}{\Sigma :: \Gamma \vdash \Delta, B \vee C} \vee R$$

$$\frac{\Sigma \Vdash t : \tau \quad \Sigma :: \Gamma, B[t/x] \vdash \Delta}{\Sigma :: \Gamma, \forall_\tau x.B \vdash \Delta} \forall L \qquad \frac{\Sigma, y : \tau :: \Gamma \vdash \Delta, B[y/x]}{\Sigma :: \Gamma \vdash \Delta, \forall_\tau x.B} \forall R$$

$$\frac{\Sigma, y : \tau :: \Gamma, B[y/x] \vdash \Delta}{\Sigma :: \Gamma, \exists_\tau x \, B \vdash \Delta} \exists L \qquad \frac{\Sigma \Vdash t : \tau \quad \Sigma :: \Gamma \vdash \Delta, B[t/x]}{\Sigma :: \Gamma \vdash \Delta, \exists_\tau x \, B} \exists R$$

$$\frac{\Sigma :: \Gamma_1 \vdash \Delta_1, B \quad \Sigma :: C, \Gamma_2 \vdash \Delta_2}{\Sigma :: B \supset C, \Gamma_1, \Gamma_2 \vdash \Delta_1, \Delta_2} \supset L \qquad \frac{\Sigma :: B, \Gamma \vdash \Delta, C}{\Sigma :: \Gamma \vdash \Delta, B \supset C} \supset R$$

Figure 4.1 Introduction rules.

$$\frac{}{\Sigma :: B \vdash B} \, init \qquad \frac{\Sigma :: \Gamma_1 \vdash \Delta_1, B \quad \Sigma :: B, \Gamma_2 \vdash \Delta_2}{\Sigma :: \Gamma_1, \Gamma_2 \vdash \Delta_1, \Delta_2} \, cut$$

Figure 4.2 Identity rules.

$$\frac{\Sigma :: \Gamma \vdash \Delta}{\Sigma :: \Gamma, B \vdash \Delta} \, wL \qquad \frac{\Sigma :: \Gamma \vdash \Delta}{\Sigma :: \Gamma \vdash \Delta, B} \, wR$$

$$\frac{\Sigma :: \Gamma, B, B \vdash \Delta}{\Sigma :: \Gamma, B \vdash \Delta} \, cL \qquad \frac{\Sigma :: \Gamma \vdash \Delta, B, B}{\Sigma :: \Gamma \vdash \Delta, B} \, cR$$

Figure 4.3 Structural rules: Contraction and weakening.

left-introduction rule for t since it is the 0-ary version of $\wedge$. The dual argument illustrates how to derive the introduction rules for f from the rules for $\vee$.

Provability in *classical logic* is given using the notion of a **C**-proof, which is any proof using inference rules in Figures 4.1, 4.2, and 4.3. Provability in *intuitionistic logic* is given using **I**-proofs, which are **C**-proofs in which the right-hand side of all sequents in a given proof contains exactly one formula: i.e., they are *single-conclusion sequents*. A proof system that can only use such restricted sequents is called a *single-conclusion proof system*. When no such restriction is imposed on sequents (as in **C**-proofs), such a proof system is called a *multiple-conclusion proof system*.

Let Σ be a given first-order signature over the primitive types in S, let Δ and Γ be finite multisets of Σ-formulas, and let B be a Σ-formula. We write $\Sigma :: \Delta \vdash_c \Gamma$ if the sequent $\Sigma :: \Delta \vdash \Gamma$ has a **C**-proof. We write $\Sigma :: \Delta \vdash_I B$ if the sequent $\Sigma :: \Delta \vdash B$ has an **I**-proof.

The restriction on **I**-proofs (that all sequents in the proof have singleton right-hand sides) implies that **I**-proofs do not contain occurrences of structural rules on the right (i.e., no occurrences of cR and wR) and that every occurrence of the $\supset L$ rule and the *cut* rule are instances of the following two inference rules.

$$\frac{\Sigma :: \Gamma_1 \vdash B \quad \Sigma :: C, \Gamma_2 \vdash E}{\Sigma :: B \supset C, \Gamma_1, \Gamma_2 \vdash E} \supset L \qquad \frac{\Sigma :: \Gamma_1 \vdash B \quad \Sigma :: B, \Gamma_2 \vdash E}{\Sigma :: \Gamma_1, \Gamma_2 \vdash E} \, cut.$$

That is, the formula on the right-hand side of the conclusion must move to the right premise and not to the left premise. These observations can give an alternative characterization of **I**-proofs.

> **Proposition 4.2.** *Let Ξ be a **C**-proof of $\Sigma :: \Gamma \vdash B$. Then Ξ is an **I**-proof if and only if Ξ contains no occurrences of either cR or wR and, in every occurrence in Ξ of an $\supset L$ and a cut rule, the right-hand side of the conclusion is the same as the right-hand side of the right premise.*

Proof: The forward direction is immediate. Thus, assume that the **C**-proof Ξ of $\Sigma :: \Gamma \vdash B$ satisfies the two conditions of the converse. We proceed by induction on the structure of proofs. Consider the last inference rule of Ξ. If that rule is an instance of the *init*, tR, or fL rules, the conclusion is immediate. Otherwise, if that last inference rule is an instance of either $\supset L$ or *cut*, then, given the inductive restrictions, the premises have proofs satisfying the same restrictions, namely that the two premises are single-conclusion sequents. Thus, by the inductive assumption, the proofs of the premises must be **I**-proofs. The inductive argument holds trivially if the last rule of Ξ is any other inference rule (the wR and cR rules are not possible). □

This alternative characterization of **I**-proofs as restricted **C**-proofs prefigures two important features of linear logic (Chapter 6). The first condition

4.1 Classical and Intuitionistic Inference Rules

$$
\cfrac{\cfrac{\cfrac{\cfrac{\cfrac{B \vdash B}{B \vdash B,\mathsf{f}} \text{wR}}{\vdash B, B \supset \mathsf{f}} \supset\!\text{R}}{\vdash B, B \vee (B \supset \mathsf{f})} \vee\text{R}}{\vdash B \vee (B \supset \mathsf{f}), B \vee (B \supset \mathsf{f})} \vee\text{R}}{\vdash B \vee (B \supset \mathsf{f})} \text{cR} \quad \text{init}
$$

Figure 4.4 A **C**-proof of the excluded middle.

(on the absence of wR and cR) means that the contexts used to describe intuitionistic logic are *hybrid*: The left-hand-side of sequents allows structural rules while the right-hand-side of sequents does not. This hybrid use of contexts will be exploited in richer ways in linear logic. The second condition means that something special is hidden in the intuitionistic implication and, as we shall see in Section 6.2, that special feature is captured by the ! *exponential* of linear logic.

Gentzen's formulation of sequent calculus treated *negation* as a logical connective. However, when we write the negation of a formula, $\neg B$, we shall mean $B \supset \mathsf{f}$. We return to these two different treatments of negation in Section 4.5.

A formula of the form $B \vee \neg B$ is an example of the *excluded middle*: In terms of truth values, B is either true or false, and there is no third possibility. Figure 4.4 contains a **C**-proof of this formula.

A slight variation of this proof yields a **C**-proof of $B \vee (B \supset C)$ for any formulas B and C.

Exercise 4.3. (‡) *Provide proofs for each of the following sequents. If an **I**-proof exists, present that proof. Assume that the signature for non-logical constants is* $\Sigma_0 = \{p : o, q : o, r : i \to o, s : i \to i \to o, a : i, b : i\}$.

1. $(p \wedge (p \supset q) \wedge (p \wedge q \supset r)) \supset r$
2. $(p \supset q) \supset (\neg q \supset \neg p)$
3. $(\neg q \supset \neg p) \supset (p \supset q)$
4. $p \vee (p \supset q)$
5. $((p \supset q) \supset p) \supset p$
6. $(r\,a \wedge r\,b \supset q) \supset \exists x.(r\,x \supset q)$
7. $\exists y.\forall x.(r\,x \supset r\,y)$
8. $\forall x.\forall y.(s\,x\,y) \supset \forall z.(s\,z\,z)$

Exercise 4.4. (‡) *Take the formulas in Exercise 4.3 which have **C**-proofs but no **I**-proofs and reorganize them into **I**-proofs in which appropriate instances of the excluded middle are added to the left-hand context. For example, give an **I**-proof of the sequent $\Sigma :: r\,a \vee \neg r\,a \vdash (r\,a \wedge r\,b \supset q) \supset \exists x.(r\,x \supset q)$.*

Exercise 4.5. (‡) *Let A be an atomic formula. Describe all pairs of formulas $\langle B, C \rangle$ where B and C are different members of the set*

$$\{A, \neg A, \neg\neg A, \neg\neg\neg A\}$$

*such that $B \vdash C$ has a **C**-proof. Make the same list such that $B \vdash C$ has an **I**-proof.*

Exercise 4.6. *The multiplicative version of $\wedge R$ is the inference rule*

$$\frac{\Sigma :: \Gamma_1 \vdash B, \Delta_1 \qquad \Sigma :: \Gamma_2 \vdash C, \Delta_2}{\Sigma :: \Gamma_1, \Gamma_2 \vdash B \wedge C, \Delta_1, \Delta_2}.$$

*Show that a sequent has a **C**-proof (resp. **I**-proof) if and only if it has one in the proof system that results from replacing $\wedge R$ with the multiplicative version. Similarly, consider the multiplicative version of the $\vee L$ rule, namely,*

$$\frac{\Sigma :: B, \Gamma_1 \vdash \Delta_1 \qquad \Sigma :: C, \Gamma_2 \vdash \Delta_2}{\Sigma :: B \vee C, \Gamma_1, \Gamma_2 \vdash \Delta_1, \Delta_2}.$$

*Show that a sequent has a **C**-proof if and only if it has a **C**-proof where the additive $\vee L$ is replaced with this multiplicative rule.*

The notion of provability based on sequents given in this section differs slightly from common presentations of classical and intuitionistic logic found in, say, Gentzen [1935], Prawitz [1965], Fitting [1969], and Troelstra [1973]. Those presentations do not make the eigenvariable signatures explicit, and substitution terms (the terms used in $\forall L$ and $\exists R$) are not constrained to be built from such signatures. The following example illustrates the main difference.

4.1 CLASSICAL AND INTUITIONISTIC INFERENCE RULES

Let S be the set $\{i, o\}$ of two sorts and let Σ_0, the signature of non-logical constants, be just $\{p : i \to o\}$. Now consider the sequent

$$\cdot :: \forall_i x \, (p \, x) \vdash \exists_i x \, (p \, x).$$

This sequent has no proof even though $\exists_i x \, (p \, x)$ follows from $\forall_i x \, (p \, x)$ in the traditional presentations of classical and intuitionistic logics. This difference is because there are no $\{p : i \to o\}$-terms of type i: That is, the type i is *empty* in this signature. Thus, we need the following additional definition. The signature Σ *inhabits* the set of primitive types S if, for every $\tau \in S$ different than o, there is a Σ-term of type τ. When Σ inhabits S, the notion of provability defined above coincides with the more traditional presentations.

The sequent calculus proof systems for classical and intuitionistic logics will be used as the standard by which we shall judge other proof systems. This comparison is broken into two parts called *soundness* and *completeness*. In particular, assume we have a sequent proof system called $\mathcal{Y}$. We say that $\mathcal{Y}$ is *sound* for classical logic if every sequent $\Gamma \vdash B$ provable in $\mathcal{Y}$ is also provable in classical logic (i.e., $\Gamma \vdash B$ has a **C**-proof). Conversely, $\mathcal{Y}$ is *complete* for classical logic if every sequent $\Gamma \vdash B$ with a **C**-proof also has a $\mathcal{Y}$ proof. Soundness and completeness for intuitionistic logic are stated similarly by using **I**-proofs instead of **C**-proofs. For example, Gentzen's theorem (Theorem 4.13) about eliminating the cut rule can be seen as a completeness theorem for the proof system that results from removing the cut rule from the rules for **C**-proofs. It is worth noting that since $p \vee (p \supset q)$ has a **C**-proof but no **I**-proof, it is the case that **I**-proofs are not complete for **C**-proofs and that **C**-proofs are not sound for **I**-proofs.

Exercise 4.7.(‡) *Assume that the set of sorts S contains the two tokens i and j and that the only non-logical constant is $f : i \to j$. In particular, assume that no constants of type i are declared in the non-logical signature. Is there an **I**-proof of $(\exists_j x \, t) \vee (\forall_i y \exists_j x \, t)$? Under the same assumption, does the formula $(\exists_j x \, t) \vee (\forall_i x \, t)$ have a **C**-proof? An **I**-proof? What comparison can you draw between proving this formula and the formula in Exercise 4.3(4)?*

As we noted at the beginning of this chapter, there are many ways to describe the difference between classical and intuitionistic logics. The following exercise contains yet another way to present this difference.

> **Exercise 4.8.** (‡) *Consider adding the rule (taken from Gabbay [1985])*
>
> $$\frac{\Sigma :: \Gamma \vdash B}{\Sigma :: \Gamma \vdash C} \text{ restart}$$
>
> *to **I**-proofs. This rule has the proviso that on the path from the occurrence of this rule to the root of the proof, there is a sequent with B as its right-hand side. The spirit of this rule is that during the search for a proof of single-conclusion sequents, one can ignore the right-hand side of a sequent (here, C) and restart an attempt to prove a previous right-hand side (here, B). Prove that a formula has a **C**-proof if and only if it has an **I**-proof with the restart rule added.*

4.2 The Identity Rules and Their Elimination

As it turns out, almost all forms of the identity rules can be eliminated from proofs without losing completeness in both classical and intuitionistic logics. In particular, all initial rules involving non-atomic formulas and all cut rules can be eliminated.

An occurrence of the initial rule of the form $\Sigma :: B \vdash B$ is an *atomic initial rule* if B is an atomic formula. A proof is *atomically closed* if every occurrence of the initial rule in it is an atomic initial rule. In classical and intuitionistic logics, we can restrict the initial rule to be atomic initial rules.

> **Theorem 4.9.** *If a sequent has a **C**-proof (resp, an **I**-proof) then it has a **C**-proof (resp, an **I**-proof) in which all occurrence of the init rule are atomic initial rules.*

Proof: We need to prove that every sequent of the form $B \vdash B$ has a proof containing only atomic initial rules. We proceed by induction on the structure of B. Consider the cases where B is of the form $B_1 \supset B_2$ and of the form $\forall_\tau x.Bx$ and consider the following two derivations.

4.2 THE IDENTITY RULES AND THEIR ELIMINATION

$$\frac{\dfrac{B_1 \vdash B_1 \quad B_2 \vdash B_2}{B_1, B_1 \supset B_2 \vdash B_2} \supset L}{B_1 \supset B_2 \vdash B_1 \supset B_2} \supset R \qquad \frac{\dfrac{\Sigma, y : \tau :: By \vdash By}{\Sigma, y : \tau :: \forall_\tau x.Bx \vdash By} \forall L}{\Sigma :: \forall_\tau x.Bx \vdash \forall_\tau x.Bx} \forall R.$$

Clearly, in these two cases, one instance of an initial rule can be replaced by other instances of the initial rule involving smaller formulas. Applying the inductive hypothesis on the premises of these derivations completes the proof for these cases. We leave the remaining cases to the reader to complete. □

The fact that the initial rules involving non-atomic formulas can be replaced by introduction rules and initial rules on subformulas is an important and desirable property of a proof system. However, atomic initial rules cannot be removed from proofs. Atoms are built from non-logical constants, such as predicates and function systems, and their meaning comes from outside logic. In particular, we shall eventually introduce *logic programs* to provide methods for proving atomic formulas that specify how to sort lists and represent transition systems. Although the logical constants have a fixed meaning given by proof systems, the non-logical constants that form atoms (predicate symbols) are the plugs for programmers to impact the development of proofs (we turn our attention to logic programs in Chapter 5).

The cut rule can also be restricted to atomic formulas, although it is more complex to prove that restriction. For example, consider the following occurrence of the cut rule.

$$\frac{\overset{\Xi_1}{\Sigma :: \Gamma_1 \vdash B, \Delta_1} \quad \overset{\Xi_2}{\Sigma :: \Gamma_2, B \vdash \Delta_2}}{\Sigma :: \Gamma_1, \Gamma_2 \vdash \Delta_1, \Delta_2} \; cut.$$

To argue that this cut can be eliminated, we need to consider the many cases that might arise when examining the last inference rule in both the Ξ_1 and Ξ_2 subproofs. Ultimately, we hope to rewrite the proof displayed above into another proof of the same endsequent in which the last inference rule is no longer the cut rule. We highlight only those cases where the last inference rule in Ξ_1 is the right-introduction rule for B and Ξ_2 is the left-introduction rule for B.

Consider a proof that contains the following cut with a conjunctive formula in which the two occurrences of that conjunction are immediately introduced in the two subproofs to cut.

$$
\dfrac{\dfrac{\Xi_1}{\Sigma :: \Gamma_1 \vdash A_1, \Delta_1 \quad \dfrac{\Xi_2}{\Sigma :: \Gamma_1 \vdash A_2, \Delta_1}}{\Sigma :: \Gamma_1 \vdash A_1 \land A_2, \Delta_1} \land R \quad \dfrac{\dfrac{\Xi_3}{\Sigma :: \Gamma_2, A_i \vdash \Delta_2}}{\Sigma :: \Gamma_2, A_1 \land A_2 \vdash \Delta_2} \land L}{\Sigma :: \Gamma_1, \Gamma_2 \vdash \Delta_1, \Delta_2} \; cut.
$$

Here, i is either 1 or 2. This derivation can be rewritten to

$$
\dfrac{\dfrac{\Xi_i}{\Sigma :: \Gamma_1 \vdash A_i, \Delta_1} \quad \dfrac{\Xi_3}{\Sigma :: \Gamma_2, A_i \vdash \Delta_2}}{\Sigma :: \Gamma_1, \Gamma_2 \vdash \Delta_1, \Delta_2} \; cut.
$$

In the process of reorganizing the proof in this manner, either Ξ_1 or Ξ_2 is discarded, and the new occurrence of cut is on a strict subformula of $A_1 \land A_2$.

Consider a proof that contains the following cut on an implicational formula and where the two occurrences of that implication are immediately introduced in the two premises of the cut.

$$
\dfrac{\dfrac{\Xi_1}{\Sigma :: \Gamma_1, A_1 \vdash A_2, \Delta_1}}{\Sigma :: \Gamma_1 \vdash A_1 \supset A_2, \Delta_1} \supset R \quad \dfrac{\dfrac{\Xi_2}{\Sigma :: \Gamma_2 \vdash A_1, \Delta_2} \quad \dfrac{\Xi_3}{\Sigma :: \Gamma_3, A_2 \vdash \Delta_3}}{\Sigma :: \Gamma_2, \Gamma_3, A_1 \supset A_2 \vdash \Delta_2, \Delta_3} \supset L
$$
$$
\overline{\Sigma :: \Gamma_1, \Gamma_2, \Gamma_3 \vdash \Delta_1, \Delta_2, \Delta_3} \; cut.
$$

This derivation can be rewritten to

$$
\dfrac{\dfrac{\dfrac{\Xi_2}{\Sigma :: \Gamma_2 \vdash A_1, \Delta_2} \quad \dfrac{\Xi_1}{\Sigma :: \Gamma_1, A_1 \vdash A_2, \Delta_1}}{\Sigma :: \Gamma_1, \Gamma_2 \vdash \Delta_1, \Delta_2, A_2} \; cut \quad \dfrac{\Xi_3}{\Sigma :: \Gamma_3, A_2 \vdash \Delta_3}}{\Sigma :: \Gamma_1, \Gamma_2, \Gamma_3 \vdash \Delta_1, \Delta_2, \Delta_3} \; cut.
$$

In the process of reorganizing the proof in this manner, the cut on $A_1 \supset A_2$ is replaced by two instances of cut, one on A_1 and the other one A_2.

Consider a proof that contains the following cut with $\forall$ in which the two occurrences of that quantifier are immediately introduced in the two subproofs to cut. Recall that the formula $\forall x.Bx$ is an abbreviation for $(\forall (\lambda x.Bx))$, which, in turn, is η-convertible to just $\forall B$. Hence, an instance of this quantifier can be written as (Bt).

4.2 The Identity Rules and Their Elimination

$$\dfrac{\dfrac{\Xi_1}{\Sigma, x :: \Gamma_1 \vdash Bx, \Delta_1}}{\Sigma :: \Gamma_1 \vdash \forall x.Bx, \Delta_1}\forall R \quad \dfrac{\dfrac{\Xi_2}{\Sigma :: \Gamma_2, Bt \vdash \Delta_2}}{\Sigma :: \Gamma_2, \forall x.Bx \vdash \Delta_2}\forall L$$
$$\overline{\Sigma :: \Gamma_1, \Gamma_2 \vdash \Delta_1, \Delta_2}\; cut$$

Here, t is a Σ-term. By Exercise 4.20, the proof Ξ_1 of $\Sigma, x :: \Gamma_1 \vdash Bx, \Delta_1$ can be transformed into a proof Ξ_1' of $\Sigma :: \Gamma_1 \vdash Bt, \Delta_1$ (notice that x is not free in any formula of Γ_1 and Δ_1 nor in the abstraction B). The above instance of cut can now be rewritten as

$$\dfrac{\dfrac{\Xi_1'}{\Sigma :: \Gamma_1 \vdash Bt, \Delta_1} \quad \dfrac{\Xi_2}{\Sigma :: \Gamma_2, Bt \vdash \Delta_2}}{\Sigma :: \Gamma_1, \Gamma_2 \vdash \Delta_1, \Delta_2}\; cut.$$

> **Exercise 4.10.** *Repeat the above rewriting of cut inference rules when the cut formula is* f, *a disjunction, or an existential quantifier.*

Consider a proof that contains the following cut with t in which the left premise is proved with the tR.

$$\dfrac{\dfrac{}{\Sigma :: \Gamma_1 \vdash t, \Delta_1}tR \quad \dfrac{\Xi}{\Sigma :: \Gamma_2, t \vdash \Delta_2}}{\Sigma :: \Gamma_1, \Gamma_2 \vdash \Delta_1, \Delta_2}\; cut.$$

Since there is no matching left-introduction rule for t, the elimination of this cut is different from those proceeding. This proof can be changed to remove this cut occurrence entirely as follows. First, the proof Ξ of $\Sigma :: \Gamma_2, t \vdash \Delta_2$ can be rewritten to the proof Ξ' of $\Sigma :: \Gamma_2 \vdash \Delta_2$ by removing the occurrence of t in the endsequent and, hence, all the other occurrences of t that can be traced to that occurrence. (See Exercise 4.19.) Furthermore, Ξ' can be transformed to a proof Ξ'' of $\Sigma :: \Gamma_1, \Gamma_2 \vdash \Delta_1, \Delta_2$ by simply adding weakening rules to it. The proof Ξ'' contains one fewer instances of the cut-rule than the original displayed proof above.

The above rewriting of cut rules suggests that each of the logical connectives, in isolation, has been given the appropriate left- and right-introduction rules. As mentioned in Section 3.7, each logical connective is given two senses: A small collection of right-introduction rules provides the means to prove a logical connective and a small collection of left-introduction rules provides the means to argue from a logical connective as an assumption.

The cut-elimination procedure (partially described above) and the non-atomic-initial-sequent elimination procedure provide some justification that these two senses belong to the same connective.

> **Exercise 4.11.** (‡) *Define a new binary logical connective, written $\diamond$, giving it the left-introduction rules for $\wedge$ but the right-introduction rules for $\vee$. Can cut be eliminated from proofs involving $\diamond$? Can init be restricted to only atomic formulas? Prior [1960] called this connective "tonk."*

Sometimes, cuts can be permuted locally, although they cannot be eliminated globally. Consider adding to the **C**-proof system a *definition* mechanism for propositional formulas (the restriction to propositional formulas is only to simplify the presentation). Specifically, let $\mathcal{D}$ be a finite set of definitions which are pairs $A := B$ of a propositional symbol A and a propositional formula B. Also, add to the proof system in Section 4.1 the following two introduction rules for defined atoms (assuming the definition $A := B$ is a member of $\mathcal{D}$).

$$\frac{\Gamma, B \vdash \Delta}{\Gamma, A \vdash \Delta} \text{ defL} \qquad \frac{\Gamma \vdash \Delta, B}{\Gamma \vdash \Delta, A} \text{ defR}.$$

Note that locally, the cut rule interacts well with these two introduction rules. For example, if the cut formulas in the premise of a cut rule are immediately introduced by these definition rules, we can have the following derivation.

$$\frac{\dfrac{\Gamma_1 \vdash \Delta_1, B}{\Gamma_1 \vdash \Delta_1, A} \text{ defR} \quad \dfrac{\Gamma_2, B \vdash \Delta_2}{\Gamma_2, A \vdash \Delta_2} \text{ defL}}{\Gamma_1, \Gamma_2 \vdash \Delta_1, \Delta_2} \text{ cut}.$$

The cut rule can be applied to the premises of *defR* and *defL* as follows.

$$\frac{\Gamma_1 \vdash \Delta_1, B \quad \Gamma_2, B \vdash \Delta_2}{\Gamma_1, \Gamma_2 \vdash \Delta_1, \Delta_2} \text{ cut}.$$

In this case, one instance of cut on the atomic formula A is replaced by another instance of cut on the possibly larger formula B. Without further restrictions on the class of formulas allowed in definitions, cuts cannot be eliminated. Exercise 4.12 illustrates that a logic extended with definitions can be inconsistent.

Exercise 4.12. (‡) *Let p be a non-logical constant of type o. Let $\mathcal{D}$ contain just the definition $p := (p \supset f)$. Show how it is possible to write proofs without the cut rule for both $p \vdash f$ and $\vdash p$. [Hint: the cR rule is needed.] As a consequence, there is a proof with a cut of $\vdash f$. Describe what happens when one attempts to eliminate the cut in this proof of f.*

4.3 Cut Elimination and Its Consequences

A proof is a *cut-free proof* if it contains no occurrences of the cut rule. The main theorem in Gentzen [1935] is the following.

Theorem 4.13 (Cut-elimination). *If a sequent has a **C**-proof (respectively, **I**-proof) then it has a cut-free **C**-proof (respectively, **I**-proof).*

We will eventually prove cut-elimination theorems for *focused* versions of sequent calculi: Theorem 5.28 proves this result for a fragment of intuitionistic logic, and Theorem 7.15 proves it for linear logic. A consequence of those theorems is cut-elimination theorem for unfocused proof systems: see Theorems 5.30 and 7.19.

4.3.1 The Duality of Cut and Initial

We mentioned in Section 3.2.2 that the initial and cut rules express dual aspects of $\vdash$. To illustrate that, let Σ be some signature and $\mathcal{T}$ be the set of formulas $B \supset B$ such that B is a Σ-formula. The *init* rule can prove all members of $\mathcal{T}$. On the other hand, the *cut* rule can be seen as using members of this set as an assumption. In particular, a cut-inference rule can be replaced with an $\supset$L rule as follows.

$$\frac{\Sigma :: \Gamma \vdash \Delta, B \quad \Sigma :: B, \Gamma' \vdash \Delta'}{\Sigma :: \Gamma, \Gamma' \vdash \Delta, \Delta'} \text{ cut} \qquad \frac{\Sigma :: \Gamma \vdash \Delta, B \quad \Sigma :: B, \Gamma' \vdash \Delta'}{\Sigma :: B \supset B, \Gamma, \Gamma' \vdash \Delta, \Delta'} \supset \text{L}.$$

Thus a proof of $\Sigma :: \Gamma \vdash \Delta$ can be converted to a cut-free proof of $\Sigma :: \mathcal{T}', \Gamma \vdash \Delta$, where $\mathcal{T}'$ is a finite subset of $\mathcal{T}$. Thus, *init* provides (cut-free) proofs of members of $\mathcal{T}$, and *cut* provides cut-free proofs using members of $\mathcal{T}$ as assumptions.

4.3.2 Eliminating Cuts Can Cause a Size Explosion

The following example illustrates that a proof without cuts can be much larger than a proof with cuts of the same sequent. Fix the non-logical signature to be $\{a\!:\!i, f\!:\!i \to i, p\!:\!i \to o\}$. The notation ($f^n\ t$) denotes the term that results from n applications of f to the term t: i.e., $(f\ (f\ \ldots\ (f\ t)\ldots))$, where there are n occurrences of f applied to t. Let $\mathcal{P}$ be the multiset $\{p\ a, \forall x.(p\ x \supset p\ (f\ x))\}$. Clearly, the sequent $\mathcal{P} \vdash p(f^n a)$ is provable for all $n \geq 0$. For example, the following cut-free proof proves that $p(f(f(f\ a)))$ is a consequence of $\mathcal{P}$.

$$\cfrac{\cfrac{\cfrac{\overline{\mathcal{P} \vdash pa} \quad \overline{\mathcal{P}, p(fa) \vdash p(fa)}}{\mathcal{P}, pa \supset p(fa) \vdash p(fa)}}{\mathcal{P} \vdash p(fa)} \dagger \quad \overline{\mathcal{P}, p(f^2a) \vdash p(f^2a)}}{\cfrac{\cfrac{\mathcal{P}, p(fa) \supset p(f^2a) \vdash p(f^2a)}{\mathcal{P} \vdash p(f^2a)} \dagger \quad \overline{\mathcal{P}, p(f^3a) \vdash p(f^3a)}}{\cfrac{\mathcal{P}, p(f^2a) \supset p(f^3a) \vdash p(f^3a)}{\mathcal{P} \vdash p(f^3a)} \dagger}}$$

The key inference steps in this proof, marked with †, involve cL and $\forall L$. This style of proof could be generalized so that proving $p(f^n a)$ involves n instances of this combination of rules.

Exercise 4.14. *Show that the shortest cut-free I-proof of $\mathcal{P} \vdash p(f^n a)$ has height that is linear in n. Here, the height of a proof is the maximum number of occurrences of inference rules on a path from an initial rule to the endsequent.*

Exercise 4.15. (‡) *Show that it is possible to have proofs with cut of $p(f^{2^n} a)$ from $\mathcal{P}$ whose height is linear in n instead of in 2^n (as in the cut-free proofs mentioned in Exercise 4.14). Do this by proving a series of lemmas when constructing that proof.*

A consequence of these two exercises is that moving from a proof with cuts to a proof without cuts can make proofs grow (at least) exponentially bigger.

4.3.3 Logical Equivalence

Another consequence of the cut-elimination theorem is that it justifies the common practice of manipulating formulas by replacing subformulas with equivalent ones.

The expression $B \equiv C$ is an abbreviation for $(B \supset C) \wedge (C \supset B)$. Two Σ-formulas B and C are *equivalent* in classical (resp., intuitionistic) logic if the sequent $\Sigma :: \cdot \vdash B \equiv C$ is provable in classical (resp., intuitionistic). Clearly, if two formulas are equivalent in intuitionistic logic, they are equivalent in classical logic. The converse is, however, not true. For example, $p \vee (p \supset q)$ is classically equivalent to $(p \supset p) \vee q$, but these are not equivalent in intuitionistic logic.

Equivalences can rewrite one logical formula to another logical formula so that equivalence is maintained. Thus, algebraic-style reasoning can be done on formulas. Sequences of rewritings provide a flexible way to prove equivalences without the explicit need to use the sequent calculus.

A common way to define the replacement of a subformula occurrence within a formula is to introduce a syntax such as $C[A]$ and to think of $C[\Box]$ as a formula with possibly several occurrences of the hole $\Box$. In that setting, if the formulas C and D can be written as $C[A]$ and $C[B]$, respectively, then we say that D results from replacing zero or more occurrences of the subformula A in C with B in D. Another definition is available via the inductive definition given by the proof system in Figure 4.5. Let C and D be Σ-formulas. We say that D arises from replacing zero or more subformula occurrences of A in C with the formula B if $\Sigma :: C \bowtie D$ is provable. Note that we use Σ as a binding mechanism for variables in the same style as we used Σ to bind eigenvariables in sequents.

$$\frac{}{\Sigma :: C \bowtie C} \qquad \frac{\Sigma :: C \bowtie E \quad \Sigma :: D \bowtie F}{\Sigma :: C \wedge D \bowtie E \wedge F} \qquad \frac{\Sigma :: C \bowtie E \quad \Sigma :: D \bowtie F}{\Sigma :: C \vee D \bowtie E \vee F}$$

$$\frac{\Sigma :: C \bowtie E \quad \Sigma :: D \bowtie F}{\Sigma :: C \supset D \bowtie E \supset F} \qquad \frac{x : \tau, \Sigma :: C \bowtie D}{\Sigma :: \forall_\tau x.C \bowtie \forall_\tau x.D} \qquad \frac{x : \tau, \Sigma :: C \bowtie D}{\Sigma :: \exists_\tau x.C \bowtie \exists_\tau x.D}$$

$$\frac{}{\Sigma :: A\theta \bowtie B\theta}\ \dagger$$

The variables C, D, E, and F are quantified per inference rule. Also, A and B are fixed $\hat{\Sigma}$-formulas for which we have proved $\hat{\Sigma} :: \vdash A \equiv B$. The proviso $\dagger$ requires that θ is a substitution of the variables in $\hat{\Sigma}$ with Σ-terms.

Figure 4.5 The inductive definition for replacing some occurrences of A with B within a formula.

Proposition 4.16. *Let A and B be $\hat{\Sigma}$-formulas such that $\hat{\Sigma} :: \cdot \vdash A \equiv B$ is provable in classical (resp., intuitionistic) logic. If $\Sigma :: C \bowtie D$ is provable using the rules in Figure 4.5, then $\Sigma :: \cdot \vdash C \equiv D$ is provable in classical (resp., intuitionistic) logic.*

Proof: Let A and B be $\hat{\Sigma}$-formulas and assume that $A \equiv B$ is provable in, say, intuitionistic logic. Hence both $\hat{\Sigma} :: A \vdash B$ and $\hat{\Sigma} :: B \vdash A$ have **I**-proofs. Also, assume that $\Sigma :: C \bowtie D$ is provable using the inference rules in Figure 4.5. The proof of this proposition follows from a straightforward induction on the structure of such proofs. We illustrate one case. Assume that the last rule involved implications: Thus, C is $C' \supset C''$ and D is $D' \supset D''$ and we know that $\Sigma :: C' \bowtie D'$ and $\Sigma :: C'' \bowtie D''$. The proof that $\Sigma :: C' \supset C'' \vdash D' \supset D''$ is built with the following derivation

$$\cfrac{\cfrac{\Sigma :: D' \vdash C' \quad \Sigma :: C'' \vdash D''}{\Sigma :: C' \supset C'', D' \vdash D''} \supset L}{\Sigma :: C' \supset C'' \vdash D' \supset D''} \supset R$$

and with the proofs that are guaranteed by the inductive hypothesis applied to the proofs of $\Sigma :: C' \bowtie D'$ and $\Sigma :: C'' \bowtie D''$. This style argument also applies to the other connectives. There are two base cases, one of which is immediate and the other is $\Sigma :: A\theta \bowtie B\theta$. In that case, we use the result in Exercise 4.20 to transform **I**-proofs of $\hat{\Sigma} :: A \vdash B$ and $\hat{\Sigma} :: B \vdash A$, into **I**-proofs of $\Sigma :: A\theta \vdash B\theta$ and $\Sigma :: B\theta \vdash A\theta$. If we substitute classical for intuitionistic provability, this argument remains the same. □

Although we occasionally use such reasoning by logical equivalence, we shall not incorporate equivalences into any inference rules within sequent calculus proof systems.

4.3.4 Invertible Introduction Rules

The cut-elimination theorem can prove that certain inference rules are invertible. As defined in Section 3.5, an inference rule is *invertible* if, whenever its conclusion is provable, all of its premises are provable.

Proposition 4.17. *The inference rules tR, $\vee L$, $\wedge R$, fL, $\forall R$, $\exists L$, and $\supset R$ from Figure 4.1 are invertible.*

Proof: The invertibility of tR and fL is immediate. To show that the $\supset$R rule is invertible, let Ξ be a **C**-proof of $\Gamma \vdash B \supset C, \Delta$ and consider the following proof involving Ξ.

$$\cfrac{\cfrac{\Xi}{\Gamma \vdash B \supset C, \Delta} \quad \cfrac{\cfrac{}{B \vdash B}\text{ init} \quad \cfrac{}{C \vdash C}\text{ init}}{B, B \supset C \vdash C}\supset\text{L}}{\cfrac{\Gamma, B \vdash C, \Delta}{\Gamma \vdash B \supset C, \Delta}\supset\text{R.}}\text{cut}$$

If we apply the cut-elimination procedure to this proof, only inference rules above the cut are affected: In particular, the result of eliminating the cut will yield a proof that ends with the introduction of $B \supset C$. In this way, we have used cut-elimination to transform Ξ into a proof that immediately introduces an occurrence of $\supset$, thereby proving the invertibility of $\supset$R □

Exercise 4.18. (‡) *Repeat the argument above to prove the invertibility of $\vee$L, $\wedge$R, $\forall$R, and $\exists$L.*

4.4 Derivable and Admissible Rules

Let us call the inference rules used to present a proof system the *primitive* rules of the system: For example, the primitive rules for **C**-proofs are given in Figures 4.1, 4.2, and 4.3. A *derivable rule* is an inference rule that can be seen as being built from possibly several primitive rules. For example, the inference rule

$$\cfrac{\Sigma :: \Gamma, B_i \vdash \Delta}{\Sigma :: \Gamma, B_1 \wedge B_2 \wedge \cdots \wedge B_n \vdash \Delta}$$

is derivable from **C**-proof primitive rules for any values of $n \geq 2$ and $1 \leq i \leq n$. (Recall from Section 2.4 that we assume that $\wedge$ associates to the left.) Eventually, in Section 5.7, we introduce the concept of *synthetic inference rules*. These rules are derived from primitive rules by leveraging the structure of *focused proof systems*.

An inference rule is *admissible* if adding it to the collection of primitive inference rules does not change the collection of provable sequents. In all the cases we encounter here, we prove that a given inference rule, say

$$\frac{S_1 \quad \cdots \quad S_n}{S_0},$$

where $n \geq 0$ and $S_0, \ldots, S_n$ are sequents, is admissible by describing how to take proofs of $S_1, \ldots, S_n$ and produce a proof of S_0. Clearly, a derivable inference rule is an admissible inference rule. However, showing the admissibility of an inference rule is generally more involved than simply assembling primitive inference rules.

Cut elimination can be rephrased using the notion of admissibility. In particular, let $\mathbf{C}^-$ be the same as the $\mathbf{C}$ proof system except that the cut rule is dropped. Theorem 4.13 implies that the cut rule is admissible in the $\mathbf{C}^-$ proof system.

The following two exercises illustrate two additional examples of admissible inference rules for **C**-proof and **I**-proof systems. The structural rule of weakening allows for adding a formula into the left or right side of sequents (reading the inference rule from premise to conclusion). A *strengthening rule* is an inference rule that allows for deleting a formula from either the left or right side of a sequent. In general, strengthening is not an admissible rule. The following exercise provides a trivial instance of when strengthening is possible.

Exercise 4.19. *Show that if there is a **C**-proof (resp., an **I**-proof) of $\Sigma :: \Gamma, t \vdash \Delta$ then there is a **C**-proof (an **I**-proof) of $\Sigma :: \Gamma \vdash \Delta$.*

The following inference rule resembles the cut rule but at the level of terms.

$$\frac{\Sigma \Vdash t : \tau \qquad \Sigma, x : \tau :: \Delta \vdash \Gamma}{\Sigma :: \Delta[t/x] \vdash \Gamma[t/x]} \; instan.$$

The following exercise states that this rule is admissible.

Exercise 4.20. *Let Ξ be a **C**-proof (resp., **I**-proof) of $\Sigma, x : \tau :: \Gamma \vdash \Delta$ and let t be a Σ-term. The result of substituting t for the bound variable x in this sequent and the bound variables corresponding to x in all other sequents in Ξ yields a **C**-proof (resp., **I**-proof) Ξ' of the sequent $\Sigma :: \Gamma[t/x] \vdash \Delta[t/x]$. The arrangement of inference rules in Ξ and in Ξ' are the same.*

4.5 Negation, False, and Minimal Logic

Our formalization of classical and intuitionistic provability using **C**-proofs and **I**-proofs is essentially the same as Gentzen's formulation of these logics using the *LK* and *LJ* proof systems. One difference between these proof systems is that Gentzen did not include the units t and f within his sequent calculi, while he did include negation as a logical connective. Thus, his proof systems included left- and right-introduction rules for negation: In particular, both *LK* and *LJ* contained the rules

$$\frac{\Gamma \vdash B, \Delta}{\neg B, \Gamma \vdash \Delta} \neg L \quad \text{and} \quad \frac{\Gamma, B \vdash \Delta}{\Gamma \vdash \neg B, \Delta} \neg R.$$

These inference rules cannot be added directly to **I**-proofs since the $\neg L$ rule cannot work with the requirement that *exactly* one formula is on the right-hand side. Gentzen's intuitionistic proof system *LJ* is defined as a restriction on *LK* in which all sequents have *at most one* formula on the right. With that restriction, an occurrence of the $\neg L$ rule is restricted, so its conclusion has an empty right-hand side. Instances of *wR* can also appear in Gentzen's version of *LJ* proofs.

> **Exercise 4.21.** Minimal logic *is sometimes defined as intuitionistic logic without the* ex falso quodlibet *rule: from false, anything follows. Formally, we define an **M**-proof as an **I**-proof in which the fL rule does not appear. Since fL is the only inference rule for f in Figure 4.1, f is not treated as a logical connective within **M**-proofs. In particular, let B be a formula and let q be a non-logical symbol of type o that does not occur in B. Let B' be the result of replacing all occurrences of f in B with q. Show that B has an **M**-proof if and only if B' has an **I**-proof.*

The following lemma shows that the *ex falso quodlibet* inference rule is admissible in **I**-proofs.

> **Lemma 4.22.** *If Ξ is an **I**-proof of $\Sigma :: \Gamma \vdash f$ then for any Σ-formula B, there is an **I**-proof Ξ' that has the same structure as Ξ but which proves $\Sigma :: \Gamma \vdash B$.*

Proof: The proof is by induction on the structure of Ξ. Essentially, some occurrences of f on the right of sequents are changed to *B*. Ultimately, an occurrence of a leaf sequent of the form $\Gamma', f \vdash f$ is converted to $\Gamma', f \vdash B$. Another way to view this transformation of Ξ to Ξ' is to consider permuting the following cut up into the left premise.

$$\dfrac{\dfrac{\Xi}{\Gamma \vdash f} \quad \dfrac{}{f \vdash B}\,\text{fL}}{\Gamma \vdash B}\,\text{cut.}$$

□

We can now show that Gentzen's original *LJ* proof system, in which negation is a logical connective and where wR can appear, can be emulated directly by **I**-proofs. Formally, define a **G**-proof to be a **C**-proof in which the rules for negation above are allowed and where the right-hand side of sequents are restricted to have at most one formula. We now show that every **G**-proof can be directly translated to an **I**-proof in which negation is replaced by "implies false." To this end, define the mapping $(B)°$ that replaces every occurrence of $\neg C$ in B with $C \supset f$. Similarly, we extend this function to multisets of formulas: $(\Gamma)° = \{(B)° \mid B \in \Gamma\}$. Finally, we further extend this mapping to work on sequents, as follows:

$$(\Gamma \vdash \Delta)° = \begin{cases} (\Gamma)° \vdash (\Delta)° & \text{if } \Delta \text{ is not empty} \\ (\Gamma)° \vdash f & \text{if } \Delta \text{ is empty.} \end{cases}$$

Clearly, the image of a sequent in a **G**-proof is a sequent with exactly one formula on the right-hand side.

Proposition 4.23. *Every G-proof of the sequent* $\Sigma :: \Gamma \vdash \Delta$ *can be converted to an I-proof of the sequent* $\Sigma :: (\Gamma)° \vdash (\Delta)°$.

Proof: All identity and introduction rules other than those for negation translate immediately from **G**-proofs to **I**-proofs. The case for negation rules is simple as well:

$$\dfrac{\Gamma \vdash B}{\neg B, \Gamma \vdash \cdot}\,\neg L \quad \longrightarrow \quad \dfrac{(\Gamma)° \vdash (B)° \quad \dfrac{}{f \vdash f}\,\text{fL}}{(B)° \supset f, (\Gamma)° \vdash f}\,\supset L$$

$$\dfrac{\Gamma, B \vdash \cdot}{\Gamma \vdash \neg B}\,\neg R \quad \longrightarrow \quad \dfrac{(\Gamma)°, (B)° \vdash f}{(\Gamma)° \vdash (B)° \supset f}\,\neg R.$$

The only non-trivial change in proofs results when the **G**-proof ends with wR. In that case, the **G**-proof inference rule

$$\frac{\Gamma \vdash \cdot}{\Gamma \vdash B} \; wR$$

would allow us to conclude that the translation of the upper sequent, i.e., $(\Gamma)° \vdash f$ has an **I**-proof. By Lemma 4.22, we can conclude that $(\Gamma)° \vdash (B)°$ has an **I**-proof. □

Thus, we can translate away Gentzen's use of negation in such a way that the role of wR in his *LJ* system can be absorbed into the f*L* rule. As a result, we have a proof system – namely, **I**-proofs – for intuitionistic logic that has neither weakening nor contraction on the right. Thus, **I**-proofs will have the *ex falso quodlibet* rule while not having wR: The **G**-proof system, on the contrary, has both the *ex falso quodlibet* rule and the wR rule.

Exercise 4.24. (‡) *Consider the following two inference rules.*

$$\frac{\Gamma \vdash B \quad \Gamma \vdash \neg B}{\Gamma \vdash C} \; explode \qquad \frac{\Gamma, B \vdash C \quad \Gamma, \neg B \vdash C}{\Gamma \vdash C} \; excluded\ middle$$

*(The names of these inference rules can be found in Kamide [2024].) Show that the first of these rules is derivable using **I**-proofs (meaning that if its two premises have **I**-proofs then its conclusion must have an **I**-proof). Similarly, show that the second inference rule is derivable using **C**-proofs. Of course, the negation $\neg B$ is translated as $B \supset f$.*

4.6 Choices to Consider during the Search for Proofs

Although Gentzen's original calculus provides an excellent framework for proving that the cut rule can be eliminated, its direct application to computational tasks presents several challenges. A primary hurdle is that when we consider proof search as a computational model, Gentzen's sequent calculus requires us to explore numerous options at each step of proof construction. These multiple choices arise in proof search in the following ways.

1. It is possible to use the cut rule to attempt a proof of any sequent.
2. The structural rules of contractions and weakening can always be applied to make additional copies of a formula or to remove formulas.
3. A sequent may contain many non-atomic formulas, and we can generally apply an introduction rule to each one.
4. One can also check if a given sequent is initial.

Some of these choices produce sub-choices. For example, choosing the cut rule requires inventing a cut formula; choosing ∨R requires selecting a disjunct; choosing ∧L requires selecting a conjunct; choosing ∀L or ∃R requires choosing a term t to instantiate a quantifier, and using the ⊃L or *cut* rules require splitting the surrounding multiset contexts into pairs (for which there can be exponentially many splits).

However, all this freedom in searching for proofs is not needed, and greatly reducing the sets of choices can still result in complete proof procedures. Most of the choices above can be addressed as follows.

1. Given the cut-elimination theorem, we do not need to consider the cut rule and the sub-problem of selecting a cut formula. Such a choice forces us to move into a domain where proofs are more like computation traces than witnesses of mathematical arguments (see the discussion in Section 3.7). However, since our goal here is the specification of computation, we shall generally live with this choice.
2. Structural rules can often be built into inference rules. For example, weakening can be delayed until the leaves of a proof, and it can be built into the *init* rule. Also, instead of attempting to split the contexts when applying the ⊃L rule, we can use the contraction rule to duplicate all the formulas and then place one copy on the left branch and one on the right branch.
3. The problem of determining appropriate substitution terms in the ∀L and ∃R rules is a serious problem whose solution falls outside our investigations here. When systems based on proof search are implemented, they generally use techniques such as employing *logic variables* and *unification* to determine instantiation terms lazily. Although such techniques are entirely standard, we shall not discuss them here.
4. Although there is significant nondeterminism involved in choosing among many possible introduction rules, that nondeterminism can be classified as either *don't-know nondeterminism*, where choices might need to be undone in order to find a proof, and *don't-care nondeterminism*, where choices do not need to be undone.

An example of don't-care nondeterminism is the choice of what order to use *invertible rules* (as defined in Section 3.5): These rules can be used in any order without losing completeness. Although non-invertible introduction rules represent genuine choices (i.e., don't-know nondeterminism) in the search for proofs, we will also provide some structure to those choices in Chapter 5.

4.7 Bibliographic Notes

Natural deduction was introduced in Gentzen [1935]. Gentzen's plan in that paper was to use natural deduction to show that proofs in intuitionistic and classical logics can be *analytic*, i.e., that they can be free of lemmas. Although it seems clear that Gentzen knew how to use natural deduction to prove this result for intuitionistic logic (see von Plato and Gentzen [2008]), he did not see how to use natural deduction to prove this same result for classical logic. Gentzen then invented the sequent calculus, and, in that setting, he provided a single procedure that transforms any proof to a proof without lemmas, and this procedure (called *cut elimination*) worked for both logics. From what we have illustrated in this chapter, it is not surprising that natural deduction has not served as a unifying framework for these two logics since (1) an essential difference between sequent calculus proofs for classical and intuitionistic logics is the presence or absence of contraction and weakening on the right, and (2) natural deduction does not support those structural rules since the conclusion of a natural deduction proof is always a single formula (even when applied to classical logic).

There are many well-known proofs for cut-elimination for proof systems resembling C-proofs and I-proofs. For the detailed proofs of such cut-elimination theorems, see Gentzen [1935] as well as more modern treatments available in Gallier [1986], Girard et al. [1989], Negri and von Plato [2001], and Bimbó [2015].

Girard et al. [1989] points out that the initial rule (recall Figure 4.2) implies that the left occurrence of B is stronger than the right occurrence of B. In contrast, the meaning of the cut rule is the opposite: A right occurrence of B is stronger than the left occurrence of B. This duality is also apparent in other presentations of these inference rules, such as in the Calculus of Structures (see Guglielmi [2007]) and uses of linear logic as a metalogic for the sequent calculus (see Section 8.7 and Miller and Pimentel [2004, 2013]).

As was mentioned in Section 4.2, logic programs will be viewed in this book as theories that attribute meaning to programmer-supplied non-logical symbols. For example, we may want to specify how to sort a list of numbers. In that case, we introduce a binary predicate, say, *sort*, to denote the relationship between lists of numbers and sorted lists of numbers. The logic program that describes how to compute this *sort* predicate is, in fact, a theory (a collection of assumptions). (See Figure 5.6 for an explicit presentation of a logic program for specifying sorting.) Different proof-theoretic approaches to logic programming are available that do not use non-logical symbols in this way. For example, Hallnäs and Schroeder-Heister [1991] encodes logic programs as *definitions* (which are given left- and right-introduction rules, as in Section 4.2). The proof theory of Horn clause logic programs has a rather direct and elegant encoding in proof-theoretic approaches to fixed points, as shown in Baelde et al. [2010].

Although Gentzen did not classify inference rules as invertible or not, Ketonen [1944] (translated in Ketonen [2022]) explicitly identified some rules as being invertible. He also exploited invertibility to design decision algorithms for classical propositional logic. The proof in Section 4.3.4 that certain inference rules are invertible follows the style of proof used by Ketonen.

Church [1936] proved that first-order classical logic is undecidable. Since provability of first-order intuitionistic logic can be encoded into first-order classical logic (using techniques such as negative translations [Gödel, 1932]), provability for first-order intuitionistic logic is also undecidable. If we restrict to only the propositional fragment, then provability of classical proposition logic is co-NP complete [Cook and Reckhow, 1979], while for intuitionistic propositional logic it is PSPACE complete [Statman, 1979].

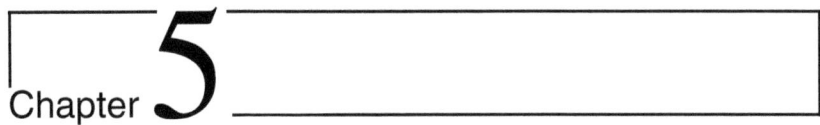

Chapter 5

Two Abstract Logic Programming Languages

We now apply the **C** and **I** proof systems to describe logic programming in a high-level and implementation-independent fashion.

5.1 Goal-Directed Proof Search

One approach to modeling logic programming is to view *logic programs* as assumptions, *goals* as queries to make against a logic program, and *computation* as the process of attempting to prove a goal from a program. The state of an idealized interpreter can be represented as the two-sided sequent $\Sigma :: \mathcal{P} \vdash G$, where Σ is the signature that declares a set of eigenvariables, $\mathcal{P}$ is a collection of Σ-formulas denoting a program, and G is a Σ-formula denoting the goal we wish to prove from $\mathcal{P}$.

It is compelling to view computation in logic programming as being based on the following restricted form of proof search. If G is not atomic, then its top-level logical connective should determine which inference rules should be used to prove $\Sigma :: \mathcal{P} \vdash G$. In particular, a right-introduction rule must be attempted. Thus, the *search semantics* for a logical connective at the head of a goal is fixed by the proof system and is independent of the program. Only when the goal is atomic (i.e., when its top-level symbol is *non-logical*) is the program $\mathcal{P}$ consulted: The program is available to provide meaning for the non-logical predicate constants at the head of atomic formulas.

If we instantiate the above view of computation using the introduction rules given in Figure 4.1, we derive the following set of proof search strategies.

1. Reduce an attempt to prove $\Sigma :: \mathcal{P} \vdash B_1 \wedge B_2$ to the attempts to prove the two sequents $\Sigma :: \mathcal{P} \vdash B_1$ and $\Sigma :: \mathcal{P} \vdash B_2$.
2. Reduce an attempt to prove $\Sigma :: \mathcal{P} \vdash B_1 \vee B_2$ to an attempt to prove either $\Sigma :: \mathcal{P} \vdash B_1$ or $\Sigma :: \mathcal{P} \vdash B_2$.
3. Reduce an attempt to prove $\Sigma :: \mathcal{P} \vdash \exists_\tau x.B$ to an attempt to prove $\Sigma :: \mathcal{P} \vdash B[t/x]$, for some Σ-term t of type τ.
4. Reduce an attempt to prove $\Sigma :: \mathcal{P} \vdash B_1 \supset B_2$ to an attempt to prove $\Sigma :: \mathcal{P}, B_1 \vdash B_2$.
5. Reduce an attempt to prove $\Sigma :: \mathcal{P} \vdash \forall_\tau x.B$ to an attempt to prove $\Sigma, y : \tau :: \mathcal{P} \vdash B[y/x]$, where c is a token not in Σ.
6. Attempting to prove $\Sigma :: \mathcal{P} \vdash \mathsf{t}$ yields an immediate success.

These strategies suggest the following technical definition to formalize the notion of *goal-directed proof search*: A cut-free **I**-proof Ξ is a *uniform proof* if every occurrence of a sequent in Ξ that has a non-atomic right-hand side is the conclusion of a right-introduction rule. Searching for uniform proofs means applying right-introduction rules when the right-hand side has a logical connective. No left-introduction, identity, or structural rules can be considered when the right-hand side is a non-atomic formula. The definition of uniform proofs provides no guidance for proof search when the right-hand side of a sequent is atomic. Such guidance will, however, soon appear.

> **Exercise 5.1.** *Show that uniform proofs are always atomically closed.*

There are provable sequents for which no uniform proof exists. For example, let the non-logical constants be $\Sigma_0 = \{p : o, q : o, r : i \to o, a : i, b : i\}$ and let Σ be a signature. The sequents

$$\Sigma :: (r\ a \wedge r\ b) \supset q \vdash \exists_i x(r\ x \supset q) \quad \text{and} \quad \Sigma :: \cdot \vdash p \vee (p \supset q)$$

have **C**-proofs but no **I**-proofs (see Exercise 4.3), so clearly, they have no uniform proofs. The two sequents

$$\Sigma :: p \vee q \vdash q \vee p \quad \text{and} \quad \Sigma :: \exists_i x.\ r\ x \vdash \exists_i x.\ r\ x$$

have **I**-proofs but no uniform proofs.

One high-level way to define logic programming is to consider those collections of programs and goals for which uniform proofs are, in fact, complete (in the sense described in Section 4.1). An *abstract logic programming language* is a triple $\langle \mathcal{D}, \mathcal{G}, \vdash_{\mathcal{X}} \rangle$ such that for all signatures Σ, for all finite sets $\mathcal{P}$ of Σ-formulas from $\mathcal{D}$, and all Σ-formulas G from $\mathcal{G}$, we have $\Sigma : \mathcal{P} \vdash_{\mathcal{X}} G$ if and only if $\Sigma :: \mathcal{P} \vdash G$ has a uniform proof. Here, $\vdash_{\mathcal{X}}$ is the provability relation associated with some particular logic, say, first-order classical or intuitionistic logic.

Both the definitions of uniform proof and abstract logic programming language are restricted to **I**-proofs. We shall refer to this as the *single-conclusion* version of these notions. After introducing linear logic, we will present, in Section 6.7, a generalization of uniform proofs to multiple-conclusion proof systems.

Let Δ be a finite multiset of formulas. This multiset satisfies the *disjunction property* if the provability of $\Sigma :: \Delta \vdash B \vee C$ implies the provability of either $\Sigma :: \Delta \vdash B$ or $\Sigma :: \Delta \vdash C$. Similarly, this multiset satisfies the *existence property* if the provability of $\Sigma :: \Delta \vdash \exists_\tau x. B$ implies the existence of a Σ-term t of type τ such that $\Sigma :: \Delta \vdash B[t/x]$ is provable. Whenever uniform proofs are complete, both the disjunction and existence properties hold.

5.2 Horn Clauses

Early characterizations of the computational nature of logic programs did not employ a *proof* procedure. Instead, they employed a *refutation* procedure, specifically the resolution refutation framework pioneered by Robinson [1965]. The decision to focus on refutation rather than proving led to defining first-order Horn clauses as the universal closure of disjunctions of *literals* (atomic formulas or their negation) that contain at most one positive literal (an atomic formula). That is, a Horn clause is a closed formula of the form

$$\forall x_1 \ldots \forall x_n [. \neg A_1 \vee \cdots \vee \neg A_m \vee B_1 \vee \cdots \vee B_p],$$

where $A_1, \ldots, A_m, B_1, \ldots, B_p$ are atomic formulas, $n, m, p \geq 0$, and $p \leq 1$. If $n = 0$, then the quantifier prefix is not written, and if $m = p = 0$, then the body of the clause is considered to be f. If the clause contains exactly one positive literal ($p = 1$), it is a *positive* Horn clause. It is a *negative* Horn clause if it contains no positive literal ($p = 0$).

When we shift from the search for refutations to the search for sequent calculus proofs, it is natural to change the presentation of Horn clauses to one of the following. Let τ be a syntactic variable that ranges over $S\backslash\{o\}$ (i.e., primitive types other than the type of formulas), and let A be a syntactic variable over atomic formulas. Consider the following recursive definitions of the two syntactic categories of *program clauses* (*definite clauses*), given by the syntactic variable D, and *goals*, given by the syntactic variable G.

$$G ::= \quad A \mid G \wedge G$$
$$D ::= A \mid G \supset A \mid \forall_\tau x\, D. \tag{5.1}$$

Program clauses using this presentation are of the form

$$\forall x_1. \cdots \forall x_n.(A_1 \wedge \cdots \wedge A_m \supset A_0),$$

where we adopt the convention that if $m = 0$ then the implication is not written. A second, richer definition of these syntactic classes is the following.

$$G ::= \mathsf{t} \mid A \mid G \wedge G \mid G \vee G \mid \exists_\tau x.G$$
$$D ::= \mathsf{t} \mid A \mid G \supset D \mid D \wedge D \mid \forall_\tau x.D. \tag{5.2}$$

Finally, a compact presentation of program clauses and goals is possible using only implication and universal quantification.

$$G ::= \quad A$$
$$D ::= A \mid A \supset D \mid \forall_\tau x.\, D. \tag{5.3}$$

This last definition describes a program clause as a formula built from implications and universals such that there are no occurrences of logical connectives to the left of an implication. Program clauses using this presentation are of the form

$$\forall \bar{x}_1(A_1 \supset \forall \bar{x}_2(A_2 \supset \cdots \supset \forall \bar{x}_m(A_m \supset \forall \bar{x}_0 A_0)\ldots)),$$

where $\bar{x}_0, \ldots, \bar{x}_m$ are (possibly empty) lists of variables.

We use the symbol *fohc* to refer informally to the logic programming languages based on one of these three descriptions of *first-order Horn clauses*. Definition (5.1) above corresponds closely to the definition of Horn clauses given using disjunction of literals. In this case, positive clauses correspond to the D-formulas, and the negation of G-formulas would all be negative clauses. Let $\mathcal{D}_1$ be the set of D-formulas and $\mathcal{G}_1$ be the set of G-formulas satisfying the recursion (5.2).

5.2 HORN CLAUSES

Exercise 5.2. *Show that the clausal order (see Section 2.4) of a formula in $\mathcal{G}_1$ is 0 and of a formula in $\mathcal{D}_1$ is 0 or 1.*

The following formulas, sometimes called the *curry/uncurry equivalences*, are provable in intuitionistic logic.

1. $t \supset E \equiv E$
2. $(B \wedge C) \supset E \equiv (B \supset C \supset E)$
3. $(B \vee C) \supset E \equiv (B \supset E) \wedge (C \supset E)$
4. $(\exists x.B) \supset E \equiv \forall x.(B \supset E)$.

They can be used (in part) to prove Exercise 5.3.

Exercise 5.3. *Let D be a Horn clause using (5.2). Show that there is a set $\mathcal{P}$ of Horn clauses using description (5.1) or (5.3) (your pick) such that D is equivalent to the conjunction of formulas in $\mathcal{P}$. Show that this rewriting might make the resulting conjunction exponentially larger than the original clause. (Take as the measure of a formula the number of occurrences of logical connectives it contains.)*

Exercise 5.4. *Let Σ be a signature, let $\mathcal{P}$ be a multiset of Σ-formulas in $\mathcal{D}_1$, and let G be a Σ-formula in $\mathcal{G}_1$. Let Ξ be a cut-free **C**-proof of $\Sigma :: \mathcal{P} \vdash G$. Show that every sequent in Ξ is of the form $\Sigma :: \mathcal{P}' \vdash \Delta$ such that $\mathcal{P}'$ is a multiset of formulas in $\mathcal{D}_1$ and Δ is a multiset of formulas in $\mathcal{G}_1$. Show also that the only introduction rules that can appear in Ξ are $\forall L, \wedge L, \supset L, \wedge R, \vee R, \exists R,$ and tR.*

The following proposition demonstrates that although classical logic can prove more sequents than intuitionistic logic, if we limit our attention to the Horn clause setting, both logics prove precisely the same (restricted) sequents.

Proposition 5.5. *Let Σ be a signature, let $\mathcal{P}$ be a multiset of Σ-formulas in $\mathcal{D}_1$, and let G be a Σ-formula in $\mathcal{G}_1$. If $\Sigma :: \mathcal{P} \vdash G$ has a **C**-proof then it has an **I**-proof.*

Proof: We show the following stronger result: If Δ is a multiset of G-formulas and $\Sigma :: \mathcal{P} \vdash \Delta$ has a cut-free **C**-proof then there is a $G \in \Delta$ such that

$\Sigma :: \mathcal{P} \vdash G$ has an **I**-proof. We prove this by induction on the structure of a cut-free **C**-proof Ξ for $\Sigma :: \mathcal{P} \vdash \Delta$.

There are three base cases for Ξ: fL is not possible since f is not a member of $\mathcal{P}$, and the two other cases of tR and *init* are immediate.

If the last inference rule in Ξ is a structural rule, the proof is straightforward again. For example, suppose the last inference rule in Ξ is a cR. In that case, this proof is of the form

$$\frac{\Sigma :: \mathcal{P} \vdash G, G, \Delta}{\Sigma :: \mathcal{P} \vdash G, \Delta} \; cR \; .$$

By the inductive hypothesis, there is an H in the multiset G, G, Δ such that $\Sigma :: \mathcal{P} \vdash H$ has an **I**-proof: Clearly, H is also a member of the multiset G, Δ. The case when the last inference rule in Ξ is wR is treated similarly. The cases for wL and cL are similarly straightforward.

Now consider all possible introduction rules that might be the last inference rule of Ξ (see Exercise 5.4). If that last rule is $\supset L$, then the proof has the form

$$\frac{\Sigma :: \mathcal{P}_1 \vdash \Delta_1, G \qquad \Sigma :: D, \mathcal{P}_2 \vdash \Delta_2}{\Sigma :: G \supset D, \mathcal{P}_1, \mathcal{P}_2 \vdash \Delta_1, \Delta_2} \; \supset L \; .$$

By the inductive assumption, there is a formula $H_1 \in \Delta_1 \cup \{G\}$ for which $\Sigma :: \mathcal{P}_1 \vdash H_1$ has an **I**-proof and a formula $H_2 \in \Delta_2$ for which $\Sigma :: D, \mathcal{P}_2 \vdash H_2$ has an **I**-proof. In the case that $H_1 \in \Delta_1$, the **I**-proof of the sequent $\Sigma :: \mathcal{P}_1 \vdash H_1$ can be extended with a series of wL rules to yield a proof of $\Sigma :: G \supset D, \mathcal{P}_1, \mathcal{P}_2 \vdash H_1$. On the other hand, if $H_1 = G$, we build an **I**-proof using the following instance of an inference rule

$$\frac{\Sigma :: \mathcal{P}_1 \vdash G \qquad \Sigma :: D, \mathcal{P}_2 \vdash H_2}{\Sigma :: G \supset D, \mathcal{P}_1, \mathcal{P}_2 \vdash H_2} \; \supset L,$$

and the two promised **I**-proofs of the premises.

If that last rule is $\wedge R$, then the proof has the form

$$\frac{\Sigma :: \mathcal{P} \vdash G_1, \Delta \qquad \Sigma :: \mathcal{P} \vdash G_2, \Delta}{\Sigma :: \mathcal{P} \vdash G_1 \wedge G_2, \Delta} \; \wedge R.$$

By the inductive assumption, there is a formula $H_1 \in \Delta \cup \{G_1\}$ for which $\Sigma :: \mathcal{P} \vdash H_1$ has an **I**-proof and a formula $H_2 \in \Delta \cup \{G_2\}$ for which $\Sigma :: \mathcal{P} \vdash H_2$ has an **I**-proof. In the case that $H_1 \in \Delta$, the **I**-proof of the sequent

5.2 HORN CLAUSES

$\Sigma :: \mathcal{P} \vdash H_1$ is the required proof. In the case that $H_2 \in \Delta$, the **I**-proof of the sequent $\Sigma :: \mathcal{P} \vdash H_2$ is the required proof. The only remaining case occurs when H_1 is G_1 and H_2 is G_2. In that case, the required **I**-proof results from applying the inference rule ∧L to the two subproofs provided by the inductive assumptions.

All the remaining cases of introduction rules can be treated similarly. □

Exercise 5.6. (‡) *Prove that Horn clause programs are always consistent by proving that for any signature Σ and any finite multiset of Horn clauses $\mathcal{P}$, the sequent $\Sigma :: \mathcal{P} \vdash f$ is not provable.*

Exercise 5.7. *Show that a cut-free **I**-proof of $\Sigma :: \mathcal{P} \vdash G$, where $\mathcal{P}$ is a finite multiset of formulas in $\mathcal{D}_1$ and $G \in \mathcal{G}_1$, is also an **M**-proof.*

Exercise 5.8. (‡) *Assume that the Σ-formulas $D_0, \ldots, D_n$ ($n \geq 0$) are Horn clauses using description (5.3). Prove that if the sequent $\Sigma :: D_1, \ldots, D_n \vdash D_0$ has a **C**-proof then it has an **I**-proof.*

We can now conclude that $\langle \mathcal{D}_1, \mathcal{G}_1, \vdash_{\mathcal{X}} \rangle$ is an abstract logic programming language if $\vdash_{\mathcal{X}}$ is taken to be $\vdash_C$, $\vdash_I$, or $\vdash_M$.

If we use the (5.2) presentation of Horn clauses, then it is only atoms or conjunctions of atoms (including the empty conjunction t) that are both goals and program clauses. All the other connectives are either dismissed (such as f) or are restricted to just half their "meaning:" when a disjunction and existential quantifier is encountered in proof search, only its right-introduction rule is needed, and when an implication and a universal quantification is encountered, only its left-introduction rule is needed.

Exercise 5.9. (‡) *Let $\mathcal{I}$ be the set of formulas using only implications and atomic formulas that are provable classically but have no uniform proofs. Peirce's formula $((p \supset q) \supset p) \supset p$ is a member of $\mathcal{I}$. Prove that the fewest number of occurrences of implications in a formula in $\mathcal{I}$ is 3.*

Readers unfamiliar with specifying computations using Horn clauses might want to read Section 5.9 now to see examples of such specifications.

5.3 Hereditary Harrop Formulas

A natural extension to Horn clauses called the *first-order hereditary Harrop formulas* allows implications and universal quantifiers in goals (and, thus, in the body of program clauses). Whereas cut-free proofs involving Horn clauses contain left-introduction rules for implications and universal quantifiers, proofs involving this extended set of formulas can also contain right-introduction rules for implications and universal quantifiers. Parallel to the three presentations of *fohc* in Section 5.2, the following three presentations of goals and program clauses describe first-order hereditary Harrop formulas.

$$G ::= A \mid G \wedge G \mid D \supset G \mid \forall x.G$$
$$D ::= \quad A \mid G \supset A \mid \forall x.D \quad (5.4)$$

The definitions of G- and D-formulas are mutually recursive. Note that a negative (resp, positive) subformula of a G-formula is a D-formula (G-formula), and that a negative (positive) subformula of a D-formula is a G-formula (D-formula). A richer formulation is given by

$$G ::= \mathsf{t} \mid A \mid G \wedge G \mid G \vee G \mid \exists x.G \mid D \supset G \mid \forall x.G$$
$$D ::= \quad A \mid G \supset D \mid D \wedge D \mid \forall x.D \quad (5.5)$$

When referring to first-order hereditary Harrop formulas and goals, we assume this formula definition. We use $\mathcal{D}_2$ to denote the set of all such D-formulas and $\mathcal{G}_2$ for the set of all G-formulas.

A completely symmetric presentation can be given as

$$G ::= \mathsf{t} \mid A \mid D \supset G \mid G \wedge G \mid \forall x.G$$
$$D ::= \mathsf{t} \mid A \mid G \supset D \mid D \wedge D \mid \forall x.D \quad (5.6)$$

In this presentation, D and G formulas range over the same set of formulas. There is no need for a definition that allows for mutual recursion. In Section 5.5, these formulas – which are generated from the set of connectives $\{\mathsf{t}, \wedge, \supset, \forall\}$ – will be called $\mathcal{L}_0$-formulas.

We use the name *fohh* to denote *first-order hereditary Harrop formulas*. This name will refer to one of the presentations above. If the text does not explicitly state the presentation used, we will assume the second one. We shall also use *fohh* to denote, in particular, the corresponding D-formulas since the associated G-formulas are uniquely determined by being the negatively occurring subformulas of D-formulas. The same comment also applies to our use of the term *fohc*.

5.3 Hereditary Harrop Formulas

Exercise 5.10. *Let $D \in \mathcal{D}_2$. Show that D is a Horn clause (using definition (5.2)) if and only if $\text{order}(D) < 2$.*

We shall use the term *clause* not just for Horn clauses but for any formula, especially any formula that can be used as part of a logic program. Thus, for example, we often refer to hereditary Harrop formulas as clauses.

The following proposition shows that identifying the right-hand side of sequents with goals and the left-hand side with logic programs is maintained within cut-free **I**-proofs.

Proposition 5.11. *Let Σ be signature of first-order variables, $\mathcal{P}$ be a finite multiset of Σ-formulas in $\mathcal{D}_2$, G be a Σ-formula in $\mathcal{G}_2$, and Ξ be a cut-free **I**-proof of $\Sigma :: \mathcal{P} \vdash G$. If $\Sigma' :: \mathcal{P}' \vdash B$ is a sequent in Ξ, then $\mathcal{P}'$ is a multiset of Σ'-formulas in $\mathcal{D}_2$, and B is a Σ'-formula in $\mathcal{G}_2$.*

This proposition is proved by a simple induction of the structure of cut-free **I**-proofs.

The triple $\langle \mathcal{D}_2, \mathcal{G}_2, \vdash_C \rangle$ is not an abstract logic programming language. For example, the formulas numbered 4, 5, 6, and 7 in Exercise 4.3 are members of $\mathcal{G}_2$ that have classical proofs but no uniform proof. We shall use the name *fohh* to also refer to the triple $\langle \mathcal{D}_2, \mathcal{G}_2, \vdash_I \rangle$. Before we prove that *fohh* is an abstract logic programming language, we prove the following lemma.

Lemma 5.12. *Let $G \in \mathcal{G}_2$ be a non-atomic Σ-formula, and let $\mathcal{P}$ be a finite multiset whose members are Σ-formulas in $\mathcal{D}_2$. Assume that $\Sigma :: \mathcal{P} \vdash G$ has an **I**-proof in which the last inference rule is not a right-introduction rule, and all premise sequents are proved by uniform proofs. There is a uniform proof of $\Sigma :: \mathcal{P} \vdash G$.*

Proof: Let Ξ be a proof of $\mathcal{P} \vdash G$ satisfying the assumptions of this lemma. (For readability, we suppress explicitly writing the signature of a sequent.) The last inference rule of this proof is either one of two structural rules (cL or wL) or one of three left-introduction rules ($\wedge L$, $\forall L$, $\supset L$). In every case, the proof of the premises must be uniform proofs, and, as a result, at least one premise must be proved by one of five right-introduction rules ($\wedge R$, $\vee R$, $\forall R$, $\exists R$, $\supset R$). We proceed by induction on the structure of the uniform proof of the right-most premise of this inference rule. All possible left rules occurring below a right-introduction rule must be considered.

Consider when an implication-left rule is applied and the right-hand side is a conjunction.

$$
\cfrac{\cfrac{\Xi_0}{\mathcal{P}_1 \vdash G} \quad \cfrac{\cfrac{\Xi_1}{D,\mathcal{P}_2 \vdash G_1} \quad \cfrac{\Xi_2}{D,\mathcal{P}_2 \vdash G_2}}{D,\mathcal{P}_2 \vdash G_1 \wedge G_2} \wedge R}{G \supset D, \mathcal{P}_1, \mathcal{P}_2 \vdash G_1 \wedge G_2} \supset L
$$

These rules can be permuted to form the following proof.

$$
\cfrac{\cfrac{\cfrac{\Xi_0}{\mathcal{P}_1 \vdash G} \quad \cfrac{\Xi_1}{D,\mathcal{P}_2 \vdash G_1}}{G \supset D, \mathcal{P}_1, \mathcal{P}_2 \vdash G_1} \supset L \quad \cfrac{\cfrac{\Xi_0}{\mathcal{P}_1 \vdash G} \quad \cfrac{\Xi_2}{D,\mathcal{P}_2 \vdash G_2}}{G \supset D, \mathcal{P}_1, \mathcal{P}_2 \vdash G_2} \supset L}{G \supset D, \mathcal{P}_1, \mathcal{P}_2 \vdash G_1 \wedge G_2} \wedge R
$$

If this proof is not uniform, apply the inductive assumption to the two subproofs with $\supset L$ as their last rule. That induction returns a uniform proof for both $G \supset D, \mathcal{P}_1, \mathcal{P}_2 \vdash G_1$ and $G \supset D, \mathcal{P}_1, \mathcal{P}_2 \vdash G_2$, and a uniform proof for the end-sequent comes from applying $\wedge R$ to those uniform proofs.

For another case, assume that $\supset L$ is applied to a sequent with an implication on the right-hand side.

$$
\cfrac{\cfrac{\Xi_1}{\mathcal{P}_1 \vdash G} \quad \cfrac{\cfrac{\Xi_2}{D',D,\mathcal{P}_2 \vdash G'}}{D,\mathcal{P}_2 \vdash D' \supset G'} \supset R}{G \supset D, \mathcal{P}_1, \mathcal{P}_2 \vdash D' \supset G'} \supset L
$$

These rules can be permuted to form the following proof.

$$
\cfrac{\cfrac{\cfrac{\Xi_1}{\mathcal{P}_1 \vdash G} \quad \cfrac{\Xi_2}{D,D',\mathcal{P}_2 \vdash G'}}{G \supset D, D', \mathcal{P}_1, \mathcal{P}_2 \vdash G'} \supset L}{G \supset D, \mathcal{P}_1, \mathcal{P}_2 \vdash D' \supset G'} \supset R
$$

If this proof is not uniform, then apply the inductive hypothesis to the right premise of the $\supset R$ rule.

All other cases can be proved similarly: Permute a left rule up over a right-introduction rule and invoke the inductive hypothesis. □

5.3 Hereditary Harrop Formulas

> **Proposition 5.13.** *Let Σ be a signature, let $\mathcal{P}$ be a finite multiset of Σ-formulas in $\mathcal{D}_2$, and let G be a Σ-formula in $\mathcal{G}_2$. If $\Sigma :: \mathcal{P} \vdash G$ has a cut-free **I**-proof then $\Sigma :: \mathcal{P} \vdash G$ has a uniform proof.*

Proof: Assume that $\Sigma :: \mathcal{P} \vdash G$ has a cut-free **I**-proof Ξ. By Theorem 4.9, we can also assume that Ξ is an atomically closed **I**-proof. If Ξ is not uniform, then there must be occurrences of left rules (either left-introduction rules or left-structural rules) in Ξ whose conclusion is a sequent with a non-atomic right-hand side. Pick one of these occurrences so that the subproofs of its premises do not have other such occurrences. Thus, the premises of this inference rule occurrence are uniform. By Lemma 5.12, we can replace the subproof determined by this left rule with a uniform proof. In this way, we can continue to replace non-uniform subproofs with uniform proofs until such rewriting yields a uniform proof. □

This proposition formally establishes *fohh* as an abstract logic programming language.

Consider the following class of first-order formulas given by

$$H := A \mid B \supset H \mid \forall x.H \mid H_1 \wedge H_2.$$

Here, A ranges over atomic formulas and B over arbitrary first-order formulas. These H-formulas are known as *Harrop formulas*. Clearly, hereditary Harrop formulas are Harrop formulas.

> **Exercise 5.14.** (‡) *Consider the sequent $\Sigma :: \Gamma \vdash B$ where Γ is a multiset of Harrop formulas, and B is an arbitrary formula. Show that Harrop formulas are "uniform at the root"; that is, if B is non-atomic and this sequent is intuitionistically provable, then it has an **I**-proof that ends in a right-introduction rule. Are uniform proofs complete for such sequents?*

Finally, note that since hereditary Harrop formulas do not have occurrences of f in them, the triple $\langle \mathcal{D}_2, \mathcal{G}_2, \vdash_M \rangle$ describes essentially the same abstract logic programming language as *fohh*.

Readers wishing to see examples of logic programs in *fohh* before reading more about their proof theory can find some examples in Section 5.11.

5.4 Backchaining as Focused Rule Application

The restriction to uniform proofs provides some information on how to structure proofs: In the bottom-up search for proofs, right-introduction rules are attempted whenever the right-hand side is non-atomic, and left rules are attempted when the right-hand side is atomic. We now present a restriction on the application of left rules, and we will eventually show that that restriction on proofs does not result in the loss of completeness.

To better structure the rules on the left, we first make two simple changes to the proof system for **I**-proofs. Although *wL* can be applied at any point in the search for a uniform proof, it is also possible to delay applications of that rule until just before applying the *init* rule. This delay suggests that we can fold weakening into the *init* rule, yielding the derived inference rule

$$\frac{}{\Sigma :: \Gamma, B \vdash B}.$$

Adding another restriction on the use of a structural rule on the left can improve the complexity of the $\supset L$ rule when searching for a proof. As we mentioned in Section 3.3, performing proof search with a multiplicative inference rule can be expensive since there can be an exponential number of ways to split the contexts of the conclusion for use among the premises. The only multiplicative left-introduction rule is $\supset L$. Since contraction and weakening are available on the left (but not the right), the following variant of that inference rule is easily proved to be admissible (see Section 3.3).

$$\frac{\Sigma :: \Gamma \vdash \Delta_1, B \quad \Sigma :: C, \Gamma \vdash \Delta_2}{\Sigma :: B \supset C, \Gamma \vdash \Delta_1, \Delta_2}.$$

Here, the *cL* rule can double the Γ context before splitting the left context. In this rule, the left context is treated additively, and the right context is treated multiplicatively. Given that we are speaking of **I**-proofs here, this rule can be simplified even further since the single formula on the right of the concluding sequent must move to the right of the right premise. Thus, we can rewrite this rule as

$$\frac{\Sigma :: \Gamma \vdash B \quad \Sigma :: C, \Gamma \vdash E}{\Sigma :: B \supset C, \Gamma \vdash E}.$$

Now consider refining this last version of the left introduction of implication in the setting of uniform proofs. That is, consider the derivation

5.4 Backchaining as Focused Rule Application

$$\frac{\Sigma :: \mathcal{P} \vdash G \quad \Sigma :: D, \mathcal{P} \vdash A}{\dfrac{\Sigma :: G \supset D, \mathcal{P} \vdash A}{\Sigma :: \mathcal{P} \vdash A} \, cL} \supset L,$$

where A is atomic and where $G \supset D$ is a member of the multiset $\mathcal{P}$. Thus, to employ $G \supset D$ in building a proof, we first use cL to make a copy of it and then apply $\supset L$. Thus, we have reduced an attempt to prove the atomic formula A from program $\mathcal{P}$ to an attempt to prove two things, one of which is still an attempt to prove A but this time from the larger multiset $\mathcal{P} \cup \{D\}$. It would seem natural to expect these inference rules to be used because this new instance of D is directly helpful in proving A. For example, D could itself be A, or some sequence of additional left rules applied to D might reduce it to an occurrence of A.

We can formalize a proof system where left-introduction rules are used in such a direct or *focused* fashion by introducing a new style of sequent, namely, $\Sigma :: \mathcal{P} \Downarrow D \vdash A$. Although provability of this sequent will imply provability of the sequent $\Sigma :: \mathcal{P}, D \vdash A$, the formula between the $\Downarrow$ and the $\vdash$, called the *focus* of this sequent, is the only formula on which left-introduction rules can be applied. The sequents $\Sigma :: \mathcal{P} \vdash G$ and $\Sigma :: \mathcal{P} \Downarrow D \vdash A$ have $\Downarrow$ *fohh*-proofs if they have proofs using the $\Downarrow$ *fohh*-proof system in Figure 5.1. This new proof system is an example of a *focused* proof system: We shall see two more such focused proof systems when we introduce linear logic in Chapter 6.

All $\Downarrow$ *fohh*-proofs are composed of two phases. A *right-introduction phase* is a derivation composed of only right-introduction rules, and where all open premises are sequents with atomic formulas on their right-hand sides. Such a phase captures the notion of *goal reduction*. The right-introduction phase for $\Sigma :: \mathcal{P} \vdash G$ is empty (i.e., contains no inference rules) if and only if G is an atomic formula. A *left-introduction phase* is a derivation composed of left-introduction rules as well as the *init* and *decide* rules (see Figure 5.1) and where all open premises are sequents without the $\Downarrow$. A left-introduction phase for $\Sigma :: \Gamma \Downarrow B \vdash A$ can never be empty since it always contains an instance of the *decide* rule). This phase captures the notion of *backchaining*.

The proof system in Figure 5.1 is different from the original proof systems of Gentzen in that there is control over the application of introduction rules. In particular, the only way to prove a sequent that does not contain $\Downarrow$ is to perform a right-introduction rule or the *decide* rule. If a sequent contains the $\Downarrow$, then that sequent must be the conclusion of a left-introduction rule or the

$$\frac{}{\Sigma :: \mathcal{P} \vdash \mathsf{t}} \mathsf{tR} \qquad \frac{\Sigma :: \mathcal{P} \vdash G_1 \quad \Sigma :: \mathcal{P} \vdash G_2}{\Sigma :: \mathcal{P} \vdash G_1 \wedge G_2} \wedge \mathsf{R}$$

$$\frac{y : \tau, \Sigma :: \mathcal{P} \vdash G[y/x]}{\Sigma :: \mathcal{P} \vdash \forall_\tau x.G} \forall \mathsf{R} \qquad \frac{\Sigma :: D, \mathcal{P} \vdash G}{\Sigma :: \mathcal{P} \vdash D \supset G} \supset \mathsf{R}$$

$$\frac{\Sigma :: \mathcal{P} \vdash G_1}{\Sigma :: \mathcal{P} \vdash G_1 \vee G_2} \vee \mathsf{R} \qquad \frac{\Sigma :: \mathcal{P} \vdash G_2}{\Sigma :: \mathcal{P} \vdash G_1 \vee G_2} \vee \mathsf{R}$$

$$\frac{\Sigma \Vdash t : \tau \quad \Sigma :: \mathcal{P} \vdash G[t/x]}{\Sigma :: \mathcal{P} \vdash \exists_\tau x\, G} \exists \mathsf{R}$$

$$\frac{\Sigma :: \mathcal{P} \Downarrow D \vdash A}{\Sigma :: \mathcal{P} \vdash A} \textit{decide} \qquad \frac{}{\Sigma :: \mathcal{P} \Downarrow A \vdash A} \textit{init}$$

$$\frac{\Sigma :: \mathcal{P} \Downarrow D_1 \vdash A}{\Sigma :: \mathcal{P} \Downarrow D_1 \wedge D_2 \vdash A} \wedge \mathsf{L} \qquad \frac{\Sigma :: \mathcal{P} \Downarrow D_2 \vdash A}{\Sigma :: \mathcal{P} \Downarrow D_1 \wedge D_2 \vdash A} \wedge \mathsf{L}$$

$$\frac{\Sigma :: \mathcal{P} \vdash G \quad \Sigma :: \mathcal{P} \Downarrow D \vdash A}{\Sigma :: \mathcal{P} \Downarrow G \supset D \vdash A} \supset \mathsf{L} \qquad \frac{\Sigma \Vdash t : \tau \quad \Sigma :: \mathcal{P} \Downarrow D[t/x] \vdash A}{\Sigma :: \mathcal{P} \Downarrow \forall_\tau x.D \vdash A} \forall \mathsf{L}$$

In the *decide* rule, D is a member of $\mathcal{P}$. In all these rules, A is atomic.

Figure 5.1 The $\Downarrow$ *fohh* proof system.

init rule. Furthermore, contraction and weakening are not separate rules but are built into other rules.

Sections 5.1–5.3 present various theorems about the unfocused proof systems **I** and **C** and their relationship with Horn clauses and hereditary Harrop formulas. The focused proof system is much more useful than those unfocused proof systems for our purposes here. Once we have proved the soundness and completeness of the focused proof system $\Downarrow$ *fohh*, most of the results in Sections 5.1–5.3 can be reproved immediately using those theorems.

The following proposition states that whatever is provable using $\Downarrow$ *fohh*-proofs is also provable in intuitionistic proofs.

Proposition 5.15 (Soundness of $\Downarrow$ *fohh*-proofs). *Let Σ be a signature, $\mathcal{P}$ be a multiset of Σ-formulas in $\mathcal{D}_2$, and G be a Σ-formula in $\mathcal{G}_2$. If the sequent $\Sigma :: \mathcal{P} \vdash G$ has a $\Downarrow$ fohh-proof then it has an **I**-proof.*

Proof: This is proved by a simple induction on the structure of $\Downarrow$ *fohh*-proofs. In that induction, the sequents $\Sigma :: \mathcal{P} \vdash G$ and $\Sigma :: \mathcal{P} \Downarrow D \vdash A$ in $\Downarrow$ *fohh*-proofs are mapped to the sequents $\Sigma :: \mathcal{P} \vdash G$ and $\Sigma :: \mathcal{P}, D \vdash A$, respectively, in the **I**-proof system. □

It is important to point out that the search for focused proofs is not justified as being the most efficient strategy or yielding the smallest proofs. Exercise 5.16 reveals that sometimes focused proofs can be much larger than other proofs.

> **Exercise 5.16.** (‡) *Let $a_0, a_1, \ldots, a_n$ be atomic (propositional) formulas ($n \geq 0$). Define the sequence of propositional Horn clauses*
>
> $$D_n = a_0 \supset \cdots \supset a_{n-1} \supset a_n \quad (n \geq 0).$$
>
> *For example, D_0 is a_0, D_1 is $a_0 \supset a_1$, and D_2 is $a_0 \supset a_1 \supset a_2$. For a given $n \geq 0$, there are many uniform proofs of the sequent $D_0, \ldots, D_n \vdash a_n$. Among these, consider those in which the left premise of the $\supset L$ rule is trivial (proved by the initial rule). Those proofs use the formulas D_i in a forward-chaining manner. How do such proofs differ in size from proofs based only on backchaining, i.e., $\Downarrow$ fohh-proofs?*

5.5 Completeness of Focused Proofs

In order to prove the completeness of the $\Downarrow$ *fohh* proof system for hereditary Harrop formulas in intuitionistic logic (see Proposition 5.38), we shall first develop some key proof-theoretic insights into focused proofs. In particular, it is interesting to ask whether or not the rules

$$\frac{}{\Sigma :: B \vdash B} \quad \text{and} \quad \frac{\Sigma :: \Gamma \vdash B \qquad \Sigma :: B, \Gamma' \vdash E}{\Sigma :: \Gamma, \Gamma' \vdash E}$$

are admissible in $\Downarrow$ *fohh*. However, just stating the unrestricted forms of the initial and cut rules for $\Downarrow$ *fohh*-proofs requires us to limit our attention to those formulas B that are both goal formulas and definite clauses since these are the only formulas that can appear on the left and right of the sequent turnstile.

To address this issue, let $\mathcal{L}_0$ be the set of connectives $\{t, \wedge, \supset, \forall\}$ and let an $\mathcal{L}_0$-*formula* be any first-order formula, all of whose logical connectives come from $\mathcal{L}_0$.[1] In particular, such formulas do not contain occurrences of disjunctions and existential quantifiers. Note that the connectives in $\mathcal{L}_0$ have invertible right-introduction rules, while their left-introduction rules are not invertible. Until we return to the issue of dealing with disjunctions and existential quantifiers in Section 5.8, we restrict our attention to $\mathcal{L}_0$-formulas, which are also the same as *fohh* using definition (5.6).

Since $\mathcal{L}_0$-formulas have no occurrences of f, provability in intuitionistic and minimal logics coincide (see Section 4.5). Thus, for most of this chapter, we could replace references to intuitionistic logic with minimal logic when discussing the properties of $\Downarrow$ *fohh*-proofs. In addition, we emphasize the role of $\mathcal{L}_0$-formulas in this section by using the name $\Downarrow$ $\mathcal{L}_0$-*proof system* for the proof system that results from removing the right-introduction rules for $\exists$ and $\vee$ from the $\Downarrow$ *fohh*-proof system.

In the $\Downarrow$ $\mathcal{L}_0$ proof system, we have the following relationship between the two phases and nondeterminism. Let Σ be a signature and $\mathcal{P} \cup \{G\}$ be $\mathcal{L}_0$-formulas over Σ. There always exists a right-introduction phase that ends in $\Sigma :: \mathcal{P} \vdash G$, and that phase is unique up to the change of names of the eigenvariables. Thus, a right-introduction phase can be seen as a *function* that takes the endsequent $\Sigma :: \mathcal{P} \vdash G$ as input and returns the unique multiset of sequents of the form $\Sigma' :: \mathcal{P}' \vdash A$ (where A is an atomic formula) that are the premises of that right-introduction phase. On the other hand, the left-introduction phase yields a nondeterministic *relation* between its endsequent, say, $\Sigma :: \mathcal{P} \Downarrow D \vdash A$, and the multiset of sequents of the form $\Sigma :: \mathcal{P} \vdash G$ that are the premises of a left-introduction phase.

Let B be an $\mathcal{L}_0$-formula. The *paths in B* are those formulas P for which the following two-place relation $B \uparrow P$ is provable (here, A denotes an atomic formula).

$$\frac{}{A \uparrow A} \quad \frac{B \uparrow P}{B \wedge C \uparrow P} \quad \frac{C \uparrow P}{B \wedge C \uparrow P} \quad \frac{C \uparrow P}{B \supset C \uparrow B \supset P} \quad \frac{B \uparrow P}{\forall_\tau x.B \uparrow \forall_\tau x.P}.$$

A formula that is a path has the form

$$\forall \bar{x}_1.(G_1 \supset \forall \bar{x}_2.(G_2 \supset \ldots \supset \forall \bar{x}_n.(G_n \supset \forall \bar{x}_0.A)\ldots)),$$

where $n \geq 0$, A is an atomic formula, $G_1, \ldots, G_n$ is a list of $\mathcal{L}_0$-formulas, and where for each i such that $0 \leq i \leq n$, $\bar{x}_i$ is a list of variables. The formula A is the *target* of this path, the formulas $G_1, \ldots, G_n$ are the *arguments* of this path,

---

[1] In Chapter 6, we introduce two additional sets of connectives $\mathcal{L}_1$ and $\mathcal{L}_2$.

5.5 Completeness of Focused Proofs

and the result of concatenating the lists $\bar{x}_0, \ldots, \bar{x}_n$ is the list of *bound variables* of this path. (We assume that all these bound variables are distinct.) We shall also present such a path using an *associated sequent*, namely, $\bar{x}_0, \ldots, \bar{x}_n ::\allowbreak G_1, \ldots, G_n \vdash A$. Note that the formula t has no paths.

For example, the paths in $(a \wedge b) \supset (c \wedge d)$ are $(a \wedge b) \supset c$ and $(a \wedge b) \supset d$. Similarly, the formula

$$\forall x.p(x) \supset ((\forall y.q(x,y) \supset (r(x,y) \wedge r(y,x))) \wedge p(x))$$

(where p, q, and r are predicates) has the following three paths (displayed with their associated sequents):

$$\forall x.p(x) \supset \forall y.q(x,y) \supset r(x,y) \qquad x,y :: p(x), q(x,y) \vdash r(x,y)$$

$$\forall x.p(x) \supset \forall y.q(x,y) \supset r(y,x) \qquad x,y :: p(x), q(x,y) \vdash r(y,x)$$

$$\forall x.p(x) \supset p(x) \qquad x : p(x) \vdash p(x).$$

> **Exercise 5.17.** Show that if the formula B contains no occurrences of t and $\wedge$ then B has exactly one path which is B itself.

> **Exercise 5.18.** Let D be a hereditary Harrop formula defined using (5.4). Prove that D has exactly one path, which is D.

Given that the following equivalences are provable in intuitionistic logic

$$B_1 \supset (B_2 \wedge B_3) \equiv (B_1 \supset B_2) \wedge (B_1 \supset B_3)$$
$$\forall x. (B_1 \wedge B_2) \equiv (\forall x. B_1) \wedge (\forall x. B_2),$$

it is easy to prove the intuitionistic equivalence

$$B \equiv \bigwedge_{B \uparrow P} P.$$

We can state the following two much stronger relationships between B and the conjunction of all paths in B.

1. The right-introduction phase that has endsequent $\Sigma :: \Gamma \vdash B$ and the right-introduction phase that has endsequent $\Sigma :: \Gamma \vdash \bigwedge_{B \uparrow P} P$ have exactly the same premises (modulo the order in which the premises are listed and modulo alphabetic changes in the names of eigenvariables).

2. The multiset of left-introduction phases with endsequent $\Sigma :: \Gamma \Downarrow B \vdash A$ can be put in one-to-one correspondence with left-introduction phases with endsequent $\Sigma :: \Gamma \Downarrow \bigwedge_{B \uparrow P} P \vdash A$ in such a way that corresponding premises are equal (modulo the order in which the premises are listed and modulo alphabetic changes in the names of eigenvariables).

These observations are stated more formally in the following two propositions.

> **Proposition 5.19.** *Let Ξ be a $\Downarrow \mathcal{L}_0$-proof of the sequent $\Sigma :: \Gamma \vdash B$. The right-introduction phase at the bottom of Ξ has a set of premises that are in one-to-one correspondence with paths in B such that the path P corresponds to the premise $\Sigma, \Sigma' :: \Gamma, \mathcal{B} \vdash A$, where the sequent associated to P is $\Sigma' :: \mathcal{B} \vdash A$. (The variables in Σ' are chosen to be disjoint from Σ.)*

Proof: We prove this proposition by induction on the structure of the $\mathcal{L}_0$ formula B. In the case that B is t, the set of paths in B is empty, and the set of premises of the right-introduction phase is also empty. If B is atomic, the end-sequent of the right-introduction phase is the same as its unique premise, corresponding to adding no bound variables and no argument formulas (this phase is empty). If B is $B_1 \wedge B_2$, then the right-introduction phase ends with

$$\frac{\Sigma :: \Gamma \vdash B_1 \quad \Sigma :: \Gamma \vdash B_2}{\Sigma :: \Gamma \vdash B_1 \wedge B_2}.$$

The premises of this phase are divided into those which are premises of the right-introduction phase with endsequent $\Sigma :: \Gamma \vdash B_1$ and the premises of the right-introduction phase with endsequent $\Sigma :: \Gamma \vdash B_2$. Since the paths in P are either paths in B_1 or in B_2, the inductive hypothesis immediately yields the required correspondence. If B is $B_1 \supset B_2$ then the right-introduction phase ends with

$$\frac{\Sigma :: \Gamma, B_1 \vdash B_2}{\Sigma :: \Gamma \vdash B_1 \supset B_2}.$$

The premises of this phase are also premises of the right-introduction phase with endsequent $\Sigma :: \Gamma, B_1 \vdash B_2$. By the inductive hypothesis, a path P' in B_2 corresponds to the premise $\Sigma, \Sigma' :: \Gamma, B_1, \mathcal{B} \vdash A$, where $\Sigma' :: \mathcal{B} \vdash A$ is the sequent associated to P'. By the definition of paths, the only difference between the path P and P' is that the former has B_1 as an additional argument.

5.5 COMPLETENESS OF FOCUSED PROOFS

Thus, the correspondence is satisfied. The case where B is $\forall x.B'$ is similar to the previous case. □

The proposition above states that an attempt to prove $\Sigma :: \Gamma \vdash B$ in $\Downarrow \mathcal{L}_0$ leads to an attempt to prove a series of sequents, one for each path in B. Thus, paths can describe the right-introduction phase. The structure of the left-introduction phases can also be described using paths in a dual sense, as described in the following proposition.

> **Proposition 5.20.** Let Ξ be a $\Downarrow \mathcal{L}_0$-proof of the sequent $\Sigma :: \Gamma \Downarrow B \vdash A$. The left-introduction phase at the bottom of Ξ has premises
>
> $$\Sigma :: \Gamma \vdash G_1, \ldots, \Sigma :: \Gamma \vdash G_n \quad (n \geq 0)$$
>
> if and only if there is a path P in B with target A', arguments $B_1, \ldots, B_n$, and bound variables Σ', and a substitution θ that maps the variables in Σ' to Σ-terms such that $A'\theta = A$ and such that $G_1 = B_1\theta, \ldots, G_n = B_n\theta$.

Proof: We prove this proposition by induction on the structure of the $\mathcal{L}_0$ formula B. The case that B is t is impossible since there is no left-introduction rule for t. If B is atomic, then B and A are equal since we assume that $\Sigma :: \Gamma \Downarrow B \vdash A$ is the endsequent of a left-introduction phase (and the set of arguments of B is the empty set).

If B is $B_1 \wedge B_2$, we first assume that there is a left-introduction phase ending in $\Sigma :: \Gamma \Downarrow B_1 \wedge B_2 \vdash A$. Thus, there is a left-introduction phase ending in $\Sigma :: \Gamma \Downarrow B_i \vdash A$, where $i = 1$ or $i = 2$. By the inductive assumption, there is a path in B_i with target A', arguments $\mathcal{B}$, and bound variables Σ', and a substitution θ that maps the variables in Σ' to Σ-terms such that $A'\theta$ is equal to A and such that every premise of that left-introduction phase can be written as $\Sigma :: \Gamma \vdash G\theta$ for each $G \in \mathcal{B}$. That same path is also a path in B, which completes this case. The converse is proved similarly.

If B is $B_1 \supset B_2$, we first assume that there is a left-introduction phase that ends with $\Sigma :: \Gamma \Downarrow B_1 \supset B_2 \vdash A$ and the inference rule

$$\frac{\Sigma :: \Gamma \vdash B_1 \quad \Sigma :: \Gamma \Downarrow B_2 \vdash A}{\Sigma :: \Gamma \Downarrow B_1 \supset B_2 \vdash A}.$$

By the inductive hypothesis, there is a path in B_2 with target A', arguments $\mathcal{B}$, bound variables Σ', and a substitution θ that maps the variables in Σ' to Σ-terms such that $A'\theta$ is equal to A and such that every premise of that left-introduction phase can be written as $\Sigma :: \Gamma \vdash G\theta$ for each $G \in \mathcal{B}$. If we add to that path the argument B_1, then that path satisfies the required condition for a path in B. The converse is proved similarly.

Finally, assume that B is $\forall_\tau x.B'$. First, assume that there is a left-introduction phase ending in $\forall_\tau x.B'$. Thus, there is a left-introduction phase ending in $\Sigma :: \Gamma \Downarrow B'[t/x] \vdash A$ and inference rule

$$\frac{\Sigma :: \Gamma \Downarrow B'[t/x] \vdash A}{\Sigma :: \Gamma \Downarrow \forall x.B' \vdash A}$$

for some Σ-term t. By the inductive assumption, there is a path in $B'[t/x]$ with target A', arguments $\mathcal{B}$, and bound variables Σ', and a substitution θ that maps the variables in Σ' to Σ-terms such that $A'\theta$ is equal to A and such that every premise of that left-introduction phase can be written as $\Sigma :: \Gamma \vdash G\theta$ for each $G \in \mathcal{B}$. The required path through $\forall x.B'$ is the same as for $B'[t/x]$ except that the required substitution is θ extended with the mapping of x to t. The converse can be proved similarly. □

Note the dual use of paths: *All* paths of B are used to describe the right-introduction phase with endsequent $\Sigma :: \Gamma \vdash B$, while *some* path of B is used to describe the left-introduction phase with endsequent $\Sigma :: \Gamma \Downarrow B \vdash A$.

Exercise 5.21. *Prove that if the sequent $\Sigma :: \Gamma, B \vdash G$ has a $\Downarrow \mathcal{L}_0$-proof Ξ in which no occurrence of decide picks the formula B as its focus, then there is a $\Downarrow \mathcal{L}_0$-proof Ξ' of $\Sigma :: \Gamma \vdash G$ that has the same inference rules as Ξ: The only difference is the sequents labeling those inference rules do not contain B. This operation of removing an assumption in a sequent is called strengthening.*

We are now able to prove the three main theorems related to $\Downarrow \mathcal{L}_0$-proofs: the admissibility of the (non-atomic) *init* rule, the admissibility of *cut*, and the completeness of $\Downarrow \mathcal{L}_0$-proofs with respect to intuitionistic provability.

Theorem 5.22 (Admissibility of initial). *Let Γ be a multiset of $\mathcal{L}_0$ Σ-formulas. If $B \in \Gamma$ then $\Sigma :: \Gamma \vdash B$ has a $\Downarrow \mathcal{L}_0$-proof.*

Proof: We describe how to build a $\Downarrow \mathcal{L}_0$-proof of $\Sigma :: \Gamma \vdash B$ by induction on the structure of the $\mathcal{L}_0$-formula B. We first consider the right-introduction

5.5 Completeness of Focused Proofs

$$\frac{\Sigma :: \Gamma \vdash B \qquad \Sigma :: \Gamma, B \vdash C}{\Sigma :: \Gamma \vdash C} \; cut \qquad \frac{\Sigma :: \Gamma \vdash B \qquad \Sigma :: \Gamma \Downarrow B \vdash A}{\Sigma :: \Gamma \vdash A} \; cut_k$$

The cut-formula B in these rules is restricted to be an $\mathcal{L}_0$-formula.
Figure 5.2 The cut inference rules used in $\Downarrow^+\mathcal{L}_0$-proofs.

phase with the endsequent $\Sigma :: \Gamma \vdash B$. By Proposition 5.19, for every path P in B, there is a premise sequent of that right-introduction phase of the form $\Sigma, \Sigma' :: \Gamma, \mathcal{B} \vdash A$, where A, $\mathcal{B}$, and Σ' are, respectively, the target, arguments, and bound variables of P. Now consider the premise corresponding to P and use the *decide* rule to select $B \in \Gamma$ to initiate a left-introduction phase. By Proposition 5.20, there is a left-introduction phase that corresponds to P. By setting θ to the identity substitution on the variables in Σ', we have $A = A\theta$ and where the left-introduction phase has the premises (where, $\mathcal{B} = \{B_1, \ldots, B_n\}$)

$$\Sigma, \Sigma' :: \Gamma, \mathcal{B} \vdash B_1 \quad, \ldots, \quad \Sigma, \Sigma' :: \Gamma, \mathcal{B} \vdash B_n \quad (n \geq 0).$$

We can conclude now by using the inductive hypotheses on each of these premises. □

In order to prove the cut-elimination theorem for $\Downarrow \mathcal{L}_0$-proofs, we introduce the two additional inference rules in Figure 5.2. The *cut* rule involves three sequents, none containing the $\Downarrow$. In order to describe the elimination of *cut* from proofs, we use a second inference rule called the *key cut*, which contains one premise with a $\Downarrow$. The formula B in both rules is the *cut formula* for that rule. The proof system that combines these two inference rules with the rules for the $\Downarrow \mathcal{L}_0$-proof system is called the $\Downarrow^+\mathcal{L}_0$ proof system, and proofs in that system are called $\Downarrow^+\mathcal{L}_0$-proofs. A $\Downarrow^+\mathcal{L}_0$-proof is said to be *cut-free* if it contains no occurrences of these new rules; hence, a cut-free proof is a $\Downarrow \mathcal{L}_0$-proof.

The following proposition can be proved by induction on the structure of $\Downarrow^+\mathcal{L}_0$-proofs.

> **Proposition 5.23** (Weakening $\Downarrow^+\mathcal{L}_0$-proofs). *Let Σ and Σ' be signatures such that $\Sigma \subseteq \Sigma'$ and let Γ and Γ' be two multisets of $\mathcal{L}_0$-formulas such that $\Gamma \subseteq \Gamma'$. If $\Sigma :: \Gamma \vdash B$ has a $\Downarrow^+\mathcal{L}_0$-proof then $\Sigma' :: \Gamma' \vdash B$ has a $\Downarrow^+\mathcal{L}_0$-proof.*

An occurrence of either *cut* or cut_k is said to be *topmost* if the subproofs of both of its premises are cut-free.

> **Lemma 5.24** (Replace *cut* with *cut$_k$*). *Consider the following topmost occurrence of the cut rule (i.e., Ξ_l and Ξ_r are (cut-free) $\Downarrow \mathcal{L}_0$-proofs).*
>
> $$\dfrac{\begin{array}{cc}\Xi_l & \Xi_r \\ \Sigma :: \Gamma \vdash B & \Sigma :: \Gamma, B \vdash C\end{array}}{\Sigma :: \Gamma \vdash C}\ cut.$$
>
> *This proof can be transformed into a proof of the same sequent with no occurrences of the cut rule, but there may be several occurrences of the cut$_k$ rule, all of which have cut-formula B.*

Proof: We first convert Ξ_r to a new proof Ξ'_r also of $\Sigma :: \Gamma, B \vdash C$ by replacing every occurrence of the *decide* rule applied to the cut formula B within Ξ_r, such as

$$\dfrac{\begin{array}{c}\Xi_0 \\ \Sigma' :: \Gamma', B \Downarrow B \vdash A\end{array}}{\Sigma' :: \Gamma', B \vdash A}\ decide$$

(where $\Sigma \subseteq \Sigma'$ and $\Gamma \subseteq \Gamma'$), with the following occurrence of the *cut$_k$* rule

$$\dfrac{\begin{array}{cc}\hat{\Xi}_l & \Xi_0 \\ \Sigma' :: \Gamma' \vdash B & \Sigma' :: \Gamma', B \Downarrow B \vdash A\end{array}}{\Sigma' :: \Gamma', B \vdash A}\ cut_k.$$

Here, $\hat{\Xi}_l$ results from weakening Ξ_l (Proposition 5.23). The resulting proof Ξ'_r has no occurrences of *decide* on B but may have several occurrences of *cut$_k$* with the cut formula B. Although Ξ'_r is a proof of $\Sigma :: \Gamma, B \vdash C$, since there are no occurrences of *decide* on B in Ξ'_r, we can strengthen Ξ'_r to get a proof Ξ_s of $\Sigma :: \Gamma \vdash C$ (see Exercise 5.21). As a result, we can replace the original proof of $\Sigma :: \Gamma \vdash C$ with the proof Ξ_s. □

The following proposition can be proved by induction on the structure of $\Downarrow^+ \mathcal{L}_0$-proofs.

> **Proposition 5.25** (Substitution into $\Downarrow^+ \mathcal{L}_0$-proofs). *Let Σ be a signature, x a variable not declared in Σ, and τ a primitive type. If $\Sigma, x : \tau : \Gamma \vdash B$ has a $\Downarrow^+ \mathcal{L}_0$-proof and t is a Σ-term of type τ then $\Sigma :: \Gamma[t/x] \vdash B[t/x]$ has a $\Downarrow^+ \mathcal{L}_0$-proof.*

5.5 Completeness of Focused Proofs

The size of a formula B, written as $|B|$, is the number of occurrences of logical connectives in B. The *size* of a formula is zero if and only if that formula is atomic.

> **Lemma 5.26** (Replace cut_k with cut). *Consider the following topmost occurrence of the cut_k rule, where Ξ_l and Ξ_r are (cut-free) $\Downarrow \mathcal{L}_0$-proofs.*
>
> $$\dfrac{\begin{array}{c}\Xi_l\\ \Sigma :: \Gamma \vdash B\end{array} \qquad \begin{array}{c}\Xi_r\\ \Sigma :: \Gamma \Downarrow B \vdash C\end{array}}{\Sigma :: \Gamma \vdash C}\ cut_k.$$
>
> *We can transform this proof into a proof of $\Sigma :: \Gamma \vdash C$ with no occurrences of cut_k but with possibly several instances of the cut rule, all of which have cut-formulas with measure strictly smaller than $|B|$.*

Proof: Consider a topmost occurrence of the cut_k rule as displayed above. If B is atomic, then B and C are equal, and the result of eliminating this cut_k is Ξ_l. In the case that B is not atomic, Ξ_l ends in a nonempty, right-introduction phase, and Ξ_r ends in a left-introduction phase. By Proposition 5.20, there is a path P in B with associated sequent $\Sigma' :: B_1, \ldots, B_n \vdash A'$ such that the premises and subproofs of that left-introduction phase are

$$\begin{array}{ccc}\Xi_1 & & \Xi_n \\ \Sigma :: \Gamma \vdash B_1\theta, & \ldots, & \Sigma :: \Gamma \vdash B_n\theta\end{array} \quad (n \geq 0)$$

and where $A'\theta$ is A, for some substitution θ. By Proposition 5.19, there is a premise in the right-introduction phase that corresponds to path P and is the sequent $\Sigma, \Sigma' :: \Gamma, B_1, \ldots, B_n \vdash A'$ with subproof Ξ_0. By repeated application of Proposition 5.25, we know that the sequent $\Sigma :: \Gamma, B_1\theta, \ldots, B_n\theta \vdash A'\theta$ has a $\Downarrow \mathcal{L}_0$-proof, say, $\Xi_0\theta$. We can arrange these various $\Downarrow \mathcal{L}_0$-proofs as the following n occurrences of the *cut* rule (remembering that A equals $A'\theta$).

$$\dfrac{\begin{array}{c}\Xi_1\\ \Sigma :: \Gamma \vdash B_1\theta\end{array} \qquad \begin{array}{c}\Xi_0\theta\\ \Sigma :: \Gamma, B_1\theta, \ldots, B_n\theta \vdash A\end{array}}{\Sigma :: \Gamma, B_2\theta, \ldots, B_n\theta \vdash A}\ cut$$

$$\vdots$$

$$\dfrac{\begin{array}{c}\Xi_n\\ \Sigma :: \Gamma \vdash B_n\theta\end{array} \qquad \Sigma :: \Gamma, B_n\theta \vdash A}{\Sigma :: \Gamma \vdash A}\ cut$$

Note that the size of each of the cut formulas $B_1\theta, \ldots, B_n\theta$ is strictly less than the size of the original cut formula B. □

Thus, Lemma 5.24 describes how one occurrence of *cut* on B can be replaced with several occurrences of cut_k on B, and Lemma 5.26 describes how an occurrence of cut_k on B can be replaced by several occurrences of *cut* on strictly smaller formulas than B.

Lemma 5.27. *A $\Downarrow^+\mathcal{L}_0$ proof that ends with a cut rule in which both premises have a cut-free proof can be replaced with a cut-free proof of the same endsequent.*

Proof: Consider the following topmost occurrence of the *cut* inference rule

$$\frac{\Xi_l \qquad \Xi_r}{\Sigma :: \Gamma \vdash B \qquad \Sigma :: \Gamma, B \vdash C} \text{ cut,}$$
$$\Sigma :: \Gamma \vdash C$$

in which Ξ_l and Ξ_r are (cut-free) $\Downarrow\mathcal{L}_0$-proofs. We will show that the sequent $\Sigma :: \Gamma \vdash C$ has a cut-free $\Downarrow\mathcal{L}_0$-proof by induction on the size of the cut formula B. First, apply Lemma 5.24 to conclude that there is a proof Ξ' of $\Sigma :: \Gamma \vdash C$ that contains no occurrences of *cut* but which might have several instances of the cut_k rule with cut formula B. We can now do a second induction on the number of occurrences of cut_k in Ξ'. If that number is 0, then Ξ' is the desired cut-free proof. Otherwise, assume that there is at least one occurrence of cut_k on B in Ξ'. Now, we pick a topmost occurrence of cut_k and apply Lemma 5.26. In that case, we can convert that occurrence of cut_k to several occurrences of *cut* on strictly smaller formulas than B. Applying the inductive assumption can eliminate all of these occurrences of *cut*. We have now replaced one occurrence of the cut_k rule with a cut-free proof, and hence, we have completed our proof. □

We can combine these lemmas to prove the main cut-elimination theorem for $\Downarrow^+\mathcal{L}_0$ proofs.

Theorem 5.28 (Elimination of cuts). *If the sequent $\Sigma :: \Gamma \vdash G$ has a $\Downarrow^+\mathcal{L}_0$-proof then it has a $\Downarrow\mathcal{L}_0$-proof.*

Proof: We proceed using induction on the number of occurrences of the *cut* inference rules in a proof. In particular, pick an occurrence of the *cut* rule,

5.5 COMPLETENESS OF FOCUSED PROOFS 85

which is the endsequent of a subproof in which both premises have cut-free proofs. By applying Lemma 5.27 to that occurrence of *cut*, we can replace it with a cut-free proof of the same sequent. The proof now follows from the inductive assumption. □

A consequence of the cut-elimination theorem for $\Downarrow^+ \mathcal{L}_0$ proofs is the completeness of $\Downarrow \mathcal{L}_0$-proofs with respect of **I**-proofs (when all formulas are restricted to $\mathcal{L}_0$).

> **Theorem 5.29** (Completeness of $\Downarrow \mathcal{L}_0$-proofs for $\mathcal{L}_0$-formulas). *If the sequent $\Sigma :: \Gamma \vdash G$ has a cut-free **I**-proof then it has a $\Downarrow \mathcal{L}_0$-proof.*

For convenience, we use the notation $\Sigma :: \mathcal{P} \vdash_\Downarrow G$ to denote the proposition that the sequent $\Sigma :: \mathcal{P} \vdash G$ has a $\Downarrow \mathcal{L}_0$-proof.

Proof: We prove this by showing that the inference rules of the intuitionistic proof system **I** are admissible in the $\Downarrow \mathcal{L}_0$-proof system. Since the right-introduction rules of **I** are the same as those in $\Downarrow \mathcal{L}_0$, these rules are trivially admissible. The admissibility of the *init* rule for **I** follows immediately from Proposition 5.22. The admissibility of the *wL* rule follows from Proposition 5.23. The admissibility of the *cL* rule is easily argued as follows. In a $\Downarrow \mathcal{L}_0$-proof of $\Sigma :: \Gamma, B, B \vdash \Delta$, the *decide* rule may have been used on the two different occurrences of B. By changing all those *decide* rules to use the same occurrence of B and then deleting the other occurrence of B, we obtain a $\Downarrow \mathcal{L}_0$-proof of $\Sigma :: \Gamma, B \vdash \Delta$.

All that remains to show is that the left-introduction rules for the $\mathcal{L}_0$ connectives $\wedge$, $\supset$, and $\forall$ are admissible.

Admissibility of $\wedge L$. Assume that $B_1 \wedge B_2$ is an $\mathcal{L}_0$ Σ-formula. By Proposition 5.22, we have $\Sigma :: B_1 \wedge B_2 \vdash_\Downarrow B_1 \wedge B_2$. A $\Downarrow \mathcal{L}_0$-proof of that sequent has immediate subproofs that yield both $\Sigma :: B_1 \wedge B_2 \vdash_\Downarrow B_1$ and $\Sigma :: B_1 \wedge B_2 \vdash_\Downarrow B_2$. In order to prove that $\wedge L$ is admissible, assume that $\Sigma :: B_1, \Gamma \vdash_\Downarrow E$. Using cut-admissibility (Theorem 5.28) with this sequent and the sequent $\Sigma :: B_1 \wedge B_2 \vdash_\Downarrow B_1$, we conclude that $\Sigma :: B_1 \wedge B_2, \Gamma \vdash_\Downarrow E$. A similar argument also concludes that if $\Sigma :: B_2, \Gamma \vdash_\Downarrow E$, then $\Sigma :: B_1 \wedge B_2, \Gamma \vdash_\Downarrow E$. Hence, both $\wedge L$ rules in **I** are admissible.

Admissibility of $\supset L$. Assume that $B_1 \supset B_2$ is an $\mathcal{L}_0$ Σ-formula. By Proposition 5.22, we have $\Sigma :: B_1 \supset B_2 \vdash_\Downarrow B_1 \supset B_2$. A $\Downarrow \mathcal{L}_0$-proof of that sequent has an immediate subproof that proves $\Sigma :: B_1, B_1 \supset B_2 \vdash_\Downarrow B_2$. In order to prove that $\supset L$ is admissible, assume that both $\Sigma :: \Gamma_1 \vdash_\Downarrow B_1$ and $\Sigma :: B_2, \Gamma_2 \vdash_\Downarrow E$. Using the Proposition 5.23, we have $\Sigma :: \Gamma_1, \Gamma_2 \vdash_\Downarrow B_1$ and

$\Sigma :: B_2, \Gamma_1, \Gamma_2 \vdash_\Downarrow E$. Using cut-admissibility (Theorem 5.28), we conclude that $\Sigma :: \Gamma_1, \Gamma_2, B_1 \supset B_2 \vdash_\Downarrow B_2$ and $\Sigma :: B_1 \supset B_2, \Gamma_1, \Gamma_2 \vdash_\Downarrow E$. Hence, the $\supset L$ rule in **I** is admissible.

Admissibility of $\forall L$. Assume that $\forall_\tau x.B$ is an $\mathcal{L}_0$ Σ-formula and that τ is a primitive type. By Proposition 5.22, we have $\Sigma :: \forall_\tau x.B \vdash_\Downarrow \forall_\tau x.B$. A $\Downarrow \mathcal{L}_0$-proof of that sequent has an immediate subproof that proves $\Sigma, y : \tau : \forall x.B \vdash_\Downarrow B[y/x]$, for a variable y not present in Σ. By Proposition 5.25, we have $\Sigma :: \forall x.B \vdash_\Downarrow B[t/x]$, for any Σ-term t. In order to prove that $\forall L$ is admissible, assume that $\Sigma :: B[t/x], \Gamma \vdash E$ has a $\Downarrow \mathcal{L}_0$-proof. Then using cut elimination (Theorem 5.28), we can conclude that $\Sigma :: \forall x.B, \Gamma \vdash E$ has a $\Downarrow \mathcal{L}_0$-proof. Hence, the $\forall L$ rule in **I** is admissible. □

Another simple consequence of proving cut elimination for $\Downarrow^+ \mathcal{L}_0$-proofs is the admissibility of cut for **I**-proofs when restricted to $\mathcal{L}_0$-formulas.

Theorem 5.30 (Admissibility of cut for **I**-proofs restricted to $\mathcal{L}_0$ formulas). *The cut rule for **I**-proofs (Figure 4.2) is admissible for cut-free **I**-proofs when restricted to $\mathcal{L}_0$-formulas.*

Proof: We wish to prove that the single-conclusion version of the cut rule from Figure 4.2, namely,

$$\frac{\Sigma :: \Gamma_1 \vdash B \qquad \Sigma :: B, \Gamma_2 \vdash E}{\Sigma :: \Gamma_1, \Gamma_2 \vdash E} \text{ cut}$$

is admissible in the cut-free **I**-proof system. Thus, assume that $\Sigma :: \Gamma_1 \vdash B$ and $\Sigma :: B, \Gamma_2 \vdash E$ have (cut-free) **I**-proofs. By Theorem 5.29, $\Sigma :: \Gamma_1 \vdash B$ and $\Sigma :: B, \Gamma_2 \vdash E$ have $\Downarrow \mathcal{L}_0$-proofs. Using Proposition 5.23, both $\Sigma :: \Gamma_1, \Gamma_2 \vdash B$ and $\Sigma :: B, \Gamma_1, \Gamma_2 \vdash E$ have $\Downarrow \mathcal{L}_0$-proofs. Given the cut-elimination result (Theorem 5.28), we know that $\Sigma :: \Gamma_1, \Gamma_2 \vdash E$ has a $\Downarrow \mathcal{L}_0$-proof. Using the soundness of $\Downarrow \mathcal{L}_0$-proofs (Proposition 5.15), we conclude that $\Sigma :: \Gamma_1, \Gamma_2 \vdash E$ has an **I**-proof. □

The inference rule (where all formulas are $\mathcal{L}_0$-formulas)

$$\frac{\Sigma \Vdash t : \tau \qquad \Sigma, x : \tau :: \Gamma \vdash B}{\Sigma :: \Gamma[t/x] \vdash B[t/x]} \text{ instan}$$

is similar to the cut rule: The *instan* rule instantiates an eigenvariable while the *cut* rule instantiates a hypothesis. The following theorem shows that the *instan* rule is admissible for **I**-proofs. The proof of this theorem follows directly from Proposition 5.25.

> **Theorem 5.31** (Admissibility of *instan* for **I**-proofs restricted to $\mathcal{L}_0$ formulas)**.** *The instan rule for **I**-proofs (Figure 4.2) is admissible for cut-free **I**-proofs when restricted to $\mathcal{L}_0$-formulas.*

5.6 A Canonical Kripke Model

Most textbooks on symbolic logic introduce, alongside of proofs, a notion of *truth* formalized using *models*. Models are mathematical structures constructed using various sets and functions: We give an example of such a structure below. Generally, models are infinite objects (especially models for quantificational logics), and there are usually an infinite number of such models. In those settings where models and proofs are both present, the terms *soundness* and *completeness* are usually used as follows (in contrast to the way these terms are used in Section 4.1).

Soundness: If a formula is provable, it is true in every model.
Completeness: If a formula is true in every model, it is provable.

In this section, we briefly consider a particular kind of model that is known as a *Kripke model*. Presentations of such models are known to be sound and complete for intuitionistic logic. We show here, however, that in the setting of **I**-proofs involving only $\mathcal{L}_0$ formulas, it is possible to build one such model, a *canonical Kripke model*, so that the completeness theorem can be strengthened to be: If a formula is true in this one canonical Kripke model, then it has an **I**-proof.

A *world* is a pair $\langle \Sigma, \mathcal{P} \rangle$ where Σ is a (finite) signature and $\mathcal{P}$ is a (finite) set of $\mathcal{L}_0$ Σ-formulas. The order relation on worlds $\langle \Sigma, \mathcal{P} \rangle \preceq \langle \Sigma', \mathcal{P}' \rangle$ is defined to hold whenever $\Sigma \subseteq \Sigma'$ and $\mathcal{P} \subseteq \mathcal{P}'$. A *Kripke model* is a pair, $\langle \mathcal{W}, I \rangle$, where $\mathcal{W}$ is a (possibly infinite) set of worlds and I is a function, called an *interpretation*, that maps the worlds in $\mathcal{W}$ to sets of atomic formulas in such a way that $I(\langle \Sigma, \mathcal{P} \rangle)$ is a set of atomic Σ-formulas. The mapping I must also be order-preserving: That is, for all $w, w' \in \mathcal{W}$, if $w \preceq w'$ then $I(w) \subseteq I(w')$.

Let the pair $\langle \mathcal{W}, I \rangle$ be a Kripke model, let $\langle \Sigma, \mathcal{P} \rangle \in \mathcal{W}$, and let B be an $\mathcal{L}_0$ Σ-formula. The three-place *satisfaction* relation $I, \langle \Sigma, \mathcal{P} \rangle \Vdash B$ is defined by induction on the structure of B as follows.

1. $I, \langle \Sigma, \mathcal{P} \rangle \Vdash B$ if B is atomic and $B \in I(\langle \Sigma, \mathcal{P} \rangle)$.
2. $I, w \Vdash B \wedge B'$ if $I, w \Vdash B$ and $I, w \Vdash B'$.
3. $I, w \Vdash B \supset B'$ if for every $w' \in \mathcal{W}$ such that $w \preceq w'$ and $I, w' \Vdash B$ then $I, w' \Vdash B'$.
4. $I, \langle \Sigma, \mathcal{P} \rangle \Vdash \forall_\tau x.B$ if for every $\langle \Sigma', \mathcal{P}' \rangle \in \mathcal{W}$ such that $\langle \Sigma, \mathcal{P} \rangle \preceq \langle \Sigma', \mathcal{P}' \rangle$ and for every Σ'-term t of type τ, the relation $I, \langle \Sigma', \mathcal{P}' \rangle \Vdash B[t/x]$ holds.

Let $\langle \Sigma, \mathcal{P} \rangle$ be a world. The *canonical model* for $\langle \Sigma, \mathcal{P} \rangle$ is defined as the Kripke model with the set of worlds $\{\langle \Sigma', \mathcal{P}' \rangle \mid \langle \Sigma, \mathcal{P} \rangle \preceq \langle \Sigma', \mathcal{P}' \rangle\}$ and the interpretation I defined so that $I(\langle \Sigma', \mathcal{P}' \rangle)$ is the set of all atomic Σ'-formulas A such that $\Sigma' :: \mathcal{P}' \vdash A$ has a *cut-free* **I**-proof. Note that the canonical Kripke model is an infinite structure in the sense that it contains countably many worlds.

Note the difference in the treatment of provability and satisfaction for an implicational formula. In order to prove the formula $B_1 \supset B_2$ in the world $\langle \Sigma, \mathcal{P} \rangle$ (i.e., that the sequent $\Sigma :: \mathcal{P} \vdash B_1 \supset B_2$ is provable), we need to move to a single new world $\langle \Sigma, \mathcal{P} \cup \{B_1\} \rangle$ and try to prove B_2. In contrast, to show that $B_1 \supset B_2$ is true in the world $\langle \Sigma, \mathcal{P} \rangle$, we need to examine *all* extensions to that world and check that B_2 is true in that world if B_1 is true in that world.

As we mentioned in Section 3.7, sequent calculus inference rules provide logical connectives with *two senses* within a proof: There are different inference rules for introducing a given logical connective on the left and right of a sequent. On the other hand, in the model-theoretic setting, logical connectives are given meaning in only one sense: There is only one clause defining the satisfiability of a given logical connective. The following lemma shows how the cut-admissibility result allows us to relate these approaches to providing meaning to logical connectives.

Lemma 5.32. *The cut rule (Figure 5.2) and the instan rule (defined at the end of Section 5.5) are admissible for cut-free **I**-proofs if and only if the following holds: For every world $\langle \Sigma, \mathcal{P} \rangle$ and every Σ-formula B, it is the case that $\Sigma :: \mathcal{P} \vdash B$ has a cut-free **I**-proof if and only if $I, \langle \Sigma, \mathcal{P} \rangle \Vdash B$, where I is the canonical model for $\langle \Sigma, \mathcal{P} \rangle$.*

In other words, the admissibility of *cut* and *instan* is equivalent to the coincidence of truth in the canonical model with provability.

Proof: To prove the forward direction, assume that both the *cut* and *instan* rules are admissible for **I**-proofs. We now prove by induction on the structure of B that $\Sigma :: \mathcal{P} \vdash_I B$ if and only if $I, \langle \Sigma, \mathcal{P} \rangle \Vdash B$.

5.6 A Canonical Kripke Model   89

Case: B is atomic. The equivalence is immediate.

Case: B is $B_1 \wedge B_2$. This case is simple and immediate.

Case: B is $B_1 \supset B_2$. Assume first that $\Sigma :: \mathcal{P} \vdash_I B_1 \supset B_2$. Hence, $\Sigma :: \mathcal{P}, B_1 \vdash_I B_2$ (using the invertibility of $\supset$R.). To show $I, \langle \Sigma, \mathcal{P} \rangle \Vdash B_1 \supset B_2$, assume that $\langle \Sigma', \mathcal{P}' \rangle \in \mathcal{W}$ is such that $\langle \Sigma, \mathcal{P} \rangle \preceq \langle \Sigma', \mathcal{P}' \rangle$ and $I, \langle \Sigma', \mathcal{P}' \rangle \Vdash B_1$. By the inductive hypothesis, $\Sigma' :: \mathcal{P}' \vdash_I B_1$ and by cut admissibility, $\Sigma' :: \mathcal{P}' \vdash_I B_2$. By induction again, we have $I, \langle \Sigma', \mathcal{P}' \rangle \Vdash B_2$. Thus, $I, \langle \Sigma, \mathcal{P} \rangle \Vdash B_1 \supset B_2$. For the converse, assume $I, \langle \Sigma, \mathcal{P} \rangle \Vdash B_1 \supset B_2$. Since $\Sigma :: \mathcal{P}, B_1 \vdash_I B_1$, the inductive hypothesis yields $I, \langle \Sigma, \mathcal{P} \cup \{B_1\} \rangle \Vdash B_1$. By the definition of satisfaction of implication, we must have $I, \langle \Sigma, \mathcal{P} \cup \{B_1\} \rangle \Vdash B_2$. Using the inductive hypothesis again, $\Sigma :: \mathcal{P}, B_1 \vdash_I B_2$, and $\Sigma :: \mathcal{P} \vdash_I B_1 \supset B_2$.

Case: B is $\forall_\tau x.B_1$. Assume first that $\Sigma :: \mathcal{P} \vdash_I \forall_\tau x.B_1$ and, hence, $\Sigma, d : \tau :: \mathcal{P} \vdash_I B_1[d/x]$ for any variable d not in Σ. To show that $I, \langle \Sigma, \mathcal{P} \rangle \Vdash \forall_\tau x.B_1$, let $\langle \Sigma', \mathcal{P}' \rangle \in \mathcal{W}$ be such that $\langle \Sigma, \mathcal{P} \rangle \preceq \langle \Sigma', \mathcal{P}' \rangle$ and t be a Σ'-term of type τ. By the admissibility of the *instan* rule, we have $\Sigma' :: \mathcal{P}' \vdash_I B_1[t/x]$. By induction we have $I, \langle \Sigma', \mathcal{P}' \rangle \Vdash B_1[t/x]$. Thus, $I, \langle \Sigma, \mathcal{P} \rangle \Vdash \forall_\tau x B_1$. For the converse, assume $I, \langle \Sigma, \mathcal{P} \rangle \Vdash \forall_\tau x B_1$. Let d be a variable not a member of Σ. Since d is a $\Sigma \cup \{d\}$-term, $I, \langle \Sigma \cup \{d\}, \mathcal{P} \rangle \Vdash B_1[d/x]$ by the definition of satisfaction of universal quantification. But by the inductive hypothesis again, $\Sigma, d : \tau :: \mathcal{P} \vdash_I B_1[d/x]$ and $\Sigma :: \mathcal{P} \vdash_I \forall_\tau x B_1$.

We now show the converse by assuming the equivalence: For every world $\langle \Sigma, \mathcal{P} \rangle$ and every Σ-formula B,

$$\Sigma :: \mathcal{P} \vdash_I B \text{ if and only if } I, \langle \Sigma, \mathcal{P} \rangle \Vdash B,$$

where I is the canonical model for $\langle \Sigma, \mathcal{P} \rangle$. We now show that any sequent that can be proved using occurrences of the *cut* and *instan* rules can be proved without such rules. In particular, we claim that if $\langle \Sigma, \mathcal{P} \rangle \preceq \langle \Sigma', \mathcal{P}' \rangle$ then each of the following holds.

1. If $\Sigma' :: \mathcal{P}' \vdash_I B$ and $\Sigma :: \mathcal{P}, B \vdash_I C$ then $\Sigma' :: \mathcal{P}' \vdash_I C$.
2. If t is a Σ'-term of type τ and $\Sigma, x : \tau :: \mathcal{P} \vdash_I B$ then $\Sigma' :: \mathcal{P}' \vdash_I B[t/x]$ (of course, x does not occur in Σ).

To prove the first claim, assume that $\Sigma' :: \mathcal{P}' \vdash_I B$ and $\Sigma :: \mathcal{P}, B \vdash_I C$. Thus, $\Sigma :: \mathcal{P} \vdash_I B \supset C$. By the assumed equivalence, $I, \langle \Sigma', \mathcal{P}' \rangle \Vdash B$ and $I, \langle \Sigma, \mathcal{P} \rangle \Vdash B \supset C$. By the definition of satisfaction for implication, $I, \langle \Sigma', \mathcal{P}' \rangle \Vdash C$. By the assumed equivalence again, this yields $\Sigma' :: \mathcal{P}' \vdash_I C$.

To prove the second claim above, assume that t is a Σ'-term of type τ and that $\Sigma, x : \tau :: \mathcal{P} \vdash_I C$. Thus, $\Sigma :: \mathcal{P} \vdash_I \forall_\tau x.B$. By the assumed equivalence, $I, \langle \Sigma, \mathcal{P} \rangle \Vdash \forall_\tau x.B$. By the definition of satisfaction for universal quantification, we have $I, \langle \Sigma', \mathcal{P}' \rangle \Vdash B[t/x]$. By the assumed equivalence again, this yields $\Sigma' :: \mathcal{P}' \vdash_I B[t/x]$. □

Given Theorems 5.28 and 5.31, this lemma provides an immediate proof of the following theorem.

> **Theorem 5.33.** *Let $\langle \Sigma, \mathcal{P} \rangle$ be a world and let I be the canonical model for $\langle \Sigma, \mathcal{P} \rangle$. For all Σ-formulas B, $\Sigma :: \mathcal{P} \vdash_I B$ if and only if $I \Vdash B$. In particular, for every $B \in \mathcal{P}$, $I \Vdash B$.*

The following simple argument supports our use of the term *canonical model*. Although we have not given a general definition of Kripke models (i.e., a notion of model that is not built from formulas and terms), whatever definition is used, it needs to be sound: If $\vdash_I B$, then B is true in every generalized Kripke model. Thus, if the $\mathcal{L}_0$ Σ-formula B is true in the canonical model for $\langle \Sigma, \emptyset \rangle$ then $\Sigma :: \cdot \vdash_I B$ and, hence, B is true in every generalized Kripke model.

5.7 Synthetic Inference Rules

The left-introduction phase in $\Downarrow \mathcal{L}_0$ can be described as a single inference rule via the following generalized notion of *backchaining*. Let Σ be a signature and let Γ be a finite set of Σ-formulas. Define $|\Gamma|_\Sigma$ to be the smallest set of pairs $\langle \Delta, D \rangle$, where Δ is a multiset of formulas and D is a formula, such that

1. if $D \in \Gamma$ then $\langle \emptyset, D \rangle \in |\Gamma|_\Sigma$,
2. if $\langle \Delta, D_1 \wedge D_2 \rangle \in |\Gamma|_\Sigma$ then $\langle \Delta, D_1 \rangle \in |\Gamma|_\Sigma$ and $\langle \Delta, D_2 \rangle \in |\Gamma|_\Sigma$,
3. if $\langle \Delta, G \supset D \rangle \in |\Gamma|_\Sigma$ then $\langle \Delta \cup \{G\}, D \rangle \in |\Gamma|_\Sigma$, and
4. if $\langle \Delta, \forall_\tau x\, D \rangle \in |\Gamma|_\Sigma$ and t is a Σ-term of type τ then $\langle \Delta, D[t/x] \rangle \in |\Gamma|_\Sigma$.

The backchaining inference rule is now defined as

$$\frac{\{\Sigma :: \Gamma \vdash G \mid G \in \Delta\}}{\Sigma :: \Gamma \vdash A} \text{BC}, \quad \text{provided } A \text{ is atomic and } \langle \Delta, A \rangle \in |\Gamma|_\Sigma.$$

If Δ is empty, then this rule has no premises. Let the $\Downarrow \mathcal{L}_0'$-proof system contain the right-introduction rules in Figure 4.1 and the BC rule. Straightforward inductive arguments prove the following two lemmas and proposition.

5.7 Synthetic Inference Rules

> **Lemma 5.34.** *If P is a path in D (i.e., D ↑ P holds), and θ is a substitution, then $P\theta$ is a path in $D\theta$.*

> **Lemma 5.35.** *Let Σ be an eigenvariable signature, let Δ be a multiset of Σ-formulas, and let A and D be a Σ-formulas, where A is atomic. Then $\langle \Delta, A \rangle \in |\{D\}|_\Sigma$ if and only if there is a path in D with bound variables $\bar{x}$, arguments $G_1, \ldots, G_n$ ($n \geq 0$), and target A' and there is a substitution θ mapping the variables $\bar{x}$ to Σ-terms such that Δ and $\{G_1\theta, \ldots, G_n\theta\}$ are equal and A and $A'\theta$ are equal.*

> **Proposition 5.36.** *Let Σ be a signature, let $\mathcal{P}$ be a multiset of $\mathcal{L}_0$ Σ-formulas and G be a Σ-formula. The sequent $\Sigma :: \mathcal{P} \vdash G$ has a $\Downarrow \mathcal{L}'_0$-proof if and only if it has an **I**-proof.*

The two-phase $\Downarrow \mathcal{L}_0$-proof system can justify replacing program clauses with inference rules. For example, let $\mathcal{P}$ be the multiset containing the clauses $\forall x. \forall y.\ [\mathrm{adj}\ x\ y \supset \mathrm{path}\ x\ y]$ and $\forall x. \forall y. \forall z.[\mathrm{adj}\ x\ y \wedge \mathrm{path}\ y\ z \supset \mathrm{path}\ x\ z]$. Here, we assume the two predicates adj and path have type $i \to i \to o$. Using the *decide* rule on the second of these formulas leads to an attempt to prove the sequent $\Sigma :: \Gamma, \mathcal{P} \vdash \mathrm{path}\ s\ t$ with the following derivation.

$$\cfrac{\cfrac{\cfrac{\cfrac{\Gamma, \mathcal{P} \vdash \mathrm{adj}\ s\ u \quad \Gamma, \mathcal{P} \vdash \mathrm{path}\ u\ t}{\Gamma, \mathcal{P} \vdash \mathrm{adj}\ s\ u \wedge \mathrm{path}\ u\ t} \wedge L \quad \cfrac{\overline{\Gamma, \mathcal{P} \Downarrow \mathrm{path}\ s\ t \vdash \mathrm{path}\ s\ t}\ init}{}}{\Gamma, \mathcal{P} \Downarrow (\mathrm{adj}\ s\ u \wedge \mathrm{path}\ u\ t \supset \mathrm{path}\ s\ t) \vdash \mathrm{path}\ s\ t} \supset L}{\Gamma, \mathcal{P} \Downarrow \forall x. \forall y. \forall z.(\mathrm{adj}\ x\ y \wedge \mathrm{path}\ y\ z \supset \mathrm{path}\ x\ z) \vdash \mathrm{path}\ s\ t} \forall L \times 3}{\Gamma, \mathcal{P} \vdash \mathrm{path}\ s\ t}\ decide$$

(We suppressed the signatures associated with sequents for readability). If we ignore the seven inference rules within this derivation, we have the inference rule

$$\cfrac{\Sigma :: \Gamma, \mathcal{P} \vdash \mathrm{adj}\ s\ u \quad \Sigma :: \Gamma, \mathcal{P} \vdash \mathrm{path}\ u\ t}{\Sigma :: \Gamma, \mathcal{P} \vdash \mathrm{path}\ s\ t}.$$

Similarly, deciding to use the first of these two formulas results in the inference rule

$$\frac{\Sigma :: \Gamma, \mathcal{P} \vdash \mathsf{adj}\, s\, t}{\Sigma :: \Gamma, \mathcal{P} \vdash \mathsf{path}\, s\, t}.$$

These two derived inference rules are rather appealing since they do not mention any logical constants. Instead, they describe how an attempt to prove one atomic formula can lead to an attempt to prove one or two additional atomic formulas. Given this observation, we can *remove* these two Horn clauses from the logic program (assumptions on the left-hand side) and *insert* in the **I**-proof system the *synthetic inference rules*

$$\frac{\Sigma :: \Gamma \vdash \mathsf{adj}\, s\, t}{\Sigma :: \Gamma \vdash \mathsf{path}\, s\, t} \quad \text{and} \quad \frac{\Sigma :: \Gamma \vdash \mathsf{adj}\, s\, u \quad \Sigma :: \Gamma \vdash \mathsf{path}\, u\, t}{\Sigma :: \Gamma \vdash \mathsf{path}\, s\, t}.$$

If we are using only Horn clauses, then it is possible to replace all program clauses in the left-hand context with synthetic inference rules that mention only atomic formulas.

More formally, we say that a sequent of the form $\Sigma :: \Gamma \vdash A$, where A is an atomic formula, is a *border sequent* since such sequents appear at the border between a right-introduction phase (on the bottom) and a left-introduction phase (on the top). A synthetic inference rule is the inference rule that results from moving from a border sequent upwards through a *decide* rule and then through the resulting left-introduction phase, and then, if any sequents remain, through the right-introduction phases. Any open sequents remaining after both phases are complete will be border sequents, and these will be the premises of the associate synthetic inference rule. In other words, a synthetic inference rule combines backchaining and goal reduction into one rule.

Although focusing on Horn clauses yields synthetic inference rules that only mention atoms, focusing on formulas of higher clause order leads to synthetic rules that contain logical connectives. For example, focusing on the propositional formula $((p \supset q) \supset r) \supset s$ would justify the synthetic inference rule

$$\frac{\Gamma, p \supset q \vdash r}{\Gamma \vdash s}.$$

Exercise 5.37. *Show that the synthetic inference rules that result from deciding on an $\mathcal{L}_0$-formula of clausal order at most 2 involve only atomic formulas in its conclusion and premises.*

5.8 Disjunctive and Existential Goals

Now that we have addressed the soundness and completeness of $\Downarrow \mathcal{L}_0$-proofs for $\mathcal{L}_0$-formulas, we return to considering allowing disjunctions and existential quantifiers into formulas in the restricted setting of definition (5.5) of *fohh*. With this definition, **I**-proofs can have disjunctions and existential introduction rules on the right but not the left of its sequents. It turns out that we can capture the right-hand side proof-search behavior of these logical constants using *non-logical constants* as follows. Let $\hat{\vee}$ be a non-logical constant of type $o \to o \to o$ and $\hat{\exists}_\tau$ be a non-logical constant of type $(\tau \to o) \to o$ for every type τ. Consider the (infinite) set $\mathcal{C}$ of formulas that contains the two clauses

$$\forall_o P \, \forall_o Q \, [P \supset (P \,\hat{\vee}\, Q)] \qquad \forall_o P \, \forall_o Q \, [Q \supset (P \,\hat{\vee}\, Q)]$$

and, for every type τ, the clause

$$\forall_{\tau \to o} B \, \forall_\tau t \, [(B \, t) \supset (\hat{\exists}_\tau B)].$$

The members of $\mathcal{C}$ are Horn clauses, but they are not first-order Horn clauses since they contain quantifiers that are not of first-order type (since that type contains the type o). Such clauses are studied in more detail in Chapter 9 where we present *higher-order Horn clauses*. The clauses above correspond to the following synthetic inference rules.

$$\frac{\Sigma :: \mathcal{P}, \mathcal{C} \vdash P}{\Sigma :: \mathcal{P}, \mathcal{C} \vdash P \,\hat{\vee}\, Q} \qquad \frac{\Sigma :: \mathcal{P}, \mathcal{C} \vdash Q}{\Sigma :: \mathcal{P}, \mathcal{C} \vdash P \,\hat{\vee}\, Q} \qquad \frac{\Sigma :: \mathcal{P}, \mathcal{C} \vdash B \, t}{\Sigma :: \mathcal{P}, \mathcal{C} \vdash \hat{\exists}_\tau B}.$$

Note that these rules exactly correspond to the $\vee$R and $\exists$R rules. Given this observation, we can now prove the following completeness theorem.

> **Proposition 5.38** (Completeness of $\Downarrow$ fohh-proofs for *fohh*). *Let Γ be a fohh logic program and G a fohh goal. If the sequent $\Sigma :: \Gamma \vdash G$ has an **I**-proof then it has a $\Downarrow$ fohh-proof.*

Proof: Assume that $\Sigma :: \Gamma \vdash G$ has an **I**-proof Ξ. Let $\mathcal{C}(\Xi)$ be the smallest set of clauses such that the following holds. (When we write $\forall \Sigma'$, we mean a string of universal quantifiers, one for each variable in Σ'.)

1. If Ξ contains the inference rule

$$\frac{\Sigma, \Sigma' :: \Gamma' \vdash B_i}{\Sigma, \Sigma' :: \Gamma' \vdash B_1 \vee B_2} \,\vee\text{R}$$

then $\mathcal{C}(\Xi)$ contains the clause $\forall \Sigma' [B_i \supset (B_1 \,\hat{\vee}\, B_2)]$.

2. If Ξ contains the inference rule

$$\frac{\Sigma, \Sigma' \Vdash t : \tau \qquad \Sigma, \Sigma' :: \Gamma' \vdash B[t/x]}{\Sigma, \Sigma' :: \Gamma' \vdash \exists_\tau x.B} \; \exists R$$

then $\mathcal{C}(\Xi)$ contains the clause $\forall \Sigma'[B[t/x] \supset (\hat{\exists}_\tau x.B)]$.

The set $\mathcal{C}(\Xi)$ is a set of essentially first-order Horn clauses: the only reason that they are not exactly members of *fohc* is that they can contain atomic formulas that might contain logical connectives (such atomic formulas have top-level symbols $\hat{\vee}$ and $\hat{\exists}$). Otherwise, only first-order quantification is used within these clauses. We shall assume here that this mild extension to *fohc* does not affect the proof theory results that we have already established for them. Chapter 9 will formally justify this assumption.

Let $\hat{\Gamma}$ and $\hat{G}$ be the result of replacing all occurrences of $\vee$ with $\hat{\vee}$ and of $\exists_\tau$ with $\hat{\exists}_\tau$. It is now straightforward to convert the **I**-proof Ξ of $\Sigma :: \Gamma \vdash G$ into an **I**-proof of $\Sigma :: \mathcal{C}(\Xi), \hat{\Gamma} \vdash \hat{G}$. This conversion takes the rule

$$\frac{\Sigma, \Sigma' :: \Gamma' \vdash B_i}{\Sigma, \Sigma' :: \Gamma' \vdash B_1 \vee B_2} \; \vee R$$

and rewrites it into

$$\frac{\frac{\frac{\Sigma, \Sigma' :: \mathcal{C}(\Xi), \hat{\Gamma} \vdash \hat{B}_i \qquad \overline{\Sigma, \Sigma' :: \hat{B}_1 \hat{\vee} \hat{B}_2 \vdash \hat{B}_1 \hat{\vee} \hat{B}_2} \; \text{init}}{\Sigma, \Sigma' :: \mathcal{C}(\Xi), \hat{\Gamma}, \hat{B}_i \supset \hat{B}_1 \hat{\vee} \hat{B}_2 \vdash \hat{B}_1 \hat{\vee} \hat{B}_2} \; \supset L}{\Sigma, \Sigma' :: \mathcal{C}(\Xi), \forall \Sigma'[B_i \supset (B_1 \hat{\vee} B_2)], \hat{\Gamma}' \vdash \hat{B}_1 \hat{\vee} \hat{B}_2} \; \forall L}{\Sigma, \Sigma' :: \mathcal{C}(\Xi), \hat{\Gamma}' \vdash \hat{B}_1 \hat{\vee} \hat{B}_2} \; cL \; .$$

A similar conversion must also be done with the $\exists R$ inference rule. Thus, the original proof can be converted into an **I**-proof involving only $\mathcal{L}_0$-formulas. By Theorem 5.29, we know that the sequent $\Sigma :: \mathcal{C}(\Xi), \hat{\Gamma} \vdash \hat{G}$ also has a $\Downarrow \mathcal{L}_0$-proof. Given that $\vee$ and $\exists$ cannot be top-level connectives of *fohh* program clauses, the left-hand context $\hat{\Gamma}$ will never get additional assumptions with target atoms containing $\hat{\vee}$ or $\hat{\exists}$ as their predicate symbol. This $\Downarrow \mathcal{L}_0$-proof can then be converted directly into a $\Downarrow \mathcal{L}_0$-proof of $\Sigma :: \Gamma \vdash B_1 \vee B_2$ by noting that the only times a *decide* rule is used with a formula from $\mathcal{C}(\Xi)$ occurs when we emulate either an $\vee R$ or $\exists R$ rule. The conversion of the proof is completed by replacing such *decide* rules and the phase above them with the right-introduction rule they are emulating. $\square$

5.9 Examples of *fohc* Logic Programs

Figure 5.3 presents some examples of Horn clauses and two kinds of declarations. The syntax there follows the λProlog conventions. The `kind` declaration is used to declare members of the set of sorts S. In particular, the `kind` declaration in Figure 5.3 declares that the token `nat` is to be used as a primitive type. The expressions

```
type tok    <type expression>.
```

declares that the non-logical signature should contain the declaration of `tok` at the associated type expression. Logic program clauses are the remaining entries. In those entries, the infix symbol `:-` denotes the converse of $\supset$, a semicolon denotes a disjunction, a comma (which binds tighter than `:-` and the semicolon) denotes a conjunction of G-formulas, and `&` denotes a conjunction of D-formulas. (In our current setting, both the comma and `&` denote the same logical connective $\wedge$. When we move to linear logic, these tokens will be mapped to different linear logic conjunctions: see Section 6.5.) Tokens with initial capital letters are universally quantified with scope around individual clauses (which are terminated by a period).

In Figure 5.3, after the symbol `nat` is declared a primitive type, both `z` and `s` are declared as constructors for natural numbers denoting zero and successor. The symbol `sum` is declared to be a relation of three natural numbers, while the two symbols `leq` and `greater` are declared to be binary relations on natural numbers. The remaining lines in that figure provide the logic programming specification of these three predicates. For example, if the `sum` predicate holds for the triple M, N, and P then $N + M = P$: This relation is described recursively using the fact that $0 + N = N$ and if $N + M = P$ then

```
kind nat              type.
type z                nat.
type s                nat -> nat.
type sum              nat -> nat -> nat -> o.
type leq, greater     nat -> nat -> o.

sum z N N.
sum (s N) M (s P)  :- sum N M P.
leq z N.
leq (s N) (s M)    :- leq N M.
greater N M        :- leq (s M) N.
```

The type o denotes o, the type of formulas (see Section 2.4).

Figure 5.3 The *fohc* specification of three relations on natural numbers.

```
kind list                  type -> type.
type nil                   list A.
type ::                    A -> list A -> list A.
infixr ::                  5.
type sumup, max            list nat -> nat -> o.
type maxx                  list nat -> nat -> nat -> o.

sumup nil z.
sumup (N::L) S    :- sumup L T, sum N T S.

max L M           :- maxx L z M.
maxx nil A A.
maxx (X::L) A M   :- leq X A,     maxx L A M.
maxx (X::L) A M   :- greater X A, maxx L X M.
```

Figure 5.4 Some relations between natural numbers and lists.

```
kind node                 type.
type a, b, c, d, e, f     node.
type adj, path            node -> node -> o.

adj a b & adj b c & adj c d & adj a c & adj e f.
path X X.
path X Z :- adj X Y, path Y Z.
```

Figure 5.5 Encoding a directed graph.

$(N + 1) + M = (P + 1)$. Similarly, relations describing $N \leq M$ and $N > M$ are also specified. Figure 5.4 introduces the type for lists and two constructors for lists: the empty list constructor `nil` and the nonempty list constructor, the infix symbol `::`. Here we are using the λProlog notation for polymorphic typing of lists, even though the formal theory of terms and types used in this book are simple types without type variables. The keyword `infixr` is used to declare that a given token should be used as an infix operator that associates to the right (with a certain priority).

Also, in Figure 5.4, the binary predicate `sumup` relates a list of natural numbers with the sum of those numbers. The binary predicate `max` relates a non-empty list of numbers with the largest number in that list and the empty list with the number 0. The predicate `maxx` is an auxiliary predicate used to help compute the `max` relation.

Exercise 5.39. *Informally describe the predicates specified by the clauses in Figures 5.5 and 5.6.*

5.10 DYNAMICS OF PROOF SEARCH FOR *fohc*

```
type memb      A         -> list A -> o.
type append    list A    -> list A -> list nat -> o.
type sort      list nat  -> list nat -> o.
type split     nat -> list nat ->
                         list nat -> list nat -> o.
memb X (X::L).
memb X (Y::L) :- memb X L.

append nil L L.
append (X::L) K (X::M) :- append L K M.

split X nil nil nil.
split X (A::L) (A::S) B :- leq A X,      split X L S B.
split X (A::L) S (A::B) :- greater A X,  split X L S B.
sort nil nil.
sort (X::L) S :- split X L Sm Bg, sort Sm SmS,
                 sort Bg BgS, append SmS (X::BgS) S.
```

Figure 5.6 More examples of Horn clause programs.

Exercise 5.40. *Take a standard definition of a Turing machine and show how to define an interpreter for a Turing machine in fohc. The specification should encode the fact that a given machine accepts a given word if and only if some atomic formula is provable.*

5.10 Dynamics of Proof Search for *fohc*

Let $\mathcal{P}$ be a *fohc* program and G a *fohc* goal such that $\Sigma :: \mathcal{P} \vdash G$ has an **I**-proof. By the completeness of $\Downarrow$ *fohh*-proofs (Theorem 5.38), this sequent must have a $\Downarrow$ *fohh*-proof, say, Ξ. Since there are no occurrences of $\supset$R or $\forall$R in Ξ, every sequent occurring in Ξ has Σ as its signature and $\mathcal{P}$ as its left-hand side. Thus, if a program clause is ever needed (via the decide rule) during the search for a proof, it must be present at the beginning of that computation, along with all other clauses that might be needed during the computation. Thus, the logic of *fohc* does not directly support hierarchical programming in which certain program clauses are meant to be local within a particular scope. Similarly, data structures are first-order terms built from a non-logical signature. Since signatures do not change during the search for proofs using first-order Horn clauses, all the constructors for data structures that need to be built during proof search must be available globally. In other words, *fohc* does not directly support hiding the internal details of data structures, an abstraction mechanism available in many programming languages via *abstract data types*.

If we only look at border sequents in $\Downarrow \mathcal{L}_0$-proofs in *fohc*, the only parts of sequents that change when moving from border to border are the atomic right-hand sides. Given that we allow first-order terms (which can encode structures such as natural numbers, lists, trees, and Turing machine tapes), it is easy to see that proof search in *fohc* has sufficient dynamics to encode general computation. Unfortunately, *all* of that dynamics occurs within *non-logical* contexts, namely, within atomic formulas. As a result, logical techniques for analyzing computation via proof theory have limited impact on what can be said directly about non-logical contexts. Thus, reasoning about specific Horn clause programs will benefit little from proof-theoretic analysis; most reasoning about Horn clause programs will be based on induction. Chapter 11 provides an exception in which a static analysis of Horn clauses relies entirely on structural proof theory instead of reducing Horn clause provability to inductive reasoning.

5.11 Examples of *fohh* Logic Programs

McCarthy [1989] presented the challenge of formally defining a sterile jar as one containing only dead bacteria. Consider proving that if a jar j is heated, then that jar is sterile (given that heating a jar kills all bacteria in that jar). The *fohh* specification of this problem is given in Figure 5.7. The expression pi x\ denotes the universal quantification of the variable x with a scope that extends as far to the right as consistent with parentheses or the end of the expression. The first of the clauses above can be written as

$$\forall x.(\forall y.(\text{in } y\ x \supset \text{dead } y) \supset \text{sterile } x).$$

```
kind jar, bacterium     type.
type j                  jar.
type sterile, heated    jar -> o.
type dead               bacterium -> o.
type in                 bacterium -> jar -> o.

sterile X :- pi y\ in y X => dead y.
dead X    :- heated Y, in X Y.
heated j.
```

Figure 5.7 Heating a jar makes it sterile.

5.11 Examples of *fohh* Logic Programs

The synthetic inference rule associated with this clause is

$$\frac{y : \mathtt{bacterium}, \Sigma :: \mathcal{P}, \mathtt{in}\ y\ x \vdash \mathtt{dead}\ y}{\Sigma :: \mathcal{P} \vdash \mathtt{sterile}\ x}.$$

Note that no constructors for type `bacterium` are provided in Figure 5.7, and no explicit assumptions about the binary predicate `in` are given.

> **Exercise 5.41.** *Construct the* $\Downarrow \mathcal{L}_0$*-proof of the goal formula* `sterile j` *from the logic program in Figure 5.7.*

Another way to prove that a jar is sterile would be to use a microscope and search out every bacterium in the jar and confirm that they are dead. Unfortunately, this style of proof is not available in *fohh* (see Exercise 5.45), although such proof strategies are possible in the stronger setting of model checking: See Heath and Miller [2019] for a proof-theoretic treatment of some aspects of model checking.

A specification for the binary predicate that relates a list with the reverse of that list can be given in *fohc* using the following program clauses.

```
reverse L K :- rev L nil K.
rev nil L L.
rev (X::M) N L :- rev M (X::N) L.
```

Here, `reverse` is a binary relation on lists, and the auxiliary predicate `rev` is a ternary relation on lists. By moving to *fohh*, it is possible to write the following specification instead.

```
reverse L K :- rv nil K => rv L nil.
rv (X::M) N :- rv M (X::N).
```

Here, the auxiliary predicate `rv` is also a binary predicate on lists. With this second specification, the use of non-logical contexts is slightly reduced in the sense that the atomic formula (`rev M K L`) in the first specification is encoded using the logical formula (`rv nil L => rv M K`) in the second specification. Note that the definition of reverse above has clausal order 2. It is possible to specify reverse with a single clause of order 3 as follows.

```
reverse L K :-
   (pi X\ pi M\ pi N\ rv (X::M) N :- rv M (X::N)) =>
     rv nil K => rv L nil.
```

Here, both the base case for `rv` and the recursive case are assumed in the body of `reverse`. Given this encoding of reverse, no other program clauses can access either of these two clauses for rv: They are only available during a proof of reverse.

> **Exercise 5.42.** *Reversing a pile of papers can informally be described as: Start by allocating an additional empty pile and then systematically moving the original pile's top member to the top of the newly allocated pile. When the original pile is empty, the other pile contains the reverse. Using the last specification of* reverse *above, show where this informal computation takes place in the construction of a proof of the reverse relation.*

Note that *fohh* allows for a simple notion of modular logic programming. For example, let classify, scanner, and misc name (possibly large) conjunctions of program clauses that have some specific role within a larger programming task: For example, scanner might contain code to convert a list of characters into a list of tokens before parsing. Consider the following goal formula.

$$\text{misc} \supset ((\text{classify} \supset G_1) \wedge (\text{scanner} \supset G_2) \wedge G_3).$$

Attempting a proof of this goal will cause attempts of the three goals G_1, G_2, and G_3 with respect to different programs: misc and classify are used to prove G_1; misc and scanner are used to prove G_2; and misc is used to prove G_3. Thus, implicational goals can be used to structure the runtime environment of a program. For example, the code in classify is unavailable during the proof attempt of G_2.

What it means to accumulate clauses from two different sources is worth noting. For example, assume that the predicate aux is described by two sets of clauses in misc and scanner, respectively. The description of aux in the accumulation of misc and scanner is given by mixing the clauses in these two separate sources. The resulting description of aux might not have a simple relationship to its descriptions in misc and scanner separately.

Classical logic does not support this discipline for the scoping of clauses. For example, the three-goal formulas

$$D \supset (G_1 \vee G_2), \quad (D \supset G_1) \vee G_2, \quad \text{and} \quad G_1 \vee (D \supset G_2)$$

all provide different scopes for the clause D. However, in classical logic, the scoping of D is the same for all of these goals: Given that $B \supset C \equiv \neg B \vee C$ is classically provable, all three of these formulas are classically equivalent to $\neg D \vee G_1 \vee G_2$. In other words, classical logic allows for *scope extrusion*: That is, while the scope of D in $(D \supset G_1) \vee G_2$ appears to be limited to G_1, that scope actually extrudes over the disjunction $G_1 \vee G_2$. Thus, classical logic does not support the notion of scope that one usually wants from a module system.

5.12 Dynamics of Proof Search for *fohh*

Proof search using *fohh* programs and goals is a bit more dynamic than for *fohc*. In particular, both logic programs and signatures can grow. In this setting, every sequent in a $\Downarrow \mathcal{L}_0$-proof of the sequent $\Sigma :: \mathcal{P} \vdash G$ is either of the form

$$\Sigma, \Sigma' :: \mathcal{P}, \mathcal{P}' \vdash G' \quad \text{or} \quad \Sigma, \Sigma' :: \mathcal{P}, \mathcal{P}' \Downarrow D \vdash A.$$

Thus, the signature can grow by the addition of Σ' and the logic program can grow by the addition of $\mathcal{P}'$ (a *fohh* program over $\Sigma \cup \Sigma'$). More generally, it is the case that if the clausal order of $\mathcal{P}$ is $n \geq 1$ and the clausal order of G is at most $n - 1$, then the clausal order of $\mathcal{P}'$ is at most $n - 2$.

Since the terms used to instantiate quantifiers in the concluding sequent of the $\exists R$ and $\forall L$ inference rules range over the signature of that sequent, more terms are available for instantiation as proof search progresses. These additional terms include the eigenvariables of the proof that are introduced by $\forall R$ inference rules. Note that once an eigenvariable is introduced, it is not instantiated by the proof search process. As a result, eigenvariables do not actually vary and, hence, act as locally scoped constants.

5.13 Limitations to *fohc* and *fohh* Logic Programs

Both *fohc* and *fohh* have certain limitations in how they can be used to represent computations. In the analysis of finite state machines and regular languages, the *pumping lemmas* help to circumscribe their expressive power. This section contains several exercises that similarly illustrate limits to the expressive power of *fohc* and *fohh* logic programs.

An immediate consequence of Proposition 5.23 is the following *monotonicity property* of intuitionistic provability: If $\Sigma :: \Gamma \vdash_I G$ and if Γ' is a set of Σ-formulas containing Γ, then $\Sigma :: \Gamma' \vdash_I G$. This proposition can be applied to solve Exercises 5.43 and 5.44.

Exercise 5.43. (‡) *Consider the collection of declarations that accumulates the primitive types and non-logical constants in Figure 5.3 along with declarations for* a *and* maxa, *which make them into predicates of one argument with sort* nat. *Assume that a nonempty set of natural numbers* $N = \{n_1, \ldots, n_k\}$ *is encoded by the multiset of atomic formulas* $\mathcal{A}(N) = \{$a $n_1, \ldots,$ a $n_k\}$. *Show that there is no fohh logic program* $\mathcal{P}$ *such that* $\mathcal{A}(N), \mathcal{P} \vdash$ maxa m *has an **I**-proof if and only if m is the maximum of the set N.*

As was illustrated in Figure 5.4, the maximum of a set of numbers can be computed in *fohc* if that set of numbers is stored as a list within the non-logical context of an atomic formula and not in the logical context as required by Exercise 5.43.

Exercise 5.44. (‡) *Given the encoding of directed graphs as is illustrated in Figure 5.5, show that it is not possible to specify in fohh a predicate that is true of two nodes if and only if there is no path between them. Similarly, show that there is no specification in fohh of a predicate that holds of a node if and only if that node is not adjacent to another node.*

As this exercise illustrates, while it is possible to capture *reachability* within a graph, it is not, in general, possible to capture *non-reachability*, at least when the adjacency graph is encoded as a set of atomic formulas as is the case in Figure 5.5.

Exercise 5.45. *Consider extending the typing information in Figure 5.7 with a finite set of tokens* $\mathcal{B}$ *that denote bacteria (i.e., they are given type* bacterium*), and let* $\mathcal{C}$ *be a subset of* $\mathcal{B}$ *denoting the set of dead bacteria. Let* $\mathcal{H}$ *be the set of atomic formulas that contains* (in b j) *for every* $b \in \mathcal{B}$ *and* (dead b) *for every* $b \in \mathcal{C}$. *Show that there is no specification, say,* $\mathcal{P}$ *in fohh of a predicate, say, p of type* jar -> o *such that* $\mathcal{H} \vdash$ (p j) *hold exactly when* $\mathcal{B}$ *and* $\mathcal{C}$ *are equal sets (i.e., when the jar j is sterile). Of course, the specification* $\mathcal{P}$ *should be general in the sense that it does not contain tokens for any of the specific bacteria mentioned in* $\mathcal{B}$.

The following example illustrates a second class of weaknesses of *fohh* specifications. Consider the problem of specifying the removal of an element

5.13 LIMITATIONS TO *fohc* AND *fohh* LOGIC PROGRAMS

from a list. In particular, assume that we have the following signature Σ, written concretely as follows.

```
kind i              type.
type a, b, c        i.
type remove         i -> list i -> list i -> o.
```

Here, the type i contains three elements. It is easy to show that it is impossible to find a specification, say $\mathcal{P}$, in *fohh* for the predicate remove such that

1. (remove *x l k*) is provable from Σ and $\mathcal{P}$ if and only if the list *k* is the result of removing *all* occurrences of *x* from *l*, and
2. the specification $\mathcal{P}$ does not contain occurrences of a, b, or c.

The last of these restrictions essentially says that remove should work no matter what terms of the type i exist. The proof of impossibility is immediate. If such a specification $\mathcal{P}$ existed, then $\mathcal{P}$ must necessarily prove (remove a [a,b,a] [b]). Since a and b are not free in $\mathcal{P}$, then the universal quantification of such a goal is also provable: That is, $\mathcal{P}$ must also prove

```
pi a\ pi b\ remove a (a::b::a::nil) (b::nil)).
```

But since that goal is provable, any instance of these quantifiers is also provable. Thus, (remove a [a,a,a] [a]) is provable, which should not be the case.

This weakness results from the inability to specify the inequality of terms within the logic without explicitly referring to the constructor of terms. Suppose we allow the specification of remove to use the specific information about the structure of type i. In that case, it is possible to write the following specification of remove, which first specifies inequality on the type i.

```
type notequal     i -> i -> o.

notequal a b & notequal b a.
notequal a c & notequal c a.
notequal b c & notequal c b.

remove X nil nil.
remove X (X::L) K        :- remove X L K.
remove X (Y::L) (Y::K)   :- notequal X Y, remove L K.
```

Consider the type declarations in Figure 5.8: Here *i* and *j* are primitive types. Note that terms of type *i* exist in contexts where constants or variables of type *j* are declared. Figure 5.8 contains a specification of predicate subSome such that the goal (subSome *x s t r*) is provable if and only if *r* is the result

```
type c              j -> i.
type f              i -> i.
type g              i -> i -> i.
type subSome        j -> i -> i -> i -> o.

subSome X T (c X)    T.
subSome X T (c Y)    (c Y).
subSome X T (f U)    (f W)    :- subSome X T U W.
subSome X T (g U V)  (g W Y)  :- subSome X T U W,
                                 subSome X T V Y.
```

Figure 5.8 Substitution of some occurrences.

of substituting *some* occurrences of x (actually, of $(c\ x)$) in t with s. Exercises 5.46 and 5.47 are concerned with the specification of predicates related to subSome.

Exercise 5.46. (‡) *Prove that it is not possible in fohh to write a specification of* subAll *such that* (subAll x s t r) *is provable if and only if r is the result of substituting* all *occurrences of x in t with s. Note that this specification would need to work in any extension of the non-logical signature (in particular, for extensions that contain constants of type j that do not occur in the specification of* subAll*).*

Exercise 5.47. *Write a fohh specification of* subOne *such that the goal* (subOne x s t r) *is provable if and only if r is the result of substituting exactly one occurrence of x in t with s. One might think that* subAll *can be specified using repeated calls to* subOne*. Given the previous exercise, this is not possible. Explain why.*

5.14 Bibliographic Notes

The early literature on logic programming did not use sequent calculus to encode proofs using Horn clauses: In fact, that literature used *refutations* instead of proof. For example, the papers by Emden and Kowalski [1976] and by Apt and Emden [1982] described logic programming using a restricted form of *resolution refutation* called *SLD resolution*. The textbooks by Gallier

[1986] and Lloyd [1987] provide more details about this approach to logic programming in classical logic.

A central design choice in our description of logic programming is the use of *goal-directed proof search* and the identification of the right-hand side of sequents with the goal and the left-hand side of sequents with the logic program. This design choice dates back to Miller and Nadathur [1986] and Miller [1986]. A more general treatment of goal-directed proof search is given in the book by Gabbay and Olivetti [2000]. The book by Miller and Nadathur [2012] focuses on λProlog and presents several examples of logic programs using first-order (and higher-order) hereditary Harrop formulas. The λProlog programming language has had a number of implementations. The two most recent implementations that allow directly executing the examples in this chapter are Teyjus [Nadathur and Mitchell, 1999] and Elpi [Dunchev et al., 2015; Tassi, 2025].

The focused proof system $\Downarrow \mathcal{L}_0$ takes the symbol $\Downarrow$ and the term "focus" from Andreoli [1992]. The first proofs of cut elimination for a focused proof system were done within linear logic: See Section 6.10 for some references.

The focused proof system *LJF* of Liang and Miller [2009] extends the $\Downarrow \mathcal{L}_0$ proof system by directly treating disjunctions and existential quantifiers and allowing atomic formulas to be polarized. In particular, if atomic formulas have negative polarity, then the backchaining-style proofs presented in Section 5.4 appear. On the other hand, if atomic formulas have positive polarity, then the forward-chaining-style proofs mentioned in Exercise 5.16 appear.

Harrop formulas were defined and shown to have the disjunction and existence properties in Harrop [1960].

Kripke first introduced his eponymous models for intuitionistic logic in Kripke [1965], some years after he proposed such models for various modal logics in Kripke [1959]. The canonical Kripke model described in Section 5.6 is a simplified version of a model construction given in Miller [1992]. The Kripke lambda models built by Mitchell and Moggi [1991] are similar but more abstract and general than the model presented here.

The notion that *synthetic inference rules* (Section 5.7) can systematically be derived from formulas was an early project of Negri and von Plato [2001]. A more general form of that early work is given in Marin et al. [2022], where focused proof systems for intuitionistic and classical logics are used to build synthetic inference rules for those two logics.

One of the applications of hereditary Harrop formulas for logic programming is to help design modular programming abstractions for logic programming. Miller [1989b] proposed an early approach to modular programming in logic programming, which later developed into the module system for λProlog in Kwon et al. [1993] and Miller [1994]. Numerous logic-based module designs for logic programming are surveyed in Bugliesi et al. [1994].

The emulation of Turing machines by first-order Horn clauses (see Exercise 5.40) shows that proving goals from a Horn clause logic program is undecidable. An early encoding of Turing machines as *fohc* clauses can be found in Tärnlund [1977].

As a result of Exercise 5.46, the implementation of substitution, typically needed when specifying theorem provers or operations that transform programs, must be *signature dependent*. That is, the constructors of certain types must be explicit in the specification. The use of copy-clauses as a flexible and general avenue for making items in a signature available to a logic specification is explored more in Miller [1991a] and Miller and Nadathur [2012].

As pointed out in Section 5.13, many important queries about graphs cannot be encoded using adjacency information stored as atomic facts. More generally, queries that involve discovering that some information is missing (e.g., there are no paths from, say, c to a) cannot be captured in *fohh* since we view logic programs as theories (sets of formulas) and since logical conclusions remain after additional formulas are added to a theory. A different way to view logic programs is as *inductive definitions* or explicit *least fixed points* instead of a set of implications. Such an approach has been proposed by, for example, Clark [1978], Girard [1992], Schroeder-Heister [1993], and Denecker et al. [2001]. In that setting, logic programs are closed by their definitions and cannot be extended. This change in perspective makes it possible to capture aspects of *negation-as-failure* as well as properties such as non-reachability and simulation (see McDowell et al. [2003]; Tiu et al. [2005]) as well as various other model-checking problems (see Heath and Miller [2019]). Although this approach to logic programs can greatly enrich the expressiveness of this topic, we shall maintain our treatment of logic programs as extensible theories, pushing this perspective into the areas of linear logic and higher-order quantification.

Chapter 6

Linear Logic

From the proof-theoretic perspective, the analysis of goal-directed proof search for classical and intuitionistic logics given in Chapter 5 has at least the following three problems.

First, that analysis holds only for subsets of classical and intuitionistic logics. As we have seen, uniform provability, along with backchaining, provides an analysis of proof search for the $\mathcal{L}_0 = \{t, \wedge, \supset, \forall\}$ fragment of intuitionistic logic, which is not a complete set of connectives for intuitionistic logic (when quantification is restricted to be first-order).

Second, that analysis did not extend to multiple-conclusion sequents, which is unfortunate since that setting allowed for a unified view of classical and intuitionistic proofs. Limiting proof search to single-conclusion sequents will restrict our ability to use negation and De Morgan dualities to reason about logic programs.

Third, the proof search dynamics for our richest logic programming language so far, *fohh*, is relatively weak. As we pointed out in Section 5.12, the left-hand side of border sequents within ⇓ *fohh* proofs can only increase during proof search, and while the right-hand side can change richly, those changes occur within atomic formulas (i.e., non-logical contexts). If sequents could change in more complex ways during proof search, logic programming could be more expressive and allow more direct uses of logic to reason about the computations specified.

As we shall see in this chapter, linear logic allows us to expand our analysis of proof search to address all three of these limitations. In particular, we will eventually analyze a multiple conclusion proof system for a set of connectives that captures all of linear logic.

6.1 Reflections on the Structural Inference Rules

Before we present linear logic, we discuss several issues related to the role of contraction and weakening in **C**-proofs and **I**-proofs.

Controlling contractions improves proof search If the contraction rules are deleted from the classical and intuitionistic (unfocused) proof systems in Section 4.1, then the height of a cut-free proof can be bounded by the number of occurrences of logical connectives in the endsequent. It would then follow that it is decidable whether or not a sequent has a cut-free proof in such a modified proof system. Using a more clever set of observations, Gentzen [1935] derived a decision procedure for propositional intuitionistic logic by seeing a way to limit the applications of contraction in that setting. The focused proof system $\Downarrow \mathcal{L}_0$ is a significant improvement over unfocused **I**-proofs in part because the structural rules are tightly regulated within $\Downarrow \mathcal{L}_0$-proofs: In particular, wL is built into the *init* rule, and cL is built into the *decide* rule as well as the $\supset L$ rule (to turn the usual multiplicative treatment of the left context into an additive treatment).

Invertible rules and contraction There is an interplay between structural rules and invertible introduction rules. Consider, for example, the following two introduction rules taken from the **C**-proof system (Section 4.1).

$$\frac{\Sigma :: B, \Gamma \vdash \Delta \qquad \Sigma :: C, \Gamma \vdash \Delta}{\Sigma :: B \vee C, \Gamma \vdash \Delta} \vee L \qquad \frac{\Sigma :: B_i, \Gamma \vdash \Delta}{\Sigma :: B_1 \wedge B_2, \Gamma \vdash \Delta} \wedge L \, .$$

The $\vee L$ rule is *invertible*, meaning that if the conclusion is provable its two premises are provable. In this case, cL never needs to be applied to the formula $B \vee C$. On the other hand, the $\wedge L$ rule is not invertible, and one might need to apply cL to this conjunction to access both conjunctions. For example, a cut-free **I**-proof of the formula $(p \wedge q) \supset (p \supset q \supset r) \supset r$ requires an application of cL to $p \wedge q$. Since controlling contraction can help one design proof-search procedures, it is valuable to know that the applicability of contraction can be limited to those formula occurrences with non-invertible introduction rules.

Selecting between multiplicative and additive connectives If one of the introduction rules for a connective is multiplicative, we say that that connective is *multiplicative*. If one of the introduction rules for a connective is additive, we say that that connective is *additive*. In typical proof systems, such as our **I** and **C** proof systems (as well as Gentzen's *LJ* and *LK*), one must select an additive or a multiplicative version of each connective: In the case of our proof system here, $\wedge$ and $\vee$ are additive while $\supset$ is multiplicative. In a fuller picture of proof theory, it seems unfortunate that we must pick just one of these variants. Although it is the case that the presence of weakening and contraction allows one to interchange the additive and multiplicative versions, we are considering proof systems where there are various restrictions on weakening and contraction. Thus, these different variants might be expected to behave differently within such proofs.

The collision of cut and the structural rules The interaction between the cut and the structural rules can lead to undesirable dynamics in the usual way to perform cut elimination. For example, consider the following instance of the cut rule.

$$\frac{\Gamma \vdash C \qquad \Gamma', C \vdash B}{\Gamma, \Gamma' \vdash B} \; cut \qquad\qquad (*)$$

If the right premise is proved by a left-contraction rule from the sequent $\Gamma', C, C \vdash B$, then cut-elimination proceeds by permuting the *cut* rule to the right premises, yielding the derivation

$$\cfrac{\Gamma \vdash C \qquad \cfrac{\cfrac{\Gamma \vdash C \qquad \Gamma', C, C \vdash B}{\Gamma, \Gamma', C \vdash B} \; cut}{\Gamma, \Gamma, \Gamma' \vdash B}}{\Gamma, \Gamma' \vdash B} \; cL.$$

In the single-conclusion variant of the sequent calculus, it is impossible for the occurrence of *C* in the left premise of (∗) to be contracted. If the cut rule in (∗) takes place in a classical proof system, the left premise might be the conclusion of a contraction applied to $\Gamma \vdash C, C$. In that case, cut elimination can also proceed by permuting the cut rule to the left premise.

$$\frac{\dfrac{\Gamma \vdash C, C \quad \Gamma', C \vdash B}{\Gamma, \Gamma' \vdash C, B} \; cut \quad \Gamma', C \vdash B}{\dfrac{\Gamma, \Gamma', \Gamma' \vdash B, B}{\Gamma, \Gamma' \vdash B} \; cL, cR} \; cut.$$

Thus, in **C**-proofs, it is possible for both occurrences of C in (∗) to be contracted and, hence, the elimination of this cut rule is nondeterministic since the cut rule can move to both the left and right premises. Such nondeterminism in cut elimination is even more pronounced when we consider the collision of the cut rule with weakening in the following derivation.

$$\frac{\dfrac{\Xi_1}{\vdash B}}{\vdash C, B} \; wR \quad \dfrac{\dfrac{\Xi_2}{\vdash B}}{C \vdash B} \; wL$$
$$\dfrac{\vdash B, B}{\vdash B} \; cR \quad cut.$$

Cut-elimination here can yield either Ξ_1 or Ξ_2: Thus, nondeterminism arising from weakening can lead to entirely different proofs of B. This kind of example does not occur in the intuitionistic (single-sided) version of the sequent calculus.

As we mentioned in Section 1.2, the functional programming paradigm can be built on top of a *deterministic* cut-elimination process. As a result, proof systems that allow this collision between cut and the structural rules are not natural foundations for functional programming.

Linear logic will address these various issues, especially once we present focused proof systems for all of linear logic in Section 6.7.

6.2 *LK* vs *LJ*: An Origin Story for Linear Logic

Gentzen restricted his *LJ* proof system for intuitionistic logic to be *LK* proofs in which there is at most one formula on the right. As we argued in Section 4.5, this restriction translates to the restriction that **I**-proofs are **C**-proofs in which the right-hand sides of all sequents have exactly one formula. As we proved in Proposition 4.2, the following two restrictions guarantee that all sequents in a **C**-proof of the endsequent $\vdash B$ have exactly one formula in the right-hand context.

6.2 LK vs LJ: An Origin Story for Linear Logic

1. No structural rules are permitted on the right: That is, proofs do not contain occurrences of *wR* and *cR*.
2. The two multiplicative rules, $\supset L$ and *cut*, are restricted so that the formula on the right-hand side of the conclusion must also be the formula on the right-hand side of the right premise.

To illustrate again this second restriction, recall the form of the $\supset L$ rule.

$$\frac{\Sigma :: \Gamma_1 \vdash \Delta_1, B \qquad \Sigma :: C, \Gamma_2 \vdash \Delta_2}{\Sigma :: B \supset C, \Gamma_1, \Gamma_2 \vdash \Delta_1, \Delta_2} \supset L .$$

If the right-hand side of the conclusion contains one formula, that formula can move to the right-hand side of either the left or right premise. This extra restriction, however, forces that formula to move only to the right premise and not to the left. Thus, the $\supset L$ rule does two things: It introduces a connective *and* moves a side formula to a particular place. In this sense, implication within intuitionistic logic is different from all other logic connectives: The introduction rules of these other connectives are only involved in introducing a connective (in an additive or multiplicative fashion). In Section 4.2, we noted that the *cut* rule could be emulated using the $\supset L$ rule and a trivial implication. Using this observation, the restriction on $\supset L$ can explain the similar restriction on *cut*. In summary, the restriction on **I**-proofs can be used to say that (1) structural rules are only allowed on the left of the sequent, and (2) implication seems to have more internal structure than is immediately apparent.

These two restrictions can motivate a central and novel feature of linear logic. In particular, the fact that in intuitionistic proofs, some occurrences of formulas in a proof can be contracted while some cannot will be captured in linear logic using the two operators ! and ? (pronounced "bang" and "question mark", respectively). In particular, a formula of the form $!B$ on the left-hand side and a formula of the form $?B$ on the right-hand side can be weakened and contracted. In linear logic, these structural rules will not apply to any other occurrences of formulas. Thus, sequents in **C**-proofs can be encoded in linear logic using sequents of the form $!B_1, \ldots, !B_n \vdash ?C_1, \ldots, ?C_m$ ($n, m \geq 0$) and sequents in **I**-proofs can be encoded in linear logic using sequents of the form $!B_1, \ldots, !B_n \vdash B_0$, where B_0 does not have ? as its top-level connective.

The ! operator can also be used to explain the behavior of the intuitionistic implication. Since the $\supset R$ rule applied to the formula $B \supset C$ moves B to the left-hand side, it seems necessary to encode such an implication as, say, $(!\,B) \multimap C$, where $\multimap$ is the *linear implication*. Such an encoding ensures that $!$ is affixed to B as a new member of the left-hand side. This decomposition of the intuitionistic implication also explains the second restriction listed above. In particular, consider the following inference rule in which the conclusion is a single-conclusion sequent encoded as described above.

$$\frac{\Sigma :: \Gamma_1 \vdash \Delta_1, !\,B \qquad \Sigma :: C, \Gamma_2 \vdash \Delta_2}{\Sigma :: (!\,B) \multimap C, \Gamma_1, \Gamma_2 \vdash \Delta_1, \Delta_2} \multimap\text{L}.$$

As is described in more detail in Section 6.3.3, the right-introduction rule for $!$ with a conclusion of the form $\Gamma_1 \vdash \Delta_1, !\,B$ is only permitted if Γ_1 contains only !'ed formulas and Δ_1 contains only ?'ed formulas. Given our encoding, the right-hand side will have one formula that is not a top-level ?: Thus, Δ_1 must be empty, and Δ_2 must be that single formula. In this way, the second restriction on the structure of $\supset$L in **I**-proofs can be explained.

6.3 Sequent Calculus Proof Systems for Linear Logic

The two-sided proof system for linear logic, called **L**, is formed by putting together all of the inference rules in Figures 6.1, 6.2, 6.3, and 6.4. Keeping with the conventions described in Section 2.4, all binary logical connectives of linear logic have the type $o \rightarrow o \rightarrow o$, the units have the type o, negation and the exponentials ($!$ and $?$) have the type $o \rightarrow o$, and the quantifiers $\forall_\tau$ and $\exists_\tau$ have type $(\tau \rightarrow o) \rightarrow o$ (for all types τ). Formulas built from the connectives explicitly mentioned in the **L** proof system are called ***L**-formulas*. The treatment of the quantifiers and signatures in linear logic will be essentially the same as in classical and intuitionistic logics. As such, many of the same conventions surrounding quantifiers will be used in the linear logic setting: That is, type subscripts and signatures of sequents are often not displayed when their value is not important or can be inferred from context.

6.3.1 An Informal Semantics for Some of Linear Logic

Before further developing the proof theory of linear logic, we briefly provide some informal semantics to help understand a few inference rules in Figure 6.4.

6.3 SEQUENT CALCULUS PROOF SYSTEMS FOR LINEAR LOGIC

$$\frac{\Sigma :: \Gamma \vdash \Delta}{\Sigma :: \Gamma, 1 \vdash \Delta} \; 1L \qquad \frac{}{\Sigma :: \cdot \vdash 1} \; 1R \qquad \frac{}{\Sigma :: \Gamma \vdash \top, \Delta} \; \top R$$

$$\frac{}{\Sigma :: \Gamma, 0 \vdash \Delta} \; 0L \qquad \frac{}{\Sigma :: \bot \vdash \cdot} \; \bot L \qquad \frac{\Sigma :: \Gamma \vdash \Delta}{\Sigma :: \Gamma \vdash \bot, \Delta} \; \bot R$$

$$\frac{\Sigma :: \Gamma, B_i \vdash \Delta}{\Sigma :: \Gamma, B_1 \& B_2 \vdash \Delta} \; \&L \; (i=1,2) \qquad \frac{\Sigma :: \Gamma \vdash B, \Delta \quad \Sigma :: \Gamma \vdash C, \Delta}{\Sigma :: \Gamma \vdash B \& C, \Delta} \; \&R$$

$$\frac{\Sigma :: \Gamma, B \vdash \Delta \quad \Sigma :: \Gamma, C \vdash \Delta}{\Sigma :: \Gamma, B \oplus C \vdash \Delta} \; \oplus L \qquad \frac{\Sigma :: \Gamma \vdash B_i, \Delta}{\Sigma :: \Gamma \vdash B_1 \oplus B_2, \Delta} \; \oplus R \; (i=1,2)$$

$$\frac{\Sigma :: \Gamma, B_1, B_2 \vdash \Delta}{\Sigma :: \Gamma, B_1 \otimes B_2 \vdash \Delta} \; \otimes L \qquad \frac{\Sigma :: \Gamma_1 \vdash B, \Delta_1 \quad \Sigma :: \Gamma_2 \vdash C, \Delta_2}{\Sigma :: \Gamma_1, \Gamma_2 \vdash B \otimes C, \Delta_1, \Delta_2} \; \otimes R$$

$$\frac{\Sigma :: \Gamma_1, B \vdash \Delta_1 \quad \Sigma :: \Gamma_2, C \vdash \Delta_2}{\Sigma :: \Gamma_1, \Gamma_2, B \;\mathrm{⅋}\; C \vdash \Delta_1, \Delta_2} \; \mathrm{⅋}L \qquad \frac{\Sigma :: \Gamma \vdash B, C, \Delta}{\Sigma :: \Gamma \vdash B \;\mathrm{⅋}\; C, \Delta} \; \mathrm{⅋}R$$

$$\frac{\Sigma :: \Gamma \vdash B, \Delta}{\Sigma :: \Gamma, B^\perp \vdash \Delta} \; (\cdot)^\perp L \qquad \frac{\Sigma :: \Gamma, B \vdash \Delta}{\Sigma :: \Gamma \vdash B^\perp, \Delta} \; (\cdot)^\perp R$$

Figure 6.1 The introduction rules for the propositional connectives.

$$\frac{}{\Sigma :: B \vdash B} \; init \qquad \frac{\Sigma :: \Gamma \vdash B, \Delta \quad \Sigma :: \Gamma', B \vdash \Delta'}{\Sigma :: \Gamma, \Gamma' \vdash \Delta, \Delta'} \; cut$$

Figure 6.2 The two identity rules.

$$\frac{\Sigma \Vdash t : \tau \quad \Sigma :: \Gamma, B[t/x] \vdash \Delta}{\Sigma :: \Gamma, \forall_\tau x.B \vdash \Delta} \; \forall L \qquad \frac{y : \tau, \Sigma :: \Gamma \vdash B[y/x], \Delta}{\Sigma :: \Gamma \vdash \forall_\tau x.B, \Delta} \; \forall R$$

$$\frac{y : \tau, \Sigma :: \Gamma, B[y/x] \vdash \Delta}{\Sigma :: \Gamma, \exists_\tau x.B \vdash \Delta} \; \exists L \qquad \frac{\Sigma \Vdash t : \tau \quad \Sigma :: \Gamma \vdash B[t/x], \Delta}{\Sigma :: \Gamma \vdash \exists_\tau x.B, \Delta} \; \exists R$$

Figure 6.3 The introduction rules for the quantifiers.

Some of the distinctions embedded in linear logic can be motivated by viewing it as a logic for dealing with *resources* instead of *truth values*.

Consider being someone who has built two digital fonts and wants to sell them. Linear logic provides two different packaging concepts for pricing the pairing of those two fonts based on its two conjunctions.

$$\frac{\Sigma :: \Gamma \vdash \Delta}{\Sigma :: \Gamma, !B \vdash \Delta} \, !W \qquad \frac{\Sigma :: \Gamma, !B, !B \vdash \Delta}{\Sigma :: \Gamma, !B \vdash \Delta} \, !C \qquad \frac{\Sigma :: \Gamma, B \vdash \Delta}{\Sigma :: \Gamma, !B \vdash \Delta} \, !D$$

$$\frac{\Sigma :: \Gamma \vdash \Delta}{\Sigma :: \Gamma \vdash ?B, \Delta} \, ?W \qquad \frac{\Sigma :: \Gamma \vdash ?B, ?B, \Delta}{\Sigma :: \Gamma \vdash ?B, \Delta} \, ?C \qquad \frac{\Sigma :: \Gamma \vdash B, \Delta}{\Sigma :: \Gamma \vdash ?B, \Delta} \, ?D$$

$$\frac{\Sigma :: !\Gamma, B \vdash ?\Delta}{\Sigma :: !\Gamma, ?B \vdash ?\Delta} \, ?L \qquad \frac{\Sigma :: !\Gamma \vdash B, ?\Delta}{\Sigma :: !\Gamma \vdash !B, ?\Delta} \, !R$$

Figure 6.4 The rules for the exponentials.

1. The right introduction rule for $\otimes$ suggests that one such packaging: If Γ_1 resources (such resources might be the hour spent designing fonts and computer expenses) were used to build font B_1 and Γ_2 resources were used to build font B_2, then we should price the pair of fonts $B_1 \otimes B_2$ to be based on the accumulation Γ_1, Γ_2. The left rule suggests that once someone has paid for such a pair, the buyer should have simultaneous access to both fonts B_1 and B_2. In other words, if it costs 3€ to build one font and 7€ to build the other, this kind of pairing should cost 10€.

2. The right introduction rule for & suggests another packaging: if both fonts B_1 and B_2 each required Γ resources separately, then we can price the pair of fonts B_1 & B_2 also with Γ. The left introduction rule for & suggests that the buyer should be able to access either font but when one of the fonts is picked, the other font is no longer accessible. In other words, if it costs 5€ to build one font and 5€ to build the other, this kind of pairing should still cost 5€.

We can informally view the formula $!B$ as an unbounded number of copies of B, an observation that is easily supported by the left rules for !, namely, $!W$, $!C$, $!D$. The $!R$ rule, also called the *promotion rule* for !, is more interesting. Consider, for example, a restaurant that would like to offer their clients unlimited french fries with their meals. One way to ensure this is to ensure that the cook has access to unlimited amounts of oil, salt, and potatoes and can make one french fry. This strategy is the informal meaning of the promotion rule for !. Dually, the $?L$ rule is the promotion rule for ?.

In these two informal descriptions, we have provided an interpretation of sequents that may have multiple formulas on the left but only one on the right. We will provide an informal semantics for inference rules involving sequents

6.3 SEQUENT CALCULUS PROOF SYSTEMS FOR LINEAR LOGIC

that contain multiple formulas on the right when we discuss the specification of concurrent processes Section 12.1.

6.3.2 Multiplicative Additive Linear Logic

Multiplicative additive linear logic, or MALL for short, is the subset of linear logic that results from collecting together the inference rules in Figures 6.1 and 6.2. MALL contains the additive and multiplicative versions of the classical disjunction, conjunction, and their units. Since MALL does not contain weakening or contraction, the additive and multiplicative versions of these connections are not inter-admissible within proofs (see Exercise 4.6). The eight logical connectives of MALL are classified in the following table as either the additive or multiplicative variant of an associated classical connective.

Classical	Linear Additive	Linear Multiplicative
t	$\top$ (top)	$\mathbf{1}$ (one)
f	$\mathbf{0}$ (zero)	$\bot$ (bottom)
$\wedge$	& (with)	$\otimes$ (tensor)
$\vee$	$\oplus$ (o-plus)	$\invamp$ (par)

Here, $\mathbf{1}$ is the unit for $\otimes$, $\top$ is the unit for &, $\bot$ is the unit for $\invamp$, and $\mathbf{0}$ is the unit for $\oplus$. Our presentation of linear logic will also accept negation as a first-class connective, written as $(\cdot)^\bot$: The inference rules for negation in Figure 6.1 are the same as used by Gentzen (see Section 4.5).

Exercise 6.1. *Let p, q, and r be propositional constants (constants of type o). Provide **L** proofs of the following sequents.*

1. $\vdash p \invamp p^\bot$
2. $(p \otimes q) \otimes r \vdash (r \otimes q) \otimes p$
3. $(p \invamp q) \invamp r \vdash (r \invamp q) \invamp p$
4. $p \otimes (q \invamp r) \vdash (p \otimes q) \invamp r$
5. $p \otimes (q \invamp r) \vdash (p \otimes r) \invamp q$
6. $r \vdash p \invamp (p^\bot \otimes q) \invamp (q^\bot \otimes r)$
7. $p^\bot \otimes q^\bot \vdash (p \invamp q)^\bot$
8. $(p \invamp q)^\bot \vdash p^\bot \otimes q^\bot$

Let B be the formula $\mathbf{1} \invamp \mathbf{1}$. It is the case that neither B nor its negation, namely $\bot \otimes \bot$, are provable in linear logic.

> **Exercise 6.2.** (‡) *In the sequent $\vdash p \otimes q, p^\perp \otimes q, p \otimes q^\perp, p^\perp \otimes q^\perp$, all occurrences of the constants p and q can be matched with an occurrence of its negation. Show, however, that this sequent is not provable in **L**.*

It is shown in Lincoln et al. [1992] that determining the provability of a *MALL* formula is PSPACE-complete. Augmenting *MALL* with the rules for first-order quantifiers (as depicted in Figure 6.3, where τ is a primitive type other than o) enhances the expressiveness of the resulting logic, yet the resulting logic still maintains PSPACE-completeness.

6.3.3 Linear Logic as MALL Plus Exponentials

Full linear logic is the strengthening of MALL with the addition of the quantifiers ∀ and ∃ and the two operators ! and ?, collectively called the *exponentials*. These operators reintroduce weakening and contraction into linear logic but only for some occurrences of formulas marked by them. In particular, Figure 6.4 contains four rules for each of these exponentials. Of those four, one permits weakening, and another permits contraction for the formulas they mark. The other two rules are essentially introduction rules. The *dereliction rules* $!D$ and $?D$ can be understood (reading rules from conclusion to premise) as saying that formulas that can be weakened and contracted can drop this privilege. The *promotion rules* $!R$ and $?L$ can similarly be read as saying that one way to show that a formula can gain the privilege of being weakened and contracted is to show that that formula can be proved in a context where every other formula has that privilege.

We say that two formulas B and C are *equivalent in linear logic* if the two sequents $B \vdash C$ and $C \vdash B$ are provable in **L**. We sometimes abbreviate this statement to $B \dashv\vdash C$.

> **Exercise 6.3.** *Show that the following equivalences between the exponential, additive, and multiplicative connectives hold in linear logic.*
>
> $!\top \dashv\vdash \mathbf{1} \quad !(B \mathbin{\&} C) \dashv\vdash\; !B \otimes\, !C \quad ?\mathbf{0} \dashv\vdash \bot \quad ?(B \oplus C) \dashv\vdash\, ?B \mathbin{⅋} ?C$
>
> *These equivalences are inspired by the algebraic equation $x^{m+n} = x^m \times x^n$.*

6.3 Sequent Calculus Proof Systems for Linear Logic

Exercise 6.4. (‡) *An exponential prefix is a finite sequence of zero or more occurrences of* ! *and* ?. *Let* π *be an exponential prefix. Prove that* $\pi\pi B \dashv\vdash \pi B$ *holds for all formulas B. Use that result to show that there are only seven exponential prefixes in linear logic up to equivalence: the empty prefix,* !, ?, !?, ?!, !?!, *and* ?!?.

Exercise 6.5. *Add a second tensor to linear logic, say,* $\hat{\otimes}$, *with the same inference rules as* $\otimes$. *Show that* $B \otimes C \dashv\vdash B \hat{\otimes} C$. *In this sense, the inference rules for tensor define it uniquely. Show that this is true for all logical connectives of linear logic except for the exponentials* ! *and* ?.

6.3.4 Duality and Polarity

The familiar De Morgan dualities of classical logic hold in a comprehensive fashion in linear logic. Not only do the binary connectives, units, and quantifiers have De Morgan duals, but the exponentials do as well. Here, we list the De Morgan duals for all the logical connectives in linear logic.

connective	$\top$	&	$\mathbf{1}$	$\otimes$	$\bot$	$\invamp$	$\mathbf{0}$	$\oplus$	!	?	$\forall$	$\exists$
De Morgan dual	$\mathbf{0}$	$\oplus$	$\bot$	$\invamp$	$\mathbf{1}$	$\otimes$	$\top$	&	?	!	$\exists$	$\forall$

This table encodes several linear logic equivalences. For example, the following equivalences hold.

$$(B \invamp C)^\bot \dashv\vdash B^\bot \otimes C^\bot \qquad (B \mathbin{\&} C)^\bot \dashv\vdash B^\bot \oplus C^\bot \qquad \top^\bot \dashv\vdash \mathbf{0}$$

$$(\exists x.B)^\bot \dashv\vdash \forall x.(B^\bot) \qquad (?B)^\bot \dashv\vdash !(B^\bot).$$

As a result of equivalences of this form, it is possible to rewrite every formula in linear logic into an equivalent formula in which negation has atomic scope. Such formulas are said to be in *negation normal form*. If we restrict our attention to only formulas in such normal forms, it is possible to give a one-sided sequent calculus proof system for linear logic, such as Figure 6.5. By exploiting dualities, this proof system has about half the number of inference rules as the two-sided inference system for linear logic. Note that in Figure 6.5, the negation symbol that appears in *init* and *cut* is no longer a logical connective (since it has no introduction rules) but should be understood as the operator that negates its argument and then puts the result into negation normal

$$\frac{}{\Sigma :: \vdash \top, \Delta} \top R \qquad \frac{\Sigma :: \vdash B, \Delta \qquad \Sigma :: \vdash C, \Delta}{\Sigma :: \vdash B \mathbin{\&} C, \Delta} \mathbin{\&} R$$

$$\frac{}{\Sigma :: \vdash \mathbf{1}} \mathbf{1}R \qquad \frac{\Sigma :: \vdash B, \Delta_1 \qquad \Sigma :: \vdash C, \Delta_2}{\Sigma :: \vdash B \otimes C, \Delta_1, \Delta_2} \otimes R$$

$$\frac{\Sigma :: \vdash \Delta}{\Sigma :: \vdash \bot, \Delta} \bot R \qquad \frac{\Sigma :: \vdash B, C, \Delta}{\Sigma :: \vdash B \mathbin{\bindnasrepma} C, \Delta} \mathbin{\bindnasrepma} R$$

$$\frac{\Sigma :: \vdash B_i, \Delta}{\Sigma :: \vdash B_1 \oplus B_2, \Delta} \oplus R \; (i = 1, 2)$$

$$\frac{y : \tau, \Sigma :: \vdash B[y/x], \Delta}{\Sigma :: \vdash \forall_\tau x.B, \Delta} \forall R \qquad \frac{\Sigma \Vdash t : \tau \qquad \Sigma :: \vdash B[t/x], \Delta}{\Sigma :: \vdash \exists_\tau x.B, \Delta} \exists R$$

$$\frac{\Sigma :: \vdash \Delta}{\Sigma :: \vdash ?B, \Delta} ?W \qquad \frac{\Sigma :: \vdash ?B, ?B, \Delta}{\Sigma :: \vdash ?B, \Delta} ?C \qquad \frac{\Sigma :: \vdash B, \Delta}{\Sigma :: \vdash ?B, \Delta} ?D$$

$$\frac{\Sigma :: \vdash B, ?\Delta}{\Sigma :: \vdash \,!B, ?\Delta} \,!R$$

$$\frac{}{\Sigma :: \vdash B, B^\perp} \text{init} \qquad \frac{\Sigma :: \vdash B, \Delta \qquad \Sigma :: \vdash B^\perp, \Delta'}{\Sigma :: \vdash \Delta, \Delta'} \text{cut}$$

Figure 6.5 A one-sided sequent calculus proof system for linear logic.

form. We shall, however, make only limited use of this one-sided sequent system for linear logic. Instead, we shall continue to use two-sided sequents in what follows.

An important and exciting aspect of linear logic is the following. It is easy to confirm that in *MALL*, the right-introduction rule of a logical connective is invertible if and only if the left-introduction rule of that connective (or the right-introduction rule of its De Morgan dual) is not invertible. This observation leads to attributing a *polarity* to connectives. In particular, we say that a connective is *negative* if its right-introduction rule is invertible and *positive* if its left-introduction rule is invertible. The negative connectives are $\bot, \top, \mathbin{\bindnasrepma}, \mathbin{\&}$, and $\forall$. The positive connectives are $\mathbf{1}, \mathbf{0}, \otimes, \oplus$, and $\exists$.

Another perspective on the polarity of linear logic connectives is the following. If the right-introduction rule for a connective requires information from an oracle or its context, then that rule introduces a positive connective. For example, the $\oplus R$ rule requires knowing which disjunct should be selected, the $\otimes R$ rule needs to know how to split a context, the $1R$ rule needs to know if its surrounding context is empty, and the $\exists R$ rule needs to be given a term. Dually, the right-introduction rules for negative connectives do not need any additional information for their successful application. (Note that the eigenvariable condition for the $\forall R$ rule requires that the eigenvariable is not currently free in the sequent: However, it is a simple matter to organize things so that new names are always selected independently from the context.) In this latter sense, it is possible to then classify ! as a positive connective since its right rule (the promotion rule $!R$), requires the information from the context that all formulas in the context are marked appropriately with an exponential. As a result, we also consider ? (the De Morgan dual of !) as negative.

The polarity of a non-atomic formula is negative or positive depending only on the polarity of its topmost connective. We adopt the convention that atoms have negative polarity to extend the notion of polarity to all linear logic formulas. This convention was initially adopted by Andreoli [1992] since it provided a natural connection to uniform proofs.

Exercise 6.6. *Let B and C be two formulas for which $B \dashv\vdash !B$ and $C \dashv\vdash !C$ are provable. Show that the following equivalences using the positive connectives are also provable: $1 \dashv\vdash !1$, $0 \dashv\vdash !0$, $B \otimes C \dashv\vdash !(B \otimes C)$, $\exists x.B \dashv\vdash !\exists x.B$, $B \oplus C \dashv\vdash !(B \oplus C)$. Dually, let B and C be two formulas such that $B \dashv\vdash ?B$ and $C \dashv\vdash ?C$ are provable. Show that the following equivalences using the negative connectives are also provable: $\bot \dashv\vdash ?\bot$, $\top \dashv\vdash ?\top$, $B \parr C \dashv\vdash ?(B \parr C)$, $B \& C \dashv\vdash ?(B \& C)$, $\forall x.B \dashv\vdash ?\forall x.B$.*

Exercise 6.7. *Let B be a linear logic formula. Prove that if the only occurrences of atomic formulas and negative connectives in B are in the scope of occurrences of !, then $B \dashv\vdash !B$ holds. Dually, prove that if the only occurrences of atomic formulas and positive connectives are in the scope of occurrences of ?, then $B \dashv\vdash ?B$ holds.*

Exercise 6.8. *Assuming that we have the cut-elimination theorem for the L proof system, prove the invertibility of $\& R$, $\parr R$, $\otimes L$, and $\oplus L$ using the style argument in the proof of Proposition 4.17.*

Exercise 6.9. *The following three entailments hold in classical logic.*

$$
\begin{array}{ll}
\textit{mix:} & A \wedge B \vdash A \vee B \\
\textit{switch:} & (A \vee B) \wedge C \vdash A \vee (B \wedge C) \\
\textit{medial:} & (A \wedge C) \vee (B \wedge D) \vdash (A \vee B) \wedge (C \vee D)
\end{array}
$$

(The names for these entailments are taken from Guglielmi [2007].) Consider mapping the pair of classical logic connectives $\langle \wedge, \vee \rangle$ into one of the four pairs of linear logic connectives $\langle \otimes, \mathbin{\invamp} \rangle$, $\langle \otimes, \oplus \rangle$, $\langle \&, \mathbin{\invamp} \rangle$, and $\langle \&, \oplus \rangle$. For each of the above three classical logic entailments, find which of these mappings of connectives yields an entailment provable in linear logic. For example, applying the first of these mappings to the Mix entailment yields $A \otimes B \vdash A \mathbin{\invamp} B$, which is not generally provable in linear logic.

Exercise 6.10. *The connectives of MALL can be given four attributes: arity (0 for a unit or 2 for a binary connective), additive/multiplicative, polarity (positive/negative), and conjunctive/disjunctive. Show that if we fix the arity, then, given any two of the remaining three attributes, the third can be determined uniquely. For example, there is a unique binary connective that is conjunctive and positive (the multiplicative $\otimes$) and a unique unit that is disjunctive and additive (the positive **0**). Show also that the De Morgan dual of a connective flips polarity and the conjunctive/disjunctive attribute while leaving the other two attributes unchanged.*

6.3.5 Introducing Implications

Since implication has played a large role in the design of the logic programming languages we have seen in earlier chapters, we add implication as a logical connective into linear logic. In fact, we add two implications, namely the *linear implication* $\multimap$ and the *intuitionistic implication* $\Rightarrow$. The linear implication $B \multimap C$ can be defined as $B^\perp \mathbin{\invamp} C$ and the intuitionistic implication $B \Rightarrow C$ can be defined as $(!\,B) \multimap C$. Since both of these implications are based on the multiplicative disjunction $\mathbin{\invamp}$, these connectives are multiplicative and have negative polarity. Instead of introducing implications as definitions, we choose to make them proper connectives by providing them with left- and right-introduction rules. The left- and right-introduction rules for $\multimap$ are the following.

6.3 Sequent Calculus Proof Systems for Linear Logic

$$\frac{\Sigma :: \Gamma_1 \vdash B, \Delta_1 \quad \Sigma :: \Gamma_2, C \vdash \Delta_2}{\Sigma :: \Gamma_1, \Gamma_2, B \multimap C \vdash \Delta_1, \Delta_2} \multimap L \qquad \frac{\Sigma :: \Gamma, B \vdash C, \Delta}{\Sigma :: \Gamma \vdash B \multimap C, \Delta} \multimap R.$$

We sometimes write $B \multimap\!\!\!\circ\!\!\!\multimap C$ as an abbreviation for $(B \multimap C) \& (C \multimap B)$. Since the right introduction rules for & and ⅋ are invertible (see Exercise 6.8), the formula $(B \multimap C) \& (C \multimap B)$ is provable in linear logic if and only if $B \dashv\vdash C$ holds.

> **Exercise 6.11.** *Prove the following* curry/uncurry *equivalences are provable in linear logic.*
>
> $$1 \multimap H \multimap\!\!\!\circ\!\!\!\multimap H \qquad (B \otimes C) \multimap H \multimap\!\!\!\circ\!\!\!\multimap B \multimap C \multimap H$$
>
> $$0 \multimap H \multimap\!\!\!\circ\!\!\!\multimap \top \qquad (B \oplus C) \multimap H \multimap\!\!\!\circ\!\!\!\multimap (B \multimap H) \& (C \multimap H)$$
>
> $$(\exists x. B\, x) \multimap H \multimap\!\!\!\circ\!\!\!\multimap \forall x. (B\, x \multimap H)$$

Many presentations of linear logic make little or no use of implications since they often focus on the rich symmetries allowed by the negation of linear logic. In particular, every logical connective of linear logic, except for the implications $\multimap$ and $\Rightarrow$, have other logical connectives that are their De Morgan duals. In what follows, we will view $B^\perp$ as an abbreviation for $B \multimap \bot$.

One issue with adding the intuitionistic implication directly to a proof system for linear logic is deciding how to specify its left- and right-introduction rules. For example, it is tempting to write the following candidate introduction rules for $\Rightarrow$.

$$\frac{\Sigma :: \Gamma_1 \vdash\, !B, \Delta_1 \quad \Sigma :: \Gamma_2, C \vdash \Delta_2}{\Sigma :: \Gamma_1, \Gamma_2, B \Rightarrow C \vdash \Delta_1, \Delta_2} \qquad \frac{\Sigma :: \Gamma, !B \vdash C, \Delta}{\Sigma :: \Gamma \vdash B \Rightarrow C, \Delta}.$$

These rules, however, break the usual pattern for introduction rules in sequent calculus: Exactly one occurrence of a logical connective appears in the conclusion while no new occurrences of a logical connective appears in a premise. In both of these rules, the occurrence of ! in the premise violates this pattern. This pattern has already been violated, in principle, by the rules for the exponentials. In particular, the contraction rule !C inserts two occurrences of ! into a premise while !R requires possibly many occurrences of ! and ? to be present in the conclusion. We address these issues around the implications and the exponentials by introducing a new style of sequent calculus proof system in Section 6.4.

> **Exercise 6.12.** Let p be a propositional constant and let B be the formula $p \otimes !(p \multimap (p \otimes p)) \otimes !(p \multimap 1)$. Show that the sequents $B \vdash B \otimes B$ and $B \vdash 1$ are provable in **L**.

6.4 Introducing Zones into Sequents

One of our hopes with introducing linear logic is to provide a means to enrich the logic programming languages described in Chapter 5. To that end, we will analyze goal-directed proofs, backchaining, and focused proof systems within linear logic. This analysis will show that *all* of linear logic can be presented as an abstract logic programming language. Before showing that result, we show how to relate proofs in linear logic with **I**-proofs and **C**-proofs.

If linear logic does serve as a more refined and low-level setting for both classical and intuitionistic logics, then we might expect that simply replacing the logical connectives in $\Downarrow \mathcal{L}_0$, namely $\{t, \wedge, \supset, \forall\}$ (see Section 5.5), with the corresponding linear logic connectives $\{\top, \&, \Rightarrow, \forall\}$ should allow us to reproduce intuitionistic proofs within linear logic. If that is indeed the case, adding $\multimap$ to this last set of connectives might provide us with an *extension* to *fohh*. We will soon show that such an extension does exist.

Let $\mathcal{L}_1$ be the set of logical connectives $\{\top, \&, \multimap, \Rightarrow, \forall\}$. An $\mathcal{L}_1$-*formula* is any first-order formula whose logical connectives come from $\mathcal{L}_1$. Figure 6.6 presents an (unfocused) proof system **P** for the formulas taken from $\mathcal{L}_1$. To solve the problem of specifying introduction rules for $\Rightarrow$ mentioned at the end of Section 6.3, the **P** proof system features an innovation: The left-hand context in sequents is divided into two *zones*. In particular, this proof system uses sequents of the form $\Sigma :: \Psi; \Gamma \vdash B$. Here, both Ψ and Γ are multisets of $\mathcal{L}_1$ formulas, and B is an $\mathcal{L}_1$ formula. We say that Ψ is the *left-unbounded zone* while Γ is the *left-bounded zone* of this sequent. We shall also refer to the right-hand side of a **P** sequent as its *right-bounded zone*. The informal reading of the sequent $B_1, \ldots, B_n; C_1, \ldots, C_m \vdash E$ is given by the linear logic sequent $! B_1, \ldots, ! B_n, C_1, \ldots, C_m \vdash E$. All the introduction rules in Figure 6.6 have the desired property that the conclusion has one occurrence of a logical connective and the premises have no explicit mention

6.4 INTRODUCING ZONES INTO SEQUENTS

$$\frac{}{\Sigma :: \Psi; A \vdash A} \text{ init} \qquad \frac{\Sigma :: \Psi, B; \Gamma, B \vdash C}{\Sigma :: \Psi, B; \Gamma \vdash C} \text{ absorb} \qquad \frac{}{\Sigma :: \Psi; \Gamma \vdash \top} \top R$$

$$\frac{\Sigma :: \Psi; \Gamma, B_i \vdash C}{\Sigma :: \Psi; \Gamma, B_1 \& B_2 \vdash C} \&L\ (i = 1, 2) \qquad \frac{\Sigma :: \Psi; \Gamma \vdash B \quad \Sigma :: \Psi; \Gamma \vdash C}{\Sigma :: \Psi; \Gamma \vdash B \& C} \&R$$

$$\frac{\Sigma :: \Psi; \Gamma \vdash B \quad \Sigma :: \Psi; \Gamma', C \vdash E}{\Sigma :: \Psi; \Gamma, \Gamma', B \multimap C \vdash E} \multimap L \qquad \frac{\Sigma :: \Psi; \Gamma, B \vdash C}{\Sigma :: \Psi; \Gamma \vdash B \multimap C} \multimap R$$

$$\frac{\Sigma :: \Psi; \cdot \vdash B \quad \Sigma :: \Psi; \Gamma, C \vdash E}{\Sigma :: \Psi; \Gamma, B \Rightarrow C \vdash E} \Rightarrow L \qquad \frac{\Sigma :: \Psi, B; \Gamma \vdash C}{\Sigma :: \Psi; \Gamma \vdash B \Rightarrow C} \Rightarrow R$$

$$\frac{\Sigma :: \Psi; \Gamma, B[t/x] \vdash C}{\Sigma :: \Psi; \Gamma, \forall x.B \vdash C} \forall L \qquad \frac{y : \tau, \Sigma :: \Psi; \Gamma \vdash B[y/x]}{\Sigma :: \Psi; \Gamma \vdash \forall_\tau x.B} \forall R$$

$$\frac{\Sigma :: \Psi; \Gamma \vdash B \quad \Sigma :: \Psi; \Gamma', B \vdash C}{\Sigma :: \Psi; \Gamma, \Gamma' \vdash C} cut_l \qquad \frac{\Sigma :: \Psi; \cdot \vdash B \quad \Sigma :: \Psi, B; \Gamma \vdash C}{\Sigma :: \Psi; \Gamma \vdash C} \text{ cut !}$$

Figure 6.6 The single-conclusion, two-zone proof system **P** for $\mathcal{L}_1$.

of logical connectives. The presences of two zones on the left of sequents also necessitates having two versions of the cut rule, cut_l and $cut\,!$, and two versions of the decide rule, $decide_l$ and $decide\,!$.

The additive rules treat formulas occurring in these two zones the same; that is, a context formula occurrence in either the left- or right-bounded zone or the left-unbounded zone of the conclusion also occurs in the corresponding zone in all premises. The multiplicative rules have a more hybrid behavior: A context formula occurring in the left-unbounded zone of the conclusion also occurs in the left-unbounded zone of all premises, while a context formula occurring in either the left- or right-bounded zone occurs in the corresponding zone in exactly one premise. This hybrid behavior for the multiplicative inference rules is possible because contraction is available for the left-unbounded zone. For example, the following derivation illustrates how the multiplicative $\multimap L$ rule plus contraction (!L) can justify this hybrid treatment.

$$\frac{\dfrac{!\Psi, \Gamma_1 \vdash B \quad !\Psi, \Gamma_2, C \vdash E}{!\Psi, !\Psi, \Gamma_1, \Gamma_2, B \multimap C \vdash E}}{!\Psi, \Gamma_1, \Gamma_2, B \multimap C \vdash E} !C$$

Two inference rules in Figure 6.6, namely $\Rightarrow$L and *cut* !, require the bounded part of one of its premises to be empty. When that context is empty, as in $B_1, \ldots, B_n; \cdot \vdash E$, the corresponding linear logic sequent is $!B_1, \ldots, !B_n \vdash E$. When that sequent is provable in linear logic, then $!B_1, \ldots, !B_n \vdash !E$ is also provable (using the $!R$ rule in Figure 6.4). Thus, requiring a premise to have an empty left-bounded zone can also guarantee that a (hidden) ! formula is proved from the left-unbounded context.

The *absorb* rule in Figure 6.6 is a combination of the contraction and dereliction rules for !: It allows for a formula in the left-unbounded zone to be copied into the left-bounded context.

The following function translates formulas that may involve implications into formulas where those implications are replaced by their definitions. Let B° be the result of repeatedly replacing within B all occurrences of $C_1 \Rightarrow C_2$ with $(!C_1)^\perp \parr C_2$ and all occurrences of $C_1 \multimap C_2$ with $C_1^\perp \parr C_2$. We also allow $\circ$ to be applied to a multiset of formulas, which results in the multiset of $\circ$ applied to each member. The following proposition relates the **P** and **L** proof systems.

Proposition 6.13. *Let B be an $\mathcal{L}_1$-formula and let Ψ and Γ be multisets of $\mathcal{L}_1$-formulas. The sequent $\Psi; \Gamma \vdash B$ has a **P**-proof if and only if the sequent $!(\Psi^\circ), \Gamma^\circ \vdash B^\circ$ has an **L** proof.*

Proving the forward direction is a straightforward induction on the structure of proofs. Proving the converse is more challenging and not given here since it will follow directly from the proof of the completeness of the focused proof system $\Downarrow \mathcal{L}_2$ (displayed in Figure 6.11) given in Chapter 7.

Although several properties of the **P** proof system could be stated and proved, this unfocused proof system is not best suited for studying generalizations of goal-directed search and backchaining. We now motivate a focused version of the **P** proof system.

As in Section 5.4, we organize the left-hand rules using the backchaining discipline. We do this by presenting two proof systems: the first uses $\Downarrow$ to denote the focus of the backchain rule, and a second proof system in which backchaining is described as a single inference rule BC.

Figure 6.7 contains a proof system in which the left-introduction rules are applied to a designated formula from the left (compare these rules to those in Figure 5.1). The new sequent, written as $\Sigma :: \Psi; \Gamma \Downarrow D \vdash A$, displays that designated formula between the $\Downarrow$ and the $\vdash$. That displayed formula is the

6.4 Introducing Zones into Sequents

$$\frac{}{\Sigma :: \Psi; \Gamma \vdash \top} \; \top R \qquad \frac{\Sigma :: \Psi; \Gamma \vdash B \quad \Sigma :: \Psi; \Gamma \vdash C}{\Sigma :: \Psi; \Gamma \vdash B \,\&\, C} \; \&R$$

$$\frac{\Sigma :: \Psi; \Gamma, B \vdash C}{\Sigma :: \Psi; \Gamma \vdash B \multimap C} \; \multimap R \qquad \frac{\Sigma :: \Psi, B; \Gamma \vdash C}{\Sigma :: \Psi; \Gamma \vdash B \Rightarrow C} \; \Rightarrow R$$

$$\frac{y : \tau, \Sigma :: \Psi; \Gamma \vdash B[y/x]}{\Sigma :: \Psi; \Gamma \vdash \forall_\tau x.B} \; \forall R$$

$$\frac{\Sigma :: \Psi, D; \Gamma \Downarrow D \vdash A}{\Sigma :: \Psi, D; \Gamma \vdash A} \; \text{decide}! \qquad \frac{\Sigma :: \Psi; \Gamma \Downarrow D \vdash A}{\Sigma :: \Psi; \Gamma, D \vdash A} \; \text{decide}_l$$

$$\frac{}{\Sigma :: \Psi; \cdot \Downarrow A \vdash A} \; \text{init} \qquad \frac{\Sigma \Vdash t : \tau \quad \Sigma :: \Psi; \Gamma \Downarrow D[t/x] \vdash A}{\Sigma :: \Psi; \Gamma \Downarrow \forall_\tau x.D \vdash A} \; \forall L$$

$$\frac{\Sigma :: \Psi; \Gamma \Downarrow D_i \vdash A}{\Sigma :: \Psi; \Gamma \Downarrow D_1 \,\&\, D_2 \vdash A} \; \&L \; (i = 1, 2)$$

$$\frac{\Sigma :: \Psi; \Gamma_1 \vdash G \quad \Sigma :: \Psi; \Gamma_2 \Downarrow D \vdash A}{\Sigma :: \Psi; \Gamma_1, \Gamma_2 \Downarrow G \multimap D \vdash A} \; \multimap L$$

$$\frac{\Sigma :: \Psi; \cdot \vdash G \quad \Sigma :: \Psi; \Gamma \Downarrow D \vdash A}{\Sigma :: \Psi; \Gamma \Downarrow G \Rightarrow D \vdash A} \; \Rightarrow L$$

Figure 6.7 The focused proof system $\Downarrow \mathcal{L}_1$.

only one on which left-introduction rules may be applied. The two decide rules are used to turn the attempt to prove an atomic formula into an attempt to use a focused formula. The sequent $\Sigma :: \Psi; \Gamma \vdash G$ or the sequent $\Sigma :: \Psi; \Gamma \Downarrow D \vdash A$ has a $\Downarrow \mathcal{L}_1$-proof if it has a proof using the rules in Figure 6.7.

Note that the rule for $\multimap L$ requires splitting the bounded zone into two parts (when reading the rule bottom-up). There are, of course, 2^n such splittings if that zone has $n \geq 0$ distinct formulas.

The soundness and completeness of the $\Downarrow \mathcal{L}_1$ proof system for sequents using formulas only from $\mathcal{L}_1$ will follow from a stronger result that we shall prove in some detail in Section 7.4.

Consider the following definition for a second (less proof-theoretic) description of backchaining. Let the syntactic variable B range over $\mathcal{L}_1$-formulas. Define $\|B\|_\Sigma$ to be the smallest set of triples of the form $\langle \Psi, \Gamma, B' \rangle$, where Ψ and Γ are multisets of formulas, such that

$$\frac{\Sigma :: \Psi; \cdot \vdash B_1 \ \ldots \ \Sigma :: \Psi; \cdot \vdash B_n \quad \Sigma :: \Psi; \Gamma_1 \vdash C_1 \ \ldots \ \Sigma :: \Psi; \Gamma_m \vdash C_m}{\Sigma :: \Psi; \Gamma_1, \ldots, \Gamma_m, B \vdash A} \, BC$$

provided $n, m \geq 0$, $\langle \{B_1, \ldots, B_n\}, \{C_1, \ldots, C_m\}, A \rangle \in \|B\|_\Sigma$, and A is atomic.

Figure 6.8 Backchaining for the linear logic fragment $\mathcal{L}_1$.

1. $\langle \emptyset, \emptyset, B \rangle \in \|B\|_\Sigma$;
2. if $\langle \Psi, \Gamma, B_1 \& B_2 \rangle \in \|B\|_\Sigma$ then $\langle \Psi, \Gamma, B_1 \rangle \in \|B\|_\Sigma$ and $\langle \Psi, \Gamma, B_2 \rangle \in \|B\|_\Sigma$;
3. if $\langle \Psi, \Gamma, B_1 \Rightarrow B_2 \rangle \in \|B\|_\Sigma$ then $\langle \Psi \cup \{B_1\}, \Gamma, B_2 \rangle \in \|B\|_\Sigma$;
4. if $\langle \Psi, \Gamma, B_1 \multimap B_2 \rangle \in \|B\|_\Sigma$ then $\langle \Psi, \Gamma \cup \{B_1\}, B_2 \rangle \in \|B\|_\Sigma$; and
5. if $\langle \Psi, \Gamma, \forall_\tau x. B' \rangle \in \|B\|_\Sigma$ and t is a Σ-term of type τ, then

$$\langle \Psi, \Gamma, B'[t/x] \rangle \in \|B\|_\Sigma.$$

Let $\Downarrow \mathcal{L}_1'$ be the proof system that results from replacing *init* and the four left-introduction rules in Figure 6.7 with the *backchaining* inference rule in Figure 6.8.

Proposition 6.14. *Let* $\{B\} \cup \Psi \cup \Gamma$ *be a multiset of* $\mathcal{L}_1$-*formulas. The sequent* $\Sigma :: \Psi; \Gamma \vdash B$ *has a* $\Downarrow \mathcal{L}_1$ *proof if and only if it has a* $\Downarrow \mathcal{L}_1'$ *proof.*

This proposition follows directly from the completeness of the $\Downarrow \mathcal{L}_1$ proof system, following the same lines used to prove the analogous results in Section 5.7. Using the terminology introduced in Section 3.3, the BC rule in Figure 6.8 is multiplicative if we take the occurrences of A and B in the conclusion to be the target occurrences of this rule.

It is now clear from the $\Downarrow \mathcal{L}_1$-proof system that the dynamics of proof search in this setting has improved beyond that described for *fohh* (Section 5.12). In particular, every sequent in a $\Downarrow \mathcal{L}_1$-proof of the sequent $\Sigma :: \Psi; \Gamma \vdash G$ is either of the form $\Sigma, \Sigma' :: \Psi, \Psi'; \Gamma' \vdash G'$ or $\Sigma, \Sigma' :: \Psi, \Psi'; \Gamma' \Downarrow D \vdash A$. Just as with *fohh*, the signature can grow by adding Σ' and the unbounded zone can grow by adding Ψ'. However, the bounded zone, Γ', can change in much more general and arbitrary ways. Formulas in the bounded zone that were present at the root of a proof may not necessarily be present later (higher) in the proof. As we shall see later, we can use formulas in the bounded zone to represent, say, the state of a computation or a switch that is off but later on.

6.5 Embedding *fohh* into Linear Logic

The abstract logic programming language $\langle \mathcal{L}_1, \mathcal{L}_1, \vdash_\mathcal{L} \rangle$ has been also called Lolli (after the lollipop shape of the $\multimap$). As a programming language, Lolli appears to be $\mathcal{L}_0$ with $\multimap$ added. To make this connection more precise, we should show how $\mathcal{L}_0$ can be embedded into Lolli (since, technically, they use different sets of connectives). Girard [1987] has presented a mapping of intuitionistic logic into linear logic that preserves not only provability but also proofs. On the fragment of intuitionistic logic containing t, $\wedge$, $\supset$, and $\forall$, his translation is given by:

$$(A)^0 = A, \text{ where } A \text{ is atomic,}$$
$$(t)^0 = \top,$$
$$(B_1 \wedge B_2)^0 = (B_1)^0 \mathbin{\&} (B_2)^0,$$
$$(B_1 \supset B_2)^0 = (B_1)^0 \Rightarrow (B_2)^0,$$
$$(\forall x.B)^0 = \forall x.(B)^0.$$

However, if we are willing to focus attention on only cut-free proofs in intuitionistic and linear logic, it is possible to define a different translation. Consider the following two translation functions.

$$(A)^+ = (A)^- = A, \text{ where } A \text{ is atomic}$$
$$(t)^+ = \mathbf{1} \qquad (t)^- = \top$$
$$(B_1 \wedge B_2)^+ = (B_1)^+ \otimes (B_2)^+$$
$$(B_1 \wedge B_2)^- = (B_1)^- \mathbin{\&} (B_2)^-$$
$$(B_1 \supset B_2)^+ = (B_1)^- \Rightarrow (B_2)^+$$
$$(B_1 \supset B_2)^- = (B_1)^+ \multimap (B_2)^-$$
$$(\forall x.B)^+ = \forall x.(B)^+$$
$$(\forall x.B)^- = \forall x.(B)^-$$

If we allow positive occurrences of $\vee$ and $\exists$ within cut-free proofs, as in proofs involving the hereditary Harrop formulas, we need to include the following two clauses.

$$(B_1 \vee B_2)^+ = (B_1)^+ \oplus (B_2)^+$$
$$(\exists x.B)^+ = \exists x.(B)^+.$$

> **Proposition 6.15.** *Let Σ be a signature, B be a Σ-formula and Δ a set of Σ-formulas, all over the logical constants $\mathbf{t}, \wedge, \supset$, and $\forall$. Define Δ^- to be the multiset $\{C^- \mid C \in \Delta\}$. Then, the sequent $\Sigma :: \Delta \vdash B$ has an **I**-proof if and only if the sequent $\Sigma :: \Delta^-; \cdot \vdash B^+$ has a cut-free proof in $\Downarrow \mathcal{L}_1$.*

This proposition is a consequence of the more general Proposition 7.18. In fact, if one considers $\Downarrow \mathcal{L}_0$-proofs instead of **I**-proofs, then $\Downarrow \mathcal{L}_0$-proofs of $\Sigma :: \Delta \vdash B$ are essentially $\Downarrow \mathcal{L}_1$-proofs of $\Sigma :: \Delta^-; \cdot \vdash B^+$. This suggests how to design the concrete syntax of a linear logic programming language so that the interpretation of Prolog and λProlog programs remains unchanged when embedded into this new setting. In particular, the Prolog syntax

$$A_0 :- A_1, \ldots, A_n$$

is traditionally intended to denote (the universal closure of) the formula

$$(A_1 \wedge \cdots \wedge A_n) \supset A_0.$$

Given the negative translation above, such a Horn clause is translated to the linear logic formula

$$(A_1 \otimes \cdots \otimes A_n) \multimap A_0.$$

Thus, the comma in Prolog denotes $\otimes$ and $:-$ denotes the converse of $\multimap$.

Another example is the natural deduction rule for the introduction of implication, often expressed using the diagram

$$\begin{array}{c} (A) \\ \vdots \\ B \\ \hline A \supset B \end{array},$$

which can be written as the following first-order formula for specifying a provability predicate:

$$\forall A. \forall B.((\mathtt{prov}(A) \supset \mathtt{prov}(B)) \supset \mathtt{prov}(A \text{ imp } B)).$$

Here, the domain of quantification is over propositional formulas of the object-language and `imp` is the object-level implication. This formula is written in λProlog using the syntax

```
prov (A imp B)   :-   prov A => prov B.
```

Given the above proposition, this formula can be translated to the formula

$$\forall A.\forall B.((\mathtt{prov}(A) \Rightarrow \mathtt{prov}(B)) \multimap \mathtt{prov}(A \text{ imp } B)),$$

which means that the λProlog symbol => should denote $\Rightarrow$. Thus, in the implication introduction rule displayed above, the metalevel implication represented as three vertical dots can be interpreted as an intuitionistic implication while the metalevel implication represented as the horizontal bar can be interpreted as a linear implication.

6.6 A Model of Resource Consumption

This book does not present many details about the implementation of proof search, but the following considerations seem high-level and useful to mention. As we discussed in Section 6.4, an attempt to apply the multiplicative inference rule $\multimap$L from either Figure 6.6 or Figure 6.7 requires splitting a multiset of formulas into two multisets: In general, an exponential number of such splittings is possible. A better strategy than trying each possible splitting is needed if the logic $\mathcal{L}_1$ is to be the foundation of a usable logic programming language. Such a strategy is possible and rests on two observations. First, instead of splitting the formulas in the left-bounded zone at the moment of applying the $\multimap$L rule, we can send all the formulas in the bounded zone to the process searching for a proof of the left premise. If a proof of that premise is found, some of those bounded formulas are consumed. The remaining unconsumed, bounded formulas can then be sent to the right premise to be consumed there. Second, the decide inference rule in Figure 6.7 consumes a bounded formula.

Figure 6.9 contains the IO proof system, which is a modification of the $\Downarrow \mathcal{L}_1$ proof system in Figure 6.7 in which the bounded zone (written using the schematic variable Γ) is replaced by the pairing $[I \parallel O]$, where I and O denote, respectively, collections of *input* and *output* formulas. Since we need to support the process of *deleting* formulas from an input to arrive at an output, the structures encoding I and O will be lists of *option formulas*. By an option formula we mean a term of the form $\langle B \rangle$, for B a formula, or ∘, which denotes that a formula has been deleted. The `pick` relation used in the *decide$_l$* rule in Figure 6.9 is used to select an occurrence of a formula from an input list and return the result of deleting that occurrence in the output list. The formal

$$\frac{\text{subcontext } O\ I}{\Sigma :: \Psi; [I \parallel O] \vdash \top} \top R$$

$$\frac{\Sigma :: \Psi; [I \parallel O] \vdash B \quad \Sigma :: \Psi; [I \parallel O] \vdash C}{\Sigma :: \Psi; [I \parallel O] \vdash B \& C} \&R$$

$$\frac{\Sigma :: \Psi; [\langle B \rangle :: I \parallel \circ :: O] \vdash C}{\Sigma :: \Psi; [I \parallel O] \vdash B \multimap C} \multimap R$$

$$\frac{\Sigma :: \Psi, B; [I \parallel O] \vdash C}{\Sigma :: \Psi; [I \parallel O] \vdash B \Rightarrow C} \Rightarrow R$$

$$\frac{y : \tau, \Sigma :: \Psi; [I \parallel O] \vdash B[y/x]}{\Sigma :: \Psi; [I \parallel O] \vdash \forall_\tau x.B} \forall R$$

$$\frac{\Sigma :: \Psi, D; [I \parallel O] \Downarrow D \vdash A}{\Sigma :: \Psi, D; [I \parallel O] \vdash A} \text{ decide!}$$

$$\frac{\text{pick } I\ D\ M \quad \Sigma :: \Psi; [M \parallel O] \Downarrow D \vdash A}{\Sigma :: \Psi; [I \parallel O] \vdash A} \text{ decide}_l$$

$$\frac{}{\Sigma :: \Psi; [I \parallel I] \Downarrow A \vdash A} \text{ init}$$

$$\frac{\Sigma \Vdash t : \tau \quad \Sigma :: \Psi; [I \parallel O] \Downarrow D[t/x] \vdash A}{\Sigma :: \Psi; [I \parallel O] \Downarrow \forall_\tau x.D \vdash A} \forall L$$

$$\frac{\Sigma :: \Psi; [I \parallel O] \Downarrow D_i \vdash A}{\Sigma :: \Psi; [I \parallel O] \Downarrow D_1 \& D_2 \vdash A} \&L\ (i \in \{1,2\})$$

$$\frac{\Sigma :: \Psi; [I \parallel M] \vdash G \quad \Sigma :: \Psi; [M \parallel O] \Downarrow D \vdash A}{\Sigma :: \Psi; [I \parallel O] \Downarrow G \multimap D \vdash A} \multimap L$$

$$\frac{\Sigma :: \Psi; [I \parallel I] \vdash G \quad \Sigma :: \Psi; [I \parallel O] \Downarrow D \vdash A}{\Sigma :: \Psi; [I \parallel O] \Downarrow G \Rightarrow D \vdash A} \Rightarrow L$$

The symbol :: is used both as the list constructor (in the supporting code in Figure 6.10) as well as the symbol separating a signature from the rest of a sequent.

Figure 6.9 The IO proof system.

6.6 A Model of Resource Consumption

```
kind opt          type -> type.
type none         opt A.
type some         A -> opt A.
type pick         list (opt A) -> A -> list (opt A)-> o.
type subcontext   list (opt A)                -> list (opt A)-> o.

pick (some B::I) B (none::I).
pick (C::I)      B (C::O)       :- pick I B O.

subcontext nil         nil.
subcontext (C::O)      (C::I)       :- subcontext O I.
subcontext (none::O)   (some B::I)  :- subcontext O I.
```

As with the type for lists, the type for options is also given a polymorphic typing: Here, A is a type variable.

Figure 6.10 The formal definition of the predicates used in Figure 6.9.

definition of the `pick` and `subcontext` predicates is given using the Horn clauses displayed in Figure 6.10.

Exercise 6.16. *The predicate* `subcontext` *can be removed from the proof system in Figure 6.9 by making use of the* `pick` *predicate instead. In particular, show that the one rule in Figure 6.9 that references* `subcontext` *can be replaced by the following two rules.*

$$\frac{}{\Sigma :: \Psi; [I \parallel I] \vdash \top} TR \qquad \frac{pick\, I\, D\, M \quad \Sigma :: \Psi; [M \parallel O] \vdash \top}{\Sigma :: \Psi; [I \parallel O] \vdash \top} TR$$

There are several observations to make about the rules in Figure 6.9.

1. Most rules are such that when the pair $[I \parallel O]$ appears in the conclusion, it also appears in all its premises. The exceptions are described next.
2. When reading inference rules from conclusion to premises, the $\multimap R$ rule can be seen as taking the pair $[I \parallel O]$ and giving to the premise the input $\langle B \rangle$ (encoded as `(some B)` in Figure 6.10). At the same time, the corresponding output structure contains $\circ$ (encoded as `none`), which denotes the deletion of B. As a result, this modified rule indicates that B must be consumed to prove the premise.
3. The *decide$_l$* rule employs the `pick` predicate to nondeterministically select a formula D from the input structure while marking it deleted in the output structure.

4. The left premise of the ⇒L rule contains the pairing [$I \parallel I$]. Such a pairing means that all formulas in the input are also in the output: No formulas have been deleted. The *init* rule uses a similar pairing.
5. The condition (`subcontext O I`) appearing in the premise of the TR is true if O results from deleting some formulas occurring in I.

In order to prove the correctness of the proof system in Figure 6.9, we define the formal difference, $I - O$, whenever it is the case that `subcontext O I` holds: In particular, $I - O$ is the multiset of formulas D such that $\langle D \rangle$ occurs in I and the corresponding position in O is the symbol ∘. The following lemma states some simple properties of this difference operator.

Lemma 6.17. *Given a list of option formulas I, the difference $I - I$ is the empty multiset. Whenever `subcontext I M` and `subcontext M O` hold then `subcontext I O` holds and $I - O$ is the multiset union of $I - M$ and $M - O$. Finally, if `pick I D O` holds, then $I - O$ is the multiset containing one occurrence of D.*

The following lemma is proved by a simple induction on the structure of IO-proofs.

Lemma 6.18. *If $\Sigma :: \Psi; [I \parallel O] \vdash G$ has an IO-proof then `subcontext O I` holds. The same is true if $\Sigma :: \Psi; [I \parallel O] \Downarrow D \vdash G$ has an IO-proof.*

The following proposition shows that this approach to the lazy splitting of contexts is sound.

Proposition 6.19. *If $\Sigma :: \Psi; [I \parallel O] \vdash G$ has an IO-proof then $\Sigma :: \Psi; I - O \vdash G$ has a $\Downarrow \mathcal{L}_1$-proof. Similarly, if $\Sigma :: \Psi; [I \parallel O] \Downarrow D \vdash G$ has an IO-proof then $\Sigma :: \Psi; I - O \Downarrow D \vdash G$ has a $\Downarrow \mathcal{L}_1$-proof.*

Proof: Let Ξ be an IO-proof of $\Sigma :: \Psi; [I \parallel O] \vdash G$. We can convert Ξ to a $\Downarrow \mathcal{L}_1$-proof by simply replacing every occurrence of the pairing [$I \parallel O$] in Ξ with the multiset $I - O$. For example, consider the IO inference rule

$$\frac{\Sigma :: \Psi; [I \parallel M] \vdash G \qquad \Sigma :: \Psi; [M \parallel O] \Downarrow D \vdash A}{\Sigma :: \Psi; [I \parallel O] \Downarrow G \multimap D \vdash A} \multimap\text{L}.$$

If we set Γ_1 and Γ_2 to be, respectively, $I-M$ and $M-O$, then by Lemma 6.17, $I-O$ is the multiset union of Γ_1 and Γ_2. Thus, the rule above is converted to the $\Downarrow \mathcal{L}_1$ inference rule

$$\frac{\Sigma :: \Psi; \Gamma_1 \vdash G \qquad \Sigma :: \Psi; \Gamma_2 \Downarrow D \vdash A}{\Sigma :: \Psi; \Gamma_1, \Gamma_2 \Downarrow G \multimap D \vdash A} \multimap L.$$

The remaining cases all follow as simply as this case. □

6.7 Multiple-Conclusion Uniform Proofs

Our current treatment of linear logic proof theory via goal-directed search and backchaining captures only a part of linear logic. As we will see in Exercise 6.20 below, if we extend the $\mathcal{L}_1$ collection of connectives with $\bot$, we can encode all of linear logic's connectives. This fact suggests that adding the unit for the multiplicative disjunction might be interesting, especially since it has the negative polarity like the other connectives in $\mathcal{L}_1$. It also seems sensible to add not just $\bot$ but also $\invamp$ and ? since they are all negative polarity connectives and they represent the 0-ary, 2-ary, and "∞-ary" multiplicative disjunction. To that end, we define $\mathcal{L}_2$ to be the set of connectives

$$\mathcal{L}_2 = \mathcal{L}_1 \cup \{\bot, \invamp, ?\} = \{\top, \&, \multimap, \Rightarrow, \forall, \bot, \invamp, ?\},$$

and we say that an $\mathcal{L}_2$-formula is any first-order formula built using the $\mathcal{L}_2$ connectives. This presentation of linear logic using the logical connectives in $\mathcal{L}_2$ is called the *Forum presentation of linear logic* in Miller [1996]. The proof system we give for these additional connectives uses multiple-conclusion sequents.

Exercise 6.20. (‡) *Show that the set of connectives $\mathcal{L}_1 \cup \{\bot\}$ is complete for linear logic by defining the formulas $B^\bot$, 0, 1, $!B$, $B \oplus C$, $B \otimes C$, $\exists x.B$, $?B$, and $B \invamp C$ using only the connectives in $\mathcal{L}_1 \cup \{\bot\}$. Use the **L** proof system to present the required proofs of equivalence. Can you argue why it is the case that if $\mathcal{L}'$ is a proper subset of $\mathcal{L}_1$ then $\mathcal{L}' \cup \{\bot\}$ does not yield a complete set of connectives for linear logic.*

The set of connectives $\mathcal{L}_2$ is redundant since we can remove $\invamp$ and ? and still have a complete set of connectives for linear logic, as the provability of the following linear logic equivalences validate.

$$? B \multimap (B \multimap \bot) \Rightarrow \bot \qquad B \invamp C \multimap (B \multimap \bot) \multimap C.$$

Although the addition of $\invamp$ and ? is not strictly necessary, their presence will allow us to write natural specifications later. Also, their presence only slightly complicates the proof theory analysis in Chapter 7.

What should goal-directed search mean when there are possibly several formulas on the right of a sequent? The key aspect of goal-directed search that we wish to maintain is that goal formulas can be introduced without any restriction, no matter what other formulas are on the left or right of the sequent turnstile. Thus, it seems natural to expect that we should be able to *simultaneously* introduce all the logical connectives on the right of the sequent turnstile. Although the sequent calculus cannot deal directly with simultaneous rule application, reference to *permutations* of inference rules can indirectly address simultaneity. That is, we can require that if two or more right-introduction rules can derive a given sequent, then all possible orders of applying those right-introduction rules can, in fact, be done, and the resulting proofs are all equal modulo permutations of introduction rules.

More precisely, a cut-free sequent proof Ξ is *uniform* if for every subproof Ξ' of Ξ and for every non-atomic formula occurrence B in the right-hand side of the endsequent of Ξ', there is a proof Ξ'' that is equal to Ξ' up to permutations of inference rules and is such that the last inference rule in Ξ'' introduces the top-level logical connective of B. This notion of uniform proof clearly extends the one given in Section 5.1. We similarly extend the notion of *abstract logic programming language* to be a triple $\langle \mathcal{D}, \mathcal{G}, \vdash \rangle$ such that for all sequents with formulas from $\mathcal{D}$ on the left and formulas from $\mathcal{G}$ on the right, that sequent has a proof if and only if it has a uniform proof. Instead of discussing multiple-conclusion uniform proofs as a separate concept, we now introduce a new focused sequent system that will yield a specific kind of uniform proof system.

The $\Downarrow \mathcal{L}_2$-proof system, given in Figure 6.11, contains sequents having the form

$$\Sigma :: \Psi; \Gamma \vdash \Delta; \Upsilon \quad \text{and} \quad \Sigma :: \Psi; \Gamma \Downarrow B \vdash \Delta; \Upsilon,$$

where Σ is a signature, and Γ, Δ, Ψ and Υ are multiset of Σ-formulas from $\mathcal{L}_2$. These two sequents have Ψ as its *left-unbounded zone*, Γ as its *left-bounded zone*, Δ as its *right-bounded zone*, and Υ as its *right-unbounded zone*. The intended meanings of these two sequents in linear logic are

$$\Sigma :: \,!\Psi, \Gamma \vdash \Delta, ?\Upsilon \quad \text{and} \quad \Sigma :: \,!\Psi, \Gamma, B \vdash \Delta, ?\Upsilon,$$

6.7 MULTIPLE-CONCLUSION UNIFORM PROOFS

respectively. The $\Downarrow \mathcal{L}_2$-proof system contains right rules only for sequents of the form $\Sigma :: \Psi; \Gamma \vdash \Delta; \Upsilon$. The syntactic variable $\mathcal{A}$ used in Figure 6.11 denotes a multiset of atomic formulas. As we have seen before, left-introduction rules are applied only to the formula between the $\Downarrow$ and the $\vdash$ in its conclusion.

Returning to the terminology in Section 3.3, the right introduction rules are all additive (assuming that the formula introduced is the subject occurrence) while the left-introduction rules are all multiplicative (assuming that the formula introduced is the subject occurrence).

The **L** proof system can serve as an (unfocused) proof system for $\mathcal{L}_2$: We simply need to replace the implications in $\mathcal{L}_2$-formulas with their definitions, using the $(\cdot)^\circ$ function from Proposition 6.13. Given the intended interpretation of sequents in $\mathcal{L}_2$, the following soundness theorem can be proved by a simple induction on the structure of $\Downarrow \mathcal{L}_2$-proofs.

Theorem 6.21 (Soundness). *If the sequent* $\Sigma :: \Psi; \Gamma \vdash \Delta; \Upsilon$ *has a* $\Downarrow \mathcal{L}_2$-*proof then* $!\Psi^\circ, \Gamma^\circ \vdash \Delta^\circ, ?\Upsilon^\circ$ *has an **L** proof. If the sequent* $\Sigma :: \Psi; \Gamma \Downarrow B \vdash \mathcal{A}; \Upsilon$ *has a* $\Downarrow \mathcal{L}_2$-*proof then* $!\Psi^\circ, \Gamma^\circ, B^\circ \vdash \Delta^\circ, ?\Upsilon^\circ$ *has an **L** proof.*

We will prove in Chapter 7 that three kinds of cut rules are admissible in $\Downarrow \mathcal{L}_2$ and use that fact to prove the completeness of $\Downarrow \mathcal{L}_2$-proof.

Exercise 6.22. *The $\Downarrow \mathcal{L}_2$-proof rule for $?L$ is unlike the other left-introduction rules in that it does not maintain focus as one moves from the conclusion to a premise. Consider the following variation to that rule.*

$$\frac{\Sigma :: \Psi; \cdot \Downarrow B \vdash \cdot; \Upsilon}{\Sigma :: \Psi; \cdot \Downarrow ?B \vdash \cdot; \Upsilon} \; ?L'$$

Show that if we replace $?L$ with $?L'$ then the resulting proof system is no longer complete. Hint: consider the formula $?(a \multimap b) \multimap ?(a \multimap b)$.

Exercise 6.23. *The $\mathcal{L}_2$ presentation of linear logic uses the 8 logical connectives $\{\top, \&, \multimap, \Rightarrow, \forall, \bot, \invamp, ?\}$. Show that all the 64 pairings of the right-introduction rules for these 8 connectives permute over each other.*

$$\frac{}{\Sigma :: \Psi; \Gamma \vdash \top, \Delta; \Upsilon} \top R$$

$$\frac{\Sigma :: \Psi; \Gamma \vdash B, \Delta; \Upsilon \quad \Sigma :: \Psi; \Gamma \vdash C, \Delta; \Upsilon}{\Sigma :: \Psi; \Gamma \vdash B \& C, \Delta; \Upsilon} \&R$$

$$\frac{\Sigma :: \Psi; \Gamma \vdash \Delta; \Upsilon}{\Sigma :: \Psi; \Gamma \vdash \bot, \Delta; \Upsilon} \bot R \qquad \frac{\Sigma :: \Psi; \Gamma \vdash B, C, \Delta; \Upsilon}{\Sigma :: \Psi; \Gamma \vdash B \mathbin{\mathspace} C, \Delta; \Upsilon} \mathbin{\mathspace} R$$

$$\frac{\Sigma :: \Psi; B, \Gamma \vdash C, \Delta; \Upsilon}{\Sigma :: \Psi; \Gamma \vdash B \multimap C, \Delta; \Upsilon} \multimap R \qquad \frac{\Sigma :: B, \Psi; \Gamma \vdash C, \Delta; \Upsilon}{\Sigma :: \Psi; \Gamma \vdash B \Rightarrow C, \Delta; \Upsilon} \Rightarrow R$$

$$\frac{y:\tau, \Sigma :: \Psi; \Gamma \vdash B[y/x], \Delta; \Upsilon}{\Sigma :: \Psi; \Gamma \vdash \forall_\tau x.B, \Delta; \Upsilon} \forall R \qquad \frac{\Sigma :: \Psi; \Gamma \vdash \Delta; B, \Upsilon}{\Sigma :: \Psi; \Gamma \vdash ?B, \Delta; \Upsilon} ?R$$

$$\frac{\Sigma :: \Psi; \Gamma \Downarrow B \vdash \mathcal{A}; \Upsilon}{\Sigma :: \Psi; B, \Gamma \vdash \mathcal{A}; \Upsilon} decide_l$$

$$\frac{\Sigma :: B, \Psi; \Gamma \Downarrow B \vdash \mathcal{A}; \Upsilon}{\Sigma :: B, \Psi; \Gamma \vdash \mathcal{A}; \Upsilon} decide! \qquad \frac{\Sigma :: \Psi; \Gamma \vdash \mathcal{A}, B; B, \Upsilon}{\Sigma :: \Psi; \Gamma \vdash \mathcal{A}; B, \Upsilon} decide?$$

$$\frac{}{\Sigma :: \Psi; \cdot \Downarrow A \vdash A; \Upsilon} init \qquad \frac{}{\Sigma :: \Psi; \cdot \Downarrow A \vdash \cdot; A, \Upsilon} init?$$

$$\frac{}{\Sigma :: \Psi; \cdot \Downarrow \bot \vdash \cdot; \Upsilon} \bot L \qquad \frac{\Sigma :: \Psi; B \vdash \cdot; \Upsilon}{\Sigma :: \Psi; \cdot \Downarrow ?B \vdash \cdot; \Upsilon} ?L$$

$$\frac{\Sigma :: \Psi; \Gamma \Downarrow B_i \vdash \mathcal{A}; \Upsilon}{\Sigma :: \Psi; \Gamma \Downarrow B_1 \& B_2 \vdash \mathcal{A}; \Upsilon} \&L_i \qquad \frac{\Sigma :: \Psi; \Gamma \Downarrow B[t/x] \vdash \mathcal{A}; \Upsilon}{\Sigma :: \Psi; \Gamma \Downarrow \forall_\tau x.B \vdash \mathcal{A}; \Upsilon} \forall L$$

$$\frac{\Sigma :: \Psi; \Gamma_1 \Downarrow B \vdash \mathcal{A}_1; \Upsilon \quad \Sigma :: \Psi; \Gamma_2 \Downarrow C \vdash \mathcal{A}_2; \Upsilon}{\Sigma :: \Psi; \Gamma_1, \Gamma_2 \Downarrow B \mathbin{\mathspace} C \vdash \mathcal{A}_1, \mathcal{A}_2; \Upsilon} \mathbin{\mathspace} L$$

$$\frac{\Sigma :: \Psi; \Gamma_1 \vdash \mathcal{A}_1, B; \Upsilon \quad \Sigma :: \Psi; \Gamma_2 \Downarrow C \vdash \mathcal{A}_2; \Upsilon}{\Sigma :: \Psi; \Gamma_1, \Gamma_2 \Downarrow B \multimap C \vdash \mathcal{A}_1, \mathcal{A}_2; \Upsilon} \multimap L$$

$$\frac{\Sigma :: \Psi; \cdot \vdash B; \Upsilon \quad \Sigma :: \Psi; \Gamma \Downarrow C \vdash \mathcal{A}; \Upsilon}{\Sigma :: \Psi; \Gamma \Downarrow B \Rightarrow C \vdash \mathcal{A}; \Upsilon} \Rightarrow L$$

The rule ∀R has the proviso that y is not in the signature Σ, and the rule ∀L has the proviso that t is a Σ-term of type τ. In $\&L_i$, $i = 1$ or $i = 2$. The syntactic variable $\mathcal{A}$ ranges over multisets of atomic formulas.

Figure 6.11 The $\Downarrow \mathcal{L}_2$-proof system.

Exercise 6.24. *Assume that a, b, c, d are all propositional constants (i.e., they have type o). Prove the following formulas using the $\Downarrow \mathcal{L}_2$-proof system. Note that proving the formula B using $\Downarrow \mathcal{L}_2$ means proving the sequent $\cdot :: \cdot\, ; \, \cdot \vdash B\,; \cdot$.*

1. $((a \multimap \bot) \multimap \bot) \multimap a$
2. $(d \multimap (a \,\invamp\, b)) \multimap (1 \multimap (c \,\invamp\, d)) \multimap (a \,\invamp\, b \,\invamp\, c)$
3. $?b \multimap (b \multimap \bot) \Rightarrow \bot$ and $((b \multimap \bot) \Rightarrow \bot) \multimap ?b$
4. $(b \,\invamp\, c) \multimap (b \multimap \bot) \multimap c$ and $((b \multimap \bot) \multimap c) \multimap (b \,\invamp\, c)$

Exercise 6.25. *Show that the contrapositive of a linear implication is equivalent to the linear implication. In particular, provide a $\Downarrow \mathcal{L}_2$-proof of $(a \multimap b) \circ\!\!-\!\!\circ ((b \multimap \bot) \multimap (a \multimap \bot))$ where a and b are constants.*

By examining the $\Downarrow \mathcal{L}_2$-proof system, we can see that the dynamics of proof search in this proof system is a simple generalization of the dynamics described for $\Downarrow \mathcal{L}_1$. That is, during the search for a $\Downarrow \mathcal{L}_2$-proof, the signature and unbounded zones (on the left and right) can grow, while the changes in the bounded zones (on the left and right) can change in more general and arbitrary ways.

6.8 Conservativity Results

We say that a sequent is an $\mathcal{L}_1$-*sequent* if all formulas in that sequent (with or without a $\Downarrow$) are $\mathcal{L}_1$-formulas. Exercises 6.26 and 6.27 show that a $\Downarrow \mathcal{L}_2$-proof of an endsequent that is a single-conclusion $\mathcal{L}_1$-sequent contains only single-conclusion sequents.

Exercise 6.26. (‡) *Prove that there is no $\Downarrow \mathcal{L}_2$-proof of an $\mathcal{L}_1$ sequent with an empty right side.*

Exercise 6.27. (‡) *Prove that if Ξ is a $\Downarrow \mathcal{L}_2$-proof of a single-conclusion $\mathcal{L}_1$-sequent then all sequents in Ξ are single-conclusion sequents.*

The $\Downarrow \mathcal{L}_1$-*proof system* is defined as the $\Downarrow \mathcal{L}_2$-proof system of Figure 6.11 but without the introduction rules for $\bot$, $\invamp$, and $?$ and without the *init*? and *decide*? rules. The following proposition is a simple consequence of the observations in Exercises 6.26 and 6.27.

> **Proposition 6.28** ($\Downarrow \mathcal{L}_2$ is conservative over $\Downarrow \mathcal{L}_1$). *If B is an $\mathcal{L}_1$ Σ-formula such that $\Sigma :: \cdot; \cdot \vdash B; \cdot$ has the $\Downarrow \mathcal{L}_2$-proof Ξ then Ξ is a $\Downarrow \mathcal{L}_1$-proof.*

In Section 5.3, we defined the set of connectives $\mathcal{L}_0$ to be $\{t, \wedge, \supset, \forall\}$. Now that we have seen linear logic, it seems that this set can also be viewed as being $\{\top, \&, \Rightarrow, \forall\}$. If we allow this renaming of intuitionistic connectives to be these linear logic connectives, we have the following conservative proposition. We say that a sequent is an $\mathcal{L}_0$-*sequent* if all formulas in that sequent (with or without a $\Downarrow$) are $\mathcal{L}_0$-formulas (assuming this renaming of connectives).

> **Proposition 6.29** ($\Downarrow \mathcal{L}_2$ is conservative over $\Downarrow \mathcal{L}_0$). *If B is an $\mathcal{L}_0$ Σ-formula such that $\Sigma :: \cdot; \cdot \vdash B; \cdot$ has the $\Downarrow \mathcal{L}_2$-proof Ξ then Ξ is a $\Downarrow \mathcal{L}_0$-proof.*

It is a consequence of these propositions that the proofs in $\Downarrow \mathcal{L}_2$ are also proofs in the $\Downarrow \mathcal{L}_1$ and $\Downarrow \mathcal{L}_0$ proof systems when their endsequents are $\mathcal{L}_1$-sequents and $\mathcal{L}_0$-sequents, respectively.

6.9 Generalizing Synthetic Inference Rules

We generalize two notions introduced in Section 5.7. A *border* sequent is a sequent of the form $\Sigma :: \Psi; \Gamma \vdash \mathcal{A}; \Upsilon$, where the right-bounded zone contains only atoms. (Since occurrences of Σ in sequent denoting binders, we shall not refer to it as a zone.) A *synthetic inference rule* is then the inference rule that results from moving from a border sequent upwards through a *decide$_l$* or *decide*! rule, followed by a left-introduction phase and then a right-introduction phase: If the latter has any open premises, these are necessarily border phases. Schematically, a synthetic inference rule can be seen as composed of focused inference rules as follows.

6.9 GENERALIZING SYNTHETIC INFERENCE RULES

$$
\cfrac{
  \cfrac{
    \cfrac{
      \cfrac{\ldots \quad \Sigma, \Sigma' :: \Psi, \Psi'; \Gamma' \vdash \mathcal{A}'; \Upsilon, \Upsilon' \quad \ldots}{\vdots \quad \ldots \quad \vdots} \text{right-intro phase}
    }{} \text{left-intro phase}
  }{\vdots \quad \vdots \quad \vdots}
}{\Sigma :: \Psi; \Gamma \vdash \mathcal{A}; \Upsilon} \; decide_l \text{ or } decide\,!
$$

The *decide?* rule can also generate synthetic inferences rule but the internal structure of such a rule has an empty left-introduction phase.

Chapter 8 will present numerous examples of logic programs using $\mathcal{L}_2$ formulas that illustrate features of linear logic. We give a simple example here. Assume that we would like to move from, say, step1 to step2 in a computation (proof search), and in the process of making that change, we wish to flip a switch. In other words, we would like to write a logic specification that could justify the following inference rules.

$$\frac{\Psi; \Gamma, \mathtt{on} \vdash \mathtt{step2}}{\Psi; \Gamma, \mathtt{off} \vdash \mathtt{step1}} \qquad \frac{\Psi; \Gamma, \mathtt{off} \vdash \mathtt{step2}}{\Psi; \Gamma, \mathtt{on} \vdash \mathtt{step1}}$$

Using the Prolog-style syntax described above, the following two clauses implement these rules.

```
step1 :- off, on -o step2.
step1 :- on,  off -o step2.
```

To illustrate this specification, assume that the formulas

off $\multimap$ (on $\multimap$ step2) $\multimap$ step1   and   on $\multimap$ (off $\multimap$ step2) $\multimap$ step1

are members of Ψ. The following partial derivation in $\mathcal{L}_2$ justifies the second of these rules above.

$$
\cfrac{
  \cfrac{
    \cfrac{\cfrac{\overline{\Psi; \cdot \Downarrow \mathtt{on} \vdash \mathtt{on}} \; init}{\Psi; \mathtt{on} \vdash \mathtt{on}} \; decide_l \quad \cfrac{\cfrac{\cfrac{\Psi; \Gamma, \mathtt{off} \vdash \mathtt{step2}}{\Psi; \Gamma \vdash \mathtt{off} \multimap \mathtt{step2}} \; \multimap R \quad \overline{\Psi; \cdot \Downarrow \mathtt{step1} \vdash \mathtt{step1}} \; init}{\Psi; \Gamma \Downarrow (\mathtt{off} \multimap \mathtt{step2}) \multimap \mathtt{step1} \vdash \mathtt{step1}} \; \multimap L}{} \; \multimap L}{\Psi; \Gamma, \mathtt{on} \Downarrow \mathtt{on} \multimap (\mathtt{off} \multimap \mathtt{step2}) \multimap \mathtt{step1} \vdash \mathtt{step1}}
  }{\Psi; \Gamma, \mathtt{on} \vdash \mathtt{step1}} \; decide\,!
}{}
$$

The two occurrences of $\multimap$L require splitting the bounded zone in their conclusions. There can be many possible splittings of these multisets, depending on the size of Γ. However, in this particular setting, the bound context can only be split one way: All other splitting would not have allowed for completing the phase and, thus, completing the left-introduction phase. If $\Rightarrow$ replaced $\multimap$ in this example, the resulting inference rules would be

$$\frac{\Psi,\mathtt{off},\mathtt{on};\cdot \vdash \mathtt{step2}}{\Psi,\mathtt{off};\cdot \vdash \mathtt{step1}} \qquad \frac{\Psi,\mathtt{on},\mathtt{off};\cdot \vdash \mathtt{step2}}{\Psi,\mathtt{on};\cdot \vdash \mathtt{step1}}.$$

Clearly, this would be a poor implementation of a switch.

The partial derivation given above is not, however, a synthetic rule since it contains two decide rules: Rather, it is composed of two synthetic rules. Given that the $\Downarrow \mathcal{L}_2$-proof system has multisets on the left and the right sides of sequents, it is possible to rewrite this example by putting the state of the switch on the right of the sequent instead of on the left. In other words, we would like to write a logic specification that justifies the following inference rules.

$$\frac{\Psi;\Gamma \vdash \mathtt{step2},\mathtt{on},\Delta;\Upsilon}{\Psi;\Gamma \vdash \mathtt{step1},\mathtt{off},\Delta;\Upsilon} \qquad \frac{\Psi;\Gamma \vdash \mathtt{step2},\mathtt{off},\Delta;\Upsilon}{\Psi;\Gamma \vdash \mathtt{step1},\mathtt{on},\Delta;\Upsilon}.$$

We introduce the symbol || into our λProlog-style syntax to denote $\mathbin{\text{⅋}}$. The following two clauses implement these rules.

```
step1 || off :- on  || step2.
step1 || on  :- off || step2.
```

These clauses denote the logical formulas

(on ⅋ step2) $\multimap$ (step1 ⅋ off)   and   (off ⅋ step2) $\multimap$ (step1 ⅋ on).

In this example, the toggling of a switch is achieved via synthetic inference rules and not a combination of two of them.

6.10 Bibliographic Notes

The material in Section 6.1 is based on text by Liang and Miller [2024] while the material in Section 6.2 is based on a blog post by Miller [2022a]. Additional observations about interactions between the structural rules and cut-elimination are given by Danos et al. [1997] and Lafont in [Girard et al., 1989].

The informal semantics given in Section 6.3.1 can be elaborated into a more extensive (and still informal) semantics often called Lafont's *restaurant semantics* for linear logic: See Okada [1998]. Girard [1987] refers to ! as "of course" and ? as "why not".

6.10 Bibliographic Notes

The notion of the *polarity* of logical connectives that we have used here is due to Andreoli [1990, 1992] and Girard [1993]. Those papers also introduced the notion of multi-zone sequents to treat bounded and unbounded zones in sequents for linear logic.

As Exercise 6.5 shows, linear logic can have a collection of different exponentials. A presentation of linear logic with such additional operators was first given in Danos et al. [1993]. Since these additional operators do not necessarily need to permit weakening and contraction, these additional operators do not necessarily satisfy the exponential laws (as described in Exercise 6.3). For these reasons, such additional operators have been called *subexponentials* in Nigam and Miller [2009]: That paper also illustrates how subexponentials can enhance the expressiveness of proof search specifications based on linear logic (see also Chaudhuri [2018], Liang and Miller [2015], and Olarte et al. [2015]).

When Girard [1987] introduced linear logic, he also introduced *proof nets* as a proof system specifically designed to capture parallelism in proofs better than sequent calculus proofs. To capture parallelism in proof construction in a sequent calculus setting, Delande and Miller [2008] introduced the notion of *multifocusing* in which more than one formula can be focused on at a time. Multifocusing has been used in Chaudhuri et al. [2008a] and Chaudhuri et al. [2016] to capture parallel actions within a proof structure.

Exercise 6.6 illustrated a property of formulas B for which $B \multimap !B$ is provable. If we restrict B to come from MALL, then few formulas have this property. In full linear logic, any formula of the form $!C$ has this property since $!C \multimap !!C$ is provable. If one extends MALL with least fixed points and term equality (thus moving linear logic closer to model checking and arithmetic), then many other formulas satisfy that equivalence: See Baelde [2012], Baelde and Miller [2007], and Heath and Miller [2019].

An implementation of a programming language based on $\Downarrow \mathcal{L}_1$ was described in Hodas and Tamura [2001]. $\mathcal{L}_2$ has been given a couple of implementations: See López and Pimentel [1998] and Urban [1997]. An important part of these implementations is the *lazy splitting of multisets* during proof search, a technique described in Section 6.6. This technique was presented by Hodas and Miller [1991, 1994] and extended in Cervesato et al. [2000b], Cervesato et al. [1996], and Hodas et al. [1998]. Mackie [1994] described type inference for a linear functional programming language using a similar technique.

The $\Downarrow \mathcal{L}_2$ proof system uses multiple-conclusion sequents, similar to Gentzen's *LK* for classical logic, whereas $\Downarrow \mathcal{L}_1$ uses single-conclusion sequents, reminiscent of *LJ* for intuitionistic logic. Consequently, $\Downarrow \mathcal{L}_2$ is frequently referred to as *classical linear logic* and $\Downarrow \mathcal{L}_1$ as *intuitionistic linear logic* (see, for instance, Hodas and Miller [1994] and Laurent [2018]). A key distinction lies in the origin of the single-conclusion property. In Gentzen's work, intuitionistic logic is obtained by restricting *LK* to single conclusions. In contrast, $\Downarrow \mathcal{L}_1$'s single-conclusion property is a consequence of its inherent structure – specifically, its reduced set of connectives – rather than a deliberate restriction of $\Downarrow \mathcal{L}_2$ (Proposition 6.28).

Although the Curry paradox regarding mixing logical connectives and untyped λ-conversion can be avoided by typing, it can also be avoided if contraction is not available in the logic. In particular, the problematic λ-term $\lambda x.(x \Rightarrow f)$ mentioned in Exercise 2.5 is no longer problematic if we write $\lambda x.(x \multimap \mathbf{0})$ and work in the subset of linear logic without the exponentials: See Grishin [1981], Girard [1992], and Schroeder-Heister [1993].

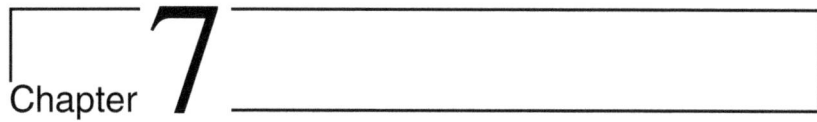

Chapter 7

Formal Properties of Linear Logic Focused Proofs

This chapter presents the main proof theory results regarding the presentation of first-order linear logic using the connectives $\mathcal{L}_2 = \{\top, \&, \multimap, \Rightarrow, \forall, \bot, \mathbin{\bindnasrepma} \mathbin{?}\}$. Readers interested mainly in specifying logic programs using linear logic can skip this chapter and continue with Chapter 8.

The outline of this chapter, which follows roughly the outline of Section 5.5 for the $\mathcal{L}_0$ subset of intuitionistic logic, is the following.

1. Define paths in $\mathcal{L}_2$-formulas and their associated sequents.
2. Use paths to describe the right-introduction and left-introduction phases.
3. Prove the admissibility of the non-atomic initial rule in $\Downarrow \mathcal{L}_2$.
4. Add four cut rules to $\Downarrow \mathcal{L}_2$ and then prove that they can be eliminated.
5. Prove the completeness of $\Downarrow \mathcal{L}_2$ with respect of the proof system **L**.
6. Prove the cut-elimination theorem for the **L** proof system.

We will not explicitly state the admissibility of cut rules for $\Downarrow \mathcal{L}_1$-proofs nor the completeness of $\Downarrow \mathcal{L}_1$-proofs for **L**, since these results follow immediately from the corresponding and stronger theorems related to the cut-elimination theorem for $\Downarrow^+ \mathcal{L}_2$-proofs (Theorem 7.15) and the completeness of $\Downarrow \mathcal{L}_2$-proofs (Theorem 7.18).

7.1 Generalized Paths and Introduction Phases

We move the notion of a path given in Section 5.5 from $\mathcal{L}_0$-formulas to $\mathcal{L}_2$-formulas. In particular, we define the relationship $\cdot \uparrow \cdot$ on $\mathcal{L}_2$-formulas as follows (here, A ranges over atomic formulas).

$$\frac{}{A \uparrow A} \quad \frac{B_1 \uparrow P}{B_1 \mathbin{\&} B_2 \uparrow P} \quad \frac{B_2 \uparrow P}{B_1 \mathbin{\&} B_2 \uparrow P} \quad \frac{B \uparrow P}{C \Rightarrow B \uparrow C \Rightarrow P} \quad \frac{B \uparrow P}{\forall_\tau x.B \uparrow \forall_\tau x.P}$$

$$\frac{}{\bot \uparrow \bot} \quad \frac{}{?B \uparrow ?B} \quad \frac{B \uparrow P}{C \multimap B \uparrow C \multimap P} \quad \frac{B_1 \uparrow P_1 \quad B_2 \uparrow P_2}{B_1 \mathbin{\bindnasrepma} B_2 \uparrow P_1 \mathbin{\bindnasrepma} P_2}$$

The elimination of $\mathbin{\&}$ from paths can be justified using the provability of the following formulas.

$$C \mathbin{\bindnasrepma} (B_1 \mathbin{\&} B_2) \mathbin{\circ\!\!-\!\!\circ} (C \mathbin{\bindnasrepma} B_1) \mathbin{\&} (C \mathbin{\bindnasrepma} B_2)$$
$$C \multimap (B_1 \mathbin{\&} B_2) \mathbin{\circ\!\!-\!\!\circ} (C \multimap B_1) \mathbin{\&} (C \multimap B_2)$$
$$C \Rightarrow (B_1 \mathbin{\&} B_2) \mathbin{\circ\!\!-\!\!\circ} (C \Rightarrow B_1) \mathbin{\&} (C \Rightarrow B_2)$$
$$\forall x. (B_1 \mathbin{\&} B_2) \mathbin{\circ\!\!-\!\!\circ} (\forall x. B_1) \mathbin{\&} (\forall x. B_2)$$

By using these equivalences (and other equivalences from Section 5.5 related to $\Rightarrow$ and $\forall$), it is possible to pull various occurrences of $\mathbin{\&}$ within a formula to the outside of the formula. That is, we have the provability of $B \mathbin{\circ\!\!-\!\!\circ} \mathbin{\&}_{B \uparrow P} P$.

Paths have a more complex structure in this setting than in Section 5.5. Fortunately, paths have a reasonably simple normal form. Using the provability of the formulas

$$B \mathbin{\bindnasrepma} (\forall x.C) \mathbin{\circ\!\!-\!\!\circ} \forall x.(B \mathbin{\bindnasrepma} C)$$
$$B \multimap (\forall x.C) \mathbin{\circ\!\!-\!\!\circ} \forall x.(B \multimap C)$$
$$B \Rightarrow (\forall x.C) \mathbin{\circ\!\!-\!\!\circ} \forall x.(B \Rightarrow C),$$

a path can be written in the form $\forall x_1. \ldots \forall x_n. P'$ where $n \geq 0$, and every occurrence of $\forall$ in P' occurs in the scope of a $?$ or to the left of either $\multimap$ or $\Rightarrow$. Similarly, using the provability of the formulas

$$(B \multimap C_1) \mathbin{\bindnasrepma} C_2 \mathbin{\circ\!\!-\!\!\circ} B \multimap (C_1 \mathbin{\bindnasrepma} C_2)$$
$$(B \Rightarrow C_1) \mathbin{\bindnasrepma} C_2 \mathbin{\circ\!\!-\!\!\circ} B \Rightarrow (C_1 \mathbin{\bindnasrepma} C_2)$$
$$B \multimap C \Rightarrow D \mathbin{\circ\!\!-\!\!\circ} C \Rightarrow B \multimap D,$$

7.1 Generalized Paths and Introduction Phases

and the unit rule $B \,\mathfrak{N}\, \bot \multimap B$, and the commutativity of $\mathfrak{N}$, all paths have the following normal form,

$$\forall \bar{x}.[C_1 \Rightarrow \ldots \Rightarrow C_n \Rightarrow B_1 \multimap \ldots \multimap B_m \multimap A_1 \,\mathfrak{N}\ldots \mathfrak{N}\, A_p \,\mathfrak{N}\, ? E_1 \ldots \mathfrak{N}\, ? E_q]$$

where n, m, p, q are non-negative integers, $A_1, \ldots, A_p$ are atomic formulas, $B_1, \ldots, B_m, C_1, \ldots, C_n, E_1, \ldots, E_q$ are $\mathcal{L}_2$-formulas, and $\forall \bar{x}$ is a list of universally quantified variables. If a path P has the normal form above, then we say that the multiset $\{C_1, \ldots, C_n\}$ is its *intuitionistic arguments*, the multiset $\{B_1, \ldots, B_m\}$ is its *linear arguments*, the multiset $\{A_1, \ldots, A_p\}$ is its *atomic targets*, and the multiset $\{E_1, \ldots, E_q\}$ is its *?-targets*. Finally, $\bar{x}$ is the list of *bound variables* of P (we assume that all these bound variables are distinct and subject to α-conversion). Since these various components of the normal form of a path are multisets, this decomposition of a path is unique. We shall also display this normal form as the sequent

$$\bar{x} :: C_1, \ldots, C_n; B_1, \ldots, B_m \vdash A_1, \ldots, A_p; E_1, \ldots, E_q.$$

Finally, we say that this sequent is *associated* to this path.

Consider the shape of the right-introduction phase and the left-introduction phase when applied to the formula

$$\forall \bar{x}(C \Rightarrow B_1 \multimap B_2 \multimap A_1 \,\mathfrak{N}\, A_2 \,\mathfrak{N}\, ? E),$$

which is its own path formula since it has no occurrences of &. The right-introduction phase can be written schematically as follows.

$$\frac{\bar{x} :: C; B_1, B_2 \vdash A_1, A_2; E}{\cdot :: \cdot; \cdot \vdash \forall \bar{x}(C \Rightarrow B_1 \multimap B_2 \multimap A_1 \,\mathfrak{N}\, A_2 \,\mathfrak{N}\, ? E); \cdot}$$

Note that the unique premise of this phase ends with the sequent associated with that path. Of course, if we place any items in any of the zones in the conclusion, they should also be placed into the same zone in the premise. The following derivation is the left-introduction phase that results from focusing on this same formula.

$$\frac{\Psi; \cdot \vdash \hat{C}; \Upsilon \quad \Psi; \Gamma_1 \vdash \hat{B}_1, \mathcal{A}_1; \Upsilon \quad \Psi; \Gamma_2 \vdash \hat{B}_2, \mathcal{A}_2; \Upsilon \quad \Psi; \hat{E} \vdash \cdot; \Upsilon}{\Psi; \Gamma_1, \Gamma_2 \Downarrow \forall \bar{x}(C \Rightarrow B_1 \multimap B_2 \multimap A_1 \,\mathfrak{N}\, A_2 \,\mathfrak{N}\, ? E) \vdash \hat{A}_1, \hat{A}_2, \mathcal{A}_1, \mathcal{A}_2; \Upsilon}.$$

Here, $\hat{A}_1, \hat{A}_2, \hat{B}_1, \hat{B}_2, \hat{C}, \hat{E}$ are the result of applying θ to the formulas in A_1, A_2, B_1, B_2, C, E, and θ is the substitution for the variables $\bar{x}$ that tabulates the substitutions used in the $\forall L$ rules.

We can view the construction of the right-introduction phase as a rewriting process. The objects that we rewrite are multisets of sequents, all of the form $\Sigma :: \Psi; \Gamma \vdash \Delta; \Upsilon$. One-step rewriting is given as follows. Select some member of this multiset: That is, write the given multiset of sequents as $\mathcal{M} \cup \{S\}$. Next, consider any right-introduction rule with conclusion S and the multiset of premises $\mathcal{M}'$ (this multiset will contain 0, 1, or 2 elements). The multiset union $\mathcal{M} \cup \mathcal{M}'$ is the result of this rewrite. When this relation holds, we write

$$\mathcal{M} \cup \{S\} \to \mathcal{M} \cup \mathcal{M}'.$$

The following observations are easy to establish about this notion of rewriting.

1. A multiset of border sequents does not rewrite. In this sense, collections of border sequents are normal forms.
2. Define the size of sequents of the form $\Sigma :: \Psi; \Gamma \vdash \Delta; \Upsilon$ to be the number of occurrences of logical connectives in Δ, and define the size of a multiset $\mathcal{M}$ to be the sum of the sizes of all sequents in $\mathcal{M}$. The length of a series of rewritings starting with $\mathcal{M}$ is bounded by the size of $\mathcal{M}$. Thus, this rewriting system is always terminating.

We wish to prove that every right-introduction phase with a fixed endsequent has the same multiset of premises. Regarding rewriting, we want to prove that our rewriting system is *confluent*. As is well-known, we only need to prove that our system is *locally confluence* to conclude that our terminating rewrite system is confluence. In our situation, proving local confluence means proving that if $\mathcal{M}$ rewrites in one step to $\mathcal{M}_1$ and to $\mathcal{M}_2$, then there exists $\mathcal{M}_0$ such that both $\mathcal{M}_1$ and $\mathcal{M}_2$ rewrite to $\mathcal{M}_0$.

Proposition 7.1. *The rewriting systems encoding the right-introduction phase are confluent.*

Proof: As we commented above, we only need to show local confluence. Thus, assume that $\mathcal{M}$ rewrites in one step to $\mathcal{M}_1$ and $\mathcal{M}_2$. We now need to prove that there exists $\mathcal{M}_0$ such that both $\mathcal{M}_1$ and $\mathcal{M}_2$ rewrite to $\mathcal{M}_0$. If the two rewrites $\mathcal{M} \to \mathcal{M}_1$ and $\mathcal{M} \to \mathcal{M}_2$ select two different sequents to apply introduction rules, then $\mathcal{M}_0$ is just the result of selecting the other sequent for rewriting in both $\mathcal{M}_1$ and $\mathcal{M}_2$. Otherwise, these two rewrites select the same sequent in $\mathcal{M}$, say, $\Sigma :: \Psi; \Gamma \vdash \Delta; \Upsilon$. Thus, there are two non-atomic formulas in Δ that are introduced. For example, the multiset

7.1 Generalized Paths and Introduction Phases

$$\mathcal{M} \cup \{\Sigma :: \Psi; \Gamma \vdash B \,⅋\, C, D \,\&\, E, \Delta'; \Upsilon\}$$

can be rewritten to both $\mathcal{M} \cup \{\Sigma :: \Psi; \Gamma \vdash B, C, D \,\&\, E, \Delta'; \Upsilon\}$ and to

$$\mathcal{M} \cup \{\Sigma :: \Psi; \Gamma \vdash B \,⅋\, C, D, \Delta'; \Upsilon, \; \Sigma :: \Psi; \Gamma \vdash B \,⅋\, C, E, \Delta'; \Upsilon\}.$$

Since the right-introduction rules for $⅋$ and $\&$ permute over each other, the desired common redex $\mathcal{M}_0$ is simply

$$\mathcal{M} \cup \{\Sigma :: \Psi; \Gamma \vdash B, C, D, \Delta'; \Upsilon, \; \Sigma :: \Psi; \Gamma \vdash B, C, E, \Delta'; \Upsilon\}.$$

All other cases can be similarly proved since all right-introduction rules for the $\mathcal{L}_2$ connectives permute over each other (Exercise 6.23). Thus, local confluence is guaranteed by the permutation of inference rules. □

The next proposition follows from the rewriting argument just given: The right-introduction phase can select one particular formula to decompose entirely before considering other formulas in the endsequent.

Proposition 7.2. *Consider a* $\Downarrow \mathcal{L}_2$*-proof* Ξ *of the sequent* $\Sigma :: \Psi; \Gamma \vdash G, \Delta; \Upsilon$. *There is a* $\Downarrow \mathcal{L}_2$*-proof* Ξ' *of this same sequent that differs only in permutations of right-introduction rules such that the formula G is decomposed first. More specially, that right-introduction phase can be written as*

$$\cfrac{\left\{ \cfrac{\Xi_i}{\Sigma, \Sigma_i :: \Psi, \Psi_i; \Gamma, \Gamma_i \vdash \mathcal{A}_i, \Delta; \Upsilon, \Upsilon_i} \right\}_{G \uparrow P_i}}{\Sigma :: \Psi; \Gamma \vdash G, \Delta; \Upsilon}$$

where the path P_i is associated with the sequent $\Sigma_i :: \Psi_i; \Gamma_i \vdash \mathcal{A}_i; \Upsilon_i$ and where Ξ_i a proof of the ith premise.

As regards left-introduction phases, we note that every premise of a left-introduction rule with endsequent $\Sigma :: \Psi; \Gamma \Downarrow B \vdash \mathcal{A}; \Upsilon$ is such that the signature and the two unbounded zones are identical to the corresponding signature and zones in the endsequent: That is, these sequents are of the form $\Sigma :: \Psi; \Gamma' \vdash \Delta'; \Upsilon$, for multisets Γ' and Δ'. Thus, only the bounded zones vary during the construction of the left-introduction phase.

Proposition 7.3. *Let Ξ be a $\Downarrow \mathcal{L}_2$-proof of the sequent $\Sigma :: \Psi; \Gamma \Downarrow B \vdash \mathcal{A}; \Upsilon$. The left-introduction phase at the bottom of Ξ, which has a multiset of premises $\mathcal{M}$, can be described as follows. There is a path P in B with the associated sequent*

$$\Sigma' :: C_1, \ldots, C_n; B_1, \ldots, B_m \vdash A_1, \ldots, A_p; E_1, \ldots, E_q;$$

and a substitution θ that maps the variables in Σ' to Σ-terms such that

1. *$\mathcal{A}$ is equal to the multiset union $\{A_1\theta, \ldots, A_p\theta\} \cup \mathcal{A}_1 \cup \cdots \cup \mathcal{A}_m$;*
2. *Γ is the multiset union $\Gamma_1 \cup \cdots \cup \Gamma_m$; and*
3. *$\mathcal{M}$ is the following multiset union,*

$$\{\Sigma :: \Psi; \cdot \vdash C_i\theta; \Upsilon\}_{i=1}^n \cup \{\Sigma :: \Psi; \Gamma_i \vdash B_i\theta, \mathcal{A}_i; \Upsilon\}_{i=1}^m$$
$$\cup \{\Sigma :: \Psi; E_i\theta \vdash \cdot; \Upsilon\}_{i=1}^q.$$

Proof: This equivalence is proved by induction on the structure of the $\mathcal{L}_2$-formula B in a fashion similar to that given in Proposition 5.20. □

7.2 Admissibility of the General Initial Rule

We can now prove the admissibility of generalized initial rules for $\mathcal{L}_2$-formulas.

Theorem 7.4 (Initial admissibility). *Let Ψ and Υ be multisets of $\mathcal{L}_2$ Σ-formulas. Let B be an $\mathcal{L}_2$ Σ-formulas.*

1. *The sequent $\Sigma :: \Psi; B \vdash B; \Upsilon$ is provable.*
2. *If B is a member of Ψ then $\Sigma :: \Psi; \cdot \vdash B; \Upsilon$ is provable.*
3. *If B is a member of Υ then $\Sigma :: \Psi; B \vdash \cdot; \Upsilon$ is provable.*

Proof: We proceed to prove all three of these claims simultaneously by induction on the structure of the formula B.

We prove the first claim by building a $\Downarrow \mathcal{L}_2$-proof of $\Sigma :: \Psi; B \vdash B; \Upsilon$. By Proposition 7.2, the right-introduction phase with the endsequent $\Sigma :: \Psi; B \vdash B; \Upsilon$ has a premise of the form

$$\Sigma, \Sigma' :: \Psi, C_1, \ldots, C_n; B, B_1, \ldots, B_m \vdash A_1, \ldots, A_p; \Upsilon, E_1, \ldots, E_q,$$

where $\Sigma' :: C_1, \ldots, C_n; B_1, \ldots, B_m \vdash A_1, \ldots, A_p; E_1, \ldots, E_q$ is the sequent associated to a path P in B. To complete the proof of the premises corresponding to path P, first use the *decide$_l$* rule to decide on B in the left-bounded zone of the premise. By Proposition 7.3, there is a left-introduction phase corresponding to the same P. By setting θ to the identity substitution on the variables in Σ', we have $\mathcal{A} = \mathcal{A}'\theta$ and $\mathcal{A}_i$ is empty for $i = 1, \ldots, m$ and the sequents

$$\{\Sigma, \Sigma' :: \Psi, C_1, \ldots, C_n; \cdot \vdash C_i; \Upsilon, E_1, \ldots, E_q\}_{i=1}^n \cup$$
$$\{\Sigma, \Sigma' :: \Psi, C_1, \ldots, C_n; B_i \vdash B_i; \Upsilon, E_1, \ldots, E_q\}_{i=1}^m \cup$$
$$\{\Sigma, \Sigma' :: \Psi, C_1, \ldots, C_n; E_i \vdash \cdot ; \Upsilon, E_1, \ldots, E_q\}_{i=1}^q$$

are all the open premises of that left-introduction phase. The first inductive assumption proves the middle group of sequents. The first group is proved using inductive assumption for the second claim, and the third group is proved using the third claim.

The proof of the second claim proceeds just as for the first claim except that the *decide!* rule is used instead of the *decide$_l$* rule.

The proof of the third claim proceeds by using the first claim to prove $\Sigma :: \Psi; B \vdash B; \Upsilon, B$ and then using *decide?* to prove $\Sigma :: \Psi; B \vdash \cdot; \Upsilon, B$. □

Exercise 7.5. *Prove that the following pairs of sequents are provable in the $\Downarrow \mathcal{L}_2$-proof system for all Σ-formulas B.*

1. $\Sigma :: \cdot; (B \multimap \bot) \multimap \bot \vdash B; \cdot$ and $\Sigma :: \cdot; B \vdash (B \multimap \bot) \multimap \bot; \cdot$
2. $\Sigma :: \cdot; (B \Rightarrow \bot) \multimap \bot \vdash B; \cdot$ and $\Sigma :: B; \cdot \vdash (B \Rightarrow \bot) \multimap \bot; \cdot$
3. $\Sigma :: \cdot; ?B \vdash \cdot; B$ and $\Sigma :: \cdot; B \vdash ?B; \cdot$

7.3 Cut Rules and Cut Elimination

Figure 7.1 introduces four cut rules involving $\mathcal{L}_2$ sequents. The first three rules in Figure 7.1 are the *regular cut rules* while the fourth, the *key cut*, is introduced for technical use within the cut-elimination procedure (compare this rule to the rule by the same name in Section 5.5). The key cut is the only cut rule containing a $\Downarrow$-sequent. The formula B is the *cut formula* in each rule. The bounded zones are treated multiplicatively in these cut inference rules, while the unbounded zones are treated additively. An occurrence of a regular cut rule

THREE REGULAR CUTS

$$\frac{\Sigma :: \Psi; \cdot \vdash B; \Upsilon \quad \Sigma :: \Psi, B; \Gamma \vdash \Delta; \Upsilon}{\Sigma :: \Psi; \Gamma \vdash \Delta; \Upsilon} \; cut\,!$$

$$\frac{\Sigma :: \Psi; \Gamma \vdash \Delta; B, \Upsilon \quad \Sigma :: \Psi; B \vdash \cdot; \Upsilon}{\Sigma :: \Psi; \Gamma \vdash \Delta; \Upsilon} \; cut\,?$$

$$\frac{\Sigma :: \Psi; \Gamma_1 \vdash B, \Delta_1; \Upsilon \quad \Sigma :: \Psi; \Gamma_2, B \vdash \Delta_2; \Upsilon}{\Sigma :: \Psi; \Gamma_1, \Gamma_2 \vdash \Delta_1, \Delta_2; \Upsilon} \; cut_l$$

THE KEY CUT

$$\frac{\Sigma :: \Psi; \Gamma_1 \vdash B, \Delta; \Upsilon \quad \Sigma :: \Psi; \Gamma_2 \Downarrow B \vdash \mathcal{A}; \Upsilon}{\Sigma :: \Psi; \Gamma_1, \Gamma_2 \vdash \Delta, \mathcal{A}; \Upsilon} \; cut_k$$

Figure 7.1 The four cut rules of the $\Downarrow^+ \mathcal{L}_2$-proof system.

is called a *border cut* if its conclusion is a border sequent. The right-premise of a border cut rule is a border sequent. An occurrence of a regular cut rule is a *non-border cut rule* occurrence if its conclusion is not a border sequent. The $\Downarrow^+\mathcal{L}_2$ proof system combines the inference rules in Figures 6.11 and 7.1. Proofs in that system are $\Downarrow^+\mathcal{L}_2$-proofs. A proof is *cut-free* if it has no occurrences of these four cut rules. In this section, we will prove the cut-elimination theorem for $\Downarrow^+\mathcal{L}_2$: If a sequent has a $\Downarrow^+\mathcal{L}_2$ proof, it has a $\Downarrow \mathcal{L}_2$-proof.

The special status of ?. Within $\mathcal{L}_2$, the ? connective provides an elegant symmetry since it is treated using an unbounded zone on the right of sequents, complementing the left unbounded zone. However, this connective is exceptional in the following senses. It is superfluous since $?B$ can be defined using other $\mathcal{L}_2$ connectives as $(B \multimap \bot) \Rightarrow \bot$: As mentioned in Section 6.7, $\mathfrak{N}$ is similarly redundant. Also, the rules related to ? in $\Downarrow \mathcal{L}_2$-proofs are different from the other rules of a similar kind. For example, the *decide?* rule does not link a left- and right-introduction phase but occurs between two adjacent right-introduction phases. Also, the left-introduction rule $?L$ does not maintain the $\Downarrow$ in its premise (see Exercise 6.22). For these reasons, we will treat ? with certain special conditions in the following proof of the cut-elimination theorem for $\Downarrow^+\mathcal{L}_2$-proofs. Although removing $\mathfrak{N}$ and ? from consideration can make the proof of cut elimination more direct, we keep these connectives for the sake of the examples and discussions that follow in this book.

7.3 Cut Rules and Cut Elimination

The cut-elimination argument uses various measurements attached to occurrences of both regular and key-cut rules. A *thread* in the $\Downarrow^+\mathcal{L}_2$-proof Ξ is a list of sequent occurrences $S_1, \ldots, S_n$ in Ξ such that $n \geq 1$, S_1 is an occurrence of the conclusion of an *init* rule, S_n is the endsequent of Ξ, and, for $i = 1, \ldots, n-1$, there is an inference rule occurrence of Ξ that has S_i as a premise and S_{i+1} as its conclusion. Such a thread is said to have length n.

The *rank* of Ξ is the maximal number of occurrences of decide and cut rules in threads in Ξ that do not contain a sequent occurrence that is the left premise of a cut_l, $cut\,!$, or cut_k. When we care about the rank of a proof, that proof will contain no occurrences of $cut\,?$. The *degree* of a formula is the number of occurrences of logical connectives in that formula.

Every occurrence of a cut rule in a given proof is given a *measure* as follows. Let Ξ be the subproof determined by having that occurrence of cut as its last inference rule. We define $|\Xi|$ to be the triple of natural numbers $\langle d, q, w \rangle$, where d is the *degree* of its cut formula, q is the number of occurrences of $cut\,?$ in Ξ, and w is the rank of Ξ. Such triples are well-ordered using the lexicographic ordering on triples. The proofs of the following two propositions follow from straightforward inductions on the structure of $\Downarrow^+\mathcal{L}_2$-proofs.

Proposition 7.6 (Weakening $\Downarrow^+\mathcal{L}_2$-proofs). *If $\Sigma :: \Psi; \Gamma \vdash \Delta; \Upsilon$ has a $\Downarrow^+\mathcal{L}_2$-proof Ξ then $\Sigma, \Sigma' :: \Psi, \Psi'; \Gamma \vdash \Delta; \Upsilon, \Upsilon'$ has a $\Downarrow^+\mathcal{L}_2$-proof Ξ'. Furthermore, every instance of a cut rule in Ξ corresponds to an instance of cut in Ξ', and they have the same measure.*

Proposition 7.7 (Substitution into $\Downarrow^+\mathcal{L}_2$-proofs). *Let Σ be a signature, x be a variable not declared in Σ, τ be a primitive type (other than o), and t be a Σ-term of type τ. If $\Sigma, x : \tau :: \Psi; \Gamma \vdash \Delta; \Upsilon$ has a $\Downarrow^+\mathcal{L}_2$-proof Ξ then $\Sigma :: \Psi[t/x]; \Gamma[t/x] \vdash \Delta[t/x]; \Upsilon[t/x]$ has a $\Downarrow^+\mathcal{L}_2$-proof Ξ'. Furthermore, every instance of a cut rule in Ξ corresponds to an instance of cut in Ξ', and they have the same measure.*

The following proposition states that if a formula occurrence in the unbounded zones of a sequent is never decided on within the proof of that sequent, then that occurrence can be removed from its zone, and the result will still be a proof with the same measure. The proof of this proposition follows from a straightforward induction on the structure of $\Downarrow^+\mathcal{L}_2$-proofs.

> **Proposition 7.8** (Strengthening $\Downarrow^+\mathcal{L}_2$-proofs). *Assume that we have a $\Downarrow^+\mathcal{L}_2$ proof Ξ of either $\Sigma :: \Psi, B; \Gamma \vdash \Delta; \Upsilon$ or $\Sigma :: \Psi, B; \Gamma \Downarrow D \vdash \Delta; \Upsilon$ in which there is no occurrence of* decide! *used with the formula B. Then there is a $\Downarrow^+\mathcal{L}_2$ proof Ξ' of either*
>
> $$\Sigma :: \Psi; \Gamma \vdash \Delta; \Upsilon \quad \text{or, respectively,} \quad \Sigma :: \Psi; \Gamma \Downarrow D \vdash \Delta; \Upsilon.$$
>
> *Furthermore, every instance of a cut rule in Ξ corresponds to an instance of cut in Ξ' and they have the same measure. Similarly, assume that we have a $\Downarrow^+\mathcal{L}_2$ proof Ξ of either $\Sigma :: \Psi; \Gamma \vdash \Delta; B, \Upsilon$ or $\Sigma :: \Psi; \Gamma \Downarrow D \vdash \Delta; B, \Upsilon$ in which there is no occurrence of* decide? *used with the formula B. Then there is a $\Downarrow^+\mathcal{L}_2$ proof Ξ' of either*
>
> $$\Sigma :: \Psi; \Gamma \vdash \Delta; \Upsilon \quad \text{or, respectively,} \quad \Sigma :: \Psi; \Gamma \Downarrow D \vdash \Delta; \Upsilon.$$
>
> *Furthermore, every instance of a cut rule in Ξ corresponds to an instance of cut in Ξ', and they have the same measure.*

An instance of the cut_k rule is called an *atomic key cut* if its cut formula is atomic. Note that the right premise of an atomic cut_k rule can only be proved using *init* or *init?*.

$$\frac{\Sigma :: \Psi; \Gamma \vdash \Delta, A; \Upsilon \quad \dfrac{}{\Sigma :: \Psi; \cdot \Downarrow A \vdash A; \Upsilon} \; init}{\Sigma :: \Psi; \Gamma \vdash \Delta, A; \Upsilon} \; cut_k$$

$$\frac{\Sigma :: \Psi; \Gamma \vdash \Delta, A; A, \Upsilon \quad \dfrac{}{\Sigma :: \Psi; \cdot \Downarrow A \vdash \cdot; A, \Upsilon} \; init?}{\Sigma :: \Psi; \Gamma \vdash \Delta; A, \Upsilon} \; cut_k$$

Both of these derivations resemble the following inferences, where A denotes an atomic formula.

$$\frac{\Sigma :: \Psi; \Gamma \vdash \Delta, A; \Upsilon}{\Sigma :: \Psi; \Gamma \vdash \Delta, A; \Upsilon} \; Rep \qquad \frac{\Sigma :: \Psi; \Gamma \vdash \Delta, A; A, \Upsilon}{\Sigma :: \Psi; \Gamma \vdash \Delta; A, \Upsilon} \; absorb$$

Here, *Rep* is a variation of the *repetition rule* used by Mints [1992] to prove a cut-elimination theorem for a different logic. An important feature of atomic key-cut rules is that their measure is always $\langle 0, 0, 1 \rangle$ since the structure of the proof of their left premise is not part of the measurement calculation. Ultimately, our cut-elimination procedure will first eliminate all cuts except for

7.3 CUT RULES AND CUT ELIMINATION

atomic key cuts. A second stage will eliminate all of these atomic key cuts – this second elimination stage does not rely on the measure (the rank) of cut formulas. In this second stage, we eliminate the *Rep* rules (trivially) and the *absorb* rules as described next.

The following lemma states the easy to prove fact that the side-formulas in the right-bounded zone for atomic key cuts (the schematic variable Δ above) in both the shape of the *Rep* and *absorb* rules, can be restricted to contain only atomic formulas: That is, the conclusion of such rules can be assumed to be border sequents.

Lemma 7.9. *By permuting Rep rules up over right-introduction rules, we can assume that all occurrences of Rep involve only border sequents. Similarly, by permuting absorb rules up over introduction rules, we can replace every absorb rule with decide? (which requires the right-bounded zone to contain only atomic formulas).*

Note that permuting right-introduction rules below a *Rep* or *absorb* rule might change the number of occurrences of such rules but will not change their measure, which is maintained at $\langle 0, 0, 1 \rangle$.

A $\Downarrow^+\mathcal{L}_2$-proof is called a $\Downarrow^a\mathcal{L}_2$-proof if the only occurrences of cut rules in it are atomic key cuts. A *redex* is a $\Downarrow^+\mathcal{L}_2$-proof where the last inference rule is a regular or key cut and where that rule's two immediate subproofs are $\Downarrow^a\mathcal{L}_2$-proofs. A redex is classified as atomic or non-atomic depending on whether the cut formula of its final cut rule is atomic or non-atomic. A redex is also classified by the kind of cut rule it ends with: For example, a *cut?*-redex is a redex in which the last inference rule is an instance of the *cut?* rule.

As a result of Lemma 7.9, the characterization of right-introduction and left-introduction phases given by Propositions 7.2 and 7.3 also works for $\Downarrow^a\mathcal{L}_2$-proofs.

We now provide several lemmas that show how various redexes can be replaced with proofs involving strictly smaller redexes.

Lemma 7.10 (Replace *cut?* with cut_l). *Let Ξ be a cut? redex. Then there exists a proof of the same endsequent in which the only instances of cut rules are either cut_l or atomic cut_k, and all such instances of cuts have a measure strictly less than $|\Xi|$.*

Proof: Consider the following redex Ξ.

$$\frac{\begin{array}{cc} \Xi_1 & \Xi_2 \\ \Sigma :: \Psi; \Gamma \vdash \Delta; B, \Upsilon & \Sigma :: \Psi; B \vdash \cdot; \Upsilon \end{array}}{\Sigma :: \Psi; \Gamma \vdash \Delta; \Upsilon} \; cut?$$

Here, the subproofs Ξ_1 and Ξ_2 are $\Downarrow^a \mathcal{L}_2$-proofs. Consider a subderivation of Ξ_1 of the form

$$\frac{\Xi' \\ \Sigma, \Sigma' :: \Psi, \Psi'; \Gamma' \vdash \mathcal{A}, B; B, \Upsilon, \Upsilon'}{\Sigma, \Sigma' :: \Psi, \Psi'; \Gamma' \vdash \mathcal{A}; B, \Upsilon, \Upsilon'} \; decide?.$$

Here, the variables bound in Σ' are not bound in Σ, and Ψ', Υ', and Γ' are multisets. This subproof can be converted to the subproof

$$\frac{\begin{array}{cc} \Xi' & \hat{\Xi}_2 \\ \Sigma, \Sigma' :: \Psi, \Psi'; \Gamma' \vdash \mathcal{A}, B; B, \Upsilon, \Upsilon' & \Sigma, \Sigma' :: \Psi, \Psi'; B \vdash \cdot; \Upsilon, \Upsilon' \end{array}}{\Sigma, \Sigma' :: \Psi, \Psi'; \Gamma' \vdash \mathcal{A}; B, \Upsilon, \Upsilon'} \; cut_l.$$

Here, $\hat{\Xi}_2$ is the necessary weakening of Ξ_2 to be used in this cut rule. In this way, we remove every occurrence of *decide?* on B in Ξ_1. The resulting derivation, say Ξ'_1, is a proof of $\Sigma :: \Psi; \Gamma \vdash \Delta; B, \Upsilon$ in which no occurrences of *decide?* on B appear. By Proposition 7.8, Ξ'_1 can be modified to yield a proof Ξ''_1 of the sequent $\Sigma :: \Psi; \Gamma \vdash \Delta; \Upsilon$. This proof can now replace our original redex. Since all new occurrences of cuts have B as their cut formula, and since we have removed an occurrence of *cut?*, the measure of all the cut-rules in Ξ''_1 is strictly smaller than $|\Xi|$. □

Lemma 7.11 (Replace *cut!* with cut_k). *Let Ξ be a cut! redex. Then there exists a proof of the same endsequent in which the only instances of cut rules are either cut_l or atomic cut_k, and all such instances of cuts have a measure strictly less than $|\Xi|$.*

Proof: Consider the following *cut!*-redex Ξ.

$$\frac{\begin{array}{cc} \Xi_l & \Xi_r \\ \Sigma :: \Psi; \cdot \vdash B; \Upsilon & \Sigma :: \Psi, B; \Gamma \vdash \Delta; \Upsilon \end{array}}{\Sigma :: \Psi; \Gamma \vdash \Delta; \Upsilon} \; cut\,!$$

7.3 Cut Rules and Cut Elimination

Here, the subproofs Ξ_l and Ξ_r are $\Downarrow^a \mathcal{L}_2$-proofs. Consider a subderivation of Ξ_r that ends in *decide*!, such as

$$\cfrac{\cfrac{\Xi_0}{\Sigma, \Sigma' :: \Psi, \Psi', B; \Gamma' \Downarrow B \vdash \mathcal{A}; \Upsilon, \Upsilon'}}{\Sigma, \Sigma' :: \Psi, \Psi', B; \Gamma' \vdash \mathcal{A}; \Upsilon, \Upsilon'} \; decide!,$$

where the variables bound in Σ' are not bound in Σ and where Ψ' and Υ' are multisets. This inference rule can be converted to the derivation

$$\cfrac{\cfrac{\hat{\Xi}_l}{\Sigma, \Sigma' :: \Psi, \Psi'; \cdot \vdash B; \Upsilon, \Upsilon'} \quad \cfrac{\Xi_0}{\Sigma, \Sigma' :: \Psi, \Psi', B; \Gamma' \Downarrow B \vdash \mathcal{A}; \Upsilon, \Upsilon'}}{\Sigma, \Sigma' :: \Psi, \Psi', B; \Gamma' \vdash \mathcal{A}; \Upsilon, \Upsilon'} \; cut_k.$$

Here, $\hat{\Xi}_l$ is the result of weakening Ξ_l using Proposition 7.6. We can thus removed all occurrences of *decide*! on B in Ξ_r to obtain the proof Ξ'_r of $\Sigma :: \Psi, B; \Gamma \vdash \Delta; \Upsilon$. By Proposition 7.8, we can strengthen Ξ'_r to get a proof Ξ''_r of $\Sigma :: \Psi; \Gamma \vdash \Delta; \Upsilon$. This proof can now replace our original redex. Since all new occurrences of cuts have B as their cut formula and since the rank part of the measure of redexes does not consider the subproof of the left premise of *cut*! and *cut$_l$*, the measure of all the cut-rules in Ξ''_r is strictly smaller than $|\Xi|$. □

The two previous lemmas were proved by replacing specific decide rules with specific cut rules. The treatment of the *cut$_l$* rule is not so easily handled. In particular, we will use the following lemma to show that the "side cut" case can be treated by moving that rule over an entire left-introduction phase.

Lemma 7.12 (Side *cut$_l$* case). *Let Ξ be a cut$_l$-redex such that a decide rule is the last inference rule of the proof of the right premise. If the formula decided on is not the cut formula, then there exists a $\Downarrow^+ \mathcal{L}_2$-proof with the same endsequent in which all instances of cuts have a measure strictly less than $|\Xi|$.*

Proof: We need to consider three cases depending on which decide rule is used in the proof of the right premise.

Let Ξ be the following proof.

$$\cfrac{\cfrac{\Xi_l}{\Sigma :: \Psi; \Gamma \vdash C, \Delta; \Upsilon} \quad \cfrac{\cfrac{\Xi_r}{\Sigma :: \Psi; \Gamma', C \Downarrow B \vdash \mathcal{A}; \Upsilon}}{\Sigma :: \Psi; \Gamma', B, C \vdash \mathcal{A}; \Upsilon} \; decide_l}{\Sigma :: \Psi; \Gamma, \Gamma', B \vdash \Delta, \mathcal{A}; \Upsilon} \; cut_l.$$

Here, the subproofs Ξ_l and Ξ_r are $\Downarrow^a\mathcal{L}_2$-proofs, and $\mathcal{A}$ is a multiset of atomic formulas. By Proposition 7.3, the sequent $\Sigma :: \Psi; \Gamma', C \Downarrow B \vdash \mathcal{A}; \Upsilon$ is the endsequent of a left-introduction phase with a multiset of premises $\mathcal{M}$ determined by a path P in B with the associated sequent

$$\Sigma' :: C_1, \ldots, C_n; B_1, \ldots, B_m \vdash A_1, \ldots, A_p; E_1, \ldots, E_q;$$

and there is a substitution θ that maps the variables in Σ' to Σ-terms such that

1. $\mathcal{A}$ is equal to the multiset union $\{A_1\theta, \ldots, A_p\theta\} \cup \mathcal{A}_1 \cup \cdots \cup \mathcal{A}_m$;
2. $\Gamma' \cup \{C\}$ is the multiset union $\Gamma_1 \cup \cdots \cup \Gamma_m$; and
3. $\mathcal{M}$ is the following multiset union,

$$\{\Sigma :: \Psi; \cdot \vdash C_i\theta; \Upsilon\}_{i=1}^n \cup \{\Sigma :: \Psi; \Gamma_i \vdash B_i\theta, \mathcal{A}_i; \Upsilon\}_{i=1}^m$$
$$\cup \{\Sigma :: \Psi; E_i\theta \vdash \cdot; \Upsilon\}_{i=1}^q.$$

Since the left-phase is multiplicative, there is a unique $k \in \{1, \ldots, m\}$ such that C occurs in Γ_k. Let Γ'_k be the result of removing one occurrence of C from Γ_k. Thus, one of the premises in $\mathcal{M}$ is

$$\Sigma :: \Psi; \Gamma'_k, C \vdash B_k\theta, \mathcal{A}_k; \Upsilon.$$

By using the cut_l rule, we have, together with a proof of the above sequent, the following proof.

$$\cfrac{\begin{array}{c}\Xi_l\\ \Sigma :: \Psi; \Gamma' \vdash C, \mathcal{A}; \Upsilon\end{array} \quad \Sigma :: \Psi; \Gamma'_k, C \vdash B_k\theta, \mathcal{A}_k; \Upsilon}{\Sigma :: \Psi; \Gamma', \Gamma'_k \vdash B_k\theta, \mathcal{A}_k, \mathcal{A}; \Upsilon} \; cut_l.$$

We can move this left-introduction phase below the cut_l rule using the same path above. Thus the original cut_l rule has been moved up, and its measure has decreased.

Let Ξ be the following proof, and assume that B is a member of Ψ.

$$\cfrac{\begin{array}{c}\Xi_l\\ \Sigma :: \Psi; \Gamma \vdash C, \Delta; \Upsilon\end{array} \quad \cfrac{\begin{array}{c}\Xi_r\\ \Sigma :: \Psi; \Gamma', C \Downarrow B \vdash \mathcal{A}; \Upsilon\end{array}}{\Sigma :: \Psi; \Gamma', C \vdash \mathcal{A}; \Upsilon} \; decide!}{\Sigma :: \Psi; \Gamma, \Gamma' \vdash \Delta, \mathcal{A}; \Upsilon} \; cut_l.$$

Here, the subproofs Ξ_l and Ξ_r are $\Downarrow^a\mathcal{L}_2$-proofs, and $\mathcal{A}$ is a multiset of atomic formulas. This case is treated the same as the previous case.

7.3 CUT RULES AND CUT ELIMINATION

Let Ξ be the following proof, and assume that B is a member of Υ.

$$\cfrac{\Xi_l \qquad \cfrac{\cfrac{\Xi_r}{\Sigma :: \Psi; \Gamma', C \vdash \mathcal{A}, B; \Upsilon}}{\Sigma :: \Psi; \Gamma', C \vdash \mathcal{A}; \Upsilon} \; decide?}{\Sigma :: \Psi; \Gamma, \Gamma' \vdash \Delta, \mathcal{A}; \Upsilon} \; cut_l.$$

Here, the subproofs Ξ_l and Ξ_r are $\Downarrow^a\mathcal{L}_2$-proofs, and $\mathcal{A}$ is a multiset of atomic formulas. If it is the case that all the formulas in Δ are atomic, then we can now permute the *decide?* and cut_l rules to get

$$\cfrac{\cfrac{\Xi_l \qquad \Xi_r}{\Sigma :: \Psi; \Gamma \vdash C, \Delta; \Upsilon \quad \Sigma :: \Psi; \Gamma', C \vdash \mathcal{A}, B; \Upsilon}}{\cfrac{\Sigma :: \Psi; \Gamma, \Gamma' \vdash \Delta, \mathcal{A}, B; \Upsilon}{\Sigma :: \Psi; \Gamma, \Gamma' \vdash \Delta, \mathcal{A}; \Upsilon} \; decide?} \; cut_l.$$

This proof has a smaller measure. If there are non-atomic formulas in Δ, we must first permute this cut instance up over the left introduction phase in Ξ_l. This permutation may produce several occurrences of cut_l, but they all have an atomic right-bounded zone. We can then permute the *decide?* and cut_l as above to reduce the measure of all these instances of cut_l. □

As a result of this lemma, an instance of cut_l on B in the endsequent can then be lifted to several instances of cut_l that are not side cuts, a change that does not affect the measure of any cuts. Now, resolve the cut/decide pairing as described in the following proof.

> **Lemma 7.13** (Replace cut_l with cut_k). *Let Ξ be a cut_l redex. Then there exists a proof of the same endsequent in which the only instances of cut rules are cut_k, and all such instances of cuts have a measure strictly less than $|\Xi|$.*

Proof: Consider the following cut_l-redex Ξ.

$$\cfrac{\cfrac{\Xi_l}{\Sigma :: \Psi; \Gamma_1 \vdash B, \Delta_1; \Upsilon} \qquad \cfrac{\Xi_r}{\Sigma :: \Psi; \Gamma_2, B \vdash \Delta_2; \Upsilon}}{\Sigma :: \Psi; \Gamma_1, \Gamma_2 \vdash \Delta_1, \Delta_2; \Upsilon} \; cut_l.$$

Here, the subproofs Ξ_l and Ξ_r are $\Downarrow^a\mathcal{L}_2$-proofs. Given the discussion above, we only need to consider the situation where the right-bounded zone contains only atomic formulas and that the last inference rule of Ξ_r is a decide rule.

Case: Ξ_r ends in the *decide$_l$* rule. If the formula selected for the focus is B, then the proof Ξ_r has the form

$$\cfrac{\cfrac{}{\Sigma :: \Psi; \Gamma'_2 \Downarrow B \vdash \Delta'_2; \Upsilon}\Xi'_r}{\Sigma :: \Psi; \Gamma'_2, B \vdash \Delta'_2; \Upsilon}\; decide_l.$$

In this case, the instance of the *cut$_l$* rule above can be replaced with the following instance of *cut$_k$*.

$$\cfrac{\cfrac{}{\Sigma :: \Psi; \Gamma_1 \vdash B, \Delta_1; \Upsilon}\Xi_l \qquad \cfrac{}{\Sigma :: \Psi; \Gamma_2 \Downarrow B \vdash \Delta_2; \Upsilon}\Xi'_r}{\Sigma :: \Psi; \Gamma_1, \Gamma_2 \vdash \Delta_1, \Delta_2; \Upsilon}\; cut_k.$$

If the formula selected for the focus is some other formula than B, then the proof Ξ_r has the form (Γ_2 is of the form C, Γ'_2)

$$\cfrac{\cfrac{}{\Sigma :: \Psi; \Gamma'_2, B \Downarrow C \vdash \Delta_2; \Upsilon}\Xi'_r}{\Sigma :: \Psi; \Gamma'_2, B, C \vdash \Delta_2; \Upsilon}\; decide_l.$$

We now use Lemma 7.12 to construct a $\Downarrow^+ \mathcal{L}_2$-proof of $\Sigma :: \Psi; \Gamma'_2, C \vdash \Delta_2; \Upsilon$ of lower right rank.

Case: Ξ_r ends in either the *decide!* or *decide?* rule. Then the redex Ξ necessarily ends in a side cut, so Lemma 7.12 provides the necessary rewriting of this redex. □

Lemma 7.14 (Reduce *cut$_k$*). *Let Ξ be a cut$_k$ redex. Then there exists a proof of the same endsequent in which all of its redexes have a measure strictly less than $|\Xi|$.*

Proof: Consider a *cut$_k$*-redex Ξ of the form

$$\cfrac{\cfrac{}{\Sigma :: \Psi; \Gamma' \vdash B, \Delta; \Upsilon}\Xi_l \qquad \cfrac{}{\Sigma :: \Psi; \Gamma'' \Downarrow B \vdash \mathcal{A}; \Upsilon}\Xi_r}{\Sigma :: \Psi; \Gamma', \Gamma'' \vdash \Delta, \mathcal{A}; \Upsilon}\; cut_k,$$

where Ξ_l and Ξ_r are $\Downarrow^a \mathcal{L}_2$-proofs. If B is atomic, then $\mathcal{A}$ is the multiset containing exactly B and the result of eliminating *cut$_k$* is Ξ_l.

Now assume that B is not atomic. Thus, Ξ_l ends in a right-introduction phase, and Ξ_r ends in a left-introduction phase. By Proposition 7.3, there is a path P in B that has the associated sequent representation

7.3 Cut Rules and Cut Elimination

$$\Sigma' :: C_1, \ldots, C_n; B_1, \ldots, B_m \vdash A_1, \ldots, A_p; E_1, \ldots, E_q$$

and there is a substitution θ that maps the variables in Σ' to Σ-terms such that $\mathcal{A}$ is the multiset union $\{A_1\theta, \ldots, A_p\theta\} \cup \mathcal{A}_1 \cup \cdots \cup \mathcal{A}_m$, Γ'' is the multiset union $\Gamma_1 \cup \cdots \cup \Gamma_m$, and this phase has $n+m+q$ premises

$$\{\Sigma :: \Psi; \cdot \vdash C_i\theta; \Upsilon\}_{i=1}^{n} \cup \{\Sigma :: \Psi; \Gamma_i \vdash B_i\theta, \mathcal{A}_i; \Upsilon\}_{i=1}^{m}$$
$$\cup \{\Sigma :: \Psi; E_i\theta \vdash \cdot; \Upsilon\}_{i=1}^{q}.$$

By Proposition 7.2, Ξ_l ends with a right-introduction phase that contains a premise of the form

$$\Xi_0$$
$$\Sigma, \Sigma' :: \Psi, C_1, \ldots, C_n; \Gamma, B_1, \ldots, B_m \vdash \mathcal{A}, A_1, \ldots, A_p; E_1, \ldots, E_q, \Upsilon.$$

By repeated application of Proposition 7.7, we know that the sequent

$$\Xi_0'$$
$$\Sigma :: \Psi, C_1\theta, \ldots, C_n\theta; \Gamma, B_1\theta, \ldots, B_m\theta \vdash \mathcal{A}, A_1\theta, \ldots, A_p\theta; E_1\theta, \ldots, E_q\theta, \Upsilon$$

has a $\Downarrow^a\mathcal{L}_2$ proof. We can take Ξ_0' and use cut_l, $cut\,!$, and $cut\,?$ with the proofs of the $n+m+q$ premises above to yield a proof with $n+m+q$ occurrences of these cut rules to build a proof of the endsequent $\Sigma :: \Psi; \Gamma', \Gamma'' \vdash \Delta, \mathcal{A}; \Upsilon$. Note that the sizes of the cut formulas $C_1\theta, \ldots, C_n\theta, B_1\theta, \ldots, B_m\theta, E_1\theta, \ldots, E_q\theta$ are strictly smaller than the size of the original cut formula B. $\square$

We can combine these lemmas to prove the main cut-elimination theorem for $\Downarrow^+\mathcal{L}_2$ proofs.

> **Theorem 7.15** (Elimination of cuts). *If a sequent has a $\Downarrow^+\mathcal{L}_2$-proof, it has a (cut-free) $\Downarrow \mathcal{L}_2$-proof.*

Proof: We divide this proof into two parts. The first part proves that if a sequent has a $\Downarrow^+\mathcal{L}_2$-proof, it has a $\Downarrow^a\mathcal{L}_2$-proof. The second part proves that if a sequent has a $\Downarrow^a\mathcal{L}_2$-proof, it has a (cut-free) $\Downarrow \mathcal{L}_2$-proof.

Thus, assume that we have a $\Downarrow^+\mathcal{L}_2$-proof. We proceed by induction on the number of occurrences of cut rules in that proof that are not atomic key cuts. If the number of such redexes is zero, we are finished with the first part of this proof. Otherwise, select a redex Ξ that is not an atomic key cut redex. We prove by induction on the measure $|\Xi|$ that this redex can be replaced by a $\Downarrow^a\mathcal{L}_2$-proof of the same endsequent. If Ξ is a $cut\,?$-redex then apply Lemma 7.10; if Ξ is a $cut\,!$-redex then apply Lemma 7.11; if Ξ is a cut_l-redex then apply Lemma 7.13; and, finally, if Ξ is a cut_k-redex then apply Lemma 7.14. The result of such applications is a proof of the same endsequent as Ξ in which all redexes have a measure strictly less than $|\Xi|$. Thus, by induction, all of these can be replaced by $\Downarrow^a \mathcal{L}_2$-proofs.

To complete the second part of this proof, we proceed to prove by induction on the number $n \geq 0$ of atomic key cuts in the $\Downarrow^a \mathcal{L}_2$-proof Ξ that there is a $\Downarrow \mathcal{L}_2$-proof of the same endsequent. If n is 0, then we are finished. Otherwise, pick any atomic key cut occurrence in Ξ. That occurrence is either of the *Rep* type, which is trivial to remove, or of the *absorb* type, in which case Lemma 7.9 guarantees that occurrence can be replaced by a *decide*? (following suitable rule permutations). □

At the end of Section 6.1, we described an interaction between the structural and cut rules in LK that makes cut elimination into a pronounced nondeterministic procedure. In the focused proof system $\Downarrow^+ \mathcal{L}_2$, such interactions cannot happen. For example, consider the *cut* ! inference rule.

$$\frac{\Sigma :: \Psi; \cdot \vdash B; \Upsilon \qquad \Sigma :: \Psi, B; \Gamma \vdash \Delta; \Upsilon}{\Sigma :: \Psi; \Gamma \vdash \Delta; \Upsilon} \; cut\,!\,.$$

The occurrence of the cut formula B in the left premise cannot be weakened since it will be the subject of a right-introduction rule. The occurrence of B in the right premise can, however, be weakened (by an application of an initial rule). A similar statement holds for the *cut*? rule while for the cut_l rule, the occurrences of the cut formula in the premises cannot be weakened in either premise. As a result, the kind of problem arising from weakening and cut that can appear in LK is avoided in $\Downarrow^+ \mathcal{L}_2$.

7.4 The Focused Proof System Is Sound and Complete

We now wish to show that the $\Downarrow \mathcal{L}_2$-proof system proves all the same theorems as the **L** proof system proves. We would also like to go one more step and show that some of the proof theory of **L** can be inferred from the proof theory of $\Downarrow \mathcal{L}_2$. Since these two proof systems use different sets of logical connectives, we must first define a mapping from formulas used in the **L** proof system into $\mathcal{L}_2$-formulas.

Recall that the negatively polarized logical connectives of **L** are $\bot$, $\top$, $\invamp$, &, $\forall$, and ? while the positively polarized logical connectives are **1**, **0**, $\otimes$, $\oplus$,

7.4 THE FOCUSED PROOF SYSTEM IS SOUND AND COMPLETE   161

$\exists$, and !. We consider a formula that is a top-level negation as being neither positively nor negatively polarized: One does not know the intended polarity of a negated formula until one considers the formula that is negated.

We define two functions, namely, $(\cdot)^\nabla$ that maps **L** formulas into $\mathcal{L}_2$-formulas and $(\cdot)^\blacktriangledown$ that maps those formulas with a positively polarized top-level logical connective into $\mathcal{L}_2$-formulas. If A is an atomic formula, then $A^\nabla = A$. These functions are defined for other formulas as follows.

$$\top^\nabla = \top \qquad\qquad \mathbf{0}^\blacktriangledown = \top$$
$$\bot^\nabla = \bot \qquad\qquad \mathbf{1}^\blacktriangledown = \bot$$
$$(B \mathbin{\bindnasrepma} C)^\nabla = B^\nabla \mathbin{\bindnasrepma} C^\nabla \qquad (B \otimes C)^\blacktriangledown = B^\nabla \multimap C^\nabla \multimap \bot$$
$$(B \mathbin{\&} C)^\nabla = B^\nabla \mathbin{\&} C^\nabla \qquad (B \oplus C)^\blacktriangledown = (B^\nabla \multimap \bot) \mathbin{\&} (C^\nabla \multimap \bot)$$
$$(\forall x.B)^\nabla = \forall x.B^\nabla \qquad (\exists x.B)^\blacktriangledown = \forall x.(B^\nabla \multimap \bot)$$
$$(?\, B)^\nabla = ?(B^\nabla) \qquad (!\, B)^\blacktriangledown = (B^\nabla) \Rightarrow \bot.$$

For formulas P with a positively polarized top-level logical connective, set $(P)^\nabla = (P)^\blacktriangledown \multimap \bot$. If the top-level connective is a negation, then $(B^\perp)^\nabla = B^\nabla \multimap \bot$. If Γ is a multiset of **L** formulas then we write Γ^∇ to denote the multiset of $\mathcal{L}_2$-formulas $\{B^\nabla \mid B \in \Gamma\}$: Assume a similar definition for $\Gamma^\blacktriangledown$ whenever all formulas in Γ have a positive polarity connective as their top-level connective.

For convenience, we use the notation $\Sigma :: \Psi; \Gamma \vdash_\Downarrow \Delta; \Upsilon$ to denote the proposition that the sequent $\Sigma :: \Psi; \Gamma \vdash \Delta; \Upsilon$ has a $\Downarrow \mathcal{L}_2$-proof.

As one expects, the following soundness property for the $(\cdot)^\nabla$ translation has a straightforward proof with many simple cases to consider.

Proposition 7.16 (Soundness of $\Downarrow \mathcal{L}_2$-proofs). *Let Γ and Δ be Σ-formulas in **L** such that $\Sigma ::\cdot; \Gamma^\nabla \vdash \Delta^\nabla; \cdot$ has a (cut-free) $\Downarrow \mathcal{L}_2$-proof. Then $\Sigma :: \Gamma \vdash \Delta$ has an cut-free proof in **L**.*

Proof: We prove the following strengthening of this proposition. Let Θ be a multiset of Σ-formulas all of which have a top-level positive connective and let $\Gamma, \Delta, \Psi,$ and Υ be multisets of Σ-formulas in **L**.

1. If $\Sigma :: \Psi^\nabla; \Gamma^\nabla, \Theta^\blacktriangledown \vdash \Delta^\nabla; \Upsilon^\nabla$ has a $\Downarrow \mathcal{L}_2$-proof then $\Sigma ::\,!\, \Psi, \Gamma \vdash \Theta, \Delta, ?\,\Upsilon$ has a cut-free proof in **L**.

2. If B is an **L** Σ-formula and $\Sigma :: \Psi^\nabla; \Gamma^\nabla, \Theta^\blacktriangledown \Downarrow B^\nabla \vdash \Delta^\nabla; \Upsilon^\nabla$ has a $\Downarrow \mathcal{L}_2$-proof then $\Sigma ::\,!\, \Psi, \Gamma, B \vdash \Theta, \Delta, ?\,\Upsilon$ has a cut-free proof in **L**.

3. If B is an **L** Σ-formula with a top-level positive connective and $\Sigma ::$ $\Psi^\nabla; \Gamma^\nabla, \Theta^\blacktriangledown \Downarrow B^\blacktriangledown \vdash \Delta^\nabla; \Upsilon^\nabla$ has a $\Downarrow \mathcal{L}_2$-proof then $\Sigma ::\ !\Psi, \Gamma \vdash B, \Theta, \Delta,\ ?\Upsilon$ has a cut-free proof in **L**.

We shall also assume that we only consider $\Downarrow \mathcal{L}_2$-proofs that satisfy the following invariant: Every sequent in a $\Downarrow \mathcal{L}_2$-proof that has an occurrence of $\bot$ in the right-bounded zone is the conclusion of the $\bot R$ inference rule (an immediate consequence of Proposition 7.2).

We proceed by mutual induction on the structure of $\Downarrow \mathcal{L}_2$-proofs of these three kinds of sequents. First, let Ξ be $\Downarrow \mathcal{L}_2$-proof of $\Sigma :: \Psi^\nabla; \Gamma^\nabla, \Theta^\blacktriangledown \vdash \Delta^\nabla; \Upsilon^\nabla$. The last inference rule in Ξ is either a right-introduction or decide rule. We consider the following cases.

1. Assume that this last inference rule introduced a negative polarity **L** connective. For example, if that rule is $\bindnasrepma R$ then Δ can be written as $B \bindnasrepma C, \Delta'$ and that last inference rule is of the form

$$\frac{\Sigma :: \Psi^\nabla; \Gamma^\nabla, \Theta^\blacktriangledown \vdash B^\nabla, C^\nabla, \Delta^\nabla; \Upsilon^\nabla}{\Sigma :: \Psi^\nabla; \Gamma^\nabla, \Theta^\blacktriangledown \vdash (B \bindnasrepma C)^\nabla, \Delta^\nabla; \Upsilon^\nabla} \bindnasrepma R.$$

By the inductive hypothesis, $\Sigma ::\ !\Psi, \Gamma \vdash B, C, \Theta, \Delta,\ ?\Upsilon$ has an **L** proof and, by the $\bindnasrepma R$ rule in **L**, we have an **L** proof of $\Sigma ::\ !\Psi, \Gamma \vdash B \bindnasrepma C, \Theta, \Delta,\ ?\Upsilon$. The remaining negative polarity connectives are handled in a simple and direct fashion.

2. Assume that the last inference rule of Ξ is $\multimap R$. (Note that $\Rightarrow R$ is not possible here.) Thus, Δ can be written as B, Δ' where B is either a negation or a top-level positive polarity connective. In the first case, write B as $C^\bot$ and the last two inference rules in Ξ are

$$\frac{\dfrac{\Sigma :: \Psi^\nabla; \Gamma^\nabla, C^\nabla, \Theta^\blacktriangledown \vdash \Delta^\nabla; \Upsilon^\nabla}{\Sigma :: \Psi^\nabla; \Gamma^\nabla, C^\nabla, \Theta^\blacktriangledown \vdash \bot, \Delta^\nabla; \Upsilon^\nabla} \bot R}{\Sigma :: \Psi^\nabla; \Gamma^\nabla, \Theta^\blacktriangledown \vdash C^\nabla \multimap \bot, \Delta^\nabla; \Upsilon^\nabla} \multimap R.$$

By the inductive hypothesis, $\Sigma ::\ !\Psi, \Gamma, C \vdash \Theta, \Delta,\ ?\Upsilon$ has an **L** proof and, by the $(\cdot)^\bot R$ rule in **L**, we have an **L** proof of $\Sigma ::\ !\Psi, \Gamma \vdash C^\bot, \Theta, \Delta,\ ?\Upsilon$. The other case to consider is when B is a top-level positive polarity connective, in which case, the last two inference rules of Ξ are

$$\frac{\dfrac{\Sigma :: \Psi^\nabla; \Gamma^\nabla, B^\blacktriangledown, \Theta^\blacktriangledown \vdash \Delta^\nabla; \Upsilon^\nabla}{\Sigma :: \Psi^\nabla; \Gamma^\nabla, B^\blacktriangledown, \Theta^\blacktriangledown \vdash \bot, \Delta^\nabla; \Upsilon^\nabla} \bot R}{\Sigma :: \Psi^\nabla; \Gamma^\nabla, \Theta^\blacktriangledown \vdash B^\blacktriangledown \multimap \bot, \Delta^\nabla; \Upsilon^\nabla} \multimap R.$$

7.4 THE FOCUSED PROOF SYSTEM IS SOUND AND COMPLETE

By the inductive hypothesis, $\Sigma :: \,!\Psi, \Gamma \vdash B, \Theta, \Delta, ?\Upsilon$ has an **L** proof, which also serves as the desired proof for this case.

3. Assume that the last inference rule of Ξ is one of the decide rules. In the case of the *decide?* inference rule, that rule translates directly to the uses of the contraction and dereliction rules ($?C$ and $?D$) for $?$. In the case of the *decide$_l$* rule, the desired **L** proof follows immediately from the mutual inductive hypothesis. Finally, in the case of the *decide!* rule, the desired **L** proof follows from the mutual inductive hypothesis and the contraction and dereliction rules ($!C$ and $!D$) for $!$.

Now consider the second mutually inductive statement. Assume that Ξ is a $\Downarrow \mathcal{L}_2$-proof of $\Sigma :: \Psi^\nabla; \Gamma^\nabla, \Theta^\blacktriangledown \Downarrow B^\nabla \vdash \Delta^\nabla; \Upsilon^\nabla$. Again, there are three cases to consider for B. If B has a top-level negative polarity logical connective, then the corresponding inference rule to use with the inductive assumption is the **L** left-introduction rule for that connective. If B is the negation $C^\perp$, then the last two inference rules of Ξ are

$$\dfrac{\Sigma :: \Psi^\nabla; \Gamma^\nabla, \Theta^\blacktriangledown \vdash C^\nabla, \Delta^\nabla; \Upsilon^\nabla \quad \dfrac{}{\Sigma :: \Psi^\nabla; \cdot \Downarrow \bot \vdash \cdot; \Upsilon^\nabla} \bot L}{\Sigma :: \Psi^\nabla; \Gamma^\nabla, \Theta^\blacktriangledown \Downarrow C^\nabla \multimap \bot \vdash \Delta^\nabla; \Upsilon^\nabla} \multimap L.$$

By the inductive assumption, $\Sigma :: \,!\Psi, \Gamma \vdash C, \Theta, \Delta, ?\Upsilon$ has a cut-free proof in **L**. The desired final proof uses the $(\cdot)^\perp L$ rule. The final case to consider for B is when it has a top-level positive logical connective. In this case, Ξ is of the form

$$\dfrac{\dfrac{\Xi'}{\Sigma :: \Psi^\nabla; \Gamma^\nabla, \Theta^\blacktriangledown \vdash B^\blacktriangledown, \Delta^\nabla; \Upsilon^\nabla} \quad \dfrac{}{\Sigma :: \Psi^\nabla; \cdot \Downarrow \bot \vdash \cdot; \Upsilon^\nabla} \bot L}{\Sigma :: \Psi^\nabla; \Gamma^\nabla, \Theta^\blacktriangledown \Downarrow B^\blacktriangledown \multimap \bot \vdash \Delta^\nabla; \Upsilon^\nabla} \multimap L.$$

Here, the definition of $(\cdot)^\blacktriangledown$ matters. We illustrate this with B being $B_1 \otimes B_2$ (the other cases are similar). In this case, Ξ' must be of the form

$$\dfrac{\dfrac{\dfrac{\dfrac{\Sigma :: \Psi^\nabla; \Gamma^\nabla, B_1^\nabla, B_2^\nabla, \Theta^\blacktriangledown \vdash \Delta^\nabla; \Upsilon^\nabla}{\Sigma :: \Psi^\nabla; \Gamma^\nabla, B_1^\nabla, B_2^\nabla, \Theta^\blacktriangledown \vdash \bot, \Delta^\nabla; \Upsilon^\nabla} \bot R}{\Sigma :: \Psi^\nabla; \Gamma^\nabla, B_1^\nabla, \Theta^\blacktriangledown \vdash B_2^\nabla \multimap \bot, \Delta^\nabla; \Upsilon^\nabla} \multimap R}{\Sigma :: \Psi^\nabla; \Gamma^\nabla, \Theta^\blacktriangledown \vdash B_1^\nabla \multimap B_2^\nabla \multimap \bot, \Delta^\nabla; \Upsilon^\nabla} \multimap R.$$

By the inductive hypothesis, we know that the sequent $\Sigma :: \,!\Psi, \Gamma, B_1, B_2 \vdash \Theta, \Delta, ?\Upsilon$ has a cut-free **L** proof. The desired **L** proof for this case follows from applying the $\otimes L$ rule of **L**.

Now consider the third and final mutually inductive statement. Assume that Ξ is a $\Downarrow \mathcal{L}_2$-proof of $\Sigma :: \Psi^\nabla; \Gamma^\nabla, \Theta^\blacktriangledown \Downarrow B^\blacktriangledown \vdash \Delta^\nabla; \Upsilon^\nabla$. Again, the definition of $(\cdot)^\blacktriangledown$ matters, and we illustrate it for $\otimes$: The other cases are done similarly. Let B be $B_1 \otimes B_2$. Thus, Ξ be of the form

$$\cfrac{\Psi^\nabla; \Gamma_1^\nabla, \Theta_1^\blacktriangledown \vdash B_1^\nabla, \Delta_1^\nabla; \Upsilon^\nabla \quad \cfrac{\Psi^\nabla; \Gamma_2^\nabla, \Theta_2^\blacktriangledown \vdash B_2^\nabla, \Delta_2^\nabla; \Upsilon^\nabla \quad \Psi^\nabla; \cdot \Downarrow \bot \vdash \cdot; \Upsilon^\nabla}{\Psi^\nabla; \Gamma_2^\nabla, \Theta_2^\blacktriangledown \Downarrow B_2^\nabla \multimap \bot \vdash \Delta_2^\nabla; \Upsilon^\nabla}}{\Psi^\nabla; \Gamma_1^\nabla, \Gamma_2^\nabla, \Theta_1^\blacktriangledown, \Theta_2^\blacktriangledown \Downarrow B_1^\nabla \multimap B_2^\nabla \multimap \bot \vdash \Delta_1^\nabla, \Delta_2^\nabla; \Upsilon^\nabla},$$

where Γ, Δ, and Θ are split into their respective pairs of multisets (the signature binder is dropped for readability). By the inductive hypothesis, there are cut-free **L** proofs for $\Sigma :: !\Psi, \Gamma_1 \vdash B_1, \Theta_1, \Delta_1, ?\Upsilon$ and $\Sigma :: !\Psi, \Gamma_2 \vdash B_2, \Theta_2, \Delta_2, ?\Upsilon$. The $\otimes R$ rule of **L** provides the final, desired **L** proof of $\Sigma :: !\Psi, \Gamma_2 \vdash B_1 \otimes B_2, \Theta_2, \Delta_2, ?\Upsilon$. $\square$

Recalling from Section 6.1, an inference rule is invertible if whenever its conclusion is provable, its premises are provable. We state an inversion lemma for $\Downarrow \mathcal{L}_2$-proofs.

Lemma 7.17. *All the right-introduction rules of $\Downarrow \mathcal{L}_2$ are invertible. Furthermore, the following equivalences hold.*

$\Sigma :: \Psi; \Gamma, (B \Rightarrow \bot) \multimap \bot \vdash_\Downarrow \Delta; \Upsilon$ *if and only if* $\Sigma :: \Psi, B; \Gamma \vdash_\Downarrow \Delta; \Upsilon$.

$\Sigma :: \Psi; \Gamma \vdash_\Downarrow ?B, \Delta; \Upsilon$ *if and only if* $\Sigma :: \Psi; \Gamma \vdash_\Downarrow \Delta; \Upsilon, B$.

Proof: The proofs that the eight right rules are invertible all follow the same pattern (see Exercise 6.8). We illustrate that pattern with two examples. Consider the $?R$ rule. Assume that $\Sigma :: \Psi; \Gamma \vdash_\Downarrow \Delta, ?B; \Upsilon$. Since the sequent $\Sigma :: \cdot; ?B \vdash \cdot; B$ has a $\Downarrow \mathcal{L}_2$-proof, then the *cut* rule and cut-elimination theorem yields $\Sigma :: \Psi; \Gamma \vdash_\Downarrow \Delta; B, \Upsilon$. For a second example, consider the $\& R$ rule. Assume that $\Sigma :: \Psi; \Gamma \vdash_\Downarrow \Delta, B_1 \& B_2; \Upsilon$. Since the sequents $\Sigma :: \cdot; B_1 \& B_2 \vdash B_i; \cdot$ have $\Downarrow \mathcal{L}_2$-proofs (for $i = 1$ and $i = 2$), then the cut rule and cut-elimination theorem yields $\Sigma :: \Psi; \Gamma \vdash_\Downarrow \Delta; B_1, \Upsilon$ and $\Sigma :: \Psi; \Gamma \vdash_\Downarrow \Delta; B_2, \Upsilon$.

Now consider the first equivalence. If we assume that $\Sigma :: \Psi; \Gamma, (B \Rightarrow \bot) \multimap \bot \vdash_\Downarrow \Delta; \Upsilon$ then, using the *cut* rule with a proof of $\Sigma :: B; \cdot \vdash (B \Rightarrow \bot) \multimap \bot; \cdot$ (see also Exercise 7.5), we have (after applying cut-elimination) a $\Downarrow \mathcal{L}_2$-proof of $\Sigma :: \Psi, B; \Gamma \vdash \Delta; \Upsilon$. Conversely, assume that $\Sigma :: \Psi, B; \Gamma \vdash \Delta; \Upsilon$ has a

7.4 THE FOCUSED PROOF SYSTEM IS SOUND AND COMPLETE

$\Downarrow \mathcal{L}_2$-proof Ξ. This proof ends with a right-introduction phase, and we list the $n \geq 0$ premises of that phase as the sequents $\Sigma, \Sigma_i :: \Psi, \Psi_i, B; \Gamma_i \vdash \mathcal{A}_i; \Upsilon, \Upsilon_i$, for $1 \leq i \leq n$. Given all of these $\Downarrow \mathcal{L}_2$-proofs, we can build the following n additional proofs (for $1 \leq i \leq n$).

$$\cfrac{\cfrac{\cfrac{\cfrac{\Sigma, \Sigma_i :: \Psi, \Psi_i, B; \Gamma_i \vdash \mathcal{A}_i; \Upsilon, \Upsilon_i}{\Sigma, \Sigma_i :: \Psi, \Psi_i, B; \Gamma_i \vdash \bot, \mathcal{A}_i; \Upsilon, \Upsilon_i} \bot R}{\Sigma, \Sigma_i :: \Psi, \Psi_i; \Gamma_i \vdash B \Rightarrow \bot, \mathcal{A}_i; \Upsilon, \Upsilon_i} \Rightarrow R \quad \cfrac{}{\Sigma, \Sigma_i :: \Psi, \Psi_i; \cdot \Downarrow \bot \vdash \cdot; \Upsilon, \Upsilon_i} \bot L}{\Sigma, \Sigma_i :: \Psi, \Psi_i; \Gamma_i \Downarrow (B \Rightarrow \bot) \multimap \bot \vdash \mathcal{A}_i; \Upsilon, \Upsilon_i} \multimap L}{\Sigma, \Sigma_i :: \Psi, \Psi_i; \Gamma_i, (B \Rightarrow \bot) \multimap \bot \vdash \mathcal{A}_i; \Upsilon, \Upsilon_i} \text{decide}_l$$

We can now build a proof of $\Sigma :: \Psi; \Gamma, (B \Rightarrow \bot) \multimap \bot \vdash \Delta; \Upsilon$ by attaching the right phase at the end of Ξ to these other premises.

Now consider the second equivalence. From $\Sigma :: \Psi; \Gamma \vdash_{\Downarrow} \Delta; \Upsilon, B$ we immediately conclude $\Sigma :: \Psi; \Gamma \vdash_{\Downarrow} \Delta, ?B; \Upsilon$ by using the $?R$ rule. Conversely, assume $\Sigma :: \Psi; \Gamma \vdash_{\Downarrow} \Delta, ?B; \Upsilon$. Since all right-introduction rules permute over each other, we can assume that the $?R$ has been applied first (reading the proof bottom-up), which has the premise $\Sigma :: \Psi; \Gamma \vdash \Delta; \Upsilon, B$. $\square$

Theorem 7.18 (Completeness of $\Downarrow \mathcal{L}_2$-proofs). *Let Δ and Γ be multisets of L formulas. If $\Sigma :: \Gamma \vdash \Delta$ has an L proof then $\Sigma :: \cdot; \Gamma^\nabla \vdash \Delta^\nabla; \cdot$ has a $\Downarrow \mathcal{L}_2$-proof.*

Proof: We prove completeness by showing that the inference rules of the **L** proof system are all admissible (via the $(\cdot)^\nabla$ mapping) in the $\Downarrow \mathcal{L}_2$-proof system. Assume that $\Sigma :: \Delta \vdash \Gamma$ has an **L** proof Ξ. We proceed by induction on the structure of Ξ.

If Ξ is an instance of the initial rule, Δ and Γ are equal and contain the single element B. By Proposition 7.4, $\Sigma :: \cdot; B^\nabla \vdash_{\Downarrow} B^\nabla; \cdot$. In the case that the last inference rule is an instance of the cut rule

$$\cfrac{\Sigma :: \Gamma_1 \vdash B, \Delta_1 \quad \Sigma :: \Gamma_2, B \vdash \Delta_2}{\Sigma :: \Gamma_1, \Gamma_2 \vdash \Delta_1, \Delta_2} \text{ cut},$$

we are allowed to assume that $\Sigma :: \cdot; \Gamma_1^\nabla \vdash_{\Downarrow} B^\nabla, \Delta_1^\nabla; \cdot$ and $\Sigma :: \cdot; \Gamma_2^\nabla, B^\nabla \vdash_{\Downarrow} \Delta_2^\nabla; \cdot$. Using the cut_l rule of $\Downarrow^+ \mathcal{L}_2$ and the cut-elimination theorem (Theorem 7.15), we know that $\Sigma :: \cdot; \Gamma_1^\nabla, \Gamma_2^\nabla \vdash_{\Downarrow} \Delta_1^\nabla, \Delta_2^\nabla; \cdot$.

Since the right-introduction rules for the connectives $\{\top, \&, \forall, \bot, \mathfrak{N}\}$ are essentially the same in the **L** and $\Downarrow \mathcal{L}_2$ proof systems, it is easy to treat the case where the proof Ξ is a right-introduction rule for one of these connectives. On the other hand, the left-introduction rules for these connectives can be applied even when the right is not a collection of atomic formulas. In these cases, we use the cut-elimination result for $\Downarrow^+\mathcal{L}_2$ proofs. For example, assume that the last inference rule for Ξ is

$$\frac{\Sigma :: \Gamma, B_i \vdash \Delta}{\Sigma :: \Gamma, B_1 \& B_2 \vdash \Delta} \ \&L\ (i = 1, 2).$$

By the inductive hypothesis, we know that $\Sigma :: \cdot; \Gamma^\nabla, B_i^\nabla \vdash_\Downarrow \Delta^\nabla; \cdot$. By Proposition 7.4 we know that $\Sigma :: \cdot; B_1^\nabla \& B_2^\nabla \vdash B_1^\nabla \& B_2^\nabla; \cdot$ has a $\Downarrow \mathcal{L}_2$-proof. Immediate subproofs of that proof are proofs of $\Sigma :: \cdot; B_1^\nabla \& B_2^\nabla \vdash B_i^\nabla; \cdot$ for $i = 1$ and $i = 2$. Using the cut-elimination result (Theorem 7.15), we can conclude that $\Sigma :: \cdot; \Gamma^\nabla, B_1^\nabla \& B_2^\nabla \vdash_\Downarrow \Delta^\nabla; \cdot$. The left-introduction rules for $\{\top, \forall, \bot, \invamp\}$ can be done similarly, invoking an application of the cut-elimination theorem.

To illustrate how to treat the introduction rules for the positive connectives $\{\mathbf{0}, \oplus, \exists, \mathbf{1}, \otimes\}$, we consider the cases where the last inference rule of Ξ is $\oplus R$ and $\oplus L$. Consider the right-introduction rule first.

$$\frac{\Sigma :: \Gamma \vdash B_i, \Delta}{\Sigma :: \Gamma \vdash B_1 \oplus B_2, \Delta} \ \oplus R\ (i = 1, 2).$$

By the inductive hypothesis, we can assume that $\Sigma :: \cdot; \Gamma^\nabla \vdash_\Downarrow B_i^\nabla, \Delta^\nabla; \cdot$. Also note that the sequent $\Sigma :: \cdot; B_i^\nabla, (B_1^\nabla \multimap \bot) \& (B_2^\nabla \multimap \bot) \vdash \cdot; \cdot$ has a $\Downarrow \mathcal{L}_2$-proof (an observation that requires the use of Theorem 7.4). These $\Downarrow \mathcal{L}_2$-proofs can be brought together to prove the $(\cdot)^\nabla$ translation of the sequent $\Sigma :: \Gamma \vdash B_1 \oplus B_2, \Delta$.

$$\cfrac{\cfrac{\cfrac{\Sigma :: \cdot; \Gamma^\nabla \vdash B_i^\nabla, \Delta^\nabla; \cdot \quad \Sigma :: \cdot; B_i^\nabla, (B_1^\nabla \multimap \bot) \& (B_2^\nabla \multimap \bot) \vdash \cdot; \cdot}{\Sigma :: \cdot; \Gamma^\nabla, (B_1^\nabla \multimap \bot) \& (B_2^\nabla \multimap \bot) \vdash \Delta^\nabla; \cdot}\ cut}{\Sigma :: \cdot; \Gamma^\nabla, (B_1^\nabla \multimap \bot) \& (B_2^\nabla \multimap \bot) \vdash \bot, \Delta^\nabla; \cdot}\ \bot R}{\Sigma :: \cdot; \Gamma^\nabla \vdash ((B_1^\nabla \multimap \bot) \& (B_2^\nabla \multimap \bot)) \multimap \bot, \Delta^\nabla; \cdot}\ \multimap R$$

Next, consider the case in which the final inference rule of Ξ is

$$\frac{\Sigma :: \Gamma, B \vdash \Delta \quad \Sigma :: \Gamma, C \vdash \Delta}{\Sigma :: \Gamma, B \oplus C \vdash \Delta}\ \oplus L.$$

By the inductive assumption, we have both $\Sigma :: \cdot; \Gamma^\nabla, B^\nabla \vdash_\Downarrow \Delta^\nabla; \cdot$ and $\Sigma :: \cdot; \Gamma^\nabla, C^\nabla \vdash_\Downarrow \Delta^\nabla; \cdot$. Attaching the $\Downarrow \mathcal{L}_2$-proofs of these two sequents to the following derivation finishes the proof for the $\oplus L$ introduction rule.

7.4 THE FOCUSED PROOF SYSTEM IS SOUND AND COMPLETE

$$\frac{\dfrac{\Sigma :: \cdot; \Gamma^\nabla, B_1^\nabla \vdash \Delta^\nabla; \cdot}{\Sigma :: \cdot; \Gamma^\nabla, B_1^\nabla \vdash \bot, \Delta^\nabla; \cdot} \quad \dfrac{\Sigma :: \cdot; \Gamma^\nabla, B_2^\nabla \vdash \Delta^\nabla; \cdot}{\Sigma :: \cdot; \Gamma^\nabla, B_2^\nabla \vdash \bot, \Delta^\nabla; \cdot}}{\dfrac{\Sigma :: \cdot; \Gamma^\nabla \vdash B_1^\nabla \multimap \bot, \Delta^\nabla; \cdot \quad \Sigma :: \cdot; \Gamma^\nabla \vdash B_2^\nabla \multimap \bot, \Delta^\nabla; \cdot}{\Sigma :: \cdot; \Gamma^\nabla \vdash (B_1^\nabla \multimap \bot) \& (B_2^\nabla \multimap \bot), \Delta^\nabla; \cdot}}.$$

Since the sequent

$$\Sigma :: \cdot; (B_1^\nabla \multimap \bot) \& (B_2^\nabla \multimap \bot), ((B_1^\nabla \multimap \bot) \& (B_2^\nabla \multimap \bot)) \multimap \bot \vdash \cdot; \cdot$$

has a $\Downarrow \mathcal{L}_2$-proof, we can use the cut-elimination theorem to obtain a proof of the $(\cdot)^\nabla$ translation of $\Sigma :: \Gamma, B_1 \oplus B_2 \vdash \Delta$.

The introduction rules for **0**, **1**, $\otimes$, and $\exists$, can be done similarly, invoking an application of the cut-elimination theorem. Thus, the remaining rules in **L** that need to be considered are the exponentials. We consider the four rules for ! in the $\Downarrow \mathcal{L}_2$-proof systems.

Assume that the last inference rule of Ξ is

$$\frac{\Sigma :: \Gamma \vdash \Delta}{\Sigma :: \Gamma, !B \vdash \Delta} \ !W.$$

By the inductive hypothesis, we know that $\Sigma :: \cdot; \Gamma^\nabla \vdash_\Downarrow \Delta^\nabla; \cdot$. By Proposition 7.6, we can weaken this sequent and conclude that $\Sigma :: B^\nabla; \Gamma^\nabla \vdash_\Downarrow \Delta^\nabla; \cdot$. By applying Lemma 7.17, we have $\Sigma :: \cdot; \Gamma^\nabla, (B^\nabla \Rightarrow \bot) \multimap \bot \vdash_\Downarrow \Delta^\nabla; \cdot$, which completes this case.

Assume that the last inference rule of Ξ is

$$\frac{\Sigma :: \Gamma, !B, !B \vdash \Delta}{\Sigma :: \Gamma, !B \vdash \Delta} \ !C.$$

By the inductive hypothesis, we know that $\Sigma :: \cdot; \Gamma^\nabla, (!B)^\nabla, (!B)^\nabla \vdash_\Downarrow \Delta^\nabla; \cdot$. Using cut-elimination on the following proof (where the proofs of the two left premises are guaranteed by Exercise 7.5),

$$\dfrac{\Sigma :: B^\nabla; \cdot \vdash (!B)^\nabla; \cdot \quad \dfrac{\Sigma :: B^\nabla; \cdot \vdash (!B)^\nabla; \cdot \quad \Sigma :: \cdot; \Gamma^\nabla, (!B)^\nabla, (!B)^\nabla \vdash \Delta^\nabla; \cdot}{\Sigma :: B^\nabla; \Gamma^\nabla, (!B)^\nabla \vdash \Delta^\nabla; \cdot} \ cut}{\Sigma :: B^\nabla; \Gamma^\nabla \vdash \Delta^\nabla; \cdot} \ cut$$

we have $\Sigma :: B^\nabla; \Gamma^\nabla \vdash_\Downarrow \Delta^\nabla; \cdot$. Using Lemma 7.17, we can conclude that $\Sigma :: \cdot; \Gamma^\nabla, (B^\nabla \Rightarrow \bot) \multimap \bot \vdash_\Downarrow \Delta^\nabla; \cdot$.

The case when the last inference rule of Ξ is

$$\frac{\Sigma :: \Gamma, B \vdash \Delta}{\Sigma :: \Gamma, !B \vdash \Delta} \;!D$$

follows simply from a use of the *cut* rule and a proof of $\Sigma :: \cdot; (!B)^\nabla \vdash B; \cdot$ (Exercise 7.5).

Assume that the last rule of Ξ is

$$\frac{\Sigma :: !\Gamma \vdash B, ?\Delta}{\Sigma :: !\Gamma \vdash !B, ?\Delta} \;!R.$$

By the inductive hypothesis, we know that $\Sigma :: \cdot; (!\Gamma)^\nabla \vdash_\Downarrow B^\nabla, (?\Delta)^\nabla; \cdot$. By repeatedly applying Lemma 7.17, we can conclude that $\Sigma :: \Gamma^\nabla; \cdot \vdash_\Downarrow B^\nabla, (?\Delta)^\nabla; \cdot$. Since all the right rules permute over each other, we can assume that the $?R$ rule is applied below the rules related to B, leading us to $\Sigma :: \Gamma^\nabla; \cdot \vdash_\Downarrow B^\nabla; \Delta^\nabla$. With a proof of that sequent, we now build the following proof.

$$\frac{\dfrac{\dfrac{\dfrac{\Sigma :: \Gamma^\nabla; \cdot \vdash B^\nabla; \Delta^\nabla \quad \dfrac{}{\Sigma :: \Gamma^\nabla; \cdot \Downarrow \bot \vdash \cdot; \Delta^\nabla}\bot L}{\Sigma :: \Gamma^\nabla; \cdot \Downarrow B^\nabla \Rightarrow \bot \vdash \cdot; \Delta^\nabla} \Rightarrow L}{\Sigma :: \Gamma^\nabla; B^\nabla \Rightarrow \bot \vdash \cdot; \Delta^\nabla} \;decide_l}{\Sigma :: \Gamma^\nabla; B^\nabla \Rightarrow \bot \vdash \bot; \Delta^\nabla}\bot R}{\Sigma :: \Gamma^\nabla; \cdot \vdash (B^\nabla \Rightarrow \bot) \multimap \bot; \Delta^\nabla} \multimap R.$$

By repeated application of Lemma 7.17, we can conclude

$$\Sigma :: \cdot; (!\Gamma)^\nabla \vdash_\Downarrow (B^\nabla \Rightarrow \bot) \multimap \bot; \Delta^\nabla$$

and by repeated application of the $?R$ rule, we have

$$\Sigma :: \cdot; (!\Gamma)^\nabla \vdash_\Downarrow (B^\nabla \Rightarrow \bot) \multimap \bot, (?\Delta)^\nabla; \cdot,$$

which provides a proof of our desired sequent.

The only remaining **L** rules to consider are the four rules for the ?-exponential. Since ? is translated directly to ? by $(\cdot)^\nabla$, the proofs involving ? are similar but simpler than for the !-exponential. We do not include these cases here. □

A simple consequence of cut elimination for $\Downarrow^+\mathcal{L}_2$-proofs is that cut can be eliminated from the **L** system.

> **Theorem 7.19.** *A sequent provable in* **L** *can be proved without the cut rule.*

Proof: We first show that a sequent in **L** that is the conclusion of the cut rule applied to two cut-free proofs can be proved by a cut-free proof. Once this is done, a simple induction can remove all instances of the cut rule from a proof. Thus, assume that $\Sigma :: B, \Delta_1 \vdash \Gamma_1$ and $\Sigma :: \Delta_2 \vdash \Gamma_2, B$ have cut-free **L** proofs. By the completeness of $\Downarrow \mathcal{L}_2$-proofs (Theorem 7.18), we know that $\Sigma :: \cdot; B^\triangledown, \Delta_1^\triangledown \vdash \Gamma_1^\triangledown; \cdot$ and $\Sigma :: \cdot; \Delta_2^\triangledown \vdash B^\triangledown, \Gamma_2^\triangledown; \cdot$ have $\Downarrow \mathcal{L}_2$-proofs. Using the *cut* inference rule of $\mathcal{L}_2$, we know that $\Sigma :: \cdot; \Delta_1^\triangledown, \Delta_2^\triangledown \vdash_\Downarrow \Gamma_1^\triangledown, \Gamma_2^\triangledown; \cdot$ has $\Downarrow^+\mathcal{L}_2$-proof. By the cut-elimination theorem for $\Downarrow^+\mathcal{L}_2$-proofs (Theorem 7.15), we know that this sequent also has a (cut-free) $\Downarrow \mathcal{L}_2$-proof. By the soundness theorem of $\Downarrow \mathcal{L}_2$-proofs (Theorem 7.16) we finally know that $\Sigma :: \Delta_1, \Delta_2 \vdash \Gamma_1, \Gamma_2$ has a cut-free proof. □

7.5 Bibliographic Notes

A one-sided sequent calculus proof system for linear logic is given in Figure 6.5. A focused variant of that proof system, which first appeared in Andreoli [1992], is given in Figure 7.2. The main difference between Andreoli's original system and the one in Figure 7.2 is that the zone between $\vdash$ and $\Uparrow$ is a list in his system while it is a multiset in Figure 7.2. The D_1 rule corresponds to the *decide$_l$* rule while the D_2 rule corresponds to the *decide!* rule. Similarly, the I_1 rule corresponds to the *init* rule while the I_2 rule corresponds to the *init?* rule. The rules $[R \Uparrow]$ and $[R \Downarrow]$ are not needed in $\Downarrow \mathcal{L}_2$-proofs given our use of only negative connectives and two-sided sequents. The right-introduction and left-introduction phases in $\Downarrow \mathcal{L}_2$ correspond to what Andreoli called the *asynchronous* and *synchronous* phases, respectively.

The first major result that one usually attempts to prove about focused proof systems is that they are complete with respect to their unfocused version. Andreoli proved this result using a permutation argument in which unfocused proofs could be made progressively more focused. The proof of the completeness of $\Downarrow \mathcal{L}_2$-proofs given in Miller [1996] directly relied on Andreoli's proof of completeness. A direct proof of cut elimination for a focused proof system for linear logic was given by Bruscoli and Guglielmi [2006] and Guglielmi [1996] for the subset of $\Downarrow \mathcal{L}_2$ that does not include

$$\frac{\Sigma \vdash \Gamma \Uparrow \Delta; \Upsilon}{\Sigma \vdash \bot, \Gamma \Uparrow \Delta; \Upsilon} \, [\bot] \qquad \frac{\Sigma \vdash F, G, \Gamma \Uparrow \Delta; \Upsilon}{\Sigma \vdash F \,\mathcal{B}\, G, \Gamma \Uparrow \Delta; \Upsilon} \, [\mathcal{B}]$$

$$\frac{\Sigma \vdash \Gamma \Uparrow \Delta; \Upsilon, F}{\Sigma \vdash ?F, \Gamma \Uparrow \Delta; \Upsilon} \, [?] \qquad \frac{}{\Sigma \vdash \top, \Gamma \Uparrow \Delta; \Upsilon} \, [\top]$$

$$\frac{\Sigma \vdash F, \Gamma \Uparrow \Delta; \Upsilon \quad \Sigma \vdash G, \Gamma \Uparrow \Delta; \Upsilon}{\Sigma \vdash F \,\&\, G, \Gamma \Uparrow \Delta; \Upsilon} \, [\&]$$

$$\frac{y : \tau, \Sigma \vdash B[y/x], \Gamma \Uparrow \Delta; \Upsilon}{\Sigma \vdash \forall_\tau x.B, \Gamma \Uparrow \Delta; \Upsilon} \, [\forall] \qquad \frac{}{\Sigma \vdash 1 \Downarrow \cdot; \Upsilon} \, [1]$$

$$\frac{\Sigma \vdash F \Downarrow \Delta_1; \Upsilon \quad \Sigma \vdash G \Downarrow \Delta_2; \Upsilon}{\Sigma \vdash F \otimes G \Downarrow \Delta_1, \Delta_2; \Upsilon} \, [\otimes] \qquad \frac{\Sigma \vdash F \Uparrow \cdot; \Upsilon}{\Sigma \vdash !F \Downarrow \cdot; \Upsilon} \, [!]$$

$$\frac{\Sigma \vdash F_i \Downarrow \Delta; \Upsilon}{\Sigma \vdash F_1 \oplus F_2 \Downarrow \Delta; \Upsilon} \, [\oplus_i] \qquad \frac{\Sigma \Vdash t : \tau \quad \Sigma \vdash B[t/x] \Downarrow \Delta; \Upsilon}{\Sigma \vdash \exists_\tau x.B \Downarrow \Delta; \Upsilon} \, [\exists]$$

$$\frac{\Sigma \vdash \Gamma \Uparrow \Delta, F; \Upsilon}{\Sigma \vdash F, \Gamma \Uparrow \Delta; \Upsilon} \, [R \Uparrow] \quad \text{provided } F \text{ is a literal or a positive formula}$$

$$\frac{\Sigma \vdash F \Uparrow \Delta; \Upsilon}{\Sigma \vdash F \Downarrow \Delta; \Upsilon} \, [R \Downarrow] \quad \text{provided that } F \text{ is a negative formula}$$

$$\frac{}{\Sigma \vdash A^\bot \Downarrow A; \Upsilon} \, [I_1] \qquad \frac{}{\Sigma \vdash A^\bot \Downarrow \cdot; \Upsilon, A} \, [I_2]$$

$$\frac{\Sigma \vdash F \Downarrow \Delta; \Upsilon}{\Sigma \vdash \cdot \Uparrow \Delta, F; \Upsilon} \, [D_1] \qquad \frac{\Sigma \vdash F \Downarrow \Delta; \Upsilon, F}{\Sigma \vdash \cdot \Uparrow \Delta; \Upsilon, F} \, [D_2]$$

The rule [∀] has the proviso that y is not in Σ. In [$\oplus_i$], $i = 1$ or $i = 2$.

Figure 7.2 A one-sided focused proof system for linear logic.

the (redundant) ? exponential and in which formulas were limited to what we call paths here. Their proofs of the cut-elimination theorem described cut elimination at the level of synthetic inference rules.

The style of completeness proof given here first proves that the generalized initial rule and the cut rule are admissible in the focused proof system. Given those results, it is then a simple matter to conclude the completeness of focusing. This approach to proving properties about focused proof systems was given in Chaudhuri [2006] and Chaudhuri et al. [2008b] for intuitionistic linear logic and was later extended by Liang and Miller [2011] and Liang and Miller [2024] to intuitionistic and classical logics. Further developments of this style of proof (along with a formal verification) are given by Simmons [2014] for propositional intuitionistic logic. Felty et al. [2021] provide a mechanically verified proof of cut admissibility for the proof system in Figure 7.2 and apply their framework to conclude various properties of object-logic proof systems that are encoded into linear logic using a technique to be presented in Section 8.7.

Section 5.6 presents a Kripke model that served as a canonical model for the intuitionistic provability of $\mathcal{L}_0$-formulas. Hodas and Miller [1994] generalized that model to a *resource-indexed model* in such a way that cut admissibility for linear logic over $\mathcal{L}_1$-formulas is equivalent to the equivalence between cut-free provability and truth in the canonical resource-indexed model (compare with Theorem 5.32).

Chapter 8

Linear Logic Programming

In this chapter, we present several small examples of linear logic programs. Subsequent chapters will present more substantial examples.

8.1 Encoding Multisets as Formulas

Consider the following encoding of multisets of terms as formulas in linear logic. Let token *item* be a predicate of one argument: The linear logic atomic formula *item x* will denote the multiset containing just the one element x occurring once. There are two natural encodings of multisets into formulas using this predicate. The *conjunctive* encoding uses **1** for the empty multiset and $\otimes$ to combine two multisets. For example, the multiset $\{1,2,2\}$ is encoded by the linear logic formula *item* 1 $\otimes$ *item* 2 $\otimes$ *item* 2. Proof search using this style encoding manipulates such multisets on the left of the sequent turnstile. This approach is favored when an intuitionistic subset of linear logic is used, such as in the $\mathcal{L}_1$ subset of linear logic (Section 6.4). The dual encoding, the *disjunctive* encoding, uses $\bot$ for the empty multiset and $\invamp$ to combine two multisets. Proof search using this style encoding manipulates such multisets on the right of the sequent turnstile, and multiple-conclusion sequents are now required, such as in the $\Downarrow \mathcal{L}_2$ presentation of linear logic (Section 6.7).

> **Exercise 8.1.** (‡) Let $A_1, \ldots, A_n, B_1, \ldots, B_m$ be atomic formulas, P_1 be $A_1 \invamp \cdots \invamp A_n$, and P_2 be $B_1 \invamp \cdots \invamp B_m$. Prove that if $P_1 \multimap P_2$ is provable in linear logic, then $P_2 \multimap P_1$ is also provable.

> **Exercise 8.2.** *Redo Exercise 8.1 but this time replace $\invamp$ with $\otimes$.*

Let S and T be the two formulas *item* s_1 $\invamp$ $\cdots$ $\invamp$ *item* s_n and *item* t_1 $\invamp$ $\cdots$ $\invamp$ *item* t_m, respectively ($n, m \geq 0$). Exercise 8.1 allows us to conclude that $S \multimap T$ is provable if and only if $T \multimap S$ is provable if and only if the two multisets $\{s_1, \ldots, s_n\}$ and $\{t_1, \ldots, t_m\}$ are equal. Now consider the following two ways to encode the multiset inclusion $S \sqsubseteq T$.

1. $S \invamp 0 \multimap T$. This formula mixes multiplicative connectives with the additive connective 0: the latter allows items in T that are not contained in S to be deleted.
2. $\exists q (S \invamp q \multimap T)$. This formula mixes multiplicative connectives with a higher-order quantifier. Intuitively, we would like to consider the instantiation for q to be the multiset difference of S from T. However, such a restriction on q is not part of this formula, and q can be instantiated with any linear logic formula.

As it turns out, these two approaches are equivalent in (higher-order) linear logic because the following formula is provable.

$$\forall S. \forall T. [(S \invamp 0 \multimap T) \multimapboth \exists q. (S \invamp q \multimap T)].$$

Recall that the expression $B \multimapboth C$ is an abbreviation for $(B \multimap C) \& (C \multimap B)$.

8.2 A Syntax for Lolli Programs

In order to present several examples in this chapter, we extend Prolog and λProlog syntax to accommodate Lolli logic programs. As we have already indicated in Section 6.5, the symbols => and :- of λProlog are used to represent $\Rightarrow$ and the converse of $\multimap$, respectively. We shall also write -o and <= to represent the $\multimap$ and the converse of $\Rightarrow$. We also use the symbols & and erase to denote, respectively, & and $\top$. Given these connectives we can define (in the sense described in Section 5.8) the symbols true, , (comma), ; (semicolon), exists, and bang which represent the linear logic connectives $\mathbf{1}$, $\otimes$, $\oplus$, $\exists$, and !, respectively. These definitions are displayed in Figure 8.1. Those clauses encode only the right-introduction rules for their respective logical connective.

```
type true     o.
type ,        o -> o -> o.
type ;        o -> o -> o.
type exists   (A -> o) -> o.
type bang     o -> o.

true.
(P , Q)  :- P :- Q.
(P ; Q)  :- P.
(P ; Q)  :- Q.
exists B :- (B T).
bang G <= G.
```

Figure 8.1 Logic programs for defining the positive polarity connectives.

8.3 Permuting a List

Since the bounded part of contexts in $\mathcal{L}$-proofs are multisets, it is simple to permute a list of items by first loading the list's members into the bounded part of a context and then unloading them. The latter operation is nondeterministic and can succeed for each permutation of the loaded list. Consider the following simple program:

```
type load      list A -> list A -> o.
type unload                list A -> o.

load nil K     :- unload K.
load (X::L) K  :- (item X -o load L K).
unload nil.
unload (X::L)  :- item X, unload L.
```

The meaning of load and unload depends on the contents of the bounded part of the context, so the correctness of these clauses must be stated relative to a context. Let Ψ be a multiset of formulas containing the four formulas displayed above and any other formulas that do not contain either item, load, or unload as their head symbol. (The *head symbol* of a clause of the form A or $G \multimap A$ is the predicate symbol that is the head of the atom A.) Let Δ be the multiset containing exactly the atomic formulas

$$\text{item}\, a_1, \ldots, \text{item}\, a_n.$$

We shall say that such a context *encodes* the multiset $\{a_1, \ldots, a_n\}$. It is now an easy matter to prove the following two assertions about load and unload.

8.3 Permuting a List

1. The sequent $\Sigma :: \Psi; \Delta \vdash$ (unload K); · is provable if and only if K is a list containing the same elements with the same multiplicity as the multiset encoded in Δ.
2. The sequent $\Sigma :: \Psi; \Delta \vdash$ (load L K); · is provable if and only if K is a list containing the same elements with the same multiplicity as in the list L together with the multiset encoded in the context Δ.

In order for load and unload to correctly permute the elements of a list, we must guarantee two things about the context: First, the predicates item, load, and unload cannot be used as head symbols in any part of the context except as specified above and, second, the bounded zone must be empty at the start of the computation of a permutation. It is possible to handle the first condition by making use of appropriate quantifiers over the predicate names item, load, and unload (we discuss such a use of higher-order quantification in Section 9.8). The second condition – that the unbounded zone is empty – can be managed by using the exponential !, which we now discuss in more detail.

Consider proving the sequent $\Sigma :: \Psi; \Delta \vdash\ ! G_1 \otimes G_2;\ \cdot$, where G_1 and G_2 are goal formulas, and ! and $\otimes$ are specified using the clauses in Figure 8.1. Given the completeness of $\Downarrow \mathcal{L}_1$, this is provable if and only if the two sequents $\Sigma :: \Psi;\ \cdot\ \vdash G_1;\ \cdot$ and $\Sigma :: \Psi; \Delta \vdash G_2;\ \cdot$ are provable. In other words, using the ! operator forces G_1 to be proved with an empty bounded zone.

It is now clear how to define the permutation of two lists given the example program above: Add either the formula

```
perm L K   :-   bang(load L K).
```

or, equivalently, the formula

```
perm L K   <=   load L K.
```

to those defining load and unload. Thus, attempting to prove (perm L K) will only reduce to an attempt to prove (load L K) if the bounded zones are empty. From the description of load above, L and K must be permutations of each other.

Exercise 8.3. *Let Ψ_0 be the collection of $\mathcal{L}_1$-formulas given in Figure 8.1, and let Ψ be a collection of $\mathcal{L}_1$-formulas that do not contain occurrences of the symbols introduced in that figure. Prove the following about provability in $\Downarrow \mathcal{L}_1$. The sequent $\Sigma :: \Psi_0, \Psi; \Delta \vdash$ bang $G;\ \cdot$ is provable if and only if $\Sigma :: \Psi_0, \Psi; \Delta \vdash$ true & $G;\ \cdot$ is provable if and only if Δ is empty and $\Sigma :: \Psi_0, \Psi;\ \cdot\ \vdash G;\ \cdot$ is provable.*

8.4 Multiset Rewriting on the Left

The ideas presented in the permutation example can easily be expanded to show how the bounded zone can be employed for multiset rewriting. Let H be the *multiset rewriting system* $\{\langle L_i, R_i\rangle \mid i \in I\}$ where for each $i \in I$ (a finite index set), L_i and R_i are finite multisets. Define the relation $M \Longrightarrow_H N$ on finite multisets to hold if there is some $i \in I$ and some multiset C such that M is $C \cup L_i$ and N is $C \cup R_i$. Let $\Longrightarrow_H^*$ be the reflexive and transitive closure of $\Longrightarrow_H$.

Given a rewriting system H, we wish to specify a binary predicate rewrite such that (rewrite L K) is provable if and only if the multisets encoded by L and K stand in the $\Longrightarrow_H^*$ relation. Let Γ_0 be the following set of formulas (these are independent of H):

```
rewrite L K      <= load L K.

load (X::L) K    :- (item X -o load L K).
load nil      K  :- rew K.

rew K            :- unload K.

unload (X::L)    :- item X, unload L.
unload nil.
```

Taken alone, these clauses give a slightly different version of the permute program of the last example. The only addition is the binary predicate rew, which will be used as a socket into which we can plug a particular rewrite system.

In order to encode a rewrite system H, each rewrite rule in H is given by a formula specifying an additional clause for the rew predicate as follows: If H contains the pair $\langle\{a_1, \ldots, a_n\}, \{b_1, \ldots, b_m\}\rangle$ then this pair is encoded by the clause:

```
rew K :- item a1,       ...,      item an,
           (item b1 -o ... -o item bm -o rew K).
```

If either n or m is zero, the appropriate portion of the formula is deleted. Operationally, this clause reads the a_i's out of the bounded zone, loads the b_i's, and then attempts another rewrite. Let Γ_H be the set resulting from encoding each pair in H. For example, if $H = \{\langle\{a,b\},\{b,c\}\rangle, \langle\{a,a\},\{a\}\rangle\}$ then Γ_H is the set containing the following two clauses.

```
rew K :-    item a, item b, (item b -o (item c -o rew K)).
rew K :-    item a, item a,             (item a -o rew K).
```

8.4 MULTISET REWRITING ON THE LEFT

One drawback of this example is that `rewrite` is a predicate on lists, though its arguments are intended to represent multisets. Unfortunately, there can be as many as $n!$ lists that denote a given multiset of n items. This redundancy might be addressed by exploring a noncommutative variant of linear logic (see references at the end of Chapter 10).

Exercise 8.4. (‡) *Consider again Exercise 5.43, in which it was argued that computing the maximum of a multiset of natural numbers was not possible if that multiset was encoded as atomic formulas in the left-side of sequents in I-proofs. It is possible to write such a program when using $\Downarrow \mathcal{L}_1$ proofs. Write a logic program $\mathcal{P}$ using $\mathcal{L}_1$-formula such that the following holds. If N is a set of natural numbers $\{n_1, \ldots, n_k\}$ and $k \geq 1$ then the $\Downarrow \mathcal{L}_1$-sequent $\cdot ::\mathcal{P}; a\,n_1, \ldots, a\,n_k \vdash \mathsf{maxa}\,m; \cdot$ is provable if and only if m is the maximum of $\{n_1, \ldots, n_k\}$.*

Exercise 8.5. (‡) *As in Exercise 8.4, let $k \geq 1$ and let N be a multiset of natural numbers $\{n_1, \ldots, n_k\}$. Write a logic program $\mathcal{P}$ that computes the sum $n_1 + \cdots + n_k$. More precisely, the $\Downarrow \mathcal{L}_1$-sequent $\cdot ::\mathcal{P}; a\,n_1, \ldots, a\,n_k \vdash \mathsf{sumup}\,m; \cdot$ is provable if and only if $m = n_1 + \cdots + n_k$. Contrast this exercise with the predicate* `sumup` *in Figure 5.4.*

Exercise 8.6. *Represent the finite graph $G = (N, E)$, with nodes N and edges $E \subseteq N \times N$, as the two sets of atomic formulas*

$$\mathcal{N} = \{\mathsf{node}(x) \mid x \in N\} \quad \text{and} \quad \mathcal{E} = \{\mathsf{edge}(x,y) \mid \langle x,y \rangle \in E\}.$$

Consider the logic program $\mathcal{P}$ that consists of the following declarations and clauses.

```
kind node            type.
type connected, loop  o.
type node, nd         node -> o.

connected :- node u, (nd u => loop).
loop.
loop :- nd u, edge u v, node v, (nd v => loop).
```

Show that the sequent $\cdot ::\mathcal{P}, \mathcal{E}; \mathcal{N} \vdash \mathsf{connected}; \cdot$ is provable in $\Downarrow \mathcal{L}_1$ if and only if the graph G is connected.

8.5 Context Management in a Theorem Prover

Logic programming provides a high-level framework for implementing theorem provers for various logics. Since such implementations deal with two logics, we call the logic underlying the logic programming language the *metalogic* and the target logic being implemented the *object logic*.

Intuitionistic logic is a useful metalogic for specifying provability in various object logics. For example, consider specifying *natural deduction* provability in propositional, intuitionistic logic over the logical symbols `imp`, `and`, and `or`, denoting object-level implication, conjunction, and disjunction (see the declarations in Figure 8.2). Natural deduction rules specify the two senses of provability for a logical connective – how to reason from and reason to (see Section 3.7) – using *elimination* and *introduction* rules, respectively. A reasonable specification of the natural deduction inference rule for implication introduction is

```
pv (A imp B) :- hyp A => pv B.
```

where `pv` and `hyp` are metalevel predicates denoting provability and hypothesis (see Figure 8.4 for their type declarations). Operationally, this formula states that one way to prove `A imp B` is to add the object-level hypothesis `A` to the context and attempt a proof of `B`. In the same setting, conjunction elimination can be expressed by the formula

```
pv G :- hyp (A and B), (hyp A => hyp B => pv G).
```

This formula states that in order to prove some object-level formula `G`, check to see if there is a conjunctive hypothesis, say `(A and B)`, in the context and, if so, attempt a proof of `G` from the context extended with the two hypotheses `A` and `B`. Other introduction and elimination rules can be specified similarly. Finally, the formula

```
pv G :- hyp G.
```

is needed to complete a proof.

```
kind fm              type.
type p, q, r         fm.
type or, and imp     fm -> fm -> fm.
infixr or      3.
infixr and     4.
infixr imp     5.
```

Figure 8.2 Declarations for the constructors of an object logic.

8.5 CONTEXT MANAGEMENT IN A THEOREM PROVER

It is easy to write a specification $\mathcal{P}$ (a multiset of $\mathcal{L}_0$ formulas) in this style so that there is a proof in the metalogic of (pv G) from $\mathcal{P}$ and the atomic formulas (hyp H_1), ..., (hyp H_i) if and only if there is a proof in the object logic of G from the assumptions $H_1, \ldots, H_i$. Unfortunately, intuitionistic logic has its drawbacks as a metalogic even in this simple setting. In particular, the set of assumptions of the form (hyp H) increases during the search for proofs, even though some assumptions need to be used at most once within some subproofs. For example, if we use the rule of cases (i.e., the elimination rule for disjunction in natural deduction) on a disjunctive assumption, then that disjunction is not needed during the search for the proofs of either subcase dealing with the disjuncts. In order to have more explicit control of the collection of hypotheses, we abandon natural deduction for sequent calculus. In particular, the sequent calculus proof system in Figure 8.3 shows one way to organize a proof system for propositional intuitionistic logic so that the only hypothesis that might be used more than once are those that are implications. This proof system uses single-conclusion sequents with multisets on the left, and it does not contain rules for either weakening or contraction. The specification of ⊃L requires that the introduced implication in its conclusion must also appear in its left premise.

The proof system in Figure 8.3 is captured by the Lolli specification in Figure 8.4, along with a (partial) specification of isatom used to recognize object-level atomic formulas. Sequents that appear in proofs involving these clauses have left-bounded zones containing only atomic formulas of the form (hyp H). Note that the two additive rules in Figure 8.3, namely, ∧R and ∨L, are encoded in the Lolli specification using the additive conjunction (&), and that the additive true (erase) is used to force the weakening of any side formulas in the *init* rule.

$$\frac{\Gamma \vdash B \quad \Gamma \vdash B}{\Gamma \vdash A \wedge B} \wedge R \qquad \frac{\Gamma, A \vdash B}{\Gamma \vdash A \supset B} \supset R \qquad \frac{\Gamma \vdash A}{\Gamma \vdash A \vee B} \vee R$$

$$\frac{\Gamma \vdash B}{\Gamma \vdash A \vee B} \vee R \qquad \frac{\Gamma, A, B \vdash G}{\Gamma, A \wedge B \vdash G} \wedge L \qquad \frac{\Gamma, A \vdash G \quad \Gamma, B \vdash G}{\Gamma, A \vee B \vdash G} \vee L$$

$$\frac{\Gamma, C \supset B \vdash C \quad \Gamma, B \vdash G}{\Gamma, C \supset B \vdash G} \supset L \qquad \frac{}{\Gamma, A \vdash A} \; init, \; A \; atomic$$

Figure 8.3 A proof system for propositional intuitionistic logic.

```
type pv, hyp, isatom      fm -> o.

pv (A and B) :- pv A & pv B.
pv (A imp B) :- hyp A -o pv B.
pv (A or  B) :- pv A.
pv (A or  B) :- pv B.
pv G :- hyp (A and B), (hyp A -o hyp B -o pv G).
pv G :- hyp (A or B),
          ((hyp A -o pv G) & (hyp B -o pv G)).
pv G :- hyp (C imp B),
          ((hyp (C imp B) -o pv C) & (hyp B -o pv G)).
pv A :- isatom A, hyp A, erase.

isatom p & isatom q & isatom r.
```

Figure 8.4 A specification of the rules in Figure 8.3.

$$\frac{\Gamma, A, B \vdash G}{\Gamma, A, A \supset B \vdash G} \supset L_1, \; A \text{ atomic} \qquad \frac{\Gamma, C \supset D \supset B \vdash G}{\Gamma, (C \wedge D) \supset B \vdash G} \supset L_2$$

$$\frac{\Gamma, C \supset B, D \supset B \vdash G}{\Gamma, (C \vee D) \supset B \vdash G} \supset L_3 \qquad \frac{\Gamma, D \supset B \vdash C \supset D \quad \Gamma, B \vdash G}{\Gamma, (C \supset D) \supset B \vdash G} \supset L_4$$

Figure 8.5 Replacements for the $\supset$L rule.

```
pv G :- hyp (A imp B), isatom A, hyp A,
          (hyp B -o hyp A -o pv G).
pv G :- hyp ((C and D) imp B),
          (hyp (C imp (D imp B)) -o pv G).
pv G :- hyp ((C or D) imp B),
          (hyp (C imp B) -o hyp (D imp B) -o pv G).
pv G :- hyp ((C imp D) imp B),
          ((hyp (D imp B) -o pv (C imp D)) &
           (hyp B -o pv G)).
```

Figure 8.6 A contraction-free formulation of $\supset$L.

The logic program in Figure 8.4 does not yield a terminating search procedure because an implication on the left can be used multiple times: For example, consider attempting to prove the sequent $p \supset p \vdash p$. Fortunately, an alternative presentation of the implication left-introduction rule can solve this particular problem. For example, proof systems given in Dyckhoff [1992] and Hudelmaier [1992] can be expressed directly in this setting. In those papers, the left-introduction rule for implication can be replaced by the four rules in Figure 8.5. Thus, consider modifying the specification in Figure 8.4 by

8.6 Multiset Rewriting on the Right

Since formulas in $\mathcal{L}_1$ are also in $\mathcal{L}_2$, the techniques for rewriting multisets using the bounded left-side zone can also be used in $\mathcal{L}_2$. However, it is also possible to use the bounded right-side zone as well. To illustrate that approach, consider the clause

$$a \,⅋\, b \circ\!\!- c \,⅋\, d \,⅋\, e.$$

When presenting examples of $\mathcal{L}_2$ specifications, we continue the habit of using $\circ\!\!-$ and $\Leftarrow$ as the converses of $-\!\!\circ$ and $\Rightarrow$ since they provide a more natural operational reading of clauses (similar to the use of : - in Prolog). Here, $⅋$ binds tighter than $\circ\!\!-$ and $\Leftarrow$. Consider the $\Downarrow \mathcal{L}_2$ sequent $\Sigma :: \Psi; \Delta \vdash a,b,\Gamma;\Upsilon$, where the above clause is a member of Ψ. A proof of this sequent can proceed as follows.

$$\dfrac{\dfrac{\dfrac{\Sigma :: \Psi; \Delta \vdash c,d,e,\Gamma;\Upsilon}{\dfrac{\Sigma :: \Psi; \Delta \vdash c,d \,⅋\, e,\Gamma;\Upsilon}{\Sigma :: \Psi; \Delta \vdash c \,⅋\, d \,⅋\, e,\Gamma;\Upsilon}} \quad \dfrac{\Sigma :: \Psi;\cdot \Downarrow a \vdash a;\Upsilon \quad \Sigma :: \Psi;\cdot \Downarrow b \vdash b;\Upsilon}{\Sigma :: \Psi;\cdot \Downarrow a \,⅋\, b \vdash a,b;\Upsilon}}{\Sigma :: \Psi; \Delta \Downarrow c \,⅋\, d \,⅋\, e \multimap a \,⅋\, b \vdash a,b,\Gamma;\Upsilon}}{\Sigma :: \Psi; \Delta \vdash a,b,\Gamma;\Upsilon} \; decide!.$$

We can interpret this fragment of a proof as a reduction of the multiset a,b,Γ to the multiset c,d,e,Γ by backchaining on the clause displayed above.

Of course, a clause may have multiple top-level implications. In this case, the surrounding context must be manipulated properly to prove the sub-goals that arise in backchaining. Consider using the *decide!* rule on the formula

$$A_1 \,⅋\, A_2 \Leftarrow G_4 \circ\!\!- G_3 \Leftarrow G_2 \circ\!\!- G_1$$

to prove the sequent $\Sigma :: \Psi; \Delta \vdash A_1,A_2,\mathcal{A};\Upsilon$. An attempt to prove this sequent would then lead to the attempt to prove the four sequents

$$\Sigma :: \Psi; \Delta_1 \vdash G_1,\mathcal{A}_1;\Upsilon \qquad \Sigma :: \Psi;\cdot \vdash G_2;\Upsilon$$
$$\Sigma :: \Psi; \Delta_2 \vdash G_3,\mathcal{A}_2;\Upsilon \qquad \Sigma :: \Psi;\cdot \vdash G_4;\Upsilon$$

where Δ is the multiset union of Δ_1 and Δ_2, and $\mathcal{A}$ is the multiset union of $\mathcal{A}_1$ and $\mathcal{A}_2$. In other words, those subgoals immediately to the right of an $\Leftarrow$ are attempted with empty bounded zones: The bounded zones, here Δ and $\mathcal{A}$, are divided up and used in attempts to prove those goals immediately to the right of $\circ\!\!-$.

For an example of computing using multisets on the right of $\Downarrow \mathcal{L}_2$ sequents, consider again computing the sum of a multiset of natural numbers. Assume that we take the encoding of natural numbers and addition (sum) given in Figure 5.3, and make them available as $\Downarrow \mathcal{L}_2$ formulas. Now add the following two formulas and consider the following exercise.

```
sumall M      :- acc M -o acc z.
acc N || a M  :- sum N M S, acc S.
```

> **Exercise 8.7.** Let Σ and Ψ be the signature and logic programs given above for sumall and acc. Show that the sequent
>
> $$\Sigma :: \Psi; \cdot \vdash a\, n_1 \,\mathbin{\mbox{$\mathpalette\new@parr\relax$}}\, a\, n_2 \,\mathbin{\mbox{$\mathpalette\new@parr\relax$}}\, \cdots \,\mathbin{\mbox{$\mathpalette\new@parr\relax$}}\, a\, n_i \,\mathbin{\mbox{$\mathpalette\new@parr\relax$}}\, \text{sumall}\, m; \cdot$$
>
> is provable if and only if m is the sum of $n_1, \ldots, n_i$.

More examples of specifications written using the $\mathcal{L}_2$ presentation of linear logic appear in Chapters 11, 12, and 13.

8.7 Specification of Sequent Calculus Proof Systems

In this section, we provide a different style of specification of sequent calculus rules from what was illustrated in Section 8.5 that makes use of multiset rewriting using the right-bounded zone of sequents in $\Downarrow \mathcal{L}_2$.

As we have described in Section 4.1, the distinction between sequents in classical, intuitionistic, and linear logics can be described, in part, by where the structural rules of weakening and contraction can be applied. In classical logic, these structural rules are allowed on both sides of the sequent turnstile; in intuitionistic logic, no structural rules are allowed on the right of the turnstile; and in linear logic, they are not allowed on either side of the turnstile. This suggests the following representation of sequents in these three systems. Let fm be the type of object-level propositional formulas and let $\lfloor \cdot \rfloor$ and $\lceil \cdot \rceil$ be two metalevel predicates of type $fm \to o$. Sequents in these three logics can

8.7 Specification of Sequent Calculus Proof Systems

be specified as follows: Object-logic sequents will be two-sided, and the left and right contexts will be paired using $\longrightarrow$ (following the original notation in Gentzen [1935]).

Linear: The sequent $B_1, \ldots, B_n \longrightarrow C_1, \ldots, C_m$ ($n, m \geq 0$) is represented by the metalevel formula

$$\lfloor B_1 \rfloor \,\mathbin{\mathpalette\make@circled\Re}\, \cdots \,\mathbin{\mathpalette\make@circled\Re}\, \lfloor B_n \rfloor \,\mathbin{\mathpalette\make@circled\Re}\, \lceil C_1 \rceil \,\mathbin{\mathpalette\make@circled\Re}\, \cdots \,\mathbin{\mathpalette\make@circled\Re}\, \lceil C_m \rceil.$$

Intuitionistic: The sequent $B_1, \ldots, B_n \longrightarrow C$ ($n \geq 0$) is represented by the metalevel formula

$$?\lfloor B_1 \rfloor \,\mathbin{\mathpalette\make@circled\Re}\, \cdots \,\mathbin{\mathpalette\make@circled\Re}\, ?\lfloor B_n \rfloor \,\mathbin{\mathpalette\make@circled\Re}\, \lceil C \rceil.$$

Classical: The sequent $B_1, \ldots, B_n \longrightarrow C_1, \ldots, C_m$ ($n, m \geq 0$) is represented by the metalevel formula

$$?\lfloor B_1 \rfloor \,\mathbin{\mathpalette\make@circled\Re}\, \cdots \,\mathbin{\mathpalette\make@circled\Re}\, ?\lfloor B_n \rfloor \,\mathbin{\mathpalette\make@circled\Re}\, ?\lceil C_1 \rceil \,\mathbin{\mathpalette\make@circled\Re}\, \cdots \,\mathbin{\mathpalette\make@circled\Re}\, ?\lceil C_m \rceil.$$

The $\lfloor \cdot \rfloor$ and $\lceil \cdot \rceil$ predicates are used to identify which object-level formulas appear on which side of the sequent, and the ? exponential is used to mark the formulas to which weakening and contraction can be applied.

As we now show, Figure 8.7 contains a specification of intuitionistic logic provability of the connectives $\wedge$, $\vee$, and $\supset$ using $\mathcal{L}_2$ as the metalevel logic. Expressions displayed as they are in Figure 8.7 are abbreviations for closed formulas: The intended formulas are those that result from applying ! to their universal closure. Let J be the set of clauses displayed in Figure 8.7 and let Σ_0 be the set of constants containing object-level logical connectives (as in Figure 8.2) along with the two predicates $\lfloor \cdot \rfloor$ and $\lceil \cdot \rceil$.

Now consider the synthetic inference rules that result from using the *decide*! rule with a formula in Figure 8.7. If Γ is a multiset of object-level

$$
\begin{array}{ll}
(\supset R) & \lceil A \supset B \rceil \circ\!\!-\!\! ?\lfloor A \rfloor \,\mathbin{\mathpalette\make@circled\Re}\, \lceil B \rceil. \\
(\supset L) & \lfloor A \supset B \rfloor \Leftarrow \lceil A \rceil \circ\!\!-\!\! ?\lfloor B \rfloor. \\
(\wedge R) & \lceil A \wedge B \rceil \circ\!\!-\!\! \lceil A \rceil \circ\!\!-\!\! \lceil B \rceil. \\
(\wedge L_1) & \lfloor A \wedge B \rfloor \circ\!\!-\!\! ?\lfloor A \rfloor. \\
(\wedge L_2) & \lfloor A \wedge B \rfloor \circ\!\!-\!\! ?\lfloor B \rfloor. \\
(\vee L) & \lfloor A \vee B \rfloor \circ\!\!-\!\! ?\lfloor A \rfloor \,\&\, ?\lfloor B \rfloor. \\
(\vee R_1) & \lceil A \vee B \rceil \circ\!\!-\!\! \lceil A \rceil. \\
(\vee R_2) & \lceil A \vee B \rceil \circ\!\!-\!\! \lceil B \rceil. \\
(initial) & \lceil B \rceil \,\mathbin{\mathpalette\make@circled\Re}\, \lfloor B \rfloor. \\
(cut) & \bot \circ\!\!-\!\! ?\lfloor C \rfloor \Leftarrow \lceil C \rceil.
\end{array}
$$

Figure 8.7 The specification J of a sequent calculus.

$$\frac{\Gamma, A \supset B \longrightarrow B \quad \Gamma, A \supset B, B \longrightarrow E}{\Gamma, A \supset B \longrightarrow E} \supset L \quad \frac{A, \Gamma \longrightarrow B}{\Gamma \longrightarrow A \supset B} \supset R$$

$$\frac{\Gamma, A \longrightarrow E}{\Gamma, A \wedge B \longrightarrow E} \wedge L_1 \quad \frac{\Gamma, B \longrightarrow E}{\Gamma, A \wedge B \longrightarrow E} \wedge L_2 \quad \frac{\Gamma \longrightarrow A \quad \Gamma \longrightarrow B}{\Gamma \longrightarrow A \wedge B} \wedge R$$

$$\frac{\Gamma \longrightarrow A}{\Gamma \longrightarrow A \vee B} \vee R_1 \quad \frac{\Gamma \longrightarrow B}{\Gamma \longrightarrow A \vee B} \vee R_2 \quad \frac{\Gamma, A \longrightarrow E \quad \Gamma, B \longrightarrow E}{\Gamma, A \vee B \longrightarrow E} \vee L$$

$$\frac{}{\Gamma, B \longrightarrow B} \text{ initial} \quad \frac{\Gamma \longrightarrow C \quad C, \Gamma \longrightarrow B}{\Gamma \longrightarrow B} \text{ cut}$$

Figure 8.8 The inference rules encoded by J.

formulas (terms of type fm), let $\lfloor \Gamma \rfloor$ denote the multiset $\{\lfloor B \rfloor \mid B \in \Gamma\}$. The synthetic rule resulting from using *decide!* on the $(\supset R)$ clause in Figure 8.7 is

$$\frac{\cdot :: J; \cdot \vdash \lceil B \rceil; \lfloor A \rfloor, \lfloor \Gamma \rfloor}{\cdot :: J; \cdot \vdash \lceil A \supset B \rceil; \lfloor \Gamma \rfloor}.$$

Thus, this synthetic inference rule captures exactly the object-level inference: that is, proving the object-level sequent $\Gamma \longrightarrow A \supset B$ has been successfully reduced to proving the sequent $A, \Gamma \longrightarrow B$ (see the $\supset R$ rule in Figure 8.8).

It is a simple matter to compute the synthetic inference rule that arises from using *decide!* on the (*cut*) clause, namely,

$$\frac{\cdot :: J; \cdot \vdash \lceil C \rceil; \mathcal{L} \quad \cdot :: J; \cdot \vdash \lceil B \rceil; \lfloor C \rfloor, \mathcal{L}}{\cdot :: J; \cdot \vdash \lceil B \rceil; \mathcal{L}}.$$

This metalevel synthetic rule captures the object-level inference rule called *cut* in Figure 8.8. Note that the occurrence of $\Leftarrow$ in the specification of (*cut*) is important here: Consider the following modification of the specification of the object-level cut inference rule.

$$(cut') \quad \bot \circ\!\!-\, ?\lfloor C \rfloor \circ\!\!-\, \lceil C \rceil.$$

Two synthetic inference rules result from using *decide!* on this formula, namely, the one displayed above and the following.

$$\frac{\cdot :: J; \cdot \vdash \lceil B \rceil, \lceil C \rceil; \mathcal{L} \quad \cdot :: J; \cdot \vdash \cdot; \lfloor C \rfloor, \mathcal{L}}{\cdot :: J; \cdot \vdash \lceil B \rceil; \mathcal{L}}.$$

This additional synthetic rule corresponds to the following object-level inference rule.

$$\frac{\Gamma \longrightarrow B, C \quad C, \Gamma \longrightarrow \cdot}{\Gamma \longrightarrow B}.$$

In other words, the clause (cut') does not properly restrict the occurrences of B in the premises. It is possible to prove that if B moves to the right side of the left premise, that left premise will not ultimately be provable (from J). Nonetheless, we wish to have exactly one synthetic inference rule arising from our metalevel specification of the cut rule. Hence, the (cut) rule and the $(\supset L)$ rules both have occurrences of $\Leftarrow$. Recall that in Section 6.2, we pointed out that both (cut) and $(\supset L)$ are different from other sequent calculus rules for intuitionistic logic: In J, that difference is captured by the use of $\Leftarrow$ instead of $\circ\!\!-$ in the specification of these two rules (see also Proposition 4.2).

> **Exercise 8.8.** *Show that the formula* $\forall B.\,!\lceil B\rceil \; \circ\!\!-\!\!\circ \; (?\lfloor B\rfloor)^{\perp}$, *which illustrates a duality between left and right occurrences of an object-level formula, is provable from the formulas* (initial) *and* (cut) *in Figure 8.7.*

8.8 Bibliographic Notes

Multiset rewriting provides a flexible framework for specifying a wide range of computationally interesting systems. For instance, it has been used to specify various algorithms (see Banâtre and Métayer [1993, 1996]) and several specification systems, including Petri Nets (see Engberg and Winskel [1990]; Gehlot and Gunter [1990]; Asperti et al. [1990]; Marti-Oliet and Meseguer [1991]; Kanovich [1995]; Delzanno [2002]) and process calculi (see Berry and Boudol [1992]). The connection between multiset rewriting and linear logic enabled natural encodings of these algorithms and specifications as linear logic programs (see Andreoli and Pareschi [1991a,b]; Miller [1993]).

In the 1990s, various other proposals for linear logic programming languages were proposed. Pym and Harland [1994] and Harland et al. [1996] proposed the Lygon language based on a notion of goal-directed proof in a multiple-conclusion setting that differs from that described in Section 6.7. Kobayashi and Yonezawa [1995] and Kobayashi et al. [1999] proposed the ACL language for encoding simple notions of asynchronous communication by identifying the send and read primitives with two complementary and multiplicative linear logic connectives. Miller [2004] is a survey article of early linear logic programming languages and their applications.

The examples of Lolli logic programs in Sections 8.3, 8.4, and 8.5 are taken from Hodas and Miller [1994]. The examples of $\mathcal{L}_2$ logic programs in Sections 8.6 and 8.7 are taken from Miller [1996]. The proof system in Figure 8.3 and the proof system arising from replacing the $\supset$L rule with the rules in Figure 8.5 are part of the proof systems called, respectively, G3ip and G4ip in Troelstra and Schwichtenberg [1996]. The analysis of object-level sequent systems using linear logic as a metatheory given in in Section 8.7 can be significantly extended and it can easily accommodate first-order quantifiers in the object logic: See, for example, Miller and Pimentel [2004], Miller and Pimentel [2013], Nigam et al. [2014], and Felty et al. [2021]. Miller [2023] presents a similar framework for specifying inference rules via multiset rewriting, but without the explicit use of linear logic as a metalogic.

Linear logic programming has found useful applications in parsing natural language sentences. In particular, both Pareschi and Miller [1990] and Hodas [1994, 1999] have shown how phenomena such as *gap threading* can be captured, at least in part, by Lolli specifications.

It is not surprising that a programming language directly exploiting proof theory ideas and techniques can specify a sequent calculus (as in Section 8.7) and a theorem prover (as in Section 8.5). Subsequent chapters (starting with Chapter 10) will show several other applications of linear logic programming in domains that are not overtly connected with logic and proof theory.

Chapter 9

Higher-Order Quantification

9.1 Introduction

The higher-order version of linear logic we present in this chapter uses the same connectives as $\mathcal{L}_2$, although we no longer restrict the type τ on the quantifiers $\forall_\tau$ and $\exists_\tau$. Removing this restriction on τ means that τ is allowed to have occurrences of the $\rightarrow$ constructor as well as the primitive type o. If we only accept the first of these additions, then the proof theory of the resulting logic is essentially the same as for first-order logic. Although the complex operation of λ-conversion is more pronounced in such a logic, that complexity occurs only at the level of terms. As we shall soon illustrate, if τ is allowed occurrences of o, the result of instantiating a universal quantifier can have more occurrences of logical connectives than the original universally quantified expression. Formulas that allow $\forall_\tau$ for arbitrary τ, and the other logical constants of $\mathcal{L}_2$, will be called $\mathcal{L}_2^\omega$ formulas.

In the following paragraphs, we address an array of issues that separates our logic with higher-order quantification ($\mathcal{L}_2^\omega$) from the corresponding logic with only first-order quantification ($\mathcal{L}_2$).

Soundness, completeness, and incompleteness In the remaining chapters, we give several examples of using higher-order quantification in the logic programming setting. For anyone familiar with the typed λ-calculus and λ-conversion (as presented in Chapter 2), these examples should not be challenging to understand. One might be worried, however, about other concerns often raised regarding higher-order logic. For example, since it is possible to formalize arithmetic in $\mathcal{L}_2^\omega$, Gödel's incompleteness theorems applies to this logic. However, we are not directly concerned with model-theoretic semantics for the proof systems we explore (except for the material on Kripke model semantics in Section 5.6). The fact that there are true statements of Peano Arithmetic that do not have proofs in higher-order linear logic is not particularly interesting to us here. Sequent calculus proof systems provide the only meaning we give to the logical connectives. As a result, the proposition that "a given sequent is provable in a given proof system" is always recursively enumerable. In this text, when we use the terms *soundness* and *completeness*, we generally refer to claims that provability in one proof system corresponds to provability in another.

Cut-elimination and consistency In Section 9.3, we will give two proof systems, $\Downarrow\mathcal{N}$ and $\Downarrow\mathcal{L}_2^\omega$, for $\mathcal{L}_2^\omega$. Following an argument in Section 3.7, it is easy to show that those proof systems are consistent if the cut rule is admissible in them. By Gödel's second incompleteness theorem, the proof of cut admissibility will involve inductions that are much stronger than those involved in the proof of cut elimination given for the first-order proof systems we saw in Chapter 7. Such a stronger induction can be achieved using the *candidats de réductibilité* of Girard [1972] (see also Girard et al. [1989] and Gallier [1990]).

The dynamics of instantiation of a higher-order quantifier On the surface, the instantiation of the quantifier $\forall_\tau x.B$ by a term t of type τ, written as $B[t/x]$, is the same in first-order and higher-order logic. A major difference between these two settings is that once one performs a (capture-avoiding) substitution of t for x is B, the result in first-order logic is a formula in β-normal form. In the higher-order setting, the resulting formula may have β-redexes (Section 2.1), and, since reducing these β-redexes requires doing more substitutions, the size of a term or formula can grow significantly in some cases. During such quantifier instantiations, the resulting instantiation might well have more occurrences of logical connectives than the original quantified expression. For example, if B contains $n \geq 0$ occurrences of logical connectives, then instantiating $\forall_o p.p \Rightarrow p$ with B replaces a formula with two occurrences of logic connectives with one containing $2n + 1$ such occurrences. In Section 9.5 the quantified expression $\forall p.\forall q.p \Rightarrow q$ (with three occurrences of logical connectives) is instantiated first with $\forall p.p \multimap p$ to yield $\forall q.(\forall p.p \multimap p) \Rightarrow q$ and then with $p \multimap q$ to get $(\forall p.p \multimap p) \Rightarrow (p \multimap q)$ (with four occurrences of logical connectives).

The subformula property As described in Section 3.7, cut-free proofs in first-order logic have the *subformula property*: That is, every occurrence of a formula in any sequent of a cut-free proof is a subformula of a formula in the endsequent. In that section, we also informally stated that "instantiations of quantified expressions must also be considered subformulas of that quantified formula." In the first-order setting, this is an interesting and useful definition. As the previous examples illustrate, this notion is trivialized in the general higher-order setting: For example, all formulas are subformulas of $\forall p.p$.

Logical connectives can appear in non-logical contexts In the first-order logic setting, an occurrence of a logical connective in a formula is either a top-level occurrence or in the scope of only other occurrences of logical connectives. In the higher-order logic setting, there is a third possibility: An occurrence of a logical connective can be in the scope of some non-logical constants and variables. This aspect of our higher-order logic is exploited by *higher-order programming* in logic programming, a topic we discuss more in Section 9.6.

9.2 Higher-Order Quantification

We now allow $\forall_\tau$ and $\exists_\tau$ to quantify variables of type τ where τ can be any type built from $\to$ and the primitive types $S \cup \{o\}$. The rules for introducing these two quantifiers are exactly as in Figure 4.1, namely, the following.

$$\frac{\Sigma :: \Gamma, B[t/x] \vdash \Delta}{\Sigma :: \Gamma, \forall_\tau x.B \vdash \Delta} \forall L \qquad \frac{\Sigma, c : \tau :: \Gamma \vdash \Delta, B[c/x]}{\Sigma :: \Gamma \vdash \Delta, \forall_\tau x.B} \forall R$$

$$\frac{\Sigma, c : \tau :: \Gamma, B[c/x] \vdash \Delta}{\Sigma :: \Gamma, \exists_\tau x.B \vdash \Delta} \exists L \qquad \frac{\Sigma :: \Gamma \vdash \Delta, B[t/x]}{\Sigma :: \Gamma \vdash \Delta, \exists_\tau x.B} \exists R.$$

Here, τ can now be any type. Also, recall that the result of applying the substitution operator $B[t/x]$ is always in λ-normal form. In the first-order setting, this can be a simple operation; in the higher-order setting, there can be a cascade of β-reductions following other β-reductions.

For the purposes of the following exercises, let $\mathbf{C}^\omega$ and $\mathbf{I}^\omega$ be the proof systems that result from using the higher-order versions of the quantifier introduction rules given above within $\mathbf{C}$ and $\mathbf{I}$ proof, respectively (see Section 4.1).

Exercise 9.1. (‡) *Prove that the formulas $\forall_o P.P$ is logically equivalent to f using I^ω-proofs.*

The following example illustrates how higher-order quantification can conceal (or simulate) cuts in proofs.

Exercise 9.2. *Note the similarities between the cut inference rule and an instance of the $\supset L$ rule.*

$$\frac{\Sigma :: \Gamma_1 \vdash B \quad \Sigma :: \Gamma_2, B \vdash C}{\Sigma :: \Gamma_1, \Gamma_2 \vdash C} \text{ cut} \qquad \frac{\Sigma :: \Gamma_1 \vdash B \quad \Sigma :: \Gamma_2, B \vdash C}{\Sigma :: B \supset B, \Gamma_1, \Gamma_2 \vdash C} \supset L$$

Use this similarity to prove the following result: if $\Sigma :: \Gamma \vdash C$ has a C^ω proof (respectively, an I^ω proof) then the sequent $\Sigma :: \forall_o p.(p \supset p), \Gamma \vdash \Delta$ has a cut-free C^ω proof (respectively, an I^ω proof). Provide a direct proof of this statement that does not use the cut-elimination theorem.

One approach to defining the equality of the two terms t and s is that all properties holding for one term holds for the other. This notation of equality is often referred to as *Leibniz equality* and can be defined using the formula $\forall_{i \to o} P.(Pt \supset Ps)$.

Exercise 9.3. (‡) *Let t and s be two terms of type i. Consider the binary relationship between these terms given by the provability in I^ω of the sequent $\vdash \forall_{i \to o} P.(Pt \supset Ps)$. Prove that this relation is an equivalence relation, i.e., prove that it is reflective, symmetric, and transitive. For example, symmetry can be proved by constructing an I^ω-proof of the sequent $\vdash \forall P.(Pt \supset Ps) \supset \forall P.(Ps \supset Pt)$.*

Exercise 9.4. *Let t and s be two terms of the same type τ. Repeat Exercise 9.2 replacing $\forall_o P.(P \supset P)$ with $\forall_{\tau \to o} P.(Pt \supset Ps)$.*

In $\mathcal{L}_2^\omega$, we have two choices for the implication used in the definition of Leibniz equality. Exercise 9.15 shows that these two choices result in logically equivalent formulas.

9.3 Near-Focused Proofs

An important invariant in the setting of proofs for first-order logic is that a first-order substitution applied to an atomic formula returns an atomic formula. Similarly, Proposition 7.7 states that substituting a term for a variable of primitive type (other than o) in a $\Downarrow^+\mathcal{L}_2$ proof yields another $\Downarrow^+\mathcal{L}_2$ proof. A similar property does not hold in the higher-order setting. For example, the following is a $\Downarrow^+\mathcal{L}_2$ proof.

$$\frac{}{q : i \to o, p : i \to o, a : i :: \cdot; \cdot \Downarrow pa \vdash pa; \cdot} \text{ init.}$$

If we instantiate p with the expression $\lambda w.qw \Rightarrow qa$ in this proof, we have the sequent

$$q : i \to o, a : i :: \cdot; \cdot \Downarrow qa \Rightarrow qa \vdash qa \Rightarrow qa; \cdot,$$

which does not have a $\Downarrow^+\mathcal{L}_2$ proof: Recall that the *init* rule can only be used on atomic formulas. More generally, applying a substitution for a variable with target type o can take a $\Downarrow \mathcal{L}_2$-proof to a proof-like structure that has two kinds of erroneous inference rules.

1. The initial rules *init* and *init?* may no longer involve atomic formulas.
2. The conclusion of the decide rules and most left-introduction rules may no longer contain only atoms in the right-bounded zone.

Given these observations, we introduce the *near-focused* proof system $\Downarrow \mathcal{N}$ in Figure 9.1. Here, the proof rules of $\Downarrow \mathcal{N}$ are the same as those for $\Downarrow \mathcal{L}_2$ in Figure 6.11 except for the following three modifications.

1. The formulas used in sequents can now be $\mathcal{L}_2^\omega$ formulas.
2. The initial rules are generalized so that the formula in focus can be a general formula. In particular, the schematic variable B in the two initial rules in Figure 9.1 can range over arbitrary $\mathcal{L}_2^\omega$ formulas.
3. The three decide rules are not constrained to have the right-bounded zone consisting of only atomic formulas. In particular, the schematic variable Δ in the three decide rules in Figure 9.1 can range over multisets of arbitrary $\mathcal{L}_2^\omega$ formulas.

Formally speaking, a $\Downarrow \mathcal{L}_2^\omega$-proof is a $\Downarrow \mathcal{N}$ proof in which the right-bounded zone of the concluding sequent of all left-introduction rules and all decide rules contain only atomic formulas.

$$\frac{}{\Sigma :: \Psi; \Gamma \vdash \top, \Delta; \Upsilon} \top R$$

$$\frac{\Sigma :: \Psi; \Gamma \vdash B, \Delta; \Upsilon \quad \Sigma :: \Psi; \Gamma \vdash C, \Delta; \Upsilon}{\Sigma :: \Psi; \Gamma \vdash B \,\&\, C, \Delta; \Upsilon} \,\&R$$

$$\frac{\Sigma :: \Psi; \Gamma \vdash \Delta; \Upsilon}{\Sigma :: \Psi; \Gamma \vdash \bot, \Delta; \Upsilon} \bot R \qquad \frac{\Sigma :: \Psi; \Gamma \vdash B, C, \Delta; \Upsilon}{\Sigma :: \Psi; \Gamma \vdash B \,\bindnasrepma\, C, \Delta; \Upsilon} \,\bindnasrepma R$$

$$\frac{\Sigma :: \Psi; B, \Gamma \vdash C, \Delta; \Upsilon}{\Sigma :: \Psi; \Gamma \vdash B \multimap C, \Delta; \Upsilon} \multimap R \qquad \frac{\Sigma :: B, \Psi; \Gamma \vdash C, \Delta; \Upsilon}{\Sigma :: \Psi; \Gamma \vdash B \Rightarrow C, \Delta; \Upsilon} \Rightarrow R$$

$$\frac{y:\tau, \Sigma :: \Psi; \Gamma \vdash B[y/x], \Delta; \Upsilon}{\Sigma :: \Psi; \Gamma \vdash \forall_\tau x.B, \Delta; \Upsilon} \forall R \qquad \frac{\Sigma :: \Psi; \Gamma \vdash \Delta; B, \Upsilon}{\Sigma :: \Psi; \Gamma \vdash ?B, \Delta; \Upsilon} ?R$$

$$\frac{\Sigma :: \Psi; \Gamma \Downarrow B \vdash \Delta; \Upsilon}{\Sigma :: \Psi; B, \Gamma \vdash \Delta; \Upsilon} \text{ decide}_l$$

$$\frac{\Sigma :: B, \Psi; \Gamma \Downarrow B \vdash \Delta; \Upsilon}{\Sigma :: B, \Psi; \Gamma \vdash \Delta; \Upsilon} \text{ decide}! \qquad \frac{\Sigma :: \Psi; \Gamma \vdash \Delta, B; B, \Upsilon}{\Sigma :: \Psi; \Gamma \vdash \Delta; B, \Upsilon} \text{ decide}?$$

$$\frac{}{\Sigma :: \Psi; \cdot \Downarrow B \vdash B; \Upsilon} \text{ init} \qquad \frac{}{\Sigma :: \Psi; \cdot \Downarrow B \vdash \cdot; B, \Upsilon} \text{ init}?$$

$$\frac{}{\Sigma :: \Psi; \cdot \Downarrow \bot \vdash \cdot; \Upsilon} \bot L \qquad \frac{\Sigma :: \Psi; B \vdash \cdot; \Upsilon}{\Sigma :: \Psi; \cdot \Downarrow ?B \vdash \cdot; \Upsilon} ?L$$

$$\frac{\Sigma :: \Psi; \Gamma \Downarrow B_i \vdash \Delta; \Upsilon}{\Sigma :: \Psi; \Gamma \Downarrow B_1 \,\&\, B_2 \vdash \Delta; \Upsilon} \,\&L_i \qquad \frac{\Sigma :: \Psi; \Gamma \Downarrow B[t/x] \vdash \Delta; \Upsilon}{\Sigma :: \Psi; \Gamma \Downarrow \forall_\tau x.B \vdash \Delta; \Upsilon} \forall L$$

$$\frac{\Sigma :: \Psi; \Gamma_1 \Downarrow B \vdash \Delta_1; \Upsilon \quad \Sigma :: \Psi; \Gamma_2 \Downarrow C \vdash \Delta_2; \Upsilon}{\Sigma :: \Psi; \Gamma_1, \Gamma_2 \Downarrow B \,\bindnasrepma\, C \vdash \Delta_1, \Delta_2; \Upsilon} \,\bindnasrepma L$$

$$\frac{\Sigma :: \Psi; \Gamma_1 \vdash \Delta_1, B; \Upsilon \quad \Sigma :: \Psi; \Gamma_2 \Downarrow C \vdash \Delta_2; \Upsilon}{\Sigma :: \Psi; \Gamma_1, \Gamma_2 \Downarrow B \multimap C \vdash \Delta_1, \Delta_2; \Upsilon} \multimap L$$

$$\frac{\Sigma :: \Psi; \cdot \vdash B; \Upsilon \quad \Sigma :: \Psi; \Gamma \Downarrow C \vdash \Delta; \Upsilon}{\Sigma :: \Psi; \Gamma \Downarrow B \Rightarrow C \vdash \Delta; \Upsilon} \Rightarrow L$$

The usual provisos are assumed on the rules ∀R and ∀L. In the $\&\, L_i$ rule, i is 1 or 2. There are no side conditions regarding atomic formulas in this proof system.

Figure 9.1 The near-focused proof system $\Downarrow \mathcal{N}$.

9.3 NEAR-FOCUSED PROOFS

Our goal for the rest of this section is to show that if $\Sigma :: \Psi; \Gamma \vdash \Delta; \Upsilon$ has a $\Downarrow \mathcal{N}$ proof, then it has a $\Downarrow \mathcal{L}_2^\omega$ proof. We do this in the following steps.

1. We introduce the follow definitions where the adjective *atomic* is applied to certain occurrences of inference rules. An instance of the $\multimap L$ rule is *atomic* if the right-bounded zone of its left premise (the schematic variable Δ_1 in Figure 9.1) contains only atomic formulas. An instance of a decide rule is *atomic* if the right-bounded zone of its conclusion (the schematic variable Δ in Figure 9.1 for all three kinds of decide rules) contains only atomic formulas. (Recall that an instance of *init* is *atomic* if the formula under focus is atomic.)
2. We prove that the *init?* rule is not needed in $\Downarrow \mathcal{N}$ proofs (Lemma 9.5).
3. We show that all instances of the *init* rule can be replaced by instances of an atomic *init* rule (Lemma 9.6).
4. We show how to replace occurrences of the *decide?* rule with atomic versions of that rule (Lemma 9.7).
5. Finally, we show how to replace occurrences of $\multimap L$ with atomic versions of $\multimap L$ (Lemma 9.8).

After these lemmas have been established, the proof that the existence of a near-focus proof implies the existence of a focused proof (Proposition 9.9) following easily.

Lemma 9.5 shows that within $\Downarrow \mathcal{N}$ proofs, the inference rule *init?* is not needed since that rule can systematically be replaced by a pair of *decide?* and *init* rules.

Lemma 9.5. *If* $\Sigma :: \Psi; \Gamma \vdash \Delta; \Upsilon$ *has a* $\Downarrow \mathcal{N}$ *proof, then it has a* $\Downarrow \mathcal{N}$ *proof with no occurrences of the init? rule.*

Proof: Consider a right-introduction phase of the following shape.

$$\cdots \quad \cfrac{\cfrac{}{\Sigma :: \Psi; \Gamma \Downarrow B \vdash \cdot; B, \Upsilon} \text{init?}}{\cfrac{\Xi}{\Sigma :: \Psi; \Gamma \Downarrow D \vdash \cdot; B, \Upsilon.}} \quad \cdots$$

That is, Ξ is some collection of left-introduction rules. We first prove by induction on the structure of Ξ that this collection of inference rules can be reorganized to provide a proof of

$$\cdots \quad \overline{\Sigma :: \Psi; \Gamma \Downarrow B \vdash B; B, \Upsilon} \; \textit{init} \quad \cdots$$
$$\Xi'$$
$$\Sigma :: \Psi; \Gamma \Downarrow D \vdash B; B, \Upsilon.$$

The base case occurs when the conclusion of Ξ is an occurrence of *init?*, in which case D and B must be the same formula. In that case, we use the *init* rule.

$$\overline{\Sigma :: \Psi; \Gamma \Downarrow B \vdash B; B, \Upsilon} \; \textit{init}$$

Otherwise, the last inference rule of Ξ is one of the five left-introduction rules $\&L_i$, $\forall L$, $?L$, $\multimap L$, or $\Rightarrow L$. If the last inference rule is $\&L_i$, then Ξ has the following shape.

$$\cdots \quad \overline{\Sigma :: \Psi; \Gamma \Downarrow B \vdash \cdot; B, \Upsilon} \; \textit{init?} \quad \cdots$$
$$\Xi_1$$
$$\dfrac{\Sigma :: \Psi; \Gamma \Downarrow D_i \vdash \cdot; B, \Upsilon}{\Sigma :: \Psi; \Gamma \Downarrow D_1 \& D_2 \vdash \cdot; B, \Upsilon} \; \&_i.$$

Invoking the inductive assumption yields the following inference rules.

$$\cdots \quad \overline{\Sigma :: \Psi; \Gamma \Downarrow B \vdash B; B, \Upsilon} \; \textit{init} \quad \cdots$$
$$\Xi'_1$$
$$\dfrac{\Sigma :: \Psi; \Gamma \Downarrow D_i \vdash B; B, \Upsilon}{\Sigma :: \Psi; \Gamma \Downarrow D_1 \& D_2 \vdash B; B, \Upsilon} \; \&_i.$$

If the last inference rule of Ξ is $\multimap L$, then Ξ has the following shape.

$$\cdots \quad \overline{\Sigma :: \Psi; \Gamma_2 \Downarrow B \vdash \cdot; B, \Upsilon} \; \textit{init?} \quad \cdots$$
$$\Xi_0 \qquad\qquad \Xi_1$$
$$\dfrac{\Sigma :: \Psi; \Gamma_1 \vdash D_1; B, \Upsilon \qquad \Sigma :: \Psi; \Gamma_2 \Downarrow D_2 \vdash \cdot; B, \Upsilon}{\Sigma :: \Psi; \Gamma_1, \Gamma_2 \Downarrow D_1 \multimap D_2 \vdash \cdot; B, \Upsilon} \; \multimap L.$$

Invoking the inductive assumption yields the following inference rules.

$$\cdots \quad \overline{\Sigma :: \Psi; \Gamma_2 \Downarrow B \vdash B; B, \Upsilon} \; \textit{init} \quad \cdots$$
$$\Xi_0 \qquad\qquad \Xi'_1$$
$$\dfrac{\Sigma :: \Psi; \Gamma_1 \vdash D_1; B, \Upsilon \qquad \Sigma :: \Psi; \Gamma_2 \Downarrow D_2 \vdash B; B, \Upsilon}{\Sigma :: \Psi; \Gamma_1, \Gamma_2 \Downarrow D_1 \multimap D_2 \vdash B; B, \Upsilon} \; \multimap L.$$

The remaining three cases can be proved similarly.

9.3 NEAR-FOCUSED PROOFS

Now consider the following occurrences of *init?* along with the path from it to the border sequent below it within a $\Downarrow \mathcal{N}$ proof.

$$
\cdots \quad \frac{\overline{\Sigma :: \Psi; \Gamma \Downarrow B \vdash \cdot; B, \Upsilon}\ \textit{init?}}{\begin{array}{c} \Xi \\ \dfrac{\Sigma :: \Psi; \Gamma \Downarrow D \vdash \cdot; B, \Upsilon}{\Sigma :: \Psi; \Gamma \vdash \cdot; B, \Upsilon}\ \textit{decide!} \end{array}} \quad \cdots
$$

(or the similar case where this last inference rule is $\textit{decide}_l$ instead of $\textit{decide!}$). By the previous argument, we can assemble the following inference rules.

$$
\cdots \quad \frac{\overline{\Sigma :: \Psi; \Gamma \Downarrow B \vdash B; B, \Upsilon}\ \textit{init}}{\begin{array}{c} \Xi' \\ \dfrac{\Sigma :: \Psi; \Gamma \Downarrow D \vdash B; B, \Upsilon}{\dfrac{\Sigma :: \Psi; \Gamma \vdash B; B, \Upsilon}{\Sigma :: \Psi; \Gamma \vdash \cdot; B, \Upsilon}\ \textit{decide?}.}\ \textit{decide!} \end{array}} \quad \cdots
$$

Thus, we have described how to replace an occurrence of *init?* with occurrences of *init* and *decide?*. By simply repeating this replacement process, we can finally arrive at a $\Downarrow \mathcal{N}$ proof of the same end sequent $\Sigma :: \Psi; \Gamma \vdash \Delta; \Upsilon$ but without occurrences of *init?*. $\square$

Lemma 9.6. *If $\Sigma :: \Psi; \Gamma \vdash \Delta; \Upsilon$ has a $\Downarrow \mathcal{N}$ proof, then it has a $\Downarrow \mathcal{N}$ proof with no occurrences of* init? *and every occurrence of* init *is an atomic init.*

Proof: Assume that $\Sigma :: \Psi; \Gamma \vdash \Delta; \Upsilon$ has a $\Downarrow \mathcal{N}$ proof Ξ. By Lemma 9.5, we can assume that Ξ contains no occurrences of *init?*. An occurrence of a logical connective in a formula is said to be a *top-level occurrence* if it is not in the scope of a variable or a non-logical constant. Let the *off-focus measure* of an occurrence of the inference rule *init* be the number of occurrences of top-level logical connectives in the focused formula. The off-focus measure of a $\Downarrow \mathcal{N}$ proof is the sum of the off-focus measure for every occurrence of the *init* rules. We now prove that if a $\Downarrow \mathcal{N}$ proof has a non-zero off-focus measure, we can reorganize that proof to yield a $\Downarrow \mathcal{N}$ proof with a strictly smaller off-focus measure.

An occurrence of *init* in Ξ must appear within a left-introduction phase of the form (here, $D \in \Psi$)

$$\cdots \quad \frac{\overline{\Sigma :: \Psi; \cdot \Downarrow B \vdash B; \Upsilon}\ \textit{init}}{\dfrac{\Pi}{\dfrac{\Sigma :: \Psi; \Gamma \Downarrow D \vdash B, \Delta; \Upsilon}{\Sigma :: \Psi; \Gamma \vdash B, \Delta; \Upsilon}\ \textit{decide}!}} \quad \cdots$$

(or the similar case where this last inference rule is *decide$_l$*). We shall argue that if B is not atomic, the derivation Π can be reorganized to provide a near-focus proof with a strictly smaller off-focus measure.

Consider, for example, the case where B is $B_1 \mathbin{\&} B_2$. The proof structure above is then of the form

$$\cdots \quad \frac{\overline{\Sigma :: \Psi; \cdot \Downarrow B_1 \mathbin{\&} B_2 \vdash B_1 \mathbin{\&} B_2; \Upsilon}\ \textit{init}}{\dfrac{\Pi}{\dfrac{\Sigma :: \Psi; \Gamma \Downarrow D \vdash B_1 \mathbin{\&} B_2, \Delta; \Upsilon}{\Sigma :: \Psi; \Gamma \vdash B_1 \mathbin{\&} B_2, \Delta; \Upsilon}\ \textit{decide}!.}} \quad \cdots$$

The following reorganization reduces the off-focus measure by one.

$$\cdots \quad \frac{\dfrac{\overline{\Sigma :: \Psi; \cdot \Downarrow B_1 \vdash B_1; \Upsilon}\ \textit{init}}{\Sigma :: \Psi; \cdot \Downarrow B_1 \mathbin{\&} B_2 \vdash B_1; \Upsilon}\ \mathbin{\&}L}{\dfrac{\Pi'}{\dfrac{\Sigma :: \Psi; \Gamma \Downarrow D \vdash B_1, \Delta; \Upsilon}{\Sigma :: \Psi; \Gamma \vdash B_1, \Delta; \Upsilon}\ \textit{decide}!}} \quad \cdots \quad \frac{\dfrac{\overline{\Sigma :: \Psi; \cdot \Downarrow B_2 \vdash B_2; \Upsilon}\ \textit{init}}{\Sigma :: \Psi; \cdot \Downarrow B_1 \mathbin{\&} B_2 \vdash B_2; \Upsilon}\ \mathbin{\&}L}{\dfrac{\Pi''}{\dfrac{\Sigma :: \Psi; \Gamma \Downarrow D \vdash B_2, \Delta; \Upsilon}{\Sigma :: \Psi; \Gamma \vdash B_2, \Delta; \Upsilon}\ \textit{decide}!.}}$$
$$\overline{\Sigma :: \Psi; \Gamma \vdash B_1 \mathbin{\&} B_2, \Delta; \Upsilon}\ \mathbin{\&}R$$

Here, the derivations Π' and Π'' differ from Π by replacing occurrences of $B_1 \mathbin{\&} B_2$ on the right-hand side of the sequents on the path to the designated *init* with B_1 and B_2, respectively.

Consider the case where B is $B_1 \Rightarrow B_2$.

$$\cdots \quad \frac{\overline{\Sigma :: \Psi; \cdot \Downarrow B_1 \Rightarrow B_2 \vdash B_1 \Rightarrow B_2; \Upsilon}\ \textit{init}}{\dfrac{\Pi}{\dfrac{\Sigma :: \Psi; \Gamma \Downarrow D \vdash B_1 \Rightarrow B_2, \Delta; \Upsilon}{\Sigma :: \Psi; \Gamma \vdash B_1 \Rightarrow B_2, \Delta; \Upsilon}\ \textit{decide}!.}} \quad \cdots$$

9.3 Near-Focused Proofs

These inference rules can be reorganized as below, yielding a new near-focused proof of strictly smaller off-focus measure.

$$\cfrac{\cfrac{\cfrac{\overline{\Sigma :: \Psi, B_1; B_1 \Downarrow \cdot \vdash B_1;}\ \textit{init}}{\Sigma :: \Psi, B_1; \cdot \vdash B_1; \Upsilon}\ \textit{decide}! \quad \overline{\Sigma :: \Psi, B_1; \cdot \Downarrow B_2 \vdash B_2; \Upsilon}\ \textit{init}}{\Sigma :: \Psi, B_1; \cdot \Downarrow B_1 \Rightarrow B_2 \vdash B_2; \Upsilon}\ \Rightarrow L}{\cdots}$$

$$\cfrac{\Pi'}{\cfrac{\cfrac{\Sigma :: \Psi, B_1; \Gamma \Downarrow D \vdash B_2, \Delta; \Upsilon}{\Sigma :: \Psi, B_1; \Gamma \vdash B_2, \Delta; \Upsilon}\ \textit{decide}!}{\Sigma :: \Psi; \Gamma \vdash B_1 \Rightarrow B_2, \Delta; \Upsilon}\ \Rightarrow R.}$$

Consider the case where B is $?B'$.

$$\cdots \quad \cfrac{\Pi}{\cfrac{\overline{\Sigma :: \Psi; \cdot \Downarrow ?B' \vdash ?B'; \Upsilon}\ \textit{init}}{\cfrac{\Sigma :: \Psi; \Gamma \Downarrow D \vdash ?B', \Delta; \Upsilon}{\Sigma :: \Psi; \Gamma \vdash ?B', \Delta; \Upsilon}\ \textit{decide}!.}} \quad \cdots$$

These inference rules can similarly be reorganized.

$$\cdots \quad \cfrac{\cfrac{\cfrac{\cfrac{\overline{\Sigma :: \Psi; \cdot \Downarrow B' \vdash B'; B', \Upsilon}\ \textit{init}}{\Sigma :: \Psi; B' \vdash B'; B', \Upsilon}\ \textit{decide}_l}{\Sigma :: \Psi; B' \vdash \cdot; B', \Upsilon}\ \textit{decide}?}{\Sigma :: \Psi; \cdot \Downarrow ?B' \vdash \cdot; B', \Upsilon}\ ?L}{} \quad \cdots$$

$$\cfrac{\Pi'}{\cfrac{\cfrac{\Sigma :: \Psi; \Gamma \Downarrow D \vdash \Delta; B', \Upsilon}{\Sigma :: \Psi; \Gamma \vdash \Delta; B', \Upsilon}\ \textit{decide}!.}{\Sigma :: \Psi; \Gamma \vdash ?B', \Delta; \Upsilon}\ ?R}$$

Here, the derivation Π' differs from Π by replacing occurrences of $?B'$ in the right-bounded zone with occurrences of B' in the right-unbounded zone in all sequents in Π'.

Such reorganization of right-introduction rules can be done for all the remaining cases for the top-level connective ($\bot$, $\mathbin{\text{⅋}}$, $\top$, $\multimap$) and for the cases where an occurrence of $\textit{decide}_l$ appears as the conclusion of the right-introduction phase. Thus, in all of these cases, the off-focus measure strictly decreases. Thus, by repeated application of such proof reorganization, we finally terminate with a proof with an off-focus measure of zero. Thus, all occurrences of *init* in the resulting proof are, in fact, atomic. □

Lemma 9.7. *If a sequent has a $\Downarrow \mathcal{N}$ proof, then it has a $\Downarrow \mathcal{N}$ proof for which all occurrences of* decide? *are atomic.*

Proof: Using Lemmas 9.5 and 9.6, we can restrict our attention to $\Downarrow \mathcal{N}$ proofs without occurrences of *init?* and with only atomic instances of *init*. In such proofs, we show how to replace one non-atomic instance of a *decide?* rule with possibly many instances of atomic *decide?* rules. Assume we have a proof of the following form

$$\frac{\Xi}{\Sigma :: \Psi; \Gamma \vdash \Delta; B, \Upsilon} \; decide?.$$

Here, we also assume that this occurrence of *decide?* is such that the proof Ξ contains only atomic instances of *decide?*. Using Proposition 7.2, we can reorganize this right-introduction phase so that formulas in Δ are all inserted into that phase before B is inserted. We can now permute this one occurrence of *decide?* up over the premises of this partial right-introduction phase. All of these new instances of *decide?* will have in their conclusion a right-bounded zone that contains only atomic formulas. □

Lemma 9.8. *If a sequent has a $\Downarrow \mathcal{N}$ proof, then it has a $\Downarrow \mathcal{N}$ proof for which all occurrences of* $\multimap L$ *are atomic.*

Proof: This proof is similar to the proof of Lemma 9.7 in that we need to permute right-introduction rules used to proved the left premise of $\multimap L$ below that rule. In particular, assume that we have the following occurrence of the $\multimap L$ rule.

$$\frac{\Xi}{\Sigma :: \Psi; \Gamma_1 \vdash \Delta_1, B; \Upsilon \quad \Sigma :: \Psi; \Gamma_2 \Downarrow C \vdash \Delta_2; \Upsilon}{\Sigma :: \Psi; \Gamma_1, \Gamma_2 \Downarrow B \multimap C \vdash \Delta_1, \Delta_2; \Upsilon} \; \multimap L$$

Here, we also assume that this occurrence of $\multimap L$ is such that the proof Ξ contains only atomic instances of $\multimap L$. Using Proposition 7.2, we can reorganize this right-introduction phase so that formulas in Δ_1 are all inserted into that phase before B is inserted. We can now permute this one occurrences of $\multimap L$ up over the premises of this partial right-introduction phase. All of these new instances of $\multimap L$ will have in their conclusion a right-bounded zone that contains only atomic formulas. □

Proposition 9.9. *If* $\Sigma :: \Psi; \Gamma \vdash \Delta; \Upsilon$ *has a* $\Downarrow \mathcal{N}$ *proof, it has a* $\Downarrow \mathcal{L}_2^\omega$ *proof.*

Proof: Assume that $\Sigma :: \Psi; \Gamma \vdash \Delta; \Upsilon$ has a $\Downarrow \mathcal{N}$ proof. By Lemma 9.6, we know that that sequent has a $\Downarrow \mathcal{N}$ proof with no occurrences of *init?* and where every occurrence of *init* is atomic. By Lemmas 9.7 and 9.8, we can additionally assume that all instances of *decide?* and $\multimap L$ in it are atomic. A simple induction of the structure of such a proof now shows that in every $\Downarrow$-sequent in Ξ, the right-bounded zone contains only atomic formulas. Hence, Ξ is, in fact, a $\Downarrow \mathcal{L}_2^\omega$ proof. □

Proposition 9.9 provides a new proof that generalized initial rules are admissible: Contrast this to the proof provided by Theorem 7.4.

Corollary 9.10. *Let B be an $\mathcal{L}_2^\omega$ Σ-formula. The following sequents have $\Downarrow \mathcal{L}_2^\omega$-proofs.*

1. $\Sigma :: \Psi, B; \cdot \vdash B; \Upsilon$
2. $\Sigma :: \Psi; B \vdash B; \Upsilon$
3. $\Sigma :: \Psi, B; \cdot \vdash \cdot; B, \Upsilon$
4. $\Sigma :: \Psi; B \vdash \cdot; B, \Upsilon$

Proof: We note that every one of these sequents has a $\Downarrow \mathcal{N}$ proof using some combination of *init*, *init?*, *decide$_l$*, and *decide!*. Thus, Proposition 9.9 entails that all these sequents also have $\Downarrow \mathcal{L}_2^\omega$ proofs. □

9.4 The Proof Theory of Higher-Order Quantification

This section states the major proof-theoretic results about $\Downarrow \mathcal{N}$ proofs and $\Downarrow \mathcal{L}_2^\omega$ proofs.

Define $\Downarrow \mathcal{N}^+$ as the proof system resulting from adding the four cut rules from Figure 7.1 to $\Downarrow \mathcal{N}$. Lemma 9.11 has a straightforward inductive proof on the structure of $\Downarrow \mathcal{N}^+$ proofs.

Lemma 9.11 (Substitution into $\Downarrow \mathcal{N}^+$-proofs). *Let Σ be a signature, x be a variable not declared in Σ, τ be a type, and t be a Σ-term of type τ. If $\Sigma, x : \tau :: \Psi; \Gamma \vdash \Delta; \Upsilon$ has an $\Downarrow \mathcal{N}^+$-proof then $\Sigma :: \Psi[t/x]; \Gamma[t/x] \vdash \Delta[t/x]; \Upsilon[t/x]$ has a $\Downarrow \mathcal{N}^+$-proof.*

Proposition 9.12 (Substitution into $\Downarrow \mathcal{L}_2^\omega$-proofs). *Let Σ be a signature, x be a variable not declared in Σ, τ be a type, and t be a Σ-term of type τ. If $\Sigma, x : \tau :: \Psi; \Gamma \vdash \Delta; \Upsilon$ has an $\Downarrow \mathcal{L}_2^\omega$-proof then $\Sigma :: \Psi[t/x]; \Gamma[t/x] \vdash \Delta[t/x]; \Upsilon[t/x]$ has a $\Downarrow \mathcal{L}_2^\omega$-proof.*

Proof: Assume that $\Sigma, x : \tau :: \Psi; \Gamma \vdash \Delta; \Upsilon$ has a $\Downarrow \mathcal{L}_2^\omega$-proof. That proof is also a $\Downarrow \mathcal{N}$ proof. As a result of Lemma 9.11, $\Sigma :: \Psi[t/x]; \Gamma[t/x] \vdash \Delta[t/x]; \Upsilon[t/x]$ has a $\Downarrow \mathcal{N}$ proof. By Proposition 9.9, this same sequent has a $\Downarrow \mathcal{L}_2^\omega$-proof. □

There are at least two major reasons why proving the cut-elimination theorem for $\Downarrow \mathcal{N}^+$ proofs (Theorem 9.13) cannot be done using the same kind of proof we gave in Chapter 7. First, the proof system for $\Downarrow \mathcal{L}_2^\omega$ and the technical device of path (see Section 7.1) both rely on the notion of atomic formulas. Since this notion is not stable under the substitution for variables of higher-order type, they cannot play a central role in the cut-elimination argument. Second, the measure of a cut (defined in Section 7.3) will not decrease in the presence of such substitutions.

Theorem 9.13 is the key result concerning $\Downarrow \mathcal{N}^+$ proofs.

Theorem 9.13 (Cut-elimination for $\Downarrow \mathcal{N}^+$-proofs). *If a sequent has a $\Downarrow \mathcal{N}^+$ proof, it has a $\Downarrow \mathcal{N}$ proof.*

We do not prove this theorem here. Many issues surrounding the permuting of the cut rules with other rules are essentially the same as in Chapter 7. The major difference is that the termination of a systematic cut-elimination procedure is significantly harder to achieve. As mentioned in the introduction of this chapter, the *candidats de réductibilité* of Girard [1972] can achieve such a termination argument. Given this theorem, the following cut-admissibility result follows immediately.

Theorem 9.14 (Cut-admissibility for $\Downarrow \mathcal{L}_2^\omega$-proofs). *The four cut rules in Figure 7.1 are admissible in $\Downarrow \mathcal{L}_2^\omega$.*

Proof: Consider the following occurrence of a *cut* ! rule where both premises have $\Downarrow \mathcal{L}_2^\omega$-proofs.

$$\frac{\Sigma :: \Psi; \cdot \vdash B; \Upsilon \qquad \Sigma :: \Psi, B; \Gamma \vdash \Delta; \Upsilon}{\Sigma :: \Psi; \Gamma \vdash \Delta; \Upsilon} \; cut\,!.$$

Thus, this endsequent has a $\Downarrow \mathcal{N}^+$ proof since every $\Downarrow \mathcal{L}_2^\omega$ proof is a $\Downarrow \mathcal{N}^+$ proof. By Theorem 9.13, this endsequent must also have a $\Downarrow \mathcal{N}$ proof. By Proposition 9.9, this same endsequent has a $\Downarrow \mathcal{L}_2^\omega$ proof. The admissibility of the other three cut rules in Figure 7.1 follow an analogous argument. □

9.5 Examples Using Quantification of Type *o*

The following are noteworthy equivalences provable in linear logic.

1. The additive units are definable using only higher-order quantification.

$$\vdash \mathbf{0} \multimap \forall p.p \qquad \vdash \top \multimap \exists p.p.$$

2. The multiplicative units are definable using higher-order quantification and multiplicative connectives.

$$\vdash \mathbf{1} \multimap \forall p.p \multimap p \qquad \vdash \bot \multimap \exists p.p \otimes p^\bot.$$

3. The additive connectives are definable using higher-order quantification, multiplicative connectives, and exponentials.

$$\vdash A \& B \multimap \exists p.\,!(p \multimap A) \otimes\, !(p \multimap B) \otimes p$$

$$\vdash A \oplus B \multimap \forall p.(A \multimap p) \Rightarrow (B \multimap p) \Rightarrow p.$$

It is worth noting that all of these equivalences are between formulas of opposite polarities.

Since it is possible to prove that $\mathbf{1}$ is equivalent to $\forall p.p \Rightarrow p$, we also have the provability of the formula $(\forall p.p \Rightarrow p) \multimap (\forall p.p \multimap p)$. Below is the (nearly complete) proof of a similar implication that instantiates two variables of type *o* with the terms $\forall p.p \multimap p$ and $p \multimap q$ in the $\forall L$ rules.

$$\cfrac{\cfrac{p_o,q_o : \cdot; p \vdash p}{p_o,q_o : \cdot; \cdot \vdash \forall p..p \multimap p} \forall R, \multimap R \qquad p_o,q_o : \cdot; p \multimap q, p \vdash q}{\cfrac{p_o,q_o : \cdot; (\forall p.p \multimap p) \Rightarrow (p \multimap q), p \vdash q}{\cfrac{p_o,q_o : \cdot; \forall p.\forall q.p \Rightarrow q, p \vdash q}{\cdot : \cdot; \forall p.\forall q.p \Rightarrow q \vdash \forall p.\forall q.p \multimap q} \forall R, \multimap R.} \forall L \times 2} \Rightarrow L$$

Exercise 9.15. (‡) *Let t and s be two Σ-terms of type τ. In $\Downarrow \mathcal{L}_2^\omega$, one can express the equality of these two terms using the Leibniz equality as either $E_1 = \forall P.(Pt \Rightarrow Ps)$ or $E_2 = \forall P.(Pt \multimap Ps)$. Prove that these two formulas are provably equivalent: i.e., provide $\Downarrow \mathcal{L}_2^\omega$-proofs of the sequents $\Sigma :: E_1; \cdot \vdash E_2; \cdot$ and $\Sigma :: E_2; \cdot \vdash E_1; \cdot.$*

The higher-order logic program used in Section 5.8 to define the disjunctive and existential goals can be written as the following $\Downarrow \mathcal{L}_2^\omega$ formulas (using λProlog syntax and its polymorphic typing).

```
type   or       o -> o -> o.
type   exists   (A -> o) -> o.

or P Q :- P.
or P Q :- Q.
exists B :- B T.
```

9.6 Higher-Order Programming

The availability of quantification over predicates makes it a simple matter to specify programs that are often referred to as *higher-order programs*. Figure 9.2 contains several examples of higher-order programs using the (polymorphic) typing and syntax of λProlog. The other predicates in that figure can be described and illustrated as follows. (Here, we assume that the logic program consists of the clauses in Figures 9.2 and 9.3).

1. The formula `forevery P L` holds if the predicate P holds for every member of the list L. For example, `forevery (x\ adj x B) [b, e]` is provable if and only if B is instantiated with the node d.
2. The formula `forsome P L` holds if the predicate P holds for some member of the list L. For example, `forsome (x\ adj x c) [b, e]` is provable, while `forsome (x\ adj e x) [a, b, c, e]` is not provable.

9.6 Higher-Order Programming

```
type forevery, forsome
              (A -> o) -> list A -> o.
type mappred  (A -> B -> o) -> list A -> list B -> o.
type sublist  (A -> o) -> list A -> list A -> o.
type ref, sym, trans
              (A -> A -> o) -> A -> A -> o.

forevery P nil.
forevery P (X::L) :- P X, forevery P L.

forsome P (X::L) :- P X; forsome P L.

mappred P nil nil.
mappred P (X::L) (Y::K) :- P X Y, mappred P L K.

sublist P (X::L) (X::K) :- P X, sublist P L K.
sublist P (X::L) K :- sublist P L K.
sublist P nil nil.

ref    R X X.
ref    R X Y :- R X Y.
sym    R X Y :- R X Y; R Y X.
trans  R X Y :- R X Y.
trans  R X Z :- R X Y, trans R Y Z.
```

Figure 9.2 Some simple higher-order logic programs.

```
kind node              type.
type a, b, c, d, e     node.
type adj               node -> node -> o.

adj a b & adj a e & adj b c & adj b d
    & adj d c & adj e d.
```

Figure 9.3 A small graph given by its adjacency relation.

3. `mappred P L K` succeeds if the corresponding elements of the lists L and K satisfy the binary predicate P. For example, the formula

   `mappred adj [a,b,d] L`

   is provable if and only if L is instantiated with one of the lists

   `[b, c, c], [b, d, c], [e, c, c], [e, d, c].`

4. `sublist P L K` succeeds if K is a sublist of L and every element of K satisfies the predicate P. For example, the formula

   `sublist (x\sigma y\ adj x y) [a,b,c,d,e] K.`

succeeds if and only if K is instantiated with the list [a, b, d, e] or with any sublist of that list (including the empty list).

5. Let R be a binary predicate on a given type. Then the three binary predicates rel R, sym R, and trans R denote, respectively, the reflexive, symmetric, and transitive closures of R. For example, the formula

sublist (x\ trans adj x e) [a,b,c,d,e] K.

succeeds if and only if K is instantiated with [a] or the empty list nil.

Note that the formula (mappred P L K) is an atomic formula since it has a non-logical constant as its head symbol. Although substitution instances of this atomic formula remain atomic, it is possible that such instances contain occurrences of logical constants since substitutions for P can contain logical constants. Such occurrences of logic constants within atomic formulas are not possible in the logics we have seen based on first-order quantification.

The concept of *tactics* and *tacticals* was introduced by Milner [1979] and Gordon et al. [1979] as a way to explicitly program in a goal-directed fashion. Although the first specifications of these concepts were given as higher-order programs in the ML functional programming language, it was later shown by Felty and Miller [1988] and Felty [1989, 1993] how the same concepts can be given a flexible and declarative specification using higher-order logic programs. We illustrate briefly how these two concepts can be specified using logic programming.

The structure of goals is given by the signature in Figure 9.4. In many implementations of tactics, goals are given as lists of primitive goals, where a list of primitive goals represents their conjunction. In general, however, one must also have an explicit representation of universally quantified goals. The signature of the type goal thus contains the constructors trueg to denote the goal with no sub-tasks, cc to denote the conjunction of two collections of goals, and allg to denote the explicitly universal quantification of a goal.

```
kind goal        type.
type trueg       goal.
type allg        (A -> goal) -> goal.
type cc          goal -> goal -> goal.
infixr cc        3.
type primgoal    goal -> o.
```

Figure 9.4 The definition of a goal structure.

9.6 HIGHER-ORDER PROGRAMMING

```
kind i, fm              type.
type q                  fm.
type p                  i -> fm.
type r                  i -> i -> fm.
type and, or, imp       fm -> fm -> fm.
type all                (i -> fm) -> fm.
type seq                list fm -> fm -> goal.
```
Figure 9.5 An example of a primitive goal.

Finally, `primgoal` is a predicate that separates primitive goals from those built from these three constructors.

A good example of a primitive goal is one that encodes an object-logic sequent. For example, the signature in Figure 9.5 describes a small first-order logic (with conjunction, disjunction, implication, universal quantification, and three predicate constants). In this case, the clause

```
primgoal (seq Gamma B).
```

declares that a structure intended to encode the two-sided sequent $\Gamma \vdash B$ is a primitive goal.

A tactic is a binary relation on goals, i.e., a tactic is a predicate of type `goal -> goal -> o`. If `tac` is a tactic, the intended meaning of the goal `tac G Gs` is that the primitive goal `G` can be achieved if all the goals in `Gs` can be achieved. A tactical is an expression whose arguments can be tactics. Thus, specifications of tactical are typically higher-order logic programs.

Examples of tactics are the predicates `andR`, `orR`, and `impR` that are specified in Figure 9.6. The tactic called `andR` states that in order to achieve the goal of proving `seq Gamma (and B C)`, one can instead attempt to achieve the two goals of proving `seq Gamma B` and `seq Gamma C`. In this example, tactics are essentially inference rules.

Tactics can be combined to form other tactics using tacticals. Figure 9.7 presents a few familiar tacticals. The `maptac` tactical is responsible for applying a tactic to all the primitive goals within a more complex goal structure. The `orelse` tactical specifies the union of two tactics, the `then` tactical describes the relational composition (natural join) of two tactics, and `repeat` allows for repeated applications of a tactic. The trivial tactic is `idtac`. For a complete description of this approach to encoding tactics and tacticals, see Felty [1993] and Miller and Nadathur [2012].

```
type andR, orR, impR, allR, init    goal -> goal -> o.

andR (seq Gamma (and B C)) ((seq Gamma B) cc
                            (seq Gamma C)).
orR  (seq Gamma (or  B C)) (seq Gamma B).
orR  (seq Gamma (or  B C)) (seq Gamma C).
impR (seq Gamma (imp B C)) (seq (B::Gamma) C).
allR (seq Gamma (all B))   (allg x\ seq Gamma (B x)).
init (seq Gamma B) trueg :- memb B Gamma.
```

Figure 9.6 Inference rules as primitive tactics.

```
type maptac          (goal -> goal -> o) ->
                     goal -> goal -> o.
type idtac           goal -> goal -> o.
type repeat          (goal -> goal -> o) ->
                     goal -> goal -> o.
type then, orelse    (goal -> goal -> o) ->
                     (goal -> goal -> o) ->
                     goal -> goal -> o.

maptac Tac trueg trueg.
maptac Tac (I1 cc I2) (O1 cc O2) :- maptac Tac I1 O1,
                                    maptac Tac I2 O2.
maptac Tac (allg I) (allg O) :-
                 pi t\ maptac Tac (I t) (O t).
maptac Tac I O :- primgoal I, Tac I O.

idtac         I I.
then   Tac1 Tac2 I O :- Tac1 I M,  maptac Tac2 M O.
orelse Tac1 Tac2 I O :- Tac1 I O ; Tac2 I O.
repeat Tac       I O :- orelse (then Tac (repeat Tac))
                               idtac I O.
```

Figure 9.7 The definition of some useful tacticals.

9.7 Proving That Reverse Is Symmetric

One of the reasons to use logic as the source code for a programming language is that the actual artifact that is the program should be amenable to direct manipulation and analysis in ways that might be challenging or impossible in more conventional programming languages. One method for reasoning directly on logic programming involves the cut rule and cut elimination. We give a first example of such reasoning in this section. We provide several more in subsequent chapters.

9.7 Proving That Reverse Is Symmetric

Although much of the motivation for designing logic programming languages based on linear logic has been to add expressiveness to such languages, linear logic can also help shed some light on conventional programs. In this section, we consider the linear logic specification for the reverse of lists and formally show that it is symmetric.

In Section 5.11, we presented two specifications of the predicate that relates two lists if the second is the reversal of the first. One of these specifications used Horn clauses, while the second used hereditary Harrop formulas. Both specifications use an auxiliary predicate. We now revisit the second of these specifications.

One way to compute the reverse of a list is illustrated using a pair of lists, the first initialized to the list we wish to reverse and the second initialized to be empty. Next, repeatedly move the top element from the first list to the top of the second list. When the first list is empty, the second list is the reverse of the original list. For example, the following is a trace of such a computation.

$(a :: b :: c :: nil)$	nil
$(b :: c :: nil)$	$(a :: nil)$
$(c :: nil)$	$(b :: a :: nil)$
nil	$(c :: b :: a :: nil)$

To design a specification to capture these dynamics, first, pick a binary relation rv to denote the pairing of lists above (this predicate will be an auxiliary predicate to *reverse*). If we wish to reverse the list L to get K, then start with the atomic formula $(rv\ L\ nil)$ and do a series of backchaining steps using the clause

$$\forall X. \forall P. \forall Q. (rv\ P\ (X :: Q) \multimap rv\ (X :: P)\ Q)$$

to get to the formula $(rv\ nil\ K)$. Once this is done, K is the result of reversing L. The entire specification of *reverse* can be given as the following formula.

$$\forall L. \forall K. [\ \forall rv. ((\forall X. \forall P. \forall Q. (rv\ P\ (X :: Q) \multimap rv\ (X :: P)\ Q)) \Rightarrow$$
$$rv\ nil\ K \multimap rv\ L\ nil) \multimap reverse\ L\ K\ ].$$

Note that the clause used for repeatedly moving the top elements of lists is to the left of an intuitionistic implication (so it can be used any number of times) while the formula representing the base case of the recursion, namely $(rv\ nil\ K)$, is to the left of a linear implication (thus, it must be used exactly once). This specification of reverse is similar to the one using hereditary Harrop formulas in Section 5.11, except that the auxiliary predicate rv is hidden using a higher-order quantifier and that the base case of the recursion is explicitly treated linearly.

Consider proving that *reverse* is symmetric: That is, if (*reverse L K*) is proved from the above clause, then so is (*reverse K L*). The informal proof of this is simple: In the table of pairs above, flip the rows and flip the columns. What results is a correct computation of reversing, but the start and final lists have exchanged roles. This informal proof is easily made formal by exploiting the metatheory of linear logic as follows. Assume that (*reverse L K*) can be proved. There is only one way to prove this (backchaining on the above clause for *reverse*). Thus the formula

$$\forall rv.((\forall X.\forall P.\forall Q.(rv\ P\ (X :: Q) \multimap rv\ (X :: P)\ Q)) \Rightarrow rv\ nil\ K \multimap rv\ L\ nil)$$

is provable. By Proposition 9.12, we can instantiate this quantifier with any binary predicate expression, and the result is still provable. So, we choose to instantiate it with the λ-expression $\lambda x \lambda y.(rv\ y\ x)^\perp$. The flip of the columns is captured by changing the order of the variables x and y between when they are abstracted and when they are arguments. The flip of the rows arises from the use of negation. The resulting formula

$$(\forall X.\forall P.\forall Q.(rv\ (X :: Q)\ P)^\perp \multimap (rv\ Q\ (X :: P))^\perp) \Rightarrow$$
$$(rv\ K\ nil)^\perp \multimap (rv\ nil\ L)^\perp$$

can be simplified by using the contrapositive rule for negation and linear implication (Exercise 6.25), and, hence, yields

$$(\forall X.\forall P.\forall Q.rv\ Q\ (X :: P) \multimap rv\ (X :: Q)\ P) \Rightarrow rv\ nil\ L \multimap rv\ K\ nil.$$

If we now universally generalize on *rv*, we again have proved the body of the reverse clause, but this time with the quantifiers for L and K switched. Note that we have succeeded in proving this fact about reverse without explicit reference to induction.

9.8 Exploiting the Hiding of Specification Details

Given that logic programs are logical formulas and computation is modeled by logical deduction, it is natural to expect that we can reason directly on logic programs in the following way. Let $\mathcal{P}$ and $\mathcal{P}'$ be $\mathcal{L}_2^\omega$ logic programs such that $\Sigma :: \mathcal{P}; \cdot \vdash G; \cdot$ has a $\Downarrow \mathcal{L}_2^\omega$-proof and $\Sigma :: \mathcal{P}'; \cdot \vdash P; \cdot$ has a $\Downarrow \mathcal{L}_2^\omega$-proof for every $P \in \mathcal{P}$ (i.e., the program $\mathcal{P}'$ entails the program $\mathcal{P}$). By repeated application of the cut-elimination theorem, there is a $\Downarrow \mathcal{L}_2^\omega$-proof for $\Sigma :: \mathcal{P}'; \cdot \vdash G; \cdot$.

9.8 Exploiting the Hiding of Specification Details

Although this syllogism is correct, it's conclusion is surprisingly weak for at least two reasons. First, the logic of $\Downarrow \mathcal{L}_2^\omega$ does not include induction, a proof technique generally used to reason about recursive programs. Second, every clause for every predicate free in program $\mathcal{P}$ must be accounted for by program $\mathcal{P}'$. For example, assume that these two logic programs provide different ways to specify the binary relation between lists L and K of natural numbers so that K is the result of sorting L in increasing order. The two programs could make use of rather different auxiliary predicates and clauses in order to specify such sorting. The requirement that all the clauses of all the auxiliary predicates of $\mathcal{P}$ must be entailed by $\mathcal{P}'$ means that all but trivial differences can exist between these two programs. At least, that is the conclusion in the first-order setting where predicates cannot be quantified and hidden. In the higher-order setting, predicates can be hidden within individual programs, and, as a result, richer entailments can be expected.

The example that proves that a particular specification of the reverse program yields a symmetric relation illustrates how using explicit quantification over variables of predicate types in a specification can hide details of an implementation. Such hiding then enables avenues for certain simple logical techniques to be used to reason about such specifications.

To illustrate in another way the usefulness of higher-order quantification for hiding details, consider again the specification of the reverse predicate first introduced in Section 5.11 using the three first-order Horn clauses and two predicates in Figure 9.8. Using higher-order quantification, it is possible to hide the predicate rev and its two clauses, as in the single formula in Figure 9.9. The formula uses rev as a local predicate only, and no other program clauses outside of this clause can invoke this predicate and its code.

Given the universal quantification in this specification, it is possible to directly manipulate this description of reverse to get a different specification of reverse. In particular, assume that reverse L K is proved from the specification in Figure 9.9. Thus, the body of that clause,

```
type reverse              list A -> list A -> o.
type rev                  list A -> list A -> list A -> o.
reverse L K :- rev L nil K.
rev nil L L.
rev (X::M) N L :- rev M (X::N) L.
```

Figure 9.8 A specification of reverse in *fohc*.

```
reverse L K :- pi rev\ (
  (pi L\ rev nil L L) =>
  (pi L\ pi M\ pi N\ pi X\
    rev (X::M) N L :- rev M (X::N) L) =>
  rev L nil K).
```

Figure 9.9 A specification of reverse using higher-order quantification.

```
reverse L K :- pi rv\ pi aux\ (
  (pi L\ rv nil L :- aux L) =>
  (pi L\ pi M\ pi N\ pi X\
    rv (X::M) L :- acc N, acc (X::N) -o rv M L) =>
  aux nil -o rv L K).
```

Figure 9.10 A specification of reverse in $\mathcal{L}_2^\omega$.

namely,

$$\forall rev.[\ (\forall L.(rev\ nil\ L\ L)) \Rightarrow$$
$$(\forall L.\forall M.\forall N.\forall X.\ rev\ M\ (X::N)\ L \multimap rev\ (X::M)\ N\ L) \Rightarrow$$
$$rev\ L\ nil\ K]$$

is provable. Since this quantified expression is provable, every instance of it must be provable (using Proposition 9.12). We then chose to instantiate rev with

$$\lambda L.\lambda K.\lambda M.aux\ K \multimap rv\ L\ M.$$

Here, we assume that aux and rv are tokens of the appropriate type. Thus, the following formula must be provable.

$$(\forall L.aux\ L \multimap rv\ nil\ L) \Rightarrow$$
$$(\forall L.\forall M.\forall N.\forall X.\ (aux\ (X::N) \multimap rv\ M\ L) \multimap aux\ N \multimap rv\ (X::M)\ L) \Rightarrow$$
$$aux\ nil \multimap rv\ L\ K.$$

(Note that the variables L and K are bound in different ways: Implicitly around the entire clause and explicitly within this clause.) Given that this formula is provable, the result of universally generalizing on the two new variables (i.e., attaching the quantifiers $\forall rv.\forall aux.$ to this formula) must also be provable. We can then see that this formula is (logically equivalent) to the body of the specification of reverse in Figure 9.10. Thus, purely logical manipulations and the metatheory of $\Downarrow \mathcal{L}_2^\omega$ proofs allow us to conclude that if the atomic formula reverse L K is provable from Figure 9.9 then it is also provable from Figure 9.10.

Exercise 9.16. *Prove the converse of the statement just made. That is, if the atomic formula* reverse L K *is provable from Figure 9.10, then it is also provable from Figure 9.9. Such a proof will likely be an inductive argument on the structure of* $\Downarrow \mathcal{L}_2^\omega$*-proofs. Explain why this converse cannot be proved if the* rev *predicate variable in the discussion above was instantiated, instead, with the term* $\lambda L.\lambda K.\lambda M.aux\ K \Rightarrow rv\ L\ M$.

9.9 Synthetic Rules and Higher-Order Logic

The concept of *synthetic inference rules* introduced in Section 5.7 allowed replacing $\mathcal{L}_0$ formulas of clause order 2 or less with inference rules involving only atomic formulas (see Exercise 5.37). Although it is possible to extend the notion of synthetic inference rule to $\mathcal{L}_1$ and $\mathcal{L}_2$ formulas, extending this notion to $\mathcal{L}_2^\omega$ is problematic since neither clause order nor the status of being atomic is stable under the substitution of higher-order variables. We illustrate two problems next.

The first problem is that the clausal order of formulas is not stable under instantiation. Consider, for example, the following simple clause.

```
type call    o -> o

call G :- G.
```

Using the definition of clausal order in Section 2.4, this formula has order 1. However, instantiating the variable G in this clause with a formula of order n results in a clause of order $n+1$. Thus, the instantiation of a Horn clause might no longer be a Horn clause.

To describe the second problem, we first introduce some terminology. We say that the formula A is a *rigid atomic formula* if A has a non-logical constant as its topmost symbol and is a *flexible atomic formula* if A has a variable as its topmost symbol. Note that the substitution instance of a rigid atomic formula is a rigid atomic formula. The second problem arises when the head of a clause is a flexible atom. In this case, a great deal of nondeterminism can be introduced into the goal-directed search for proofs. For example, consider having the clause $\forall_o p.p \supset p$ as a member of the logic program Γ. In the simple setting of two-sided sequent calculi for intuitionistic logic, the inference rule

$$\frac{\Sigma :: \Gamma \vdash B}{\Sigma :: \Gamma \vdash B}$$

is built using $\forall L$, $\supset L$, and *init*. Although Mints [1992] has considered such a repetition rule, its presence in the proof-search setting is not useful. Similarly, the use of *Leibniz equality* is also problematic. If a and b are two constants of type τ, the formula $\forall_\tau P.Pa \supset Pb$ can motivate the inference rule

$$\frac{\Sigma :: \Gamma \vdash Pb}{\Sigma :: \Gamma \vdash Pa} \; .$$

Here, the schema variable P has type $\tau \to o$, and, as a result, P can be substituted by expressions of the form $\lambda x.B$, where B can be a complex formula and x may have zero or more occurrences in B. In particular, if x is not free in B, then this rule is another instance of the above repetition rule. Even if we were to restrict this rule from being applied when the right-hand side is an atomic formula, there is much nondeterminism present with this rule. For example, assume that the right-hand side is the atomic formula A and that there are n occurrences of the constant b in A. There are 2^n terms $\lambda x.B$ such that $(\lambda x.B)b$ λ-reduces to A.

This issue with having flexible atoms at the head of clauses has led to the following definitions of higher-order versions of Horn clauses and hereditary Harrop formulas.

Higher-order Horn clauses These formulas are defined as the D-formulas in the following definition.

$$G := \mathsf{t} \mid A \mid G_1 \wedge G_2 \mid G_1 \vee G_2 \mid \exists x.G$$
$$D := A_r \mid G \supset A_r \mid \forall x.D \mid D_1 \wedge D_2.$$

Here, the syntactic variable A_r ranges over rigid atomic formulas. Additionally, all formulas are restricted so that the connectives $\supset$ and $\forall$ are not allowed within atomic formulas. It is proved in Miller and Nadathur [1986] and Nadathur and Miller [1990] that uniform proofs are complete for classical logic for sequents in which the left-hand sides are D-formulas and the right-hand sides are G-formulas. Note that the clauses displayed in Figures 9.2 and 9.7 are all examples of higher-order Horn clauses.

Higher-order hereditary Harrop formulas These formulas are defined as the D-formulas in the following definition.

$$G := t \mid A \mid G_1 \wedge G_2 \mid G_1 \vee G_2 \mid \forall x.G \mid \exists x.G \mid D \supset G$$
$$D := A_r \mid G \supset A_r \mid \forall x.D \mid D_1 \wedge D_2.$$

Again, the syntactic variable A_r ranges over rigid atomic formulas. Additionally, all formulas are restricted so that the connective $\supset$ is not allowed within atomic formulas. It is proved in Miller et al. [1991] that uniform proofs are complete for intuitionistic logic for sequents in which the left-hand side contains D-formulas, and the right-hand side is a single G-formula.

The restriction to rigid atoms in the definition of the higher-order generalizations of Horn clauses and hereditary Harrop formulas makes it possible to know how many left-introduction rules are in a left-introduction phase. For example, if D is a higher-order hereditary formula, then a left-introduction phase above a sequent of the form $\Sigma :: \Psi; \Gamma \Downarrow D \vdash \Delta; \Upsilon$ is limited by the shape of D: In particular, higher-order instantiations during the left-introduction phase will not affect this shape.

Another consequence of using rigid atomic formulas is that it is possible to conclude that a given set of higher-order hereditary Harrop formulas must be consistent in the sense that not just any formula is provable. In particular, if q is a propositional symbol that does not appear in such a set of formulas, then q cannot be proved from that set.

9.10 Bibliographic Notes

The textbooks by Andrews [1986] and Farmer [2023] provide a good background in higher-order logics similar to the Simple Theory of Types in Church [1940]. The implementation of proof search strategies for logics containing simply typed λ-terms usually starts with the problem of how to unify such terms. Huet [1975] described the (pre)unification of simply typed λ-terms, and in Huet [1973b], he also showed how such unification can be incorporated into a prover based on resolution refutations. Andrews led a long-term effort to build an automated theorem prover for Church's Simple Theory of Types. His system, the TPS theorem-proving system, described in Miller et al. [1982], Andrews et al. [1986], Andrews et al. [1996] and Andrews et al. [2000] employed Huet's unification procedure. Interpreters employing focused proof search and Huet's unification procedure have been described for higher-order

Horn clauses (see Nadathur [1987] and Nadathur and Miller [1990]) and for higher-order hereditary Harrop formulas, the foundations of λProlog (see Nadathur and Miller [1988] and Miller and Nadathur [2012]).

It is important to note that the unification of simply typed λ-terms is, in general, undecidable, and when unifiers are known to exist, there might not be a most general unifier. If one moves instead to the weaker setting of *higher-order pattern unification* introduced in Miller [1991b], one loses expressiveness but regains the decidability of unification as well as the existence of most general unifiers for unifiable terms. Both the Isabelle theorem prover (see Nipkow et al. [2002]) and the Elf implementation (see Pfenning [1991]) of the LF specification language of Harper et al. [1993] implement unification of typed λ-calculi. The handbook chapter by Benzmüller and Miller [2014] provides an overview of different approaches to the automation of higher-order logic.

Finding instantiations for predicate variables during proof search in higher-order logic is a difficult and largely open problem. Some early steps in that direction were taken by Bledsoe [1979], Bledsoe and Feng [1993], and Felty [2000].

Exercise 9.2, which is taken from Baaz and Leitsch [2000], illustrates that simple higher-order assumptions, such as $\forall p.(p \supset p)$, can mask or simulate cut rules. Benzmüller et al. [2009] show that such *cut-simulation* can also be done using other higher-order formulas such as those used by Church [1940] to formulate the axioms of extensionality and choice.

There are significant challenges to making model-theoretic semantics for higher-order versions of Horn clauses and hereditary Harrop formula, especially since the proof systems we have adopted here are not *extensional* in the sense that the equivalence $\forall_\tau x.px \equiv qx$ might be provable while the equation $p = q$ might not be provable. For example, in the proof system $\Downarrow \mathcal{L}_2^\omega$, the terms $\lambda x.px \mathbin{\&} qx$ and $\lambda x.qx \mathbin{\&} px$ are not $\beta\eta$-convertible and, hence, are not equal. Models dealing with such non-extensional logics have been considered by Andrews [1971, 1972], Benzmüller et al. [2004], Lipton and Nieva [2018], and others.

The proof that reverse is symmetric using higher-order instantiations is due to Miller [1997]. As is argued in Miller and Nadathur [2012], this proof can be done without reference to linear logic: While the same higher-order substitution involving negation and the use of contrapositive forces the underlying proof theory to move from intuitionistic to classical logic, the transformed clauses are only Horn clauses. As a result, Proposition 5.5 ensures

9.10 Bibliographic Notes

that a classical logic entailment can be replaced by an intuitionistic logic entailment.

The use of quantification to hide predicates can also be applied to hide the constructors used to build a given data structure. This approach has been used proposed by Miller [1989a] and Miller and Nadathur [2012] as a mechanism for building *abstract data types* within λProlog.

Chapter 10

Specifying Computations Using Multisets

This chapter provides an extended example that illustrates how higher-order linear logic and $\Downarrow \mathcal{L}_2^\omega$-proofs can specify some well-known concepts of computation, including finite automata and pushdown automata. Since all examples in this chapter are based on the notion of *multiset rewriting* (developed in Sections 8.4 and 8.6), we start by providing some simple illustrations of using multisets to encode data and rewriting to encode computation.

10.1 Numerals as Multisets

Figure 5.3 encodes the natural numbers with the following specification.

```
kind nat              type.
type z                nat.
type s                nat -> nat.

nat z.
nat (s X) :- nat X.
```

The following specification provides an alternative approach to encoding natural numbers, this time using atomic formulas.

```
type zero             o.
type succ             o -> o.

zero.
succ X :- X.
```

10.1 Numerals as Multisets

This second encoding makes zero a proposition denoting zero, and succ encodes successor as a predicate. If we let $\mathcal{P}$ be this logic program, then the following is easily proved: For every natural number n, $\cdot :: \mathcal{P}; \cdot \vdash \mathrm{succ}^n(\mathrm{zero}); \cdot$ has a $\Downarrow \mathcal{L}_2^\omega$-proof. Here, of course, succ^n denotes the n-fold application of succ. A following variant of this sequent is also provable for all natural numbers n.

$$\cdot :: \forall x.(x \multimap \mathrm{succ}\ x); \mathrm{zero} \vdash \mathrm{succ}^n(\mathrm{zero}); \cdot$$

Note that in this sequent, zero occurs in the left-bounded zone.

Let $\star$ be a token of type o. The natural number n can be encoded using the multiset that consists of $\star$ with multiplicity n. In particular, let $\star^n$ denote $\{\star, \ldots, \star\}$ where $\star$ occurs exactly n times. If n is 0, then $\star^n$ is the empty multiset.

Exercise 10.1. (‡) *Give a $\Downarrow \mathcal{L}_2^\omega$-proof of* $(\forall x.(x \multimap \star \mathbin{\bindnasrepma} x)) \multimap (\bot \multimap \star)$.

By reclassifying a couple of tokens from being non-logical constants to being eigenvariables, the sequent displayed above can be written as follows.

$$\mathrm{zero} : o, \mathrm{succ} : o \to o :: \forall x.(x \multimap \mathrm{succ}\ x); \mathrm{zero} \vdash \mathrm{succ}^n(\mathrm{zero}); \cdot$$

Consider the following instantiations for zero and succ.

$$\mathrm{zero} \mapsto \bot \qquad \mathrm{succ} \mapsto \lambda w. \star \mathbin{\bindnasrepma} w.$$

By using Proposition 9.12 and this substitution, as well as the equivalence from Exercise 10.1, we have that

$$\cdot :: \bot \multimap \star; \bot \vdash \star \mathbin{\bindnasrepma} \cdots \mathbin{\bindnasrepma} \star \mathbin{\bindnasrepma} \bot; \cdot$$

must be provable, where there are n occurrences of $\star$ on the right. (Of course, this simple result could be proved directly without using a higher-order instantiation argument.) This observation provides a separate characterization of natural-numbers-com-multisets: If Δ is a multiset of atomic formulas, then

$$\cdot :: \bot \multimap \star; \bot \vdash \Delta; \cdot$$

has a $\Downarrow \mathcal{L}_2^\omega$-proof if and only if Δ is $\star^n$ for some natural number n.

```
type star              o.
type zero, one, two    o.
type suc               o -> o.
type plus              o -> o -> o.

zero.
one     || star.
two     || star || star.
three   || star || star || star.
suc P   || star :- P.
plus P Q :- P :- Q.
```

Figure 10.1 Using multisets of tokens to do simple arithmetic.

Let the non-logical signature Σ_0 contain at least the declarations $\star : o$, $z :$ nat, $s :$ nat $\to$ nat, and $f :$ nat $\to o$, and let $\mathcal{P}$ be the following specification.

$$f\ z.$$
$$f\ (s\ z)\ \mathbin{\text{\textparenleft}\!\!\!\text{?}\!\!\!\text{\textparenright}}\ \star.$$
$$\forall x.\ (f\ x \multimap f\ (s\ x)) \multimap f\ (s\ (s\ x))).$$

This logic program specifies the Fibonacci numbers in the following sense. If Δ is a multiset of atomic Σ_0-formulas then the sequent

$$\cdot :: \mathcal{P};\ \cdot\ \vdash f\ (s^n\ z), \Delta;\ \cdot$$

has a $\Downarrow \mathcal{L}_2^\omega$-proof if and only if Δ is $\star^m$ where m is the nth Fibonacci number. Here, the zeroth Fibonacci number is 0, the first is 1, and the remaining are the sum of the preceding two: e.g., the twelfth Fibonacci is 144.

Exercise 10.2. Let $\mathcal{P}$ be the logic program in Figure 10.1. Prove that the following equivalence holds: If Δ is a multiset of atomic formulas then

$$\cdot :: \mathcal{P}; \bot \vdash \texttt{plus (plus (suc three) two) three}, \Delta;\ \cdot$$

has a $\Downarrow \mathcal{L}_2^\omega$-proof if and only if Δ is the multiset that contains `star` with multiplicity 9.

10.2 Letters and Words

Let Λ be a finite and nonempty set. We use this set as an *alphabet*: That is, members of this set are the tokens that denote letters used to build words.

A *word* is a finite list of letters written using concatenation. The empty word is denoted as ϵ. By Λ^*, we mean the set of all words that can be formed using the letters in Λ: For example, the set $\{a,b\}^*$ contains ϵ, *aba*, and *baabba*.

Letters in Σ are encoded in logic as constants of type $o \to o$ and a word is encoded as a term of type $o \to o$ built from the tokens denoting letters: For example, $\lambda x.(u\ (v\ (u\ x)))$, $\lambda x.(v\ (v\ x))$, and $\lambda x.x$ denote the words *uvu*, *vv*, and ϵ, respectively. Note that the concatenation of two words w and w' is given by function composition at the level of terms, namely, $\lambda x.w(w'x)$. In this chapter, the set of non-logical symbols Σ_0 will generally contain Λ.

10.3 Encoding Finite Automata

Let Q and Λ be two nonempty, finite sets of non-overlapping tokens. Elements of Q will be used as the *states* of an automaton, while Λ will be used as the *alphabet* of the input language to an automaton. A *finite automata* F is a quintuple $\langle Q, \Lambda, \delta, s, \mathcal{F} \rangle$ where Q and Λ are given as above and where

1. $s \in Q$ is the *initial state*,
2. $\mathcal{F} \subseteq Q$ is the set of *final states* (possibly empty), and
3. $\delta \subseteq Q \times \Lambda^* \times Q$ is the set of *transitions*.

We write $p \xrightarrow{w} q$ to denote the fact that $\langle p, w, q \rangle \in \delta$. The transition $p \xrightarrow{\epsilon} q$ is called an ϵ-*transition*. The three-place relation $p \xrightarrow{w}^* q$ is defined as the smallest relation such that: (*i*) $p \xrightarrow{\epsilon}^* p$ holds for all $p \in Q$, and (*ii*) if $p \xrightarrow{u} r$ and $r \xrightarrow{v}^* q$ then $p \xrightarrow{uv}^* q$. A word w is *accepted* by F if there is a final state $f \in \mathcal{F}$ such that $s \xrightarrow{w}^* f$. The set $L(F)$ is defined as the set of words accepted by F.

We now encode finite automata into linear logic in such a way that we use no primitive type other than o. The members of Q are encoded as constants of type o, and, as such, will also be members of the signature of non-logical constants Σ_0. A transition relation, δ, will be encoded as the theory $\mathcal{T}(\delta)$ composed of one clause of the form

$$\forall x.[q \mathbin{\invamp} x \multimap p \mathbin{\invamp} (w\ x)] \quad \text{for every} \langle p, w, q \rangle \in \delta.$$

The ϵ-transition $p \xrightarrow{\lambda x.x} q$ is therefore encoded as the formula $\forall x.[q \mathbin{\invamp} x \multimap p \mathbin{\invamp} x]$, which is logically equivalent to the formula $q \multimap p$. Let $\mathcal{T}'(\delta)$ be the same as $\mathcal{T}(\delta)$ except that ϵ-transitions are written as $q \multimap p$ instead of $\forall x.[q \mathbin{\invamp} x \multimap p \mathbin{\invamp} x]$. Clearly, $\mathcal{T}'(\delta)$ and $\mathcal{T}(\delta)$ prove the same formulas.

Exercise 10.3. Let $p, q \in Q$. Give $\Downarrow \mathcal{L}_2^\omega$-proofs that $\forall x.[q \mathbin{\mathpalette\BigPar@\relax} x \multimap p \mathbin{\mathpalette\BigPar@\relax} x]$ entails $q \multimap p$ and vice versa.

The formulas in $\mathcal{T}'(\delta)$ give rise to synthetic inference rules of the following two kinds.

$$\frac{\cdot :: \mathcal{T}'(\delta); \Gamma \vdash q, \Delta; \cdot}{\cdot :: \mathcal{T}'(\delta); \Gamma \vdash p, \Delta; \cdot} \langle p, \epsilon, q \rangle \qquad \frac{\cdot :: \mathcal{T}'(\delta); \Gamma \vdash q, t, \Delta; \cdot}{\cdot :: \mathcal{T}'(\delta); \Gamma \vdash p, (w\ t), \Delta; \cdot} \langle p, w, q \rangle.$$

The first of these corresponds to the ϵ-transition $p \xrightarrow{\epsilon} q$ and the second to the transition $p \xrightarrow{w} q$ where w encodes a nonempty word. Here, t is some Σ-term of type o. The following collection of inference rules in $\mathcal{L}_2$ justifies the second of these synthetic rules.

$$\cfrac{\cfrac{\cfrac{\cdot :: \mathcal{T}'(\delta); \Gamma \vdash q, t, \Delta; \cdot}{\cdot :: \mathcal{T}'(\delta); \Gamma \vdash q \mathbin{\mathpalette\BigPar@\relax} t, \Delta; \cdot} \quad \cfrac{\cdot :: \mathcal{T}'(\delta); \cdot \Downarrow p \vdash p; \cdot \quad \cdot :: \mathcal{T}'(\delta); \cdot \Downarrow (w\ t) \vdash (w\ t); \cdot}{\cdot :: \mathcal{T}'(\delta); \cdot \Downarrow p \mathbin{\mathpalette\BigPar@\relax} (w\ t) \vdash p, (w\ t); \cdot}}{\cfrac{\cdot :: \mathcal{T}'(\delta); \Gamma \Downarrow q \mathbin{\mathpalette\BigPar@\relax} t \multimap p \mathbin{\mathpalette\BigPar@\relax} (w\ t) \vdash p, (w\ t), \Delta; \cdot}{\cfrac{\cdot :: \mathcal{T}'(\delta); \Gamma \Downarrow \forall x.[q \mathbin{\mathpalette\BigPar@\relax} x \multimap p \mathbin{\mathpalette\BigPar@\relax} (w\ x)] \vdash p, (w\ t), \Delta; \cdot}{\cdot :: \mathcal{T}'(\delta); \Gamma \vdash p, (w\ t), \Delta; \cdot}}}\ \text{decide}!.$$

We can now prove that the cut-free $\Downarrow \mathcal{L}_2^\omega$-proofs can faithfully model transitions within a finite automaton.

Proposition 10.4. Let $F = \langle Q, \Lambda, \delta, s, \{f_1, \ldots, f_n\} \rangle$ be a finite automata.

1. The transition $p \xrightarrow{w}^* q$ holds if and only if the sequent

$$\cdot :: \mathcal{T}(\delta); \cdot \vdash \forall x.[q \mathbin{\mathpalette\BigPar@\relax} x \multimap p \mathbin{\mathpalette\BigPar@\relax} (w\ x)]; \cdot$$

is provable in $\Downarrow \mathcal{L}_2^\omega$.

2. The word $w \in L(F)$ if and only if the sequent

$$\cdot :: \mathcal{T}(\delta); \cdot \vdash \forall x.[(f_1\ \&\ \cdots\ \&\ f_n) \mathbin{\mathpalette\BigPar@\relax} x \multimap s \mathbin{\mathpalette\BigPar@\relax} (w\ x)]; \cdot$$

is provable in $\Downarrow \mathcal{L}_2^\omega$.

10.3 Encoding Finite Automata

Proof: To prove item 1 above, assume that $p \xrightarrow{w}{}^* q$. We proceed by induction on the definition of this proposition. Given the base case $p \xrightarrow{\epsilon}{}^* p$, it is trivial to show that $\forall x.[p \,\mathbin{\text{⅋}}\, x \multimap p \,\mathbin{\text{⅋}}\, x]$ is provable. For the inductive case, assume that there are words u and v such that w is uv and a state $r \in Q$ such that both $p \xrightarrow{u} r$ and $r \xrightarrow{v}{}^* q$ hold. By the inductive hypothesis, it is the case that

$$\cdot :: \mathcal{T}(\delta); \cdot \vdash \forall x.[q \,\mathbin{\text{⅋}}\, x \multimap r \,\mathbin{\text{⅋}}\, (v\ x)]; \cdot$$

is provable. By invertibility, it must be the case that

$$x : o :: \mathcal{T}(\delta); q \,\mathbin{\text{⅋}}\, x \vdash r, (v\ x); \cdot$$

has a $\Downarrow \mathcal{L}_2^\omega$-proof. The desired proof then adds the following synthetic inference rule plus a right-introduction phase to that proof.

$$\dfrac{\dfrac{x : o :: \mathcal{T}(\delta); q \,\mathbin{\text{⅋}}\, x \vdash r, (v\ x); \cdot}{x : o :: \mathcal{T}(\delta); q \,\mathbin{\text{⅋}}\, x \vdash p, (u\ (v\ x)); \cdot} \langle p, u, r \rangle}{\cdot :: \mathcal{T}(\delta); \cdot \vdash \forall x.[q \,\mathbin{\text{⅋}}\, x \multimap p \,\mathbin{\text{⅋}}\, (u\ (v\ x))]; \cdot}.$$

To prove the converse of item 1 above, assume that

$$\cdot :: \mathcal{T}(\delta); \cdot \vdash \forall x.[q \,\mathbin{\text{⅋}}\, x \multimap p \,\mathbin{\text{⅋}}\, (w\ x)]; \cdot$$

has a $\Downarrow \mathcal{L}_2^\omega$-proof. Since they prove the same formulas, we can replace $\mathcal{T}(\delta)$ with $\mathcal{T}'(\delta)$ in this sequent. Using the invertibility of right-introduction rules, we can conclude that the sequent

$$x : o :: \mathcal{T}'(\delta); q \,\mathbin{\text{⅋}}\, x \vdash p, (w\ x); \cdot$$

has a $\Downarrow \mathcal{L}_2^\omega$-proof say Ξ. We proceed by induction on the decide depth of Ξ. The last inference rule of Ξ is a $decide_l$ or $decide!$. If $decide_l$ is used, the focus must be on $q \,\mathbin{\text{⅋}}\, x$: this only leads to a proof if p and q are the same and w is $\lambda x.x$. Thus, $p \xrightarrow{w}{}^* q$ holds. If $decide!$ is used, this rule must select a formula in $\mathcal{T}'(\delta)$ as its focus. If that formula encodes an ϵ-transition, it is of the form $r \multimap p$ for some $r \in Q$. In this case, the proof Ξ ends in the synthetic inference rule determined by $r \multimap p$, that is, Ξ is of the form

$$\frac{\Xi'}{x : o :: \mathcal{T}'(\delta); q \; \mathfrak{P} \; x \vdash r, (w \; x); \cdot} \langle p, \epsilon, r \rangle.$$
$$x : o :: \mathcal{T}'(\delta); q \; \mathfrak{P} \; x \vdash p, (w \; x); \cdot$$

By the inductive assumption, Ξ' encodes $r \xrightarrow{w}{}^* q$, which together with the ϵ-transition $p \xrightarrow{\epsilon} r$ yields $p \xrightarrow{w}{}^* q$. On the other hand, assume that the focused formula is of the form $\forall x.[r \; \mathfrak{P} \; x \multimap p \; \mathfrak{P} \; (u \; x)]$ where u is a prefix of w (meaning that there is a word v such that w is uv) and $r \in Q$. Thus, Ξ is of the form

$$\frac{\Xi'}{x : o :: \mathcal{T}'(\delta); q \; \mathfrak{P} \; x \vdash r, (v \; x); \cdot} \langle p, u, r \rangle.$$
$$x : o :: \mathcal{T}'(\delta); q \; \mathfrak{P} \; x \vdash p, (u \; (v \; x)); \cdot$$

The inductive hypothesis ensures that $r \xrightarrow{v}{}^* q$ and, therefore, $p \xrightarrow{uv}{}^* q$.

To prove point 2 above, assume that $w \in L(F)$. Thus, there is an f_i ($i \in \{1, \ldots, n\}$) such that $s \xrightarrow{w}{}^* f_i$. By point 1 above, this implies that

$$\cdot :: \mathcal{T}(\delta); \cdot \vdash \forall x.[f_i \; \mathfrak{P} \; x \multimap s \; \mathfrak{P} \; (w \; x)]; \cdot$$

has a $\Downarrow \mathcal{L}_2^\omega$-proof. By invertibility, the sequent

$$x : o :: \mathcal{T}(\delta); f_i \; \mathfrak{P} \; x \vdash s, (w \; x); \cdot$$

also has a $\Downarrow \mathcal{L}_2^\omega$-proof. Given that there is a simple $\Downarrow \mathcal{L}_2^\omega$-proof of

$$x : o :: \cdot; (f_1 \& \cdots \& f_n) \; \mathfrak{P} \; x \vdash f_i \; \mathfrak{P} \; x; \cdot,$$

the *cut* rule Figure 7.1 along with the cut-elimination theorem (Theorem 9.13) yields a proof of $x : o :: \mathcal{T}(\delta); (f_1 \& \cdots \& f_n) \; \mathfrak{P} \; x \vdash s, (w \; x); \cdot$, which concludes the forward direction of point 2. To prove the converse, assume that

$$\cdot :: \mathcal{T}(\delta); \cdot \vdash \forall x.[(f_1 \& \cdots \& f_n) \; \mathfrak{P} \; x \multimap s \; \mathfrak{P} \; (w \; x)]; \cdot$$

has a $\Downarrow \mathcal{L}_2^\omega$-proof. Reading this proof from conclusion to premises, it is a series of synthetic rules based on formulas selected from $\mathcal{T}(\delta)$ ending with a decide rule with the conclusion

$$x : o :: \cdot; (f_1 \& \cdots \& f_n) \; \mathfrak{P} \; x \vdash f_i \; \mathfrak{P} \; x; \cdot.$$

We can now modify that proof by replacing all occurrences of $(f_1 \& \cdots \& f_n)$ with f_i and this will give us a proof of

$$\cdot :: \mathcal{T}(\delta); \cdot \vdash \forall x.[f_i \; \mathfrak{P} \; x \multimap s \; \mathfrak{P} \; (w \; x)]; \cdot$$

Thus, by point 1, this is equivalent to $s \xrightarrow{w}^* f_i$ which is also equivalent to $w \in L(F)$. □

> **Exercise 10.5.** *If we only attempt to compute words that label paths between two states (as in Proposition 10.4), then we do not need to use the $⅋$ connective. Let **par** be a new constant of type $o \to o \to o$. Show how the formula $p ⅋ t$ can systematically be replaced in $\mathcal{T}(\delta)$ by the atomic formula (**par** $p\ t$) in such a way that capturing a transition from p to q by word w is captured by proving the implication $\forall x.[(\textbf{par}\ q\ x) \multimap (\textbf{par}\ p\ (w\ x))]$. Prove also that this encoding task can be reduced further by replacing all occurrences of $\multimap$ with $\Rightarrow$. The result of such a transformation on $\mathcal{T}(\delta)$ would yield a collection of binary clauses, i.e., formulas of the form $\forall \bar{x}.[A \Rightarrow A']$, where A and A' are atomic formulas. (See also Section 13.5.)*

10.4 Properties about Finite Automata

Once finite automata are defined, one usually attempts to introduce different versions of such machines (e.g., deterministic finite automata), and to prove various properties of these various machines and the languages they accept. Many of those developments could be attempted in this setting, although there is no guarantee that our proof-theoretic setting would make establishing those results easier. We can, however, illustrate a few occasions where using the proof-theoretic setting is interesting or illuminating in this setting.

Since proofs allow for the substitution of eigenvariables and since constants can be considered eigenvariables within our higher-order logic setting, it is easy to prove the following.

Let h is a mapping from Λ to Λ^*. By the homomorphic extension of h we mean a mapping from Λ^* to Λ^* (which we also write as h) given by setting $h(u_1 u_2 \ldots u_n)$ to the concatenation of the words $h(u_1), h(u_2), \ldots, h(u_n)$.

> **Proposition 10.6.** *Let h be a mapping form Λ to Λ^*. If L is a language accepted by a finite automaton, then the language $h(L) = \{h(w) \mid w \in L\}$ is also accepted by a finite automata.*

Proof: Let $F_1 = \langle Q, \Lambda, \delta, s, \{f_1, \ldots, f_n\}\rangle$ be a finite automata that accepts L. Let Λ be the set of letters $\{v_1, \ldots, v_n\}$ ($n \geq 1$).

We first pick a new alphabet that is essentially a copy of Λ. Let $\bar{\Lambda}$ be the set of letters $\{\bar{v}_1, \ldots, \bar{v}_n\}$, all of which are assumed to be new (i.e., not members of Q or Λ). For $w \in \Lambda^*$, let $\bar{w}$ denote the word in $\bar{\Lambda}^*$ that results from relabeling the letters v in w with $\bar{v}$. Finally, let the mapping $\bar{h}$ from Λ^* to $\bar{\Lambda}^*$ be defined by $\bar{h}(w) = \overline{h(w)}$.

Let F_2 be the automaton $\langle Q, \bar{\Lambda}, \bar{h}(\delta), s, \{f_1, \ldots, f_n\}\rangle$ where its transitions are given by

$$\bar{h}(\delta) = \{p \xrightarrow{\bar{h}(w)} q \mid p \xrightarrow{w} q \in \delta\}.$$

We now show that F_2 accepts the language $\bar{h}(L)$.

Let $w \in L(F_2)$. Thus, there is $m \geq 0$, words $w_1, \ldots, w_m$ in $\bar{\Lambda}^*$, and states $p_0, \ldots, p_m$ such that p_0 is s, $p_m \in \{f_1, \ldots, f_n\}$, and the transition $p_i \xrightarrow{w_{i+1}} p_{i+1}$ is in $\bar{h}(\delta)$ ($0 \leq i < n$). Thus, there are words $\{z_1, \ldots, z_n\} \subseteq \Lambda^*$ such that $\bar{h}(z_i) = w_i$ and $p_i \xrightarrow{z_{i+1}} p_{i+1}$ is in δ ($0 \leq i < n$). Thus, the string $z_1 \cdots z_n$ is accepted by F_1 and $\bar{h}(z_1 \cdots z_n) = w$. Thus, $w \in \bar{h}(L(F_1)) = \bar{h}(L)$.

Conversely, assume that $w \in \bar{h}(L)$. Thus, there is a word $z \in L$ such that $w = \bar{h}(z)$. By Proposition 10.4, the sequent

$$\cdot :: \mathcal{T}(\delta); \cdot \vdash \forall x.[(f_1 \& \cdots \& f_n) \,\mbox{\reflectbox{$\mathbb{N}$}}\, x \multimap s \,\mbox{\reflectbox{$\mathbb{N}$}}\, (w\, x)]; \cdot$$

has a $\Downarrow \mathcal{L}_2^\omega$ proof. By repeatedly applying Proposition 7.7 with the substitutions $v \mapsto \bar{h}(v)$ ($v \in \Lambda$), we can conclude that

$$Q, \bar{\Lambda} :: \mathcal{T}(\bar{h}(\delta)); \cdot \vdash \forall x.[(f_1 \& \cdots \& f_n) \,\mbox{\reflectbox{$\mathbb{N}$}}\, x \multimap s \,\mbox{\reflectbox{$\mathbb{N}$}}\, (\bar{h}(w)\, x)]; \cdot$$

is provable. (These substitutions can be applied in any order since the letters in the domain do not appear in the range: This is the reason why the alphabet $\bar{\Lambda}$ was introduced.) Thus, $\bar{h}(w)$ is accepted by F_2.

We have now shown that $\bar{h}(L)$ is accepted by the automaton F_2. Finally, if we let F_3 be the automaton that is identical to F_2 except that all occurrences of the letter $\bar{u}_i$ are replaced by u_i, it is then the case that $h(L)$ is accepted by the automaton F_3. □

Given that this is a rather direct theorem, the use of a proof-theoretic characterization of finite automata in this proof is minor.

Assume that we have a finite automaton in which we have a transition $p \xrightarrow{uv} q$ for words u and v. It is an easy matter to modify that automaton by adding a new state, say r, and by replacing that transition with the two transitions $p \xrightarrow{u} r$ and $r \xrightarrow{v} q$. At the level of a linear logic specification, consider the following two formulas.

10.4 Properties about Finite Automata

$$D_1 = \quad \forall x.[q \;⅋\; x \multimap p \;⅋\; (u(v\,x))]$$
$$D_2 = \quad \exists r.[\;\; \forall x.[q \;⅋\; x \multimap r \;⅋\; (v\,x)] \otimes$$
$$\forall x.[r \;⅋\; x \multimap p \;⅋\; (u\,x)] \quad].$$

Let D_2' be the formula under the existential quantifier of D_2: That is, D_2 is $\exists r.D_2'$. The linear implication $D_2 \multimap D_1$ is equivalent in linear logic to $\forall r.(D_2' \multimap D_1)$. It is an easy matter to prove this formula since there is a short $\Downarrow \mathcal{L}_2^\omega$ proof of the sequent $r : o :: \cdot; D_2' \vdash D_1; \cdot$. Thus, by using cut and cut elimination with our logic specification, any word accepted by the original machine must be accepted by the modified machine. The converse entailment does not, however, hold, as is evident from the fact that the formula $p \;⅋\; (u\;\top)$ is provable from D_2 but not from D_1. Although D_2 is technically stronger than D_1, inductive arguments about $\Downarrow \mathcal{L}_2^\omega$-proofs in which the structure of atomic formulas is restricted to be related to sequences of letters can prove such a converse relation.

Given this result, we can always replace a transition with two or more letters with two transitions with shorter transitions. If we repeat this process enough, we can build a machine in which transitions are limited to either a letter or the empty word. This argument can introduce a restricted form of finite automata in which the restriction on the relation δ can be changed from being $Q \times \Lambda^* \times Q$ to being $Q \times (\Lambda \cup \{\epsilon\}) \times Q$.

The finite automata defined here are nondeterministic in the sense from state p and word w, there can be δ-transitions to several states, say, $q_1, \ldots, q_n$ ($n \geq 0$). As formulas in linear logic, $\mathcal{T}(\delta)$ can contain the clauses

$$\forall x.[q_1 \;⅋\; x \multimap p \;⅋\; wx]$$
$$\vdots$$
$$\forall x.[q_n \;⅋\; x \multimap p \;⅋\; wx].$$

The conjunction of these n formulas (using &) is logically equivalent to the single formula

$$\forall x.[(q_1 \oplus \cdots \oplus q_n) \;⅋\; x \multimap p \;⅋\; (w\,x)].$$

Thus, some aspects of nondeterminism within the specification of a finite automata can be captured using the additive disjunction in such an explicit fashion.

Given that observation, it is certainly possible to consider a variation of finite automata where this additive disjunction is replaced with an additive conjunction. That is, one could allow logic specifications such as

$$\forall x.[(q_1 \mathbin{\&} \cdots \mathbin{\&} q_n) \mathbin{\bindnasrepma} x \multimap p \mathbin{\bindnasrepma} (w\ x)].$$

Such a clause would specify that the string wu is accepted starting from p if u is accepted starting at q_i for every $i = 1, \ldots, n$. Variants of such machines are known as *alternating finite automata*.

10.5 Encoding Pushdown Automata

A simple extension to the specification we used for finite automata yields an encoding of pushdown automata. As in the definition of finite automata, let Q and Λ be a set of states and an alphabet. Let Ω be an additional set of tokens to be used as the set of *stack symbols*: This set is assumed to be finite and disjoint from Q and Λ. A *pushdown automaton* F is a sextuplet $\langle Q, \Lambda, \Omega, \delta, s, \mathcal{F} \rangle$ where Q, Λ, and Ω are given as above and where

1. $s \in Q$ is the *initial state*,
2. $\mathcal{F} \subseteq Q$ is the set of *final states* (possibly empty), and
3. $\delta \subseteq Q \times \Lambda^* \times \Omega^* \times Q \times \Omega^*$ is the set of *transitions*.

We write $p, \gamma \xrightarrow{w} q, \gamma'$ to denote the fact that $\langle p, w, \gamma, q, \gamma' \rangle \in \delta$. The fact that δ contains the tuple $\langle p, w, \gamma, q, \gamma' \rangle$ indicates that this pushdown automaton can make a transition when (*i*) the automata is in state p, (*ii*) the top of the automata's stack is γ, and (*iii*) the input word has w as a prefix. If these three conditions hold, then the automata can transition to state q, and the state is changed by dropping the γ prefix (popping symbols from the stack) followed by concatenating γ' onto the stack (pushing symbols onto the stack). Of course, the w prefix on the input string is dropped during this transition.

This informal specification can be made precise by directly encoding it into linear logic. To do this, we repeat the encoding of state and alphabet symbols as constants of type o and $o \to o$, respectively. In addition, stack symbols will also be encoded as constants of type $o \to o$. Furthermore, the transition relation, δ, is encoded as the theory $\mathcal{T}(\delta)$ composed of one clause of the form

$$\forall x. \forall y.[q \mathbin{\bindnasrepma} x \mathbin{\bindnasrepma} (\gamma' y) \multimap p \mathbin{\bindnasrepma} (w\ x) \mathbin{\bindnasrepma} (\gamma\ y)]$$

for every tuple $\langle p, w, \gamma, q, \gamma' \rangle \in \delta$. Note the difference between the treatment of the input string and the stack: When reading this implication from right to left, the input string does not grow while the stack might become longer. It is also the case, that w can be $\lambda x.x$, in which case the input string does not change during the transition. If γ is empty and γ' is not empty, then the stack is treated as a *push* with the symbols in γ'. Conversely, if γ' is empty and γ is not empty, then the stack is treated as a *pop* of the symbols in γ. If both γ and γ' are empty, the stack does not change, and if both γ and γ' are not empty, then a push and pop operation occurs simultaneously during this transition.

In the case that Ω is empty, the only member of Ω^* is the empty word. In that case, every transition will be encoded as a clause of the form

$$\forall x. \forall y. [q \mathbin{\texttt{⅋}} x \mathbin{\texttt{⅋}} y \multimap p \mathbin{\texttt{⅋}} (w\ x) \mathbin{\texttt{⅋}} y]$$

which is logically equivalent to the formula

$$\forall x. [q \mathbin{\texttt{⅋}} x \multimap p \mathbin{\texttt{⅋}} (w\ x)].$$

In this sense, a pushdown automaton with an empty set of stack symbols is a finite automaton.

In a complete analogy with finite automata, a word is accepted by the pushdown automaton $\langle Q, \Lambda, \Omega, \delta, s, \mathcal{F} \rangle$ if the following sequent is provable in linear logic.

$$\mathcal{T}(\delta) \vdash \forall x. \forall y. [(f_1 \mathbin{\&} \cdots \mathbin{\&} f_n) \mathbin{\texttt{⅋}} x \mathbin{\texttt{⅋}} y \multimap s \mathbin{\texttt{⅋}} (w\ x) \mathbin{\texttt{⅋}} y].$$

Note that the stack starts empty and must be empty again at the end of an accepting run.

10.6 Bibliographic Notes

The connection between multiset rewriting and Fibonacci numbers has been developed by Kanovich [2014] to provide new proofs of results in the theory of additive partitions of natural numbers. Kanovich [1996] has also explored the use of linear logic to specify various kinds of machine models.

The encoding of words into λ-terms given in Section 10.3 goes back to at least the proof in Huet [1973a] that *third-order unification* is undecidable, a proof that reduces the *Post correspondence problem* to solving such unification.

An important precursor to linear logic was the work of Lambek [1958, 1988], in which he studied Gentzen's original sequent calculus but without any of the structural rules: That is, he shuns the exchange rule as well as the weakening and contraction rules. In that setting, the contexts in sequents are lists and not multisets. A noncommutative variant of linear logic arises in that setting, and words can be encoded directly as lists of tokens (encoding letters) of type o instead of type $o \to o$. See the handbook chapter by Moortgat [1996] for more on this approach to deduction without exchange.

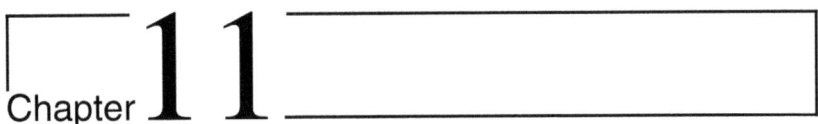

Chapter 11

Collection Analysis for Horn Clauses

In this chapter, we use both proof theory and linear logic to provide a certain kind of *static checking* – called *collection analysis* – of Horn clause logic programs.

11.1 Introduction

Static analysis of logic programs can provide useful information for programmers and compilers. Type checking, an example of a static analysis, is valuable during the development of code since type errors often represent program errors that are caught at compile time when they are easier to find and fix than at runtime when they are much harder to locate. Static-type information also provides valuable documentation of code since it provides a concise approximation to what the code does.

To illustrate what is called *collection analysis*, consider a Horn clause specification of list sorting that maintains duplicates of elements (see, for example, Figure 5.6). Part of the correctness of a sort program includes the fact that if the atomic formula $(sort\ t\ s)$ is provable, then s is a permutation of t that is in order. The proof of such a property is likely to involve inductive arguments requiring the invention of invariants: In other words, this may not be a property that can be inferred statically during compile time. On the other hand, if the lists t and s are approximated by multisets (that is, if we forget the order of items in lists), then it might be possible to establish that if the atomic formula $(sort\ t\ s)$ is provable, then the multiset associated to s is equal to the multiset

229

associated to t. If that is so, then it is immediate that the lists t and s are, in fact, permutations of one another (in other words, no elements were dropped, duplicated, or created during sorting). As we shall see, such properties based on using multisets to approximate lists can often be established statically. As a result, at least part of the correctness of the sort specification can be established automatically. Besides lists, other data structures, such as trees, can be approximated by various collections of the items they contain. Such approximations can provide partial correctness properties of Horn clause logic programs.

We present a scheme by which such collection analysis can be structured and automated. Central to this scheme is the use of linear logic as a computational logic underlying the logic of Horn clauses.

11.2 The Undercurrents

Various themes underlie this approach to inferring properties of Horn clause programs. We list them explicitly below. The rest of this chapter can be seen as a particular example of how these themes can be developed.

If typing is important, why use only one type system? Types and other static properties of programming languages have proved important on several levels. Typing can be useful for programmers: They can offer important invariants and code documentation. Compilers can also use static analysis to uncover useful structures that allow compilers to make choices that can improve execution. Although compilers might use multiple static analysis regimes, programmers do not usually have convenient access to multiple static analyses for the code they are composing. Sometimes, a programming language provides no static analysis, as is the case with Lisp and Prolog. Other programming languages offer exactly one typing discipline, such as the polymorphic typing disciplines of Standard ML and λProlog. It seems clear, however, that such code analysis, if it can be done quickly and incrementally, might have significant benefits for programmers while writing code. For example, a programmer might find it valuable to know that a particular recursive program has linear or quadratic runtime complexity or that a particular relation defines a function. An open set of properties and analysis tools is an interesting direction for designing a programming language. The collection analysis we discuss here could be just one such analysis tool.

Constants and eigenvariables During the search for cut-free proofs, eigenvariables act as *scoped constant*. Once an eigenvariable is introduced into a proof, it does not vary. When eliminating cut rules, it is the case that eigenvariables are instantiated (i.e., they act as variables): See Propositions 5.25 and 7.7. Thus, within cut-free proofs, the difference between a constant and an eigenvariable is really only one of scope: A constant has a global scope, while an eigenvariable has scope only within the subproof into which it is introduced (using the ∀R rule). This scoped nature of constants has also been hinted at by the introduction of three different kinds of signatures in Section 2.4: the signature of the logical connectives used in a logic is written as Σ_{-1}, the signature of non-logical constants used in logic programs is written as Σ_0, and the part of sequents used to bind eigenvariables is usually written as Σ. In a higher-order setting, it is possible to move all the constants in Σ_0 into Σ. In this chapter, we shall use the substitution of non-logical constants in order to "split the atom": For example, by substituting for the predicate p in the atom $p(t_1, \ldots, t_n)$, we replace that atom with a formula, which, in this chapter, will be a linear logic formula.

Linear logic underlies computational logic As we have illustrated repeatedly in this book, linear logic is able to explain the proof theory of various logic programming languages, even those that were not originally conceived as being built on linear logic. Linear logic is also able to provide natural means to reason about resources, such as items in multisets and sets. Thus, linear logic will allow us to sit within one declarative framework to describe both usual logic programming as well as "sub-atomic" reasoning about the resources implicit in the arguments of predicates.

11.3 Abstraction and Substitution in Proof Theory

We now outline three ways to instantiate items appearing within the sequent calculus.

Substituting for types The primitive type o is fixed in this book as the type used by logical formulas. All other primitive types can be considered non-logical since these are provided when one specifies logic programs. We shall allow for the formal substitution of non-logical primitive types with some simple type. It is an easy matter to show that if one takes a proof with a primitive type constant σ and replaces it everywhere with some type, say, τ, one gets another valid proof. Since we have used polymorphic typing for lists in this book, we shall consider a particular instance of the list type, e.g., (list nat) as a primitive type.

Substituting for non-logical constants Assume that the following sequent has a $\Downarrow \mathcal{L}_2^\omega$-proof.

$$\Sigma, p : \tau :: D_1, D_2, \Gamma; \cdot \vdash p(t_1, \ldots, t_m); \cdot, .$$

Here, assume that the type τ is a predicate type (i.e., it is of the form $\tau_1 \to \cdots \to \tau_m \to o$) and where p appears in, say, D_1 and D_2 and in no formula of Γ. Let θ be the substitution $[p \mapsto \lambda x_1 \ldots \lambda x_m.S]$, where S is formula (i.e., a term of type o) over the signature $\Sigma \cup \{x_1, \ldots, x_m\}$. By an application of Proposition 7.7, there is a $\Downarrow \mathcal{L}_2^\omega$-proof also of

$$\Sigma :: D_1\theta, D_2\theta, \Gamma; \cdot \vdash S[t_1/x_1, \ldots, t_m/x_m]; \cdot.$$

As this example illustrates, it is possible to instantiate a predicate (here, p) with an abstraction of a formula (here, $\lambda x_1 \ldots \lambda x_m. S$). Such instantiations carry a provable sequent to a provable sequent. Depending on the structure of the formula S, the formula $D_i\theta$ may have a complicated logical structure even if D_i is simply a first-order Horn clause.

Substituting for assumptions An instance of the cut rule is the following.

$$\frac{\Sigma :: \Gamma; \cdot \vdash C; \cdot \qquad \Sigma :: \Gamma, C; \cdot \vdash B; \cdot}{\Sigma :: \Gamma; \cdot \vdash B; \cdot} \text{ cut }!.$$

This inference rule (especially when associated with the cut-elimination procedure) provides a way to merge (substitute) the proof of a formula (here, C) with the use of that formula as an assumption. For example, consider the following situation. Continuing the example above, assume that we can prove

$$\Sigma :: \Gamma; \cdot \vdash D_1\theta; \cdot \quad \text{and} \quad \Sigma :: \Gamma; \cdot \vdash D_2\theta; \cdot$$

Using two instances of the cut rule, the proofs of these sequents, and the cut-elimination theorem, it is possible to obtain a cut-free proof of the sequent

$$\Sigma :: \Gamma; \cdot \vdash S[t_1/x_1, \ldots, t_m/x_m]; \cdot.$$

Thus, by a series of instantiations, it is possible to move from a proof of

$$\Sigma, p : \tau :: D_1, D_2, \Gamma; \cdot \vdash p(t_1, \ldots, t_m); \cdot$$

to a proof of

$$\Sigma :: \Gamma; \cdot \vdash S[t_1/x_1, \ldots, t_m/x_m]; \cdot \cdot$$

We shall use this style of reasoning several times in this chapter. Such reasoning will allow us to replace the atomic formula $p(t_1, \ldots, t_m)$ with the formula $S[t_1/x_1, \ldots, t_m/x_m]$ and to transform proofs of that atom into proofs of this new formula. In what follows, the formula S will be a linear logic formula that provides an encoding of some judgment about the data structures encoded in the terms $t_1, \ldots, t_m$.

11.4 Multiset Approximations

From the purposes of this chapter, a *multiset expression* is a formula in linear logic built from the predicate symbol *item* (denoting the singleton multiset), the linear logic multiplicative disjunction $\invamp$ (for multiset union), and the unit $\bot$ for $\invamp$ (used to denote the empty multiset). We shall also allow variables of type o to be used to denote a (necessarily open) multiset expression. An example of an open multiset expression is $item(f\ X) \invamp \bot \invamp Y$, where Y is a variable of type o, X is a first-order variable, and f is some first-order term constructor. A closed multiset expression denotes an actual multiset that arises from collecting the arguments of all items in it. If S is a closed multiset expression, we write $\ulcorner S \urcorner$ to denote this multiset of atomic formulas denoted by S. Thus, $\ulcorner item(f\ a) \invamp \bot \invamp item\ a \invamp item\ a \urcorner$ is the multiset $\{a, a, (f\ a)\}$.

Let S and T be two multiset expressions. The two *multiset judgments* that we wish to capture are multiset inclusion, written as $S \sqsubseteq T$, and equality, written as $S \stackrel{m}{=} T$. We use the syntactic variable ρ to range over these two judgments, which are formally binary relations of type $o \to o \to o$. A *multiset statement* is a formula of the form

$$\forall \bar{x}[S_1\ \rho_1\ T_1\ \&\ \cdots\ \&\ S_n\ \rho_n\ T_n \Rightarrow S_0\ \rho_0\ T_0]$$

where the quantified variables $\bar{x}$ are either first-order or of type o and formulas $S_0, T_0, \ldots, S_n, T_n$ are possibly open multiset expressions.

If S and T are closed multiset expressions, then we write $\models_m S \sqsubseteq T$ whenever $\ulcorner S \urcorner$ is contained in $\ulcorner T \urcorner$, and we write $\models_m S \stackrel{m}{=} T$ whenever the multisets $\ulcorner S \urcorner$ and $\ulcorner T \urcorner$ are equal. Similarly, we write

$$\models_m \forall \bar{x}[S_1\ \rho_1\ T_1\ \&\ \cdots\ \&\ S_n\ \rho_n\ T_n \Rightarrow S_0\ \rho_0\ T_0]$$

if for all closed substitutions θ such that $\models_m (S_i\theta) \; \rho_i \; (T_i\theta)$ for all $i = 1, \ldots, n$, it is the case that $\models_m (S_0\theta) \; \rho_0 \; (T_0\theta)$.

Assume that S and T are closed multiset expressions. The following are proved by simple inductions and references to the invertibility of $\mathfrak{R}$R and $\bot$R (see Exercise 8.1).

1. The following are equivalent: (a) the judgment $\models_{ms} S \stackrel{m}{=} T$ holds, (b) $\ulcorner S \urcorner$ and $\ulcorner T \urcorner$ are the same multiset, (c) $T \multimap S$ is provable, (d) $S \multimap T$ is provable, and (e) $S \multimap\!\!\circ T$ is provable.
2. The following are equivalent: (a) the judgment $\models_{ms} S \sqsubseteq T$ holds, (b) $\ulcorner T \urcorner$ is a multiset of the form $\ulcorner S \urcorner \cup \Delta$, for some multiset Δ of *item*-atoms, and (c) the formula $S \,\mathfrak{R}\, \mathbf{0} \multimap T$ is provable.

Proposition 11.1 is central to our use of linear logic to establish multiset statements for Horn clause programs.

Proposition 11.1. *Let $S_0, T_0, \ldots, S_n, T_n$ ($n \geq 0$) be multiset expressions, all of whose free variables are in the list of variables $\bar{x}$. For each judgment $s \; \rho \; t$ we write $s \; \hat{\rho} \; t$ to denote ($s \,\mathfrak{R}\, \mathbf{0} \multimap t$) if ρ is $\sqsubseteq$ and $s \multimap\!\!\circ t$ if ρ is $\stackrel{m}{=}$. If*

$$\forall \bar{x}[S_1 \; \hat{\rho}_1 \; T_1 \;\&\; \ldots \;\&\; S_n \; \hat{\rho}_n \; T_n \Rightarrow S_0 \; \hat{\rho}_0 \; T_0] \quad (*)$$

is provable in linear logic, then

$$\models_{ms} \forall \bar{x}[S_1 \; \rho_1 \; T_1 \;\&\; \cdots \;\&\; S_n \; \rho_n \; T_n \Rightarrow S_0 \; \rho_0 \; T_0]$$

Proof: Assume that the formula $(*)$ is provable in linear logic. Let θ be a closed substitution such that $\models_m (S_i\theta) \; \rho_i \; (T_i\theta)$ for all $i = 1, \ldots, n$. By the observations above, we have $\vdash (S_i\theta) \; \hat{\rho}_i \; (T_i\theta)$ for all $i = 1, \ldots, n$. Using the provability of $(*)$ and cut elimination, we conclude that $\vdash (S_0\theta) \; \hat{\rho}_0 \; (T_0\theta)$ and, hence, $\models_{ms} (S_0\theta) \; \hat{\rho}_0 \; (T_0\theta)$. $\square$

This proposition shows that linear logic can infer valid multiset statements. Note that the converse does not hold: The statement

$$\forall x \forall y. (x \sqsubseteq y) \;\&\; (y \sqsubseteq x) \Rightarrow (x \stackrel{m}{=} y)$$

is valid, but its translation into linear logic is not provable.

To illustrate how deduction in linear logic can establish the validity of a multiset statement, consider the first-order Horn clause program in Figure 11.1. Three predicates – append, split, sort – are defined in that figure, while

11.4 Multiset Approximations

```
type append   list nat -> list nat -> list nat -> o.
type sort     list nat -> list nat -> o.
type split    nat -> list nat ->
                     list nat -> list nat -> o.
type leq      nat -> nat -> o.
type gr       nat -> nat -> o.

append nil K K.
append (X::L) K (X::M) :- append L K M.

split X nil nil nil.
split X (A::R) (A::S) B :- leq A X, split X R S B.
split X (A::R) S (A::B) :- gr  A X, split X R S B.

sort nil nil.
sort (F::R) S:- split F R Sm B, sort Sm SS, sort B BS,
   append SS (F::BS) S.
```

Figure 11.1 Some Horn clauses for specifying a sorting relation.

two other predicates — leq, gr — denote order relations, and are apparently defined elsewhere.

If we think of lists as collections of items, then we might want to check that the sort program, as written, does not drop, duplicate, or create any elements. That is, if the atom (sort $s\ t$) is provable then the multiset of items in the list s is equal to the multiset of items in the list t. If this property holds then t and s are lists that are permutations of each other: Of course, this does not say that it is the correct permutation but this more simple fact is one that, as we show, can be inferred automatically.

Computing this property of our example logic programming follows the following three steps.

First, we provide an approximation of lists using multiset: more precisely, as *formulas* denoting multisets. The first step, therefore, must be to substitute list nat with o in the signature of Figure 11.1. Next we map the list constructors into linear logic expressions using the substitution

$$\text{nil} \mapsto \bot, \quad :: \mapsto \lambda x \lambda y.\ \textit{item}\ x\ \invamp\ y.$$

Under such a mapping, the list (1::3::2::nil) is mapped to the multiset expression *item* 1 $\invamp$ *item* 3 $\invamp$ *item* 2 $\invamp$ $\bot$.

Second, we associate with each predicate in Figure 11.1 a multiset judgment that encodes an invariant concerning the multisets denoted by the predicate's arguments. For example, if (append $r\ s\ t$) or (split $u\ t\ r\ s$) is provable then the multiset union of the items in r with those in s is equal to the multiset

$$\text{append} \mapsto \lambda x \lambda y \lambda z. (x \,\text{⅋}\, y) \multimap z$$
$$\text{split} \mapsto \lambda u \lambda x \lambda y \lambda z. (y \,\text{⅋}\, z) \multimap x$$
$$\text{sort} \mapsto \lambda x \lambda y. x \multimap y$$
$$\text{leq} \mapsto \lambda x \lambda y. \mathbf{1}$$
$$\text{gr} \mapsto \lambda x \lambda y. \mathbf{1}$$

Figure 11.2 An instantiation for various predicate symbols.

$$\forall K (\bot \,\text{⅋}\, K \multimap K)$$
$$\forall X, L, K, M (L \,\text{⅋}\, K \multimap M) \Rightarrow (\textit{item}\, X \,\text{⅋}\, L \,\text{⅋}\, K \multimap \textit{item}\, X \,\text{⅋}\, M)$$
$$\forall X (\bot \,\text{⅋}\, \bot \multimap \bot)$$
$$\forall X, A, B, R, S. (S \,\text{⅋}\, B \multimap R) \Rightarrow \mathbf{1} \Rightarrow (\textit{item}\, A \,\text{⅋}\, S \,\text{⅋}\, B \multimap \textit{item}\, A \,\text{⅋}\, R)$$
$$\forall X, A, B, R, S. (S \,\text{⅋}\, B \multimap R) \Rightarrow \mathbf{1} \Rightarrow (S \,\text{⅋}\, \textit{item}\, A \,\text{⅋}\, B \multimap \textit{item}\, A \,\text{⅋}\, R)$$
$$(\bot \multimap \bot)$$

$$\forall F, R, S, Sm, Bg, SS, BS.$$
$$[(Sm \,\text{⅋}\, B \multimap R) \,\&\, (Sm \multimap SS) \,\&\, (B \multimap BS) \,\&\,$$
$$(SS \,\text{⅋}\, \textit{item}\, F \,\text{⅋}\, BS \multimap S)] \Rightarrow$$
$$(\textit{item}\, F \,\text{⅋}\, R \multimap S)$$

Figure 11.3 The result of instantiating these various predicates.

of items in t, and if (sort s t) is provable then the multisets of items in lists s and t are equal. This association of multiset judgments to atomic formulas can be achieved formally using the substitutions in Figure 11.2. The predicates leq and gr (for the least-than-or-equal-to and greater-than relations) relate numbers and not the items being collected so that they are substituted with the trivial tautology $\mathbf{1}$. Figure 11.3 presents the result of applying these mappings to Figure 11.1.

Third, we must now attempt to prove each of the resulting formulas. In the case of Figure 11.3, all the displayed formulas are trivial theorems of linear logic.

Having taken these three steps, we now claim that we have proved the intended collection judgments associate with each of the logic programming predicates above: In particular, we have now shown that our particular sort program computes a permutation.

Exercise 11.2.(‡) *Use the same kind of argument to prove that the standard Horn clause encoding of reverse (given below) yields a permutation of its elements.*

```
reverse L K :- rev L nil K.
rev nil L L.
rev (X::M) N L :- rev M (X::N) L.
```

11.5 Formalizing the Method

The formal correctness of this three stage approach is easily justified given the substitution properties we presented in Section 11.3 for the sequent calculus presentation of linear logic.

Let Γ denote a multiset of formulas that contains those in Figure 11.1. Let θ denote the substitution described above for the type (list nat), for the constructors nil and ::, and for the predicates in Figure 11.1. If Σ is the signature for Γ then split Σ into the two signatures Σ_1 and Σ_2 so that Σ_1 is the domain of the substitution θ and let Σ_3 be the signature of the range of θ (in this case, it just contains the constant *item*). Thus, $\Gamma\theta$ is the set of formulas in Figure 11.3.

Assume now that $\Sigma_1, \Sigma_2; \Gamma \vdash sort(t,s)$ is provable. Given the discussion in Section 11.3, we know that

$$\Sigma_1, \Sigma_3; \Gamma\theta \vdash t\theta \multimap s\theta$$

is provable. Since the formulas in $\Gamma\theta$ are provable, we can use substitution into proofs (using the cut rule) to conclude that $\Sigma_1, \Sigma_3; \vdash t\theta \multimap s\theta$. Given Proposition 11.1, we can conclude that $\models_m t\theta \stackrel{m}{=} s\theta$: That is, that $t\theta$ and $s\theta$ encode the same multiset.

Consider the following model-theoretic argument for establishing similar properties of Horn clauses. Let $\mathcal{M}$ be the model that captures the invariants that we have in mind. In particular, $\mathcal{M}$ contains the atoms (append r s t) and (split u t r s) if the items in the list r added to the items in list s are the same as the items in t. Furthermore, $\mathcal{M}$ contains all closed atoms of the form (leq t s) and (gr t s), and closed atoms (sort s t) where s and t are lists that are permutations of one another. One can now show that $\mathcal{M}$ satisfies all the Horn clauses in Figure 11.1. Due to the soundness of first-order classical logic, any atom provable from the clauses in Figure 11.1 must be true in $\mathcal{M}$. By the construction of $\mathcal{M}$, the desired invariant holds for all atoms proved from the program.

The approach suggested here – using linear logic and deduction – remains syntactic and proof theoretic. In particular, deduction within linear logic replaces showing that a model satisfies a Horn clause.

11.6 Set Approximations

The method just described for using multisets to reason about list structures can be modified to reason about sets instead. In particular, we shall switch from relying on the multiplicative connective $\bindnasrepma$ to the additive connective &. In particular, the set $\{x_1, \ldots, x_n\}$ can be encoded as the formula *item* x_1 & $\cdots$ & *item* x_n.

A *set expression* is a formula in linear logic built from the predicate symbol *item* (denoting the singleton set), the linear logic additive disjunction & (for set union), and the unit $\top$ for & (used to denote the empty set). We shall also allow a predicate variable (a variable of type o) to denote a (necessarily open) set expression. An example of an open set expression is $(item\,(f\,X))\,\&\,\top\,\&\,Y$, where Y is a variable of type o, X is a first-order variable, and f is some first-order term constructor. A closed set expression denotes an actual set that arises from collecting the arguments of all items in it. If S is a closed set expression, we write $\llcorner S \lrcorner$ to denote the set of atomic formulas in S. Thus, $\llcorner item\,(f\,a)\,\&\,\top\,\&\,item\,a \lrcorner$ is the set $\{a, (f\,a)\}$.

Let S and T be two set expressions. The two *set judgments* we wish to capture are set inclusion, written as $S \subseteq T$, and set equality, written as $S \stackrel{s}{=} T$. We shall use the syntactic variable ρ to range over these two judgments, which are formally binary relations of type $o \to o \to o$. A *set statement* is a formula of the form

$$\forall \bar{x}[S_1\,\rho_1\,T_1\,\&\,\cdots\,\&\,S_n\,\rho_n\,T_n \Rightarrow S_0\,\rho_0\,T_0]$$

where the quantified variables $\bar{x}$ are either first-order or of type o and formulas $T_0, S_0, \ldots, T_n, S_n$ are possibly open set expressions.

If S and T are closed set expressions, we write $\models_s S \subseteq T$ whenever $\llcorner S \lrcorner \subseteq \llcorner T \lrcorner$ and $\models_s S \stackrel{s}{=} T$ whenever the sets $\llcorner S \lrcorner$ and $\llcorner T \lrcorner$ are equal. Finally, we write

$$\models_s \forall \bar{x}[S_1\,\rho_1\,T_1\,\&\,\cdots\,\&\,S_n\,\rho_n\,T_n \Rightarrow S_0\,\rho_0\,T_0]$$

if for all closed substitutions θ such that $\models_s (S_i\theta)\,\rho_i\,(T_i\theta)$ for all $i = 1, \ldots, n$, it is the case that $\models_s (S_0\theta)\,\rho_0\,(T_0\theta)$.

Assume that S and T are closed set expressions. It is easy to prove (using the invertibility of &R and $\top$R) that the judgment $\models_s S \subseteq T$ holds if and only if the formula $T \multimap S$ is provable. Notice also that $T \multimap S$ is provable in linear logic if and only if $T \Rightarrow S$ is provable in linear logic. Similarly, $\models_s S \stackrel{s}{=} T$ holds if and only if the formula $T \multimap\!\!\circ S$ is provable in linear logic. Also, $T \multimap\!\!\circ S$ is provable if and only if $T \Leftrightarrow S$ is provable. Here, we abbreviate $(B \to C)\,\&\,(C \to B)$ by $B \Leftrightarrow C$.

For a simple example of using sets as approximations, consider modifying the sorting program provided before so that duplicates are not kept in the sorted

11.6 Set Approximations

```
split X nil nil nil.
split X (X::R) S B :- split X R S B.
split X (A::R) (A::S) B :- lt A X, split X R S B.
split X (A::R) S (A::B) :- gr A X, split X R S B.
```

Figure 11.4 Splitting a list while dropping duplicates.

$$\forall X.((item\ X\ \&\ \top) \Leftrightarrow (item\ X\ \&\ \top\ \&\ \top))$$
$$\forall X, B, R, S.\ ((item\ X\ \&\ R) \Leftrightarrow (item\ X\ \&\ S\ \&\ B)) \Rightarrow$$
$$((item\ X\ \&\ (item\ X\ \&\ R)) \Leftrightarrow (item\ X\ \&\ S\ \&\ B))$$
$$\forall X, A, B, R, S.\ \mathbf{1}\ \&\ ((item\ X\ \&\ R) \Leftrightarrow (item\ X\ \&\ S\ \&\ B)) \Rightarrow$$
$$((item\ X\ \&\ (item\ A\ \&\ R)) \Leftrightarrow (item\ X\ \&\ item\ A\ \&\ S\ \&\ B))$$
$$\forall X, A, B, R, S.\ \mathbf{1}\ \&\ ((item\ X\ \&\ R) \Leftrightarrow (item\ X\ \&\ S\ \&\ B)) \Rightarrow$$
$$((item\ X\ \&\ (item\ A\ \&\ R)) \Leftrightarrow (item\ X\ \&\ S\ \&\ item\ A\ \&\ B))$$

Figure 11.5 The set statements produced by the `split` program above.

list. We achieve this modification by replacing the previous specification for splitting a list with the clauses in Figure 11.4. That figure contains a new definition of splitting that contains three clauses for deciding whether or not the pivot for the splitting X is equal to, less than (using the `lt` predicate), or greater than the first member of the list being split. Using the following substitutions for predicates

$$\texttt{append} \mapsto \lambda x \lambda y \lambda z.\ (x\ \&\ y) \Leftrightarrow z$$
$$\texttt{split} \mapsto \lambda u \lambda x \lambda y \lambda z.\ (item\ u\ \&\ x) \Leftrightarrow (item\ u\ \&\ y\ \&\ z)$$
$$\texttt{sort} \mapsto \lambda x \lambda y.\ x \Leftrightarrow y$$

(as well as the trivial substitution for `lt` and `ge`), we obtain new linear logic formulas: Those formulas arising from the clauses for `split` are in Figure 11.5. By proving that those formulas are all linear logic theorems, we show that `sort` relates two lists only if the same set approximates those lists.

Proposition 11.3 is analogous to Proposition 11.1.

Proposition 11.3. *Let* $S_0, T_0, \ldots, S_n, T_n$ *($n \geq 0$) be set expressions all of whose free variables are in the list of variables* $\bar{x}$. *For each judgment* $s\ \rho\ t$ *we write* $s\ \hat{\rho}\ t$ *to denote* $t \Rightarrow s$ *if* ρ *is* $\subseteq$ *and* $t \Leftrightarrow s$ *if* ρ *is* $\stackrel{s}{=}$. *If*

$$\forall \bar{x}[S_1\ \hat{\rho}_1\ T_1\ \&\ \ldots\ \&\ S_n\ \hat{\rho}_n\ T_n \Rightarrow S_0\ \hat{\rho}_0\ T_0]$$

is provable in linear logic, then

$$\models_s \forall \bar{x}[S_1\ \rho_1\ T_1\ \&\ \cdots\ \&\ S_n\ \rho_n\ T_n \Rightarrow S_0\ \rho_0\ T_0]$$

Proof: We only need to consider the case where the judgment ρ is $\subseteq$, since $\stackrel{s}{=}$ is a conjunction of two inclusion judgments. The proof here is similar and simpler than for Proposition 11.1 and the observation that the judgment $\models_s S \subseteq T$ holds if and only if the sequent $\cdot :: \cdot \, ; T \vdash S; \cdot$ has a $\Downarrow \mathcal{L}_2^\omega$-proof. □

Lists can be approximated by sets by using the following substitution:

$$\texttt{nil} \mapsto \top, \qquad :: \, \mapsto \lambda x \lambda y. \, item \, x \, \& \, y.$$

Under such a mapping, the list (1::2::2::nil) is mapped to the set expression *item* 1 & *item* 2 & *item* 2 & $\top$. This expression is equivalent (∘—∘) to the set expression *item* 1 & *item* 2.

11.7 Automation of Analysis

We describe how to automate proving the set and multiset statements described in Propositions 11.1 and 11.3.

We first consider the treatment of set statements. Note that in this case, there is no loss of generality if we only consider the subset judgment since set equality can be expressed as two inclusions. Figure 11.6 contains a small proof system that can decide if a set expression is provable. This proof system uses sequents of the form $\mathcal{R} \mid S \vdash T$ where S and T are set expressions and where $\mathcal{R}$ is a multiset of set judgments (inclusions).

$$\frac{j \in I}{\mathcal{R} \mid \&_i A_i \vdash A_j} \, \&\text{L} \qquad \frac{\{\mathcal{R} \mid D \vdash A_i \mid i \in I\}}{\mathcal{R} \mid D \vdash \&_{i \in I} A_i} \, \&\text{R}$$

$$\frac{\mathcal{R}, B \Rightarrow (\&_{i \in I} A_i) \mid D \vdash B \qquad j \in I}{\mathcal{R}, B \Rightarrow (\&_{i \in I} A_i) \mid D \vdash A_j} \, \text{BC}$$

The schematic variable A ranges over with propositional variables or formulas of the form *item t*, for some term t. A set expression can be written as $\&_{i \in I} A_i$ for some finite index set I. If that index set is the empty set, then this expression denotes $\top$.

Figure 11.6 Specialized proof rules for proving set statements.

11.7 Automation of Analysis

Proposition 11.4. *Let $S_0, T_0, \ldots, S_n, T_n$ ($n \geq 0$) be set expressions, all of whose free variables are in the list of variables $\bar{x}$. The formula*

$$\forall \bar{x}[(S_1 \Rightarrow T_1) \& \ldots \& (S_n \Rightarrow T_n) \Rightarrow (S_0 \Rightarrow T_0)]$$

is provable in linear logic if and only if the sequent

$$S_1 \Rightarrow T_1, \ldots, S_n \Rightarrow T_n \mid S_0 \vdash T_0$$

is provable using the proof system in Figure 11.6.

Proof: Given a proof using the rules in Figure 11.6, a proof in $\Downarrow \mathcal{L}_2^\omega$ can easily be constructed. The completeness of that proof system also follows simply from the completeness of $\Downarrow \mathcal{L}_2^\omega$ (Proposition 7.18). Note that this proof system treats the quantified variables $\bar{x}$ in the linear logic formula above as constants. □

It is easy to note that proof search using the rules in Figure 11.6 is decidable. In particular, when one attempts to find a proof of a sequent by searching from conclusion to premise, the left-hand side of sequents does not change, and only a finite number of atomic right-hand sides can appear. Thus, any looping proof search can be terminated.

The proof system in Figure 11.7 can characterize the structure of proofs of the linear logic encoding of multiset statements. Let

$$\forall \bar{x}[S_1 \; \hat{\rho}_1 \; T_1 \& \ldots \& S_n \; \hat{\rho}_n \; T_n \Rightarrow S_0 \; \hat{\rho}_0 \; T_0]$$

$$\frac{\Gamma \mid S \vdash \Delta}{\Gamma \mid S \vdash \bot, \Delta} \bot R \qquad \frac{\Gamma \mid S \vdash T_1, T_2, \Delta}{\Gamma \mid S \vdash T_1 \; \mathbin{\text{⅋}} \; T_2, \Delta} \mathbin{\text{⅋}} R \qquad \frac{\Gamma \mid S \vdash B, \Delta}{\Gamma \mid S \vdash A_1, \ldots, A_n, \Delta} BC$$

$$\frac{\cdot \mid S \vdash \Delta}{\Gamma \mid S \vdash \Delta} decide \qquad \frac{\cdot \mid T_1 \vdash \Delta_1 \quad \cdot \mid T_2 \vdash \Delta_2}{\cdot \mid T_1 \; \mathbin{\text{⅋}} \; T_2 \vdash \Delta_1, \Delta_2} \mathbin{\text{⅋}} L$$

$$\frac{}{\cdot \mid \bot \vdash \cdot} \bot L \qquad \frac{}{\cdot \mid \mathbf{0} \vdash \Delta} \mathbf{0} L \qquad \frac{}{\cdot \mid A \vdash A} init$$

The schematic variable A ranges over atomic formula (i.e., propositional variables or formulas of the form $item \, t$, for some term t). The *decide* and BC rules have the proviso that the right side of the conclusion contains only formulas that are either atomic or **0**. Additionally, the BC inference rule is constrained so that $n \geq 0$ and Γ contains the formula $B \multimap (A_1 \; \mathbin{\text{⅋}} \cdots \mathbin{\text{⅋}} \; A_n)$.

Figure 11.7 Specialized proof rules for proving multiset statements.

be the translation of a multiset statement into linear logic. The provability of this formula can be reduced to attempting to prove $S_0 \; \hat{\rho}_0 \; T_0$ from assumptions of the form $(B_1 \; \mathbin{\tilde{?}} \; \cdots \; \mathbin{\tilde{?}} \; B_m) \multimap (A_1 \; \mathbin{\tilde{?}} \; \cdots \; \mathbin{\tilde{?}} \; A_n)$, where $A_1, \ldots, A_n$ are atomic, and $B_1, \ldots, B_m$ are atomic or $\mathbf{0}$.

Proposition 11.5. *Let $S_0, T_0, \ldots, S_n, T_n$ ($n \geq 0$) be multiset expressions, all of whose free variables are in the list of variables $\bar{x}$. The formula*

$$\forall \bar{x}[(S_1 \multimap T_1) \mathbin{\&} \ldots \mathbin{\&} (S_n \multimap T_n) \multimap (S_0 \multimap T_0)]$$

is provable in linear logic if and only if the sequent

$$S_1 \multimap T_1, \ldots, S_n \multimap T_n \mid S_0 \vdash T_0$$

is provable using the proof system in Figure 11.7.

Proof: Since the proof system in Figure 11.7 is essentially the focused proof system for $\Downarrow \mathcal{L}_2^\omega$, soundness and completeness follow from the soundness and completeness of the $\Downarrow \mathcal{L}_2^\omega$ proof system. □

Note that the proofs using the rules in Figure 11.7 are straight-line proofs with no branching until the point where the *decide* inference rule is used. During the search for proofs, the left-hand side of sequents remains constant during this non-branching part, but the right-hand side captures multiset rewriting based on the rewrite rules encoded by the left-unbounded zone. Given this observation, this proof system captures multiset rewriting and, since such rewriting can easily encode the reachability problem of Petri Nets (as shown in Esparza and Nielsen [1994] and Leroux and Schmitz [2019]), the complexity of proving judgments in this logic has a TOWER lower bound by a result in Czerwiński et al. [2020]. It is likely that in the context of multiset collection analysis of Horn clauses representing actual Prolog programs, the proof system in Figure 11.7 is more effective than this lower bound suggests.

11.8 List Approximations

Collection analysis can be used with other structures than the lists structures we illustrated in Sections 11.4 and 11.6. For example, a binary tree might be approximated by a collection of its leaves. In such a setting, lists themselves might be a useful structure for collecting together items: That is, we might consider using lists of items instead of multisets and sets of items. Since lists have more structure than sets and multisets, encoding and reasoning with them is more involved. We only illustrate their possible encoding and use here.

Since the order of elements in a list is important, encoding lists into linear logic must involve a connective that is not commutative. Linear implication provides a good candidate for encoding the order used in lists. For example, the list (a::b::nil) can be encoded as the formula

$$(((\bot \multimap p) \multimap \mathit{item}\, b) \multimap p) \multimap \mathit{item}\, a$$

for some (fixed) propositional constant p. This formula is equivalent to

$$\mathit{item}\, a \,\mathbin{\bindnasrepma}\, (p^\bot \otimes (\mathit{item}\, b \,\mathbin{\bindnasrepma}\, p^\bot)).$$

The example above suggests that lists and list equality can be captured directly in linear logic using the following encoding:

$$\mathtt{nil} \mapsto \lambda l.\bot \qquad \mathtt{::} \mapsto \lambda x \lambda R \lambda l.\, ((R\, l) \multimap l) \multimap \mathit{item}\, x.$$

The encoding of the list (a::b::nil) is given by the λ-abstraction

$$\lambda l.(((\bot \multimap l) \multimap \mathit{item}\, b) \multimap l) \multimap \mathit{item}\, a.$$

Proposition 11.6 can be proved by induction on the length of lists.

> **Proposition 11.6.** *Let s and t be two lists (built using* nil *and* :: *) and let S and T be the translation of those lists into expressions of type $o \to o$ via the substitution above. Then $\forall l.(Sl) \multimap\!\circ (Tl)$ is provable in linear logic if and only if s and t are the same list.*

This presentation of lists can be degraded to multisets simply by applying the translation of a list to the formula $\bot$. For example, applying the translation of (a::b::nil) to $\bot$ yields the formulas

$$(((\bot \multimap \bot) \multimap \mathit{item}\, b) \multimap \bot) \multimap \mathit{item}\, a,$$

which is linear logically equivalent to $\mathit{item}\, a \,\mathbin{\bindnasrepma}\, \mathit{item}\, b$.

Given this presentation of lists, there appears to be no simple combinator for, say, list concatenation, and, as a result, there is no direct way to express the judgments of prefix, suffix, and sublist. Thus, beyond equality of lists (by virtue of Proposition 11.6) there seem to be few natural judgments that can be stated for lists.

11.9 Bibliographic Notes

Probably the most common form of static analysis of logic programs is typing. Polymorphic typing is available in λProlog: see Nadathur and Miller [1988] and Nadathur and Pfenning [1992]. Various other forms of typing have also been explored for logic programming languages: See Pfenning [1992] for a collection of papers on this topic. The Ciao system preprocessor described in Hermenegildo et al. [2005] allows a programmer to write various properties about code that the preprocessor attempts to verify statically.

In Section 11.8, the linear logic formula used to represent a list could be viewed as an asynchronous process that alternates between the output of list elements and the input of a control token. See Chapter 12 for more on encoding asynchronous processes in linear logic in this way.

In the case of determining the validity of a set statement, the use of linear logic here appears to be rather weak when compared to the large body of results for solving set-based constraint systems: See Aiken [1994] and Pacholski and Podelski [1997].

This chapter is based on two papers by Miller [2006, 2008a].

Chapter 12

Encoding Security Protocols

By extending the encoding of multiset rewriting in linear logic that was presented in Section 8.6, we find a natural setting to encode some features of communicating processes. By exploiting a mild form of higher-order quantification, we can also capture some aspects of communicating securely over a public communication structure.

12.1 Communicating Processes

The left side of Figure 12.1 depicts a common view of a data structure based on pointers. If we have access to the pointer in the top left corner, then we also have access to both resource A and resource B (computer memory serves as a good example of a resource). Viewed in this way, the pair of pointers to A and B exhibits a similarity to linear logic's $\otimes$ conjunction. Naturally, it is tempting to apply linear logic's negation to this diagram and the conjunction to obtain a dualized representation of this fundamental resource characteristic. To this end, consider the right side of the figure. Here, the arrows have been inverted, and the static resource (something that is accessed) has been dualized into a process (the entity that performs the accessing). The operational interpretation of this right-hand diagram is that two processes, P and Q, converge (synchronize) at the $\invamp$ symbol and are then replaced by a new process. This interpretation precisely aligns with the intended meaning of backchaining on a clause of the form

$$P \invamp Q \multimap R,$$

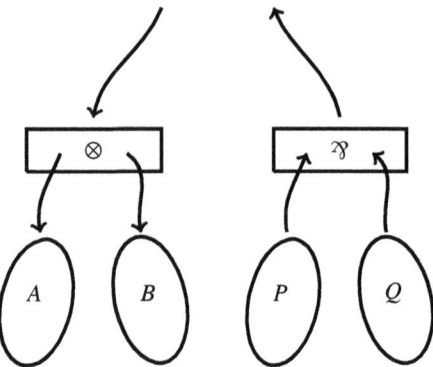

Figure 12.1 Illustrating how to interpret the operational reading of the dual connectives $\otimes$ and $\bindnasrepma$.

where R represents the process resulting from the interaction between P and Q. Therefore, the $\bindnasrepma$ connective signifies a location, a *forum*, where processes can interact. This aspect of $\bindnasrepma$ is the origin of the name "Forum" for the programming language based on the $\Downarrow \mathcal{L}_2$ proof system.

To illustrate this approach to encoding processes using linear logic as a logic programming language, we consider here briefly the π-calculus of Milner et al. [1992a]. The principle computation mechanism of the π-calculus is the synchronization of two agents during which a name is transferred from one agent to another. The expression $\bar{x}z.P$ describes an agent willing to transmit the name z on the wire with the name x. The expression $x(y).Q$ denotes an agent that is willing to receive a name on wire x and formally binds that value to y. The bound variable y in this expression is scoped over Q. The central computational step of the π-calculus is the reduction of the parallel composition $\bar{x}z.P \mid x(y).Q$ to the expression $P \mid Q[z/y]$. The agents P and $Q[z/y]$ are now able to continue their interactions with their environment independently.

Another important aspect of the π-calculus is the notion of scope restriction: In the agent expression $(x)P$, x is bound and invisible to the outside. The scoped value x, however, can be communicated outside its scope, providing a phenomenon known as *scope extrusion*. For example, $(z)(\bar{x}z.P \mid Q) \mid x(y).R$ is structurally equivalent to $(z)(\bar{x}z.P \mid Q \mid x(y).R)$, provided that z is not free in $x(y).R$. This proviso is always easy to accommodate since we assume that α-conversion is available to change the name of bound variables. This expression can be reduced to $(z)(P \mid Q \mid R[z/y])$: The restricted name z has now moved into the agent $R[z/y]$. This mechanism of generating new names (using α-conversion) and sending them outside their scope is an important part of the computational power of the π-calculus.

For an example, consider the following process expression where $a, b,$ and x are free names.

$$(x(y).\bar{y}a.\bar{y}b.\mathbf{0}) \mid (z)(\bar{x}z.z(u).z(v).\bar{u}v.\mathbf{0})$$

(Here, $\mathbf{0}$ is the null process.). Given the informal description of how a π-calculus expression evolves, the scope of the (z) restriction enlarges to yield the expression

$$(z)\Big((x(y).\bar{y}a.\bar{y}b.\mathbf{0}) \mid (\bar{x}z.z(u).z(v).\bar{u}v.\mathbf{0})\Big).$$

Next, communication can take place within the scope of the restriction, yielding the expression

$$(z)\Big((\bar{z}a.\bar{z}b.\mathbf{0}) \mid (z(u).z(v).\bar{u}v.\mathbf{0})\Big).$$

Two more internal communication steps yield the expression

$$(z)\Big(\mathbf{0} \mid (\bar{a}b.\mathbf{0})\Big).$$

Since z is not free in the scope of the restriction (z) and since $\mathbf{0}$ is the unit of parallel composition, this last expression is essentially the same as the expression $(\bar{a}b.\mathbf{0})$.

We encode some of the behavior of the π-calculus as proof search within $\Downarrow \mathcal{L}_2^\omega$ using the following primitive type and four non-logical symbols.

```
kind name      type.
type or        o -> o -> o.
type send      name -> name -> o -> o.
type get       name -> (name -> o) -> o.
type match     name -> name -> o -> o.
```

As is clear from these types, the bound variable of the input prefix get will be mapped to the λ-abstraction in logic. The following mapping translates some π-calculus expressions into linear logic.

$$\langle\!\langle P \mid Q \rangle\!\rangle = \langle\!\langle P \rangle\!\rangle \,\⅋\, \langle\!\langle Q \rangle\!\rangle \qquad \langle\!\langle (x)P \rangle\!\rangle = \forall x. \langle\!\langle P \rangle\!\rangle \qquad \langle\!\langle \mathbf{0} \rangle\!\rangle = \bot$$

$$\langle\!\langle \bar{x}y.P \rangle\!\rangle = \mathtt{send}\ x\ y\ \langle\!\langle P \rangle\!\rangle \qquad \langle\!\langle x(y).P \rangle\!\rangle = \mathtt{get}\ x\ \lambda y \langle\!\langle P \rangle\!\rangle$$

$$\langle\!\langle P + Q \rangle\!\rangle = \mathtt{or}\ \langle\!\langle P \rangle\!\rangle\ \langle\!\langle Q \rangle\!\rangle \qquad \langle\!\langle [x = y]P \rangle\!\rangle = \mathtt{match}\ x\ y\ \langle\!\langle P \rangle\!\rangle.$$

To describe the meaning of the four non-logical constants, we have the following $\mathcal{L}_2^\omega$ specification.

```
get X R || send X Y Q :- R Y || Q.
match X X P :- P.
or P Q :- P.
or P Q :- Q.
```

Note that these axioms are higher-order in the sense that they allow quantification over predicate symbols (such as P and Q) as well as variables of type *name* $\to$ *o* (such as R).

Exercise 12.1. *Show that the informal reduction of the π-calculus expressions given above can be reproduced in $\mathcal{L}_2^\omega$ as follows. Let Σ be the declaration that a and b are names, and let Ψ be the multiset of the four formulas listed above. Build the $\mathcal{L}_2^\omega$ proof of the sequent $\Sigma :: \Psi; P_0 \vdash P_1; \cdot$ where P_1 is the expression*

```
get x (y\ send y a (send y b bot)) ||
pi z\ (send x z (get z u\ (get z v\ send u v bot)))
```

and P_0 is the expression `(send a b bot)`.

Exercise 12.2. *Let Q be the expression*

```
get x y (or (match y a (send x a bot))
            (match y b (send x b bot)))
```

Also let P_a, P_b, and P_c be the expressions `(send x a bot)`, `(send x b bot)`, *and* `(send x c bot)`, *respectively. Show that the two $\mathcal{L}_2^\omega$ sequents $\Sigma :: \Psi; P_a \vdash P_a \mid Q; \cdot$ and $\Sigma :: \Psi; P_b \vdash P_b \mid Q; \cdot$ are provable but that $\Sigma :: \Psi; P_c \vdash P_c \mid Q; \cdot$ is not provable.*

A goal of this kind of encoding of process calculus into linear logic would be to identify the notion that "process P reduces to Q" with the provability of the $\mathcal{L}_2^\omega$ sequent $\Sigma :: \Psi; \langle\!\langle Q \rangle\!\rangle \vdash \langle\!\langle P \rangle\!\rangle; \cdot$. Although this encoding into linear logic captures some of the nature of computation and communication in the π-calculus, we list two of its flaws.

1. One flaw is the fact that only some combinators of the π-calculus are translated into linear logic connectives, while others are encoded using non-logical constants. For example, it is tempting to encode the π-calculus's

+ using the linear logic $\oplus$. Although the right-introduction rules for $\oplus$ in linear logic does encode the nondeterministic (local) choice of the π-calculus, the left-introduction rule for $\oplus$ would force us to accept the following reduction strategy: If P reduces to Q_1 and to Q_2, then P reduces to $Q_1 + Q_2$, which is a principle that is not generally seen as a proper reduction in the π-calculus literature. It is for this reason that the encoding of + is made with a non-logical symbol: Backchaining on its axiomatization mimics the right-hand introduction rule for $\oplus$ but does not make the left-hand introduction possible.
2. The left rule for $\forall$ is also problematic since $\forall x.\forall y.Pxy \vdash \forall x.Pxx$ is provable in every quantificational logic in this book. In the setting of the π-calculus, this would mean that we would need to accept the reduction of $(x)\bar{x}a.\bar{x}b.\mathbf{0}$ to the process $(x)(y)\bar{x}a.\bar{y}b.\mathbf{0}$, which is again not an accepted reduction in the π-calculus.

Chapter 13 contains a different specification of the π-calculus in which process expressions are not encoded as formulas but as terms. With that encoding, a more precise encoding of the π-calculus can be achieved.

In the rest of this chapter, we shall consider a calculus for communication that is, in some senses, weaker than that of the π-calculus. In this weaker setting, provability in linear logic is much more accurate and flexible.

12.2 Specifying Communication Protocols

Assume that Alice and Bob want to use a trusted server to help them establish their own private channel for communications. At the start of this protocol, Alice and Bob have private encryption keys allowing them to communicate securely with a server. At the end of this protocol's execution, Alice and Bob should be sharing an encryption key that allows them to exchange messages securely between themselves, without any additional need for the trusted server.

Figure 12.2 is a presentation of the *Needham–Schroeder Shared Key Protocol* (abbreviated NS) using a standard kind of description. Here, A, B, and S denote the agents Alice, Bob, and server, respectively. The notation $A \longrightarrow S : M$ implies that Alice (A) sends the message M to another agent, say a server (S). Encryption keys and nonces are denoted by the schematic variables k and n, respectively. Messages are tuples of data items that include

Message 1 $A \longrightarrow S: A, B, n_A$
Message 2 $S \longrightarrow A: \{n_A, B, k_{AB}, \{k_{AB}, A\}_{k_{BS}}\}_{k_{AS}}$
Message 3 $A \longrightarrow B: \{k_{AB}, A\}_{k_{BS}}$
Message 4 $B \longrightarrow A: \{n_B\}_{k_{AB}}$
Message 5 $A \longrightarrow B: \{n_B, \text{Secret}\}_{k_{AB}}$

Figure 12.2 The Needham-Schroeder Shared Key Protocol.

structures of the form $\{t_1, \ldots, t_n\}_k$, denoting the result of encrypting the tuple $t_1, \ldots, t_n$ using the key k.

One of our goals is to replace this specific syntax with one based on a direct use of logic. We do this now by identifying a sequence of aspects of this conventional presentation that can be captured in linear logic.

12.2.1 Communicating on a Public Network

The notation $A \longrightarrow B : M$ is misleading since it seems to indicate a "three-way synchronization" between Alice, Bob, and a message M. However, it is important to understand that the intended communication is, in fact, asynchronous, in the sense that Alice is meant to put the message M into a public network (say, the internet) and that at some time later, Bob is meant to retrieve that message from that network. It should be possible to interleave these two actions with some actions of an intruder who might read, delete, and/or modify the message M. Thus, a better syntax is inspired by multiset rewriting (we use $\text{N} \cdot$ to denote network messages). We use | as the multiset constructor.

$$A \longrightarrow A' \mid \text{N} M$$
$$B \mid \text{N} M \longrightarrow B'$$
$$\vdots$$
$$E \mid \text{N} M \longrightarrow E' \mid \text{N} M$$

Here, the first line indicates that Alice in state A puts a message on the network and transitions to state A'. The second line indicates that Bob in state B makes a transition only if there is a message in the network: When there is such a message, that message is consumed, and Bob moves to state B'. The last line encodes an eavesdropper E who waits for a message and after consuming it, readmits it while moving to state E'. This last state might store information contained in that message in the agent's internal memory. More generally, we can imagine that the action of an agent could be described as

12.2 Specifying Communication Protocols

$$A \mid \text{N } M_1 \mid \cdots \mid \text{N } M_p \longrightarrow A' \mid \text{N } P_1 \mid \cdots \mid \text{N } P_q$$

where $p, q \geq 0$. This line specifies that Alice in state A can consume messages $M_1, \ldots, M_p$ and then transition to state A' while posting messages $P_1, \ldots, P_q$.

12.2.2 Static Distribution of Keys

Consider a protocol containing the following steps.

$$\vdots$$
$$\text{Message } i \quad A \longrightarrow S{:}\{M\}_k$$
$$\text{Message } j \quad S \longrightarrow A{:}\{P\}_k.$$
$$\vdots$$

In the general setting, we need to declare exactly which agents have access to which keys: In the steps above, we know two places where the k is used, but we must separately declare, for example, that the key is not known to any other agents. This declaration is critical for modularity and for establishing correctness later: It can also be made statically by using a **local** declaration, such as the following

$$\text{local } k. \left\{ \begin{array}{c} \vdots \\ A \longrightarrow A' \mid \text{N}\{M\}_k \\ S \mid \text{N}\{P\}_k \longrightarrow S' \\ \vdots \end{array} \right\}.$$

This declaration appears to be similar to a quantifier. The intention is that we can statically examine all occurrences of the bound variable k in the scope of this quantifier and thereby know which agents do and do not contain occurrences of this key. If there are lines of the protocol that are outside the scope of this bound variable, then that key is not statically available to the agents and messages listed in that part of the protocol.

12.2.3 Dynamic Creation of New Symbols

During the execution of a protocol, new symbols representing nonces (used to help guarantee "freshness") and keys for encryption are needed in protocols. Using the syntax in Figure 12.2, one needs to explicitly point out that, for example, n_A, n_b, and k_{AB} need to be freshly generated symbols during the execution of this protocol. The following more explicit syntax seems better for this purpose.

$$a_1\ S \longrightarrow new\ k.\ (a_2\ k\ S) \mid N\{M\}_k.$$

This *new* operator resembles, of course, a quantifier: It should support α-conversion and seems to be a bit like reasoning generically. The scope of *new* is over the body of this rule. Here, we have also replaced the simple token denoting Alice with a structured object that encodes different stages of an agent and her memory at different points of the protocol.

12.2.4 Mapping the New Notation into Linear Logic

There are two approaches to view the new notation we have introduced as logical connectives.

	|	unit	$\longrightarrow$	*new*	*local*
disjunctive	$⅋$	$\bot$	$\multimap$	$\forall$	$\exists$
conjunctive	$\otimes$	1	$\multimap$	$\exists$	$\forall$

The disjunctive approach allows protocols to be seen as specifications within $\mathcal{L}_2^\omega$. The conjunctive approach is also popular and has been used in, say, the MSR system of Cervesato et al. [1999]. From the linear logic perspective, these two approaches yield essentially the same dynamics when doing proof search: The only difference is that what happens in the right-hand side of sequents using the disjunctive approach happens essentially unchanged on the left-hand side using the conjunctive approach.

For the rest of this chapter, we assume that the primitive types are $\mathcal{S} = \{o, d\}$. We use the type d to encode the data within messages. For convenience, we shall assume that all strings are included in this type. The tupling operator $\langle \cdot, \cdot \rangle$, for pairing data together, has type $d \to d \to d$. Expressions such as $\langle \cdot, \cdot, \ldots, \cdot \rangle$ denote pairing associated to the right.

Finally, the communications network is represented as a multiset of atomic formulas all with the predicate N of type $d \to o$. For example, the following are examples of network messages.

```
N⟨"alice","account34"⟩    N⟨"bob","45euros"⟩.
```

Such network messages could be used to facilitate a financial transaction. Since we model the public network as an evolving multiset of atomic formulas representing network messages and agents, all agents – not just Alice and Bob – can access and read all messages. It is likely that we do not intend these financial transactions to be viewable and mutable by just anyone with access to the network.

12.2.5 Encrypted Data as an Abstract Data Type

A final step of encoding communicating protocols involves encryption keys and encrypted data. We shall assume that an encryption key is a symbolic function, say, k of type $d \to d$, and that the encrypted message $\{M\}_k$ is encoded as the simple application $(k\ M)$. If an agent has access to the data constructor, which is an encryption key, then via a simple matching operation within logic, decryption can take place. If, however, the encryption key is not available to the agent, then decryption is impossible. Thus, we are representing encrypted data as an *abstract data type*: That is, as a type in which the constructors are given a limited scope using appropriate quantification. In order for encryption keys to be inserted into data objects, we introduce the postfix constructor $(\cdot)^\circ$ of type $(d \to d) \to d$ that can coerce such keys into terms of type d. The use of higher-order types means that we will also use the equations of λ-conversion when processing encrypted data.

Consider the following specification, which contains two encryption keys.

$$\exists k_{as}.\exists k_{bs}.[\quad a_1\ \langle M, S \rangle \quad \circ\!\!- a_2\ S\ ⅋\ \text{N}\,(k_{as}\ M).$$
$$b_1\ T\ ⅋\ \text{N}\,(k_{bs}\ M) \circ\!\!- b_2\ M\ T.$$
$$s_1\ ⅋\ \text{N}\,(k_{as}\ P) \quad \circ\!\!- \text{N}\,(k_{bs}\ P).\qquad]$$

(Here as elsewhere, quantification of capital letter variables is universal with scope limited to the clause in which the variable appears.) In this example, Alice (a_1, a_2) communicates with Bob (b_1, b_2) via a server (s_1). To make the communications secure, Alice uses the key k_{as} to communicate with the server while Bob uses the key k_{bs}. The server is deleted immediately after it translates one message encrypted for Alice to a message encrypted for Bob. The existential quantifiers establish that the occurrences of keys, say, between Alice and the server and Bob and the server, are the only occurrences of those keys. Even if more principals are added to this system, these occurrences are still the only ones for these keys. Thus, the existential quantifier helps determine the static or lexical scope of key distribution. Of course, as protocols evolve, keys may extrude their scope and move freely onto the network. This dynamic notion of scope extrusion is similar to that in the π-calculus.

12.3 Protocols as Theories in Linear Logic

In order to encode communication protocols as theories in linear logic, we make the following few definitions. An *agent identifier* is a symbol, say, ρ. For some number $n \geq 1$ and for $i = 1, \ldots, n$, the pair ρ_i of an agent identifier and an index is an *agent state predicate* all of whose arguments (if any) are of type d. These state predicates encode an agent's internal states as a protocol progresses. An *agent state atom* is an atomic formula of the form $\rho_i\, t_1\, \ldots\, t_m$ where $m \geq 0$, $t_1, \ldots, t_m$ are terms of type d, and ρ_i is an agent state predicate. An *agent clause* is a linear logic formula of the form

$$\forall x_1.\cdots\forall x_i.[a_1 \mathbin{\mathglyph{⅋}} \cdots \mathbin{\mathglyph{⅋}} a_m \multimapinv \forall y_1.\cdots\forall y_j.[b_1 \mathbin{\mathglyph{⅋}} \cdots \mathbin{\mathglyph{⅋}} b_n]]$$

where $m \geq 1$ and $i, j, n \geq 0$. Here, the *head* of such a clause is the formula $a_1 \mathbin{\mathglyph{⅋}} \cdots \mathbin{\mathglyph{⅋}} a_m$ and the *body* is $\forall y_1.\cdots\forall y_j.[b_1 \mathbin{\mathglyph{⅋}} \cdots \mathbin{\mathglyph{⅋}} b_n]$. Agent clauses also have the following restrictions: All the atoms $a_1, \ldots, a_m, b_1, \ldots, b_n$ are either network messages (atomic formulas with predicate N) or agent state atoms such that the following hold.

1. There must be exactly one agent state atom in the head and at most one in the body.
2. If the agent state atom in the head is $(\rho_i\, \bar{t})$ and if there is any agent state atom in the body, say, $(\rho'_j\, \bar{s})$, then ρ and ρ' must be the same agent identifier and $i < j$.

Thus, an agent clause involves, at most, a single agent (and possibly network messages): This implies that agents cannot synchronize with other agents directly, and that one agent cannot evolve into another agent. It is allowed for an agent to be deleted since no agent state atom must appear in the body. It is also the case that all agents have finite runs.

An *agent theory* is a linear logic formula of the form

$$\exists x_1.\cdots\exists x_r.\,[C_1 \otimes \cdots \otimes C_s],$$

where $r, s \geq 0$, $C_1, \ldots, C_s$ are agent clauses, $x_1, \ldots, x_r$ are variables of type d or $d \to d$, and whenever C_i and C_j have the same agent state predicate in their head then $i = j$. This last condition implies that agents in protocols are deterministic. This condition can easily be relaxed within linear logic if nondeterministic agents are of interest.

Many other restrictions or generalizations could be considered here for the definition of agent theory and agent clauses, but for our simple considerations

12.3 Protocols as Theories in Linear Logic

$\exists k_{as}.\exists k_{bs}.\{$

$\qquad\qquad\qquad\qquad a_1\ S \circ\!\!-\ \forall n_a.\ a_2\ n_a\ S\ \mathfrak{P}\ \mathrm{N}\,\langle\mathrm{alice},\mathrm{bob},n_a\rangle.$

$a_2\ N\ S\ \mathfrak{P}\ \mathrm{N}\,(k_{as}\langle N,\mathrm{bob},K,E\rangle) \circ\!\!-\qquad a_3\ K\ S\ \mathfrak{P}\ \mathrm{N}\,E.$

$\qquad a_3\ \mathrm{Key}^\circ\ S\ \mathfrak{P}\ \mathrm{N}\,(\mathrm{Key}\ N_b) \circ\!\!-\qquad a_4\ \mathfrak{P}\ \mathrm{N}\,(\mathrm{Key}\langle N_b,S\rangle).$

$\qquad b_1\ \mathfrak{P}\ \mathrm{N}\,(k_{bs}\langle\mathrm{Key}^\circ,\mathrm{alice}\rangle) \circ\!\!-\ \forall n_b.\ b_2\ n_b\ \mathrm{Key}^\circ\ \mathfrak{P}\ \mathrm{N}\,(\mathrm{Key}\ n_b).$

$\qquad b_2\ N_b\ \mathrm{Key}^\circ\ \mathfrak{P}\ \mathrm{N}\,(\mathrm{Key}\langle N_b,S\rangle) \circ\!\!-\qquad b_3\ S.$

$\qquad\qquad s_1\ \mathfrak{P}\ \mathrm{N}\,\langle\mathrm{alice},\mathrm{bob},N\rangle \circ\!\!-\ \forall k.\mathrm{N}\,(k_{as}\langle N,\mathrm{bob},k^\circ,(k_{bs}\langle k^\circ,\mathrm{alice}\rangle)\rangle).$

$\}$

Figure 12.3 Encoding the NS protocol.

here, this definition is sufficient. Ultimately, we will introduce a different syntax for agents that will not need to use these rather awkward agent state predicates.

Figure 12.3 contains a linear logic implementation of the NS protocol contained in Figure 12.2. Let $C_1,\ldots,C_6$ be the six agent clauses in Figure 12.3 (remembering that there are implicit universal quantifiers around agent clauses). It is easy to show that this protocol implements the specification

$$\forall x.[a_1\ x\ \mathfrak{P}\ b_1\ \mathfrak{P}\ s_1 \circ\!\!-\ a_4\ \mathfrak{P}\ b_3\ x],$$

in the sense that there is a simple $\Downarrow \mathcal{L}_2^\omega$-proof of the sequent

$$\Sigma, k_{as}, k_{bs} :: C_1,\ldots,C_6;\ \cdot\ \vdash\ \forall x.[a_4\ \mathfrak{P}\ b_3\ x \multimap a_1\ x\ \mathfrak{P}\ b_1\ \mathfrak{P}\ s_1];\ \cdot.$$

That is, this protocol can transform the initial states of Alice (with some secret), Bob, and the server to the final states of Alice and Bob (now with the secret).

For another example, consider the following two clauses for Alice.

$$a\ K^\circ\ \mathfrak{P}\ \mathrm{N}\,(K\ M) \circ\!\!-\ a'\ M. \qquad (3.1)$$
$$a\ \mathfrak{P}\ \mathrm{N}\,(K\ M) \circ\!\!-\ a'\ M. \qquad (3.2)$$

In the first case, Alice possesses an encryption key and uses it to decrypt a network message. In the second case, it appears that she is decrypting a message without knowing the key, an inappropriate behavior, of course. Note that (3.2) is logically equivalent (and, hence, operationally indistinguishable using proof search) to both of the formulas

$$\forall M.\forall X.[a\ \mathfrak{P}\ \mathrm{N}\,X \circ\!\!-\ a'\ M] \quad \text{and} \quad \forall X.[a\ \mathfrak{P}\ \mathrm{N}\,X \circ\!\!-\ \exists M.a'\ M].$$

This last clause clearly illustrates that Alice is not actually decoding an existing message but simply guessing (using $\exists$) at some data value M, and continues with that guess as $a'\ M$. If we think operationally instead of declaratively about proof search involving clause (3.2), we would consider possible unifiers for matching the pattern $(K\ M)$ with a network message, say, $(k\ \text{secret})$, for two constants k and secret. Unification on simply typed λ-terms yields exactly the following three distinct unifiers:

$$[M \mapsto (k\ \text{secret}), K \mapsto \lambda w.w] \quad [M \mapsto s, K \mapsto k] \quad [M \mapsto M, K \mapsto \lambda w.k\ \text{secret}].$$

Thus, M can be bound to either $(k\ \text{secret})$ or s or any term: In other words, M can be bound to any expression of type d.

Logical entailment can help in reasoning about agent clauses and theories. As the following exercise illustrates, such entailments are strengthened by the presence of quantification at type $d \to d$.

Exercise 12.3. (‡) *The following clauses specify that Alice takes a step that generates a new encryption key and then outputs a message (either m or m') using that encryption key.*

$$a_1 \circ\!\!-\ \forall k.\, N(k\ m) \qquad a_1 \circ\!\!-\ \forall k.\, N(k\ m').$$

In both cases, Alice has no continuation, and, therefore, she and access to the key disappear. These two clauses are operationally similar since they both generate an unreadable message. Show, in fact, that these two formulas are logically equivalent.

12.4 Abstracting Internal States

The internal states of agents are denoted by predicates that have limited roles: They can only be used internally by an agent. It is possible to use existential quantification over *predicates* (in particular, agent state predicates) to provide an interesting rewriting of the structure of agent theories. To illustrate this, we step back from considering only agent theories for a moment.

General n-way synchronization ($n \geq 3$) is allowed within the setting of multiset rewriting. Such synchronization can be rewritten using only 2-way synchronization by introducing new, intermediate, and hidden predicates. For example, the following two formulas are logically equivalent.

$$\exists l_1. \exists l_2. \left\{ \begin{array}{l} a \,\mathscr{B}\, b \circ\!\!-\ l_1 \\ l_1 \,\mathscr{B}\, c \circ\!\!-\ l_2 \,\mathscr{B}\, e \\ l_2 \circ\!\!-\ d \,\mathscr{B}\, f \end{array} \right\} \quad \dashv\vdash \quad a \,\mathscr{B}\, b \,\mathscr{B}\, c \circ\!\!-\ d \,\mathscr{B}\, e \,\mathscr{B}\, f.$$

The clause on the right specifies a 3-way synchronization and the spawning of 3 atomic formulas, whereas the formula on the left is limited to rewriting at most two atoms into at most 2 atoms. The proof of the forward entailment in linear logic is straightforward, while the proof of the reverse entailment involves the two higher-order substitutions of $a \mathbin{\bindnasrepma} b$ for $\exists l_1$ and $d \mathbin{\bindnasrepma} f$ for $\exists l_2$. As long as we use logical entailment, these two formulas are indistinguishable and can be used interchangeably in all contexts. If instead, we could observe possible failures in the search for proofs, then it is possible to distinguish these formulas: Consider the search for a proof of a sequent containing a and b but not c. The proof theory of linear logic we have presented here does not observe such failures since that proof theory is generally involved with reasoning about *complete* proofs.

Existential quantification over program clauses can also hide predicates encoding agents. In fact, one might argue that the various restrictions on sets of process clauses (no synchronization directly with atoms encoding agents and no agent changing into another agent) might all be considered a way to enforce locality (i.e., hiding) of predicates. Existential quantification can, however, achieve this same notion of locality but much more directly. For example, the following two formulas are logically equivalent.

$$\exists a_2. \exists a_3. \left\{ \begin{array}{l} a_1 \mathbin{\bindnasrepma} \mathrm{N}\, m_0 \circ\!\!-\, a_2 \mathbin{\bindnasrepma} \mathrm{N}\, m_1 \\ a_2 \mathbin{\bindnasrepma} \mathrm{N}\, m_2 \circ\!\!-\, a_3 \mathbin{\bindnasrepma} \mathrm{N}\, m_3 \\ a_3 \mathbin{\bindnasrepma} \mathrm{N}\, m_4 \circ\!\!-\, a_4 \mathbin{\bindnasrepma} \mathrm{N}\, m_5 \end{array} \right\} \dashv\vdash$$

$$a_1 \mathbin{\bindnasrepma} \mathrm{N}\, m_0 \circ\!\!-\, (\mathrm{N}\, m_1 \circ\!\!-\, (\mathrm{N}\, m_2 \circ\!\!-\, (\mathrm{N}\, m_3 \circ\!\!-\, (\mathrm{N}\, m_4 \circ\!\!-\, (\mathrm{N}\, m_5 \mathbin{\bindnasrepma} a_4)))))$$.

The changing of polarity that occurs when moving to the right of a $\circ\!\!-$ flips expressions from output (e.g., $\mathrm{N}\, m_1$) to input (e.g., $\mathrm{N}\, m_2$), and back again. We develop this observation further in Section 12.5.

12.5 Agents as Nested Implications

The observation that abstracting over internal states results in an equivalent syntax with nested $\circ\!\!-$ suggests an alternative syntax for agents. Consider the following two syntactic categories of linear logic formulas.

$$H ::= A \mid \bot \mid H \mathbin{\bindnasrepma} H \qquad K ::= H \mid H \circ\!\!-\, K \mid \forall x .. K.$$

Here, A denotes the class of atomic formulas encoding network messages (in particular, formulas of the form $\mathrm{N}\, \cdot$). Formulas belonging to the class H denote bundles of messages used as either input or output to the network. Formulas belonging to the class K can have deep nesting of implications. As we shall see, the nesting of $\circ\!\!-$ can model the alternation between a process that outputs a message to one that is willing to input a message. We call K formulas *agent formulas*, and they can replace agent clauses. Note that the only predicate in an agent formula is N.

To see this mechanism in the proof search setting, consider building proofs of the $\Downarrow \mathcal{L}_2^\omega$ sequent $\Sigma :: \cdot; \Gamma \vdash \Delta, \mathcal{A}; \cdot$, where both Δ and Γ are multisets of K formulas and $\mathcal{A}$ is a multiset of atomic formulas (hence, formulas with the predicate N). The right-introduction phase captures the process of performing all the possible output actions by all processes in Δ while the left-introduction phase captures the input action of any agent formula chosen to be the focus. For example, let P be the formula

$$\forall_d x. \forall_d y. (\text{N}(fx) \,\mathbin{\text{\textreferencemark}}\, \text{N}(gxy) \circ\!\!- \hat{P}xy).$$

Here, we assume that f is a constructor of type $d \to d$, g is a constructor of type $d \to d \to d$, and $\hat{P}xy$ is K-formula possibly containing x and y free. If P is on the right of a sequent, the right-introduction phase for this sequent yields the derivable inference rule

$$\frac{\Sigma, x, y :: \cdot; \Gamma, \hat{P}xy \vdash \Delta, \mathcal{A}, \text{N}(fx), \text{N}(gxy); \cdot}{\Sigma :: \cdot; \Gamma \vdash \Delta, \mathcal{A}, P; \cdot}.$$

This rule can be read as the process P creates two new tokens x and y, outputs to the network the atomic formulas $\text{N}(fx)$ and $\text{N}(gxy)$, and then moves into input mode since $\hat{P}xy$, the body of the P formula, moves to the left. If this same expression appears on the left, then the left phase yields the following derivable inference rule

$$\frac{\Sigma :: \cdot; \Gamma \vdash \Delta, \mathcal{A}, \hat{P}\,t\,s; \cdot}{\Sigma :: \cdot; \Gamma, P \vdash \Delta, \mathcal{A}, \text{N}(f\,t), \text{N}(g\,t\,s); \cdot}.$$

Here, t and s are two Σ-terms of type d.

Negation flips the status of a process from input to output and vice versa. For example, if the process formula $\bot \circ\!\!- P$ is on the right of a sequent, it outputs $\bot$, which makes no effect on the network messages, and P moves to the left into input mode. The dual statement holds if we start with $\bot \circ\!\!- P$ on the left of the sequent. Various equivalences found in linear logic also make sense from the point-of-view of asynchronous communication. For example,

12.5 Agents as Nested Implications

(Out) $\forall n_a.\, \mathrm{N}\langle \mathsf{alice}, \mathsf{bob}, n_a\rangle \circ\!\!-$
(In) $(\forall \mathsf{Key}.\forall E.\, \mathrm{N}\,(k_{as}\langle n_a, \mathsf{bob}, \mathsf{Key}^\circ, E\rangle)) \circ\!\!-$
(Out) $(\mathrm{N}\, E \circ\!\!-$
(In) $(\forall N.\, \mathrm{N}\,(\mathsf{Key}\, N) \circ\!\!-$
(Out) $(\mathrm{N}\,(\mathsf{Key}\langle N, \mathsf{secret}\rangle)) \circ\!\!-$
(Cont) $a_4)))$.

The agent for Alice

(Out) $\bot \circ\!\!-$
(In) $(\forall \mathsf{Key}.\, \mathrm{N}\,(k_{bs}\langle \mathsf{Key}^\circ, \mathsf{alice}\rangle)) \circ\!\!-$
(Out) $(\forall n_b.\, \mathrm{N}\,(\mathsf{Key}\, n_b) \circ\!\!-$
(In) $(\forall S.\, \mathrm{N}\,(\mathsf{Key}\langle n_b, S\rangle) \circ\!\!-$
(Cont) $b_3\, S)))$.

The agent for Bob

(Out) $\bot \circ\!\!-$
(In) $(\forall N.\, \mathrm{N}\langle \mathsf{alice}, \mathsf{bob}, N\rangle \circ\!\!-$
(Out) $(\forall k.\, \mathrm{N}\,(k_{as}\langle N, \mathsf{bob}, k^\circ, k_{bs}\langle k^\circ, \mathsf{alice}\rangle\rangle))))$.

The agent for the server

Figure 12.4   The agents of Alice, Bob, and a server.

if one skips a phase (by outputting or inputting an empty multiset), the two adjacent phases can be contracted as follows:

$$p \circ\!\!- (\bot \circ\!\!- (q \circ\!\!- k)) \dashv\vdash p \,⅋\, q \circ\!\!- k$$
$$p \circ\!\!- (\bot \circ\!\!- \forall x.(q\, x \circ\!\!- k\, x)) \dashv\vdash \forall x.(p \,⅋\, q\, x \circ\!\!- k\, x).$$

Figure 12.4 displays three agent formulas. The first represents Alice, the second Bob, and the final one, the server. (All agents in this figure are written in output mode: Since Bob and the server essentially start with inputs, these two agents are negated, meaning they first output nothing and then move to input mode.) These formulas are a second way to encode the NS protocol within linear logic. If the three formulas in Figure 12.4 are placed on the right-hand side of a sequent turnstile (with no formulas on the left) then the agent formula for Alice will output a message and move to the left side of the sequent turnstile (reading inference rules bottom-up). Bob and the server output nothing and move to the left-hand side. At that point, the server will need to be chosen for the focus of the left-introduction phase, causing it to input the message Alice sent and then move its continuation to the right-hand side. It will then immediately output another message, and so on.

Variations on this simple scheme can easily be explored. For example, one might want an agent, such as the server, to be persistent. In that case, the first line of Figure 12.4 for the server could be simply changed by replacing $\circ\!\!-$ with $\Leftarrow$. In a setting where one wishes to model attacks on protocols, it seems more appropriate for network messages to occur in the right-unbounded zone since adversaries can be assumed to be capable of reading and replacing every network message that appears. Thus, even if a network message were to disappear from the right-bounded zone, the adversary can be assumed to have remembered its content. In this case, the ? exponential could be used on all output messages.

The style of specification given in Figure 12.4 is similar to that of process calculus: In particular, the implication $\circ\!\!-$ is syntactically similar to the dot prefix in, say, CCS. Universal quantification can appear in two modes: In output mode, it is used to generate new eigenvariables (similar to the π-calculus restriction operator) and in input mode, it is used for variable binding (similar to value-passing CCS). If we use $\|$ to denote the parallel composition of processes and use a dot to prefix a process with an input action, then the formula scheme $a \circ\!\!- (b \circ\!\!- (c \circ\!\!- (d \circ\!\!- \cdots)))$ can denote processes described as

$$\bar{a} \| (b. (\bar{c} \| (d. \cdots))) \quad \text{or} \quad a. (\bar{b} \| (c. (\bar{d} \| \cdots)))$$

depending on which side of the sequent it occurs. This formula and its negation can also be written without linear implications as

$$a \mathbin{\char"7E} (b^\perp \otimes (c \mathbin{\char"7E} (d^\perp \otimes \ldots))) \text{ resp, } a^\perp \otimes (b \mathbin{\char"7E} (c^\perp \otimes (d \mathbin{\char"7E} \ldots))).$$

12.6 Bibliographic Notes

The encoding of parts of the π-calculus in Section 12.1 are taken from Miller [1993]. Examples such as the Needham–Schroeder Shared Key Protocol in Section 12.2 can be found in the work on MSR by Cervesato et al. [1999, 2000a] and Cervesato and Stehr [2007]. See also Durgin et al. [2004] for more about analyzing security protocols using an encoding of multisets in linear logic.

Material on using existential quantifiers at predicate types to hide the internal states of processes is taken from Miller [2003]. Andreoli [1992] used a compilation method to reduce an arbitrary linear logic formula to a collection of *bipolar* formulas. Applying his compiling technique to the formula in Figure 12.4 yields the formulas in Figure 12.3.

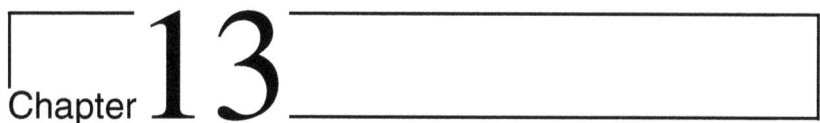

Chapter 13

Formalizing Operational Semantics

This chapter provides an overview of a few ways that logic programming can specify the operational semantics of various programming and specification languages. Establishing these links between logic and operational semantics has many advantages for operational semantics: Logic programming interpreters can animate semantic specifications; the proof-theoretic treatment of term-level binding structures can address binding structures in the syntax of programs; and the declarative nature of logical specifications provides broad avenues for reasoning about semantic specifications. We shall illustrate all of these advantages in this chapter.

This chapter will use the term "logic specification" interchangeably with "logic program" and "theory." Additionally, when we speak of "programming languages" we include specification languages such as the λ-calculus and the π-calculus.

13.1 Three Frameworks for Operational Semantics

Numerous formalisms have been employed to define the computational behavior of programming languages. When building upon these formalisms to develop various *concepts* (e.g., observational equivalence, static analysis) and *tools* (e.g., interpreters, model checkers, theorem provers), the quality of these encodings significantly impacts the success of the endeavor. This chapter uses logic to directly encode operational semantics, eschewing alternative

261

formalisms such as complete partial orders, algebras, games, and Petri nets. Proof search within this logical framework will endow logical specifications with the dynamics necessary to capture a range of operational specifications. We concentrate on three prominent frameworks for specifying operational semantics and outline the logic frameworks most naturally aligned with each.

Multiset rewriting Specifying computations by computing directly on multisets was proposed in the 1990s with the Gamma programming language of Banâtre and Métayer [1993] and the chemical abstract machine of Berry and Boudol [1992], as well as later with the specification of security protocols in Bistarelli et al. [2005], Cervesato et al. [1999], and Durgin et al. [2004]. As we have seen in Section 8.1 and Chapter 10, it is a simple matter to capture multiset rewriting using proof search in linear logic.

Structural operational semantics First introduced by Milner [1980] and Plotkin [1981, 2004], *structural operational semantics* (SOS) has been widely used to characterize a diverse range of programming language features, including concurrency, functional computation, and stateful computations. This style of specification, commonly referred to as *small-step SOS*, facilitates a natural treatment of concurrency through interleaving. *Big-step SOS*, introduced by Kahn [1987], proves particularly convenient for specifying nonconcurrent specifications, such as functional programming. Both of these operational semantics paradigms define relations using inductive systems formalized by inference rules. As we shall observe, Horn clauses and hereditary Harrop formulas typically provide suitable frameworks for encoding these inference rules.

Abstract machines A specific form of term rewriting can be interpreted as encoding *abstract machines*, where entities such as code, environments, and argument stacks are directly manipulated. The SECD machine of Landin [1964] serves as an early example of such an abstract machine. These abstract machines can frequently be represented using *binary clauses*, a restricted form of Horn clause where the clause body contains only a single atomic formula. Proof search with these clauses naturally characterizes simple, iterative algorithms. Arbitrary Horn clause programs can also be transformed into binary clauses through a continuation-passing-style transformation. Consequently, binary clauses can be viewed as encapsulating a thread of computation comprising a sequence of instructions or commands. Although binary clauses represent a retreat from logic in the sense that they employ fewer logical connectives (such as conjunction) than general Horn clauses, they offer two significant advantages: (1) the ability to explicitly specify the order of computation and (2) a foundation for an extension to linear logic that enables the natural representation of concurrency and imperative features within big-step structural operational semantics.

13.2 The Abstract Syntax of Programs-as-Terms

To encode a programming language, we first translate its syntactic expressions into terms within a suitable logic, such as Church's Simple Theory of Types (see Section 2.3) or higher-order logic ($\mathcal{L}_2^\omega$). Since most programming languages involve binding constructs, we directly represent them using λ-abstraction, a primitive concept in these logics. Language constructors are mapped to corresponding term constructors, with the latter's types reflecting the *syntactic categories* of the constructed objects. Typically, we model term construction with function application. Similarly, language binders are translated to λ-abstractions that bind variables within the encoded scope. We illustrate this encoding approach by using both the untyped λ-calculus and the π-calculus as examples.

The untyped λ-calculus (see Section 2.1) can be encoded as simply typed λ-terms using one syntactic type, say *tm*, and two constructors for application and abstraction. Using λProlog syntax, these tokens can be declared as follows.

```
kind tm      type.
type app     tm -> tm -> tm.
type abs     (tm -> tm) -> tm.
```

Note that *abs* is applied to a term-level abstraction: The argument type *tm* → *tm* acts as the syntactic type of term abstractions over terms. The following is a list of some untyped λ-terms along with their encoding as a simply type λ-term of type *tm*.

$\lambda x.x$ (*abs* $\lambda x\ x$)
$\lambda x \lambda y.x$ (*abs* λx (*abs* $\lambda y\ x$))
$\lambda x.(x\ x)$ (*abs* λx (*app* $x\ x$))
$\lambda x \lambda y \lambda z.(x\ z)(y\ z)$ (*abs* λx (*abs* λy (*abs* λz ((*app* (*app* $x\ z$) (*app* $y\ z$)))))).

It is important to observe that two untyped λ-terms are α-convertible if and only if their encodings as terms of type *tm* are βη-convertible.

As we have already seen in Section 12.1, processes in the finite π-calculus are described by the grammar

$$P ::= 0 \mid \bar{x}y.P \mid x(y).P \mid \tau.P \mid (y)P \mid [x = y]P \mid P|P \mid P + P.$$

(Many treatments of the π-calculus also include a replication operator or recursion: Their absence here is why we are describing the *finite* π-calculus.) We use the symbols P and Q to denote processes and lower case letters, for example, x, y, z to denote names. The occurrences of y in the processes $x(y).P$ and $(y)P$ are binding occurrences with P as their scope. The notions of free and bound variables are the usual ones, and we consider processes to be syntactically equal if they are equal up to α-conversion.

In Section 12.1, we suggested defining the operational semantics of π-calculus expressions by mapping them into linear logic formulas. Here, we encode π-calculus expressions as terms using the declarations of two primitives types, for names and processes, and process constructors in Figure 13.1. The precise translation of the π-calculus syntax into simply typed λ-terms is given using the following function $[\![\cdot]\!]$ that translates process expressions to $\beta\eta$-long normal terms of type p.

$$\begin{array}{rlrl}
[\![0]\!] = & \texttt{null} & [\![P + Q]\!] = & \texttt{plus } [\![P]\!] \, [\![Q]\!] \\
[\![\tau.P]\!] = & \texttt{taup } [\![P]\!] & [\![P|Q]\!] = & \texttt{par } [\![P]\!] \, [\![Q]\!] \\
[\![x(y).P]\!] = & \texttt{in } x \, (\lambda y.[\![P]\!]) & [\![\bar{x}y.P]\!] = & \texttt{out } x \, y \, [\![P]\!] \\
[\![(x)P]\!] = & \texttt{nu } (\lambda x.[\![P]\!]) & [\![[x = y]P]\!] = & \texttt{match } x \, y \, [\![P]\!].
\end{array}$$

For example, the π-calculus expression $\nu y.[x = y]\bar{x}z.0$ is translated into the expression (nu y\ match x y (out x z null)) which contains the free names x and z.

```
kind   n, p            type.

type   null            p.
type   taup            p -> p.
type   plus, par       p -> p -> p.
type   match, out      n -> n -> p -> p.
type   nu              (n -> p) -> p.
type   in              n -> (n -> p) -> p.
```

Figure 13.1 Declarations of the primitive types and constructors for the finite π-calculus.

13.4 SMALL-STEP SEMANTICS: π-CALCULUS TRANSITIONS

$$\overline{\lambda x.R \searrow \lambda x.R} \qquad \frac{M \searrow (\lambda x.R) \quad N \searrow U \quad R[U/x] \searrow V}{(M\ N) \searrow V}$$

```
type eval    tm -> tm -> o.

eval (abs R) (abs R).
eval (app M N) V :-
     eval M (abs R), eval N U, eval (R U) V.
```

Figure 13.2 Big-step specification of the call-by-value evaluation of the untyped λ-calculus via inference rules and λProlog clauses.

13.3 Big-Step Semantics: Call-by-Value Evaluation

Figure 13.2 contains a common, *big-step semantic specification* of *call-by-value evaluation* for the λ-calculus: This specification is given as both inference rules as well as Horn clause specification. The (infix) predicate symbol $\searrow$ is of type $tm \to tm \to o$ and is written simply as eval in these clauses. The encoding of the atomic evaluation judgment $R[U/x] \searrow V$ in Figure 13.2 is simply (eval (R U) V) in the clausal specification: That is, the logic specification forms the expression $(R\ U)$ and once R is instantiated with a λ-abstraction, the logic's built-in treatment of β-reduction performs the necessary substitution.

Such a specification is referred to as *big-step* since the predicate $\searrow$ relates an expression to its final value. In contrast, as we now illustrate, *small-step* specifications encode just a single computation step in a possibly long series of transitions.

13.4 Small-Step Semantics: π-Calculus Transitions

The relation of one-step (late) transition for the π-calculus in Milner et al. [1992b] is denoted by $P \xrightarrow{\alpha} Q$, where P and Q are processes and α is an action. Figure 13.3 contains a standard specification of this transition semantics for the finite π-calculus. Figure 13.4 presents this same semantic as an $\mathcal{L}_0$ logic program. This specification introduces a new primitive sort a to denote actions and uses three constructors for actions: $\tau : a$ (for the silent action) and the two constants $\downarrow$ and $\uparrow$, both of type $n \to n \to a$ (for building input and output

$$\dfrac{}{\tau.P \xrightarrow{\tau} P} \text{ TAU} \qquad \dfrac{}{x(y).P \xrightarrow{x(w)} P[w/y]} \text{ IN}, w \notin fn((y)P)$$

$$\dfrac{}{\bar{x}y.P \xrightarrow{\bar{x}y} P} \text{ OUT} \qquad \dfrac{P \xrightarrow{\alpha} P'}{[x=x]P \xrightarrow{\alpha} P'} \text{ MATCH}$$

$$\dfrac{P \xrightarrow{\alpha} P'}{P + Q \xrightarrow{\alpha} P'} \text{ SUM} \qquad \dfrac{P \xrightarrow{\alpha} P'}{P \mid Q \xrightarrow{\alpha} P' \mid Q} \text{ PAR}, bn(\alpha) \cap fn(Q) = \emptyset$$

$$\dfrac{P \xrightarrow{\alpha} P'}{(y)P \xrightarrow{\alpha} (y)P'} \text{ RES}, y \notin n(\alpha)$$

$$\dfrac{P \xrightarrow{\bar{x}y} P'}{(y)P \xrightarrow{\bar{x}(w)} P'[w/y]} \text{ OPEN}, y \neq x, w \notin fn((y)P')$$

$$\dfrac{P \xrightarrow{\bar{x}(w)} P' \quad Q \xrightarrow{x(w)} Q'}{P \mid Q \xrightarrow{\tau} (w)(P' \mid Q')} \text{ CLOSE} \qquad \dfrac{P \xrightarrow{\bar{x}y} P' \quad Q \xrightarrow{x(z)} Q'}{P \mid Q \xrightarrow{\tau} P' \mid Q'[y/z]} \text{ COMM}$$

The functions $fn(P)$ (free variables of P), $bn(P)$ (bound variables of P), and $n(P)$ (the union of $fn(P)$ and $bn(P)$) are defined in Milner et al. [1992b]. The logic specification in Figure 13.4 does not need such functions and provisos.

Figure 13.3 The late transition rules for the finite π-calculus.

actions, respectively). The free output action $\bar{x}y$, is encoded as $\uparrow xy$ while the bound output action $\bar{x}(y)$ is encoded as $\lambda y\,(\uparrow xy)$ (or the η-equivalent term $\uparrow x$). The free input action xy is encoded as $\downarrow xy$ while the bound input action $x(y)$ is encoded as $\lambda y\,(\downarrow xy)$ (or simply $\downarrow x$). Note that bound input and bound output actions have type $n \to a$ instead of a.

Our encoding splits the labeled transition relation in Figure 13.3 into two relations depending on whether or not the transition involves a free or bound action. The relation between the two processes, P and Q, and an action A is encoded using the arrow $P \xrightarrow{A} Q$: This arrow is encoded using a predicate of type $p \to a \to p \to o$. The relation between a process P, a bound action A, and an abstracted process Q is encoded using the harpoon $P \xrightharpoonup{A} Q$: This arrow is encoded using a predicate of type $p \to (n \to a) \to (n \to p) \to o$.

13.4 SMALL-STEP SEMANTICS: π-CALCULUS TRANSITIONS

$$
\begin{array}{ll}
\text{TAU:} & \top \supset \tau P \xrightarrow{\tau} P \\
\text{IN:} & \top \supset \text{in } X\, M \xrightarrow{\downarrow X} M \\
\text{OUT:} & \top \supset \text{out } x\, y\, P \xrightarrow{\uparrow xy} P \\
\text{MATCH:} & P \xrightarrow{A} Q \supset \text{match } x\, x\, P \xrightarrow{A} Q \\
 & P \xrightarrow{A} Q \supset \text{match } x\, x\, P \xrightarrow{A} Q \\
\text{SUM:} & P \xrightarrow{A} R \vee Q \xrightarrow{A} R \supset P + Q \xrightarrow{A} R \\
 & P \xrightarrow{A} R \vee Q \xrightarrow{A} R \supset P + Q \xrightarrow{A} R \\
\text{PAR:} & P \xrightarrow{A} P' \supset P \mid Q \xrightarrow{A} P' \mid Q \\
 & Q \xrightarrow{A} Q' \supset P \mid Q \xrightarrow{A} P \mid Q' \\
 & P \xrightarrow{A} M \supset P \mid Q \xrightarrow{A} \lambda n (M\, n \mid Q) \\
 & Q \xrightarrow{A} N \supset P \mid Q \xrightarrow{A} \lambda n (P \mid N\, n) \\
\text{RES:} & \forall n.(P n \xrightarrow{A} Q n) \supset \nu n.P n \xrightarrow{A} \nu n.Q n \\
 & \forall n.(P n \xrightarrow{A} P' n) \supset \nu n.P n \xrightarrow{A} \lambda m\, \nu n.P' n m \\
\text{OPEN:} & \forall y.(M y \xrightarrow{\uparrow X y} M' y) \supset \nu y.M y \xrightarrow{\uparrow X} M' \\
\text{CLOSE:} & P \xrightarrow{\downarrow X} M \wedge Q \xrightarrow{\uparrow X} N \supset P \mid Q \xrightarrow{\tau} \nu y.(M y \mid N y) \\
 & P \xrightarrow{\uparrow X} M \wedge Q \xrightarrow{\downarrow X} N \supset P \mid Q \xrightarrow{\tau} \nu y.(M y \mid N y) \\
\text{COM:} & P \xrightarrow{\downarrow X} M \wedge Q \xrightarrow{\uparrow X Y} Q' \supset P \mid Q \xrightarrow{\tau} M Y \mid Q' \\
 & P \xrightarrow{\uparrow X Y} P' \wedge Q \xrightarrow{\downarrow X} N \supset P \mid Q \xrightarrow{\tau} P' \mid N Y \\
\end{array}
$$

Figure 13.4 The inference rules in Figure 13.3 as logical formulas.

One-step transition judgments are translated to atomic formulas as follows (we extend the use of the symbol $[\![.]\!]$ from Section 13.2).

$$
\begin{array}{lll}
[\![P \xrightarrow{xy} Q]\!] = [\![P]\!] \xrightarrow{\downarrow xy} [\![Q]\!] & \quad [\![P \xrightarrow{x(y)} Q]\!] = [\![P]\!] \xrightarrow{\downarrow x} \lambda y.[\![Q]\!] \\
[\![P \xrightarrow{\bar{x}y} Q]\!] = [\![P]\!] \xrightarrow{\uparrow xy} [\![Q]\!] & \quad [\![P \xrightarrow{\bar{x}(y)} Q]\!] = [\![P]\!] \xrightarrow{\uparrow x} \lambda y.[\![Q]\!] \\
[\![P \xrightarrow{\tau} Q]\!] = [\![P]\!] \xrightarrow{\tau} [\![Q]\!]. &
\end{array}
$$

Figure 13.4 contains a set of clauses, called $\mathbf{D}_\pi$, that encodes the operational semantics of the late transition system for the finite π-calculus. As is customary when we display clauses, free variables are assumed to be universally quantified over the clause in which they appear. These variables have primitive types, such as a, n, and p as well as arrow types such as $n \to a$ and $n \to p$. As a consequence of using the notion of binders to encode π-calculus-level binders, the side conditions in the original specifications of the π-calculus Figure 13.3 are no longer present in $\mathbf{D}_\pi$. For example, the explicit side condition that $X \neq y$ in the OPEN rule is implicit in $\mathbf{D}_\pi$ since the quantification on X is outside the scope of quantification on y and, therefore, cannot be instantiated with y (substitutions into logical expressions cannot capture bound variable names). Figure 13.5 presents the same collection of clauses as in Figure 13.4 but using λProlog syntax this time.

The adequacy of this encoding is stated in Proposition 13.1 (the proof of this proposition can be found in Tiu [2004] and Tiu and Miller [2010]).

Proposition 13.1. *Let P and Q be processes and α an action. Let $\bar{n}$ be a list of free names containing the free names in P, Q, and α. The transition $P \xrightarrow{\alpha} Q$ is derivable in the π-calculus if and only if $\forall \bar{n}.[\![P \xrightarrow{\alpha} Q]\!]$ is provable from the logical theory $\mathbf{D}_\pi$.*

13.5 Binary Clauses

A reduced class of Horn clauses, called *binary clauses*, can play an important role in modeling computation. As we argue below, they can explicitly order computations, whereas such ordering is left unspecified using more general clauses: Such an explicit ordering is important when attempting to use big-step semantics to capture side effects and concurrency. They can also be used to capture the notion of abstract machines, a common device for specifying operational semantics.

13.5.1 Continuation Passing in Logic Programming

Continuation-passing style (cps) specifications are possible in logic programming using quantification over the type of formulas: See, for example, Tarau [1992]. In fact, it is possible to *cps transform* Horn clauses into binary clauses as follows. First, for every predicate p of type $\tau_1 \to \ldots \to \tau_n \to o$ ($n \geq 0$), we provide a second predicate $\hat{p}$ of type $\tau_1 \to \ldots \to \tau_n \to o \to o$: That is, an additional argument of type o is added to predicate p. Thus, the atomic formula A of the form $(p\ t_1\ \ldots\ t_n)$ is similarly transformed to the term $\hat{A} = (\hat{p}\ t_1\ \ldots\ t_n)$ of type $o \to o$. Using these conventions, the cps transformation of the formula

$$\forall z_1. \cdots \forall z_m. [(A_1 \wedge \ldots \wedge A_n) \supset A_0] \quad (m \geq 0, n > 0)$$

is the binary clause

$$\forall z_1. \cdots \forall z_m. \forall k. [(\hat{A}_1\ (\hat{A}_2(\cdots(\hat{A}_n\ k)\cdots))) \supset (\hat{A}_0\ k)].$$

13.5 Binary Clauses

```
kind   a              type.
type   tau            a.
type   dn, up         n -> n -> a.

type   one            p -> a -> p -> o.
type   oneb           p -> (n -> a) -> (n -> p) -> o.

oneb  (in X M) (dn X) M.
one   (out X Y P) (up X Y) P.
one   (taup P) tau P.
one   (match X X P) A Q :- one P A Q.
oneb  (match X X P) A M :- oneb P A M.
one   (plus P Q) A R :- one  P A R.
one   (plus P Q) A R :- one  Q A R.
oneb  (plus P Q) A M :- oneb P A M.
oneb  (plus P Q) A M :- oneb Q A M.
one   (par P Q) A (par P1 Q) :- one P A P1.
one   (par P Q) A (par P Q1) :- one Q A Q1.
oneb  (par P Q) A (x\ par (M x) Q) :- oneb P A M.
oneb  (par P Q) A (x\ par P (N x)) :- oneb Q A N.
one   (nu P) A (nu Q) :- pi x\ one  (P x) A (Q x).
oneb  (nu P) A (y\ nu x\ Q x y) :-
   pi x\ oneb (P x) A (Q x).
oneb  (nu M) (up X) N :-
   pi y\ one (M y) (up X y) (N y).
one   (par P Q) tau (nu y\ par (M y) (N y)) :-
   oneb P (dn X) M, oneb Q (up X) N.
one   (par P Q) tau (nu y\ par (M y) (N y)) :-
   oneb P (up X) M, oneb Q (dn X) N.
one   (par P Q) tau (par (M Y) T) :-
   oneb P (dn X) M, one Q (up X Y) T.
one   (par P Q) tau (par R (M Y)) :-
   oneb Q (dn X) M, one P (up X Y) R.
```

Figure 13.5 The λProlog specification of the finite π-calculus.

Similarly, the cps transformation of the formula

$$\forall z_1. \cdots \forall z_m. [A_0] \quad \text{is} \quad \forall z_1. \cdots \forall z_m. \forall k. [k \supset (\hat{A}_0\ k)].$$

If $\mathcal{P}$ is a finite set of Horn clauses and $\hat{\mathcal{P}}$ is the result of applying this cps transformation to all clauses in $\mathcal{P}$, then $\mathcal{P} \vdash A$ if and only if $\hat{\mathcal{P}} \vdash (\hat{A}\ \top)$.

$$(((abs\ R) \searrow (abs\ R))\ ;\ K) \supset K.$$
$$((M \searrow (abs\ R))\ ;\ (N \searrow U)\ ;\ ((R\ U) \searrow V)\ ;\ K) \supset ((app\ M\ N) \searrow V)\ ;\ K.$$

Figure 13.6 Binary version of call-by-value evaluation.

Consider again the specification of call-by-value evaluation in Figure 13.2. In order to add side-effecting features, this specification must be made more explicit: In particular, the exact order in which M, N, and $(R\ U)$ are evaluated must be specified. The cps transformation of that specification is given in Figure 13.6: There, evaluation is denoted by a ternary predicate, which is written using both the $\setminus$ arrow and a semicolon: For example, the relation "M evaluates to V with the continuation K" is denoted by $(M \setminus V)\ ;\ K$. If we write this evaluation predicate as evalc then the λProlog specification of the formulas in Figure 13.6 can be written as follows.

```
type evalc     term -> term -> o -> o.

evalc (abs R) (abs R) K :- K.
evalc (app M N) V K :- evalc M (abs R) (evalc N U
                                      (evalc (R U) V K)).
```

In this specification, goals are now sequenced in the sense that bottom-up proof search is forced to construct a proof of one evaluation pair before other such pairs. The goal $((M \setminus V)\ ;\ \top)$ is provable if and only if V is the call-by-value result of M. The order in which evaluation is executed is now forced not by the use of logical connectives but by the use of the non-logical constant $(\cdot \setminus \cdot)\ ;\ \cdot$.

13.5.2 Abstract Machines

Abstract machines, which are often used to specify operational semantics, can be encoded naturally using binary clauses. To support this claim, Hannan and Miller [1992] introduced the following definition of *Abstract Evaluation System* (AES), which generalizes the notion of abstract machines.

A *term rewriting system* is a pair (Σ, R) such that Σ is a signature and R is a set of directed equations $\{l_i \Rightarrow r_i\}_{i \in I}$ with $l_i, r_i \in T_\Sigma(X)$ and $\mathcal{V}(r_i) \subseteq \mathcal{V}(l_i)$. Here, $T_\Sigma(X)$ denotes the set of first-order terms with constants from the signature Σ and free variables from X, and $\mathcal{V}(t)$ denotes the set of free variables occurring in t. An *abstract evaluation system* is a quadruple (Σ, R, ρ, S) such that the pair $(\Sigma, R \cup \{\rho\})$ is a term rewriting system, ρ is not a member of R, and $S \subseteq R$.

Evaluation in an AES is a sequence of rewriting steps with the following restricted structure. The first rewrite rule must be an instance of the ρ rule. This rule can be understood as loading the machine to an initial state given an input expression. The last rewrite step must be an instance of a rule in S: These rules denote the successful termination of the machine and can be

13.5 Binary Clauses

		M	$\Rightarrow$	$\langle nil, M,$	$nil \rangle$
$\langle$	$E,$	$\lambda M, X::S \rangle$	$\Rightarrow$	$\langle X::E, M,$	$S \rangle$
$\langle$	$E,$	$M \char`\^ N, S \rangle$	$\Rightarrow$	$\langle E, M, \{E,N\}::S \rangle$	
$\langle \{E',M\}::E,$		$0, S \rangle$	$\Rightarrow$	$\langle E', M,$	$S \rangle$
$\langle$	$X::E,$	$n+1, S \rangle$	$\Rightarrow$	$\langle E, n,$	$S \rangle$
$\langle$	$E,$	$\lambda M, nil \rangle$	$\Rightarrow$	$\{E, \lambda M\}$	

Figure 13.7 The Krivine machine.

$$M \Rightarrow \langle nil, nil, M\ nil, nil \rangle$$

$\langle S, E, \lambda M\ C, D \rangle \Rightarrow \langle \{E, \lambda M\}\ S, E, C, D \rangle$
$\langle S, E, (M \char`\^ N)\ C, D \rangle \Rightarrow \langle S, E, M\ N\ ap\ C, D \rangle$
$\langle S, E, n\ C, D \rangle \Rightarrow \langle nth(n, E)\ S, E, C, D \rangle$
$\langle X\ \{E', \lambda M\}\ S, E, ap\ C, D \rangle \Rightarrow \langle nil, X\ E', M\ nil, (S, E, C)\ D \rangle$
$\langle X\ S, E, nil, (S', E', C')\ D \rangle \Rightarrow \langle X\ S', E', C', D \rangle$

$$\langle X\ S, E, nil, nil \rangle \Rightarrow X$$

Figure 13.8 The SECD machine (bottom).

understood as unloading the machine and producing the answer or final value. We also make the following significant restriction to the general notion of term rewriting: All rewriting rules must be applied to a term at its root. This restriction significantly simplifies the computational complexity of applying rewrite rules during evaluation in an AES. A term $t \in T_\Sigma(\emptyset)$ *evaluates* to the term s (with respect to the AES (Σ, R, ρ, S)) if there is a series of rewriting rules satisfying the restrictions above that rewrites t into s.

The SECD machine in Landin [1964] and Krivine machine in Curien [1991] are both AESs and variants of these are given in Figure 13.7 and Figure 13.8. There, the syntax for λ-terms uses notation introduced in De Bruijn [1972] with ^ (infix) and λ as the constructors for application and abstraction, respectively. In this notation, bound variable names are replaced by numerical indices that count the number of λ-abstractions between the variable's occurrence and its corresponding binder. The expression $\{E, M\}$ denotes the closure of term M with environment E. The first rule given for each machine is the load rule or ρ of their AES description. The last rule given for each is the unload rule. (In both examples, there is only one unload rule.) The remaining rules are state transformation rules, each one moving the machine through a computation step.

A state in the Krivine machine is a triple $\langle E, M, S \rangle$ in which E is an environment, M is a single term to be evaluated, and S is a stack of arguments. A state in the SECD machine is a quadruple $\langle S, E, C, D \rangle$ in which S is a stack of computed values, E is an environment (here just a list of terms), C is a list of commands (terms to be evaluated), and D is a dump or saved state. The expression $nth(n, E)$, used to access variables in an environment, is treated as a function that returns the $n + 1^{st}$ element of the list E. Although Landin's original description of the SECD machine used variables names, our use of De Bruijn numerals does not change the essential mechanism of that machine.

There is a natural and easy way to see a given AES as a set of binary clauses. Let *load*, *unload*, and *rewrite* be three predicates of one argument each. Given the AES (Σ, R, ρ, S) let $\mathcal{B}$ be the set of binary clauses composed of the following three groups of formulas:

1. $\forall \hat{x}.[rewrite\ r \supset load\ l]$ where ρ is the rule $l \Rightarrow r$,
2. for every rule $l \Rightarrow r$ in R, add the clause $\forall \hat{x}.[rewrite\ r \supset rewrite\ l]$, and
3. for every rule $l \Rightarrow r$ in S, add the clause $\forall \hat{x}.[unload\ r \supset rewrite\ l]$.

It is then easy to show that if we start with term t and evaluate it to get s (this can be a nondeterministic relationship), then from the set of clauses $\mathcal{B}$ we can prove *unload* $t \supset$ *load* s. In particular, if this implication is provable from $\mathcal{B}$, then it has a proof of the form displayed in Figure 13.9: There, only synthetic inference rules (Section 5.7) are displayed. The transitions of the abstract machine can be read directly from this proof: Given the term s, the machine's state is initialized to be s_1, which is then repeatedly rewritten, yielding the sequence of terms $s_2, \ldots, s_n$, at which point the machine is unloaded to get the value t.

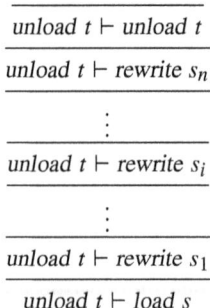

Figure 13.9 A proof involving synthetic rules based on the formulas in $\mathcal{B}$ related to the execution of an abstract machine.

13.6 LINEAR LOGIC

In order to motivate our next operational semantic framework, consider the problem of using binary clauses to specify side effects, exceptions, and concurrent (multi-threaded) computation. Since all the dynamics of computation is represented via term structures (say, within $s, s_1, \ldots, s_n, t$) all the information about these threads, reference cells, and exceptions must be maintained as, say, lists within these terms. Such an approach to specifying these features of a programming language lacks modularity and makes little use of logic. We now consider extending binary clauses so that these additional features have a much more natural and modular specification.

13.6 Linear Logic

In Sections 8.4 and 8.6, we illustrated how linear logic can capture multiset rewriting. Given that many aspects of computation can be captured using multiset rewriting, it is possible to describe a subset of linear logic that includes binary clauses but provides a natural means to capture side effects and concurrency.

13.6.1 Adding a Counter to Evaluation

Consider again the binary clause example in Figure 13.6. As we showed in Section 6.5, the top-level intuitionistic implication ⊃ of Horn clauses can be rewritten as the linear implication ⊸ without changing the operational reading of proof search. With this change, the binary clauses in that figure are also an example of multiset rewriting: In particular, one atom is repeatedly replaced by another atom (until a final continuation replaces the atom). In this way, binary clauses can be seen as modeling single-threaded computation. Now that we have embedded binary clauses within the richer setting of linear logic, it is easy to see how multi-threaded computations might be organized. We present a couple of examples here.

Consider adding to the untyped λ-calculus a single global counter that can be read and incremented. In particular, we shall place all integers into type *tm* and add two additional constructors of type *tm*, namely *get* and *inc*. The intended operational semantics of these two constants is that evaluating the first returns the counter's current value, and evaluating the second increments the counter's value and returns the counter's old value. We also assume that integers are values: That is, for every integer i, the clause $\forall k.(k \multimap (i \setminus i) ; k)$ is part of the evaluator's specification. The multiset rewriting specification of these two additional constructors can be given as the two formulas

$$\forall K.\forall V.(r\ V\ \bindnasrepma\ K \multimap ((get \setminus V) ; K)\ \bindnasrepma\ r\ V)\ \text{and}$$
$$\forall K.\forall V.(r\ (V+1)\ \bindnasrepma\ K \multimap ((inc \setminus V) ; K)\ \bindnasrepma\ r\ V).$$

Here, the atom of the form $(r\ x)$ denotes the "r-register" with value x. Let $\mathcal{D}$ contain the two formulas in Figure 13.6, the two formulas displayed above, and the formulas mentioned above describing the evaluation of integers. Then $\mathcal{D}$ is a specification of the call-by-value evaluator with one global counter in the sense that the $\mathcal{L}_2^\omega$ sequent

$$\mathcal{D}; \cdot \vdash ((M \setminus V) ; \top)\ \bindnasrepma\ r\ 0; \cdot$$

is provable exactly when we expect the program M to evaluate to V in the setting where the register r is initialized to 0.

Of course, the name of the predicate encoding a register should not be a part of the specification of a counter. Higher-order quantification over r makes it possible to hide the name of this register. Figure 13.10 contains three specifications – E_1, E_2, and E_3 – of a counter: all three specifications store the counter's value in an atomic formula as the argument of the predicate r. In these three specifications, the predicate r is existentially quantified over the specification in which it is used so that the atomic formula that stores the counter's value is itself local to the counter's specification. The first two specifications store the counter's value on the right of the sequent turnstile, and reading and incrementing the counter occurs via a synchronization between a $\setminus$-atom and an r-atom. In the third specification, the counter is stored as a linear assumption on the left of the sequent arrow, and synchronization is not used: Instead, the linear assumption is "destructively" read and then rewritten in order to specify the *get* and *inc* functions (similar to the examples in Section 8.4). Finally, in the first and third specifications, evaluating the *inc* symbol causes 1 to be added to the counter's value. In the second specification, evaluating the *inc* symbol causes 1 to be subtracted from the counter's value: To compensate for this unusual implementation of *inc*, reading a counter in the second specification returns the negative of the counter's value.

The specifications in Figure 13.10 use several linear logic connectives not formally part of $\mathcal{L}_2$. Positive connectives often appear when one uses the curry/uncurry equivalences (see Exercise 6.11). Consider proving the sequent

$$\Sigma :: \Psi; \exists r.[(r\ 0)^\perp \otimes\ !D_1 \otimes\ !D_2] \vdash G; \cdot,$$

13.6 Linear Logic

$$E_1 = \exists r.[\quad (r\ 0)^\perp \otimes$$
$$!\forall K.\forall V.(r\ V \bindnasrepma K \multimap ((get\ \backslash\ V)\ ;\ K) \bindnasrepma r\ V) \otimes$$
$$!\forall K.\forall V.(r\ (V+1) \bindnasrepma K \multimap ((inc\ \backslash\ V)\ ;\ K) \bindnasrepma r\ V)]$$

$$E_2 = \exists r.[\quad (r\ 0)^\perp \otimes$$
$$!\forall K.\forall V.(r\ V \bindnasrepma K \multimap ((get\ \backslash\ (-V))\ ;\ K) \bindnasrepma r\ V) \otimes$$
$$!\forall K.\forall V.(r\ (V-1) \bindnasrepma K \multimap ((inc\ \backslash\ (-V))\ ;\ K) \bindnasrepma r\ V)]$$

$$E_3 = \exists r.[\quad (r\ 0) \otimes$$
$$!\forall K.\forall V.(r\ V \otimes (r\ V \multimap K) \multimap ((get\ \backslash\ V)\ ;\ K)) \otimes$$
$$!\forall K.\forall V.(r\ V \otimes (r\ (V+1) \multimap K) \multimap ((inc\ \backslash\ V)\ ;\ K))]$$

Figure 13.10 Three specifications of a global counter.

where D_1, D_2, and G are $\mathcal{L}_2$ formulas. Given invertibility of $\exists L$, $\otimes L$, and $\neg L$, provability of that sequent is equivalent to the provability of the $\Downarrow \mathcal{L}_2$ sequent

$$\Sigma, r :: \Psi, D_1, D_2;\ \cdot\ \vdash G, (r\ 0);\ \cdot\ .$$

Although these three specifications of a global counter are different, they should be equivalent in the sense that the process of evaluating terms cannot tell them apart. Although there are several ways that the equivalence of such counters can be argued, the specifications of these counters are, in fact, *logically* equivalent.

> **Proposition 13.2.** *The three entailments $E_1 \vdash E_2$, $E_2 \vdash E_3$, and $E_3 \vdash E_1$ are provable in linear logic.*

Proof: The proof of each of these entailments proceeds (in a bottom-up fashion) by choosing an eigenvariable to instantiate the existential quantifier on the left-hand side and then instantiating the right-hand existential quantifier with some term involving that eigenvariable. Assume that in all three cases, the eigenvariable selected is the predicate symbol s. Then the first entailment is proved by instantiating the right-hand existential with $\lambda x.s\ (-x)$; the second entailment is proved using the substitution $\lambda x.(s\ (-x))^\perp$; and the third entailment is proved using the substitution $\lambda x.(s\ x)^\perp$. The proof of the first two entailments must also use the identities $-0 = 0$, $-(x+1) = -x-1$, and $-(x-1) = -x+1$. The proof of the third entailment requires no such identities. □

Clearly, logical equivalence is a strong equivalence: It immediately implies that evaluation cannot tell the difference between any of these different counter specifications. For example, assume $E_1 \vdash (M \setminus V)\,;\, \top$. Then by the cut inference rule and Proposition 13.2, we have $E_2 \vdash (M \setminus V)\,;\, \top$.

As was shown in Chirimar [1995] and Miller [1996], it is possible to generalize the previous example involving a single global counter to languages that have the ability to generate references dynamically, such as is possible in Algol and Standard ML.

13.6.2 Specifying Concurrency Primitives

The concurrency primitives proposed by Reppy [1991] for the design of Concurrent ML (CML) can also be specified in linear logic. We assume that the reader is familiar with this extension of ML.

Consider extending the untyped λ-calculus with the following constructors.

$$none : tm.$$
$$guard, poll, receive, some, sync : tm \to tm.$$
$$choose, transmit, wrap : tm \to tm \to tm.$$
$$spawn, newchan : (tm \to tm) \to tm.$$

The meaning of these constructors is then given using the linear logic formulas in Figure 13.11 and Figure 13.12. The clauses in Figure 13.11 specify the straightforward evaluation rules for the eight data constructors. In Figure 13.12, the predicate *event* is of type $tm \to tm \to o \to o$ and is used to store in the right-bounded zone atomic formulas with the predicate *event*. The first three clauses of that figure defined the meaning of the three special forms *sync*, *spawn*, and *newchan*. The remaining clauses specify the *event* predicate.

The formulas in Figure 13.12 allow for multiple evaluation threads. Evaluation of the *spawn* function initiates a new evaluation thread. The *newchan* function causes a new eigenvariable to be picked (via the $\forall c$ quantification) and then to assume that that eigenvariable is a value (via the assumption

$$K \multimap (none \setminus none)\,;\, K$$
$$(E \setminus V)\,;\, K \multimap ((guard\ E) \setminus (guard\ V))\,;\, K$$
$$(E \setminus V)\,;\, K \multimap ((poll\ E) \setminus (poll\ V))\,;\, K$$
$$(E \setminus V)\,;\, K \multimap ((receive\ E) \setminus (receive\ V))\,;\, K$$
$$(E \setminus V)\,;\, K \multimap ((some\ E) \setminus (some\ V))\,;\, K$$
$$(E \setminus U)\,;\, ((F \setminus V)\,;\, K) \multimap ((choose\ E\ F) \setminus (choose\ U\ V))\,;\, K$$
$$(E \setminus U)\,;\, ((F \setminus V)\,;\, K) \multimap ((transmit\ E\ F) \setminus (transmit\ U\ V))\,;\, K$$
$$(E \setminus U)\,;\, ((F \setminus V)\,;\, K) \multimap ((wrap\ E\ F) \setminus (wrap\ U\ V))\,;\, K$$

Figure 13.11 These CML-like constructors evaluate to themselves.

13.6 LINEAR LOGIC

$$(E \setminus U) \,;\, (event\ U\ V\ K) \multimap ((sync\ E) \setminus V) \,;\, K$$
$$(((R\ unit) \setminus unit) \,;\, \bot) \mathbin{\mathclap{\gamma}} K \multimap ((spawn\ R) \setminus unit) \,;\, K$$
$$\forall c.(\forall I.(I \multimap (c \setminus c) \,;\, I) \Rightarrow ((R\ c) \setminus V) \,;\, K) \multimap ((newchan\ R) \setminus V) \,;\, K$$

$$K \mathbin{\mathclap{\gamma}} L \multimap event\ (receive\ C)\ V\ K \mathbin{\mathclap{\gamma}} event\ (transmit\ C\ V)\ unit\ L$$

$$event\ E\ V\ K \multimap event\ (choose\ E\ F)\ V\ K$$
$$event\ F\ V\ K \multimap event\ (choose\ E\ F)\ V\ K$$
$$event\ E\ U\ (((app\ F\ U) \setminus V) \,;\, K) \multimap event\ (wrap\ E\ F)\ V\ K$$
$$((app\ F\ unit) \setminus U) \,;\, (event\ U\ V\ K) \multimap event\ (guard\ F)\ V\ K$$
$$(event\ E\ U\ \top)\ \&\ K \multimap event\ (poll\ E)\ (some\ E)\ K$$
$$K \multimap event\ (poll\ E)\ none\ K$$

Figure 13.12 Specifications of some primitives similar to those in Concurrent ML.

$\forall I.(I \multimap (c \setminus c) \,;\, I))$: Such a new value can designate new channels for use in synchronization. The *sync* primitive allows for synchronization between threads: Its use causes an "evaluation thread" to become an "event thread." The remaining clauses in Figure 13.12 describe the behaviors of event threads. The primitive events are *transmit* and *receive*, representing two halves of synchronization between two event threads. Note that the clause describing their meaning is the only clause in Figure 13.12 that has a head with more than one atom. The non-primitive events *choose*, *wrap*, *guard*, and *poll* are reduced to other calls to *event* and $\setminus$. The *choice* event is implemented as a local, nondeterministic choice. (Specifying global choice, as presented in CCS [Milner, 1989], would be much more involved.) The *wrap* and *guard* events chain together evaluation and synchronization but in direct orders.

The only use of *additive* linear logic connectives, in particular & and $\top$, in any of our semantic specifications, is in the specification of polling. In an attempt to synchronize with $(poll\ E)$ (with the continuation K) the goal

$$(event\ E\ U\ \top)\ \&\ K$$

is attempted (for some unimportant term U). Thus, a copy of the current evaluation threads is made, and $(event\ E\ U\ \top)$ is attempted in one of these copies. This atom is provable if and only if there is a complementary event for E in the current environment, in which case, the continuation $\top$ brings us to a quick completion, and the continuation K is attempted in the original and unspoiled context of threads. If such a complementary event is not present, then the other clause for computing a polling event can be used, in which case, the result of the poll is *none*, which signals such a failure. The semantics of polling, unfortunately, is not exactly as intended in CML since it is possible to have a polling event return *none* even if the event being tested could be synchronized. This analysis of polling is similar to the analysis of testing in process calculus as described in Miller [1993].

13.7 Bibliographic Notes

A distinction is often made between the *static semantics* and the *dynamic semantics* of programming languages (see, for example, Clement et al. [1986]). Static semantics refers to properties of program text that a compiler can infer: Typing is a typical example of static semantics, and the collection analysis in Chapter 11 is another example. Dynamic semantics refers to properties of programs that can be inferred by executing programs: Termination is a typical example of dynamic semantics. In this chapter, we have limited ourselves to the specification of dynamic semantics of some simple programming languages and to the π-calculus. Logic programming and its concomitant technologies of unification and proof search has an important role in specifying the static semantics of programming languages, particularly, in type checking and type inference: See, for example, the so-called Hindley–Milner approach to type inference in Hindley [1969] and Milner [1978].

There has been a long-standing interest in being able to formally specify and reason about the static and dynamic semantic descriptions of programming languages. Formal specifications of these using logic programming have been available since the introduction of operational semantics: See, for example, Despeyroux [1986], Hannan and Miller [1989], Hannan and Pfenning [1992], Hannan [1993], Pfenning and Schürmann [1999], and McDowell and Miller [2002] for some early references.

The treatment of bindings in data structures, such as those that encode the (untyped) λ-calculus and the π-calculus, is given a simple and declarative treatment in the logic programming setting we are using in this book. This setting provides bindings as a primitive via the availability of simply typed λ-terms and enables binder mobility through the use of eigenvariables during proof search as described in Section 3.2.3 and in Miller [2019]. The Abella proof assistant, described in Baelde et al. [2014], provides a setting in which reasoning on such logic programs can be done.

The specification of the π-calculus [Milner et al., 1992a] in Figure 13.3 is taken from Miller and Palamidessi [1999].

13.7 Bibliographic Notes

For more about translating SOS specifications of evaluation directly into abstract machines, see Hannan and Miller [1992].

Chirimar [1995] presents a linear logic specification of a programming language motivated by Standard ML (as defined in Milner et al. [1990]). In particular, a specification for the call-by-value λ-calculus is provided, and then modularly extended with the specifications of references, exceptions, and continuations: Each of these features is specified without complicating the specifications of the other features.

The general outline of this chapter is based on the short article [Miller, 2008b].

Solutions to Selected Exercises

Solution to Exercise 2.1 (page 11). Of the six terms listed, only the fourth and fifth terms do not have a β-normal form.

1. $((\lambda x.y)(\lambda x.x))$ reduces to the normal form y.
2. $((\lambda x.x)(\lambda x.x))$ reduces to the normal form $(\lambda x.x)$.
3. $((\lambda x.(xx))(\lambda x.x))$ reduces to the term above, namely, $((\lambda x.x)(\lambda x.x))$. Thus, its normal form is $(\lambda x.x)$.
4. $((\lambda x.(xx))(\lambda x.(xx)))$ reduces only to itself, and since this term is not normal, this term has no normal form.
5. Applying β-conversion to $((\lambda x.((xx)x))(\lambda x.((xx)x)))$ yields a larger term with more β-reduces, including this initial one. This term has no normal form.
6. $((\lambda x.y)((\lambda x.(xx))(\lambda x.(xx))))$ reduces to y.

Solution to Exercise 2.3 (page 11). E_2 normalizes to the Church encoding of 16. In general, E_n has the λ-normal form that encodes the number

$$\left. 2^{2^{2^{\cdot^{\cdot^{\cdot^{2}}}}}} \right\} n+1$$

There are $n + 1$ occurrences of 2 in this expression.

Solution to Exercise 2.4 (page 12). The abstraction $(\lambda x.w)$ is vacuous, i.e., x is not free in its scope (which is just the variable w). Since substitution is capture-avoiding, every instance of that term remains a vacuous abstraction. Since the term $\lambda y.y$ is not a vacuous abstraction, no such expression for N is possible.

Solution to Exercise 2.5 (page 12). Let Y denote the untyped λ-term $\lambda f.(\lambda x.f(xx))(\lambda x.f(xx))$. Let g be any untyped λ-term. Then: (Yg) β-reduces to $(\lambda x.g(xx))(\lambda x.g(xx))$ which β-reduces to $g((\lambda x.g(xx))(\lambda x.g(xx)))$, and this is equal to $g(Yg)$. Now let B be the term $\lambda x.(x \Rightarrow \mathsf{f})$. Consider the provable formula $(YB) \Rightarrow (YB)$. This formula is equal to (via β-conversions) $(YB) \Rightarrow (B(YB))$ and $(YB) \Rightarrow (YB) \Rightarrow \mathsf{f}$. This last formula is equivalent to $(YB) \Rightarrow \mathsf{f}$, which is β-convertible to $B(YB)$ and (YB). Using modus ponens, we now have a proof of f. Any formula can replace the symbol for false f, and this proof would have worked just the same.

Solution to Exercise 2.6 (page 14). The proof of uniqueness is a simple induction on the structure of typing judgment proofs. For the second part of this question, let Σ be the empty signature, and let t be the λ-term $\lambda x.x$, and assume that S contains two different primitive sorts a and b. Then we have both $\Sigma \Vdash t : a \to a$ and $\Sigma \Vdash t : b \to b$.

Solution to Exercise 3.2 (page 28). The multiplicative version of the $\wedge \mathrm{R}$ rule is

$$\frac{\Sigma :: \Gamma \vdash \Delta, B \qquad \Sigma :: \Gamma' \vdash \Delta', C}{\Sigma :: \Gamma, \Gamma' \vdash \Delta, \Delta', B \wedge C} \wedge \mathrm{R}^m.$$

The following derivation shows that weakening and the additive $\wedge \mathrm{R}$ rule can derive the multiplicative $\wedge \mathrm{R}^m$ rule.

$$\frac{\dfrac{\Sigma :: \Gamma \vdash \Delta, B}{\Sigma :: \Gamma, \Gamma' \vdash \Delta, \Delta', B} \; wR, wL \qquad \dfrac{\Sigma :: \Gamma \vdash \Delta, C}{\Sigma :: \Gamma, \Gamma' \vdash \Delta, \Delta', C} \; wR, wL}{\Sigma :: \Gamma, \Gamma' \vdash \Delta, \Delta', B \wedge C} \wedge \mathrm{R}$$

The following derivation shows that contraction and the multiplicative $\wedge \mathrm{R}^m$ rule can derive the additive $\wedge \mathrm{R}$ rule.

$$\dfrac{\dfrac{\Sigma :: \Gamma \vdash \Delta, B \qquad \Sigma :: \Gamma \vdash \Delta, C}{\Sigma :: \Gamma, \Gamma \vdash \Delta, \Delta, B \wedge C} \wedge \mathrm{R}^m}{\Sigma :: \Gamma \vdash \Delta, B \wedge C} \; cR, cL.$$

Similarly, the $\wedge \mathrm{L}^m$ rule can be derived from the $\wedge \mathrm{L}$ rule with contraction.

$$\dfrac{\dfrac{\dfrac{\Sigma :: \Gamma, B, C \vdash \Delta}{\Sigma :: \Gamma, B \wedge C, C \vdash \Delta} \wedge \mathrm{L}}{\Sigma :: \Gamma, B \wedge C, B \wedge C \vdash \Delta} \wedge \mathrm{L}}{\Sigma :: \Gamma, B \wedge C \vdash \Delta} \; cL.$$

Finally, the ∧L rule can be derived from the ∧L^m rule with weakening.

$$\frac{\dfrac{\Sigma :: \Gamma, B \vdash \Delta}{\Sigma :: \Gamma, B, C \vdash \Delta} \, wL}{\Sigma :: \Gamma, B \wedge C \vdash \Delta} \, \wedge R^m.$$

Solution to Exercise 4.1 (page 38). Since $\sqrt{2}^{\sqrt{2}}$ is either rational or irrational, we have two cases to consider. In the case that $\sqrt{2}^{\sqrt{2}}$ is rational, then set $a = b = \sqrt{2}$. In the case that $\sqrt{2}^{\sqrt{2}}$ is irrational, then set $a = \sqrt{2}^{\sqrt{2}}$ and $b = \sqrt{2}$. A more satisfying proof of this fact results from assigning $a = \sqrt{2}$ and $b = \log_2 9$. Kuzmin [1930] proved that $\sqrt{2}^{\sqrt{2}}$ is transcendental.

Solution to Exercise 4.3 (page 41). Of these examples, (3), (4), (5), (6), and (7) all have **C**-proofs but no **I**-proofs. A **C**-proof of (5) is

$$\cfrac{\cfrac{\cfrac{\cfrac{\cfrac{\cfrac{\overline{p \vdash p} \; init}{p \vdash q, p} \, wR}{\vdash p \supset q, p} \, \supset R \quad \overline{p \vdash p} \; init}{(p \supset q) \supset p \vdash p, p} \, \supset L}{(p \supset q) \supset p \vdash p} \, cR}{\cdot \vdash ((p \supset q) \supset p) \supset p} \, \supset R.$$

Solution to Exercise 4.4 (page 42). The instance of the excluded middle $B \vee (B \supset f)$ assumed as an additional assumption is given for the examples in Exercise 4.3 by specifying the instance of B. For (3), B is q. For (4), B is p. For (5), B is p. For (6), B is $r\,a$. For (7), B is $\exists y \forall x.(r\,x \supset r\,y)$. Below is the **I**-proof for (5) with the appropriate instance of the excluded middle.

$$\cfrac{\cfrac{\cfrac{\overline{p \vdash p}\; init}{p,(p \supset q) \supset p \vdash p}\, wL \quad \cfrac{\cfrac{\cfrac{\overline{p \vdash p}\; init \quad \overline{f \vdash q}\; fL}{p \supset f, p \vdash q}\, \supset L}{p \supset f \vdash p \supset q}\, \supset R \quad \overline{p \vdash p}\; init}{p \supset f, (p \supset q) \supset p \vdash p}\, \supset L}{p \vee (p \supset f), (p \supset q) \supset p \vdash p}\, \vee L}{p \vee (p \supset f) \vdash ((p \supset q) \supset p) \supset p}\, \supset R$$

SOLUTIONS TO SELECTED PROBLEMS   283

Solution to Exercise 4.5 (page 42). The list of pairs for which entailment is provable in classical logic is

$$\{\langle A, \neg\neg A\rangle, \langle \neg\neg A, A\rangle, \langle \neg A, \neg\neg\neg A\rangle, \langle \neg\neg\neg A, \neg A\rangle, \}.$$

In intuitionistic logic, the list of pairs for which entailment is provable is the same, except that the pair $\langle \neg\neg A, A\rangle$ is removed.

Solution to Exercise 4.7 (page 43). Assume that S contains the primitive types i and j. The following is an **I**-proof.

$$\cfrac{\cfrac{f : i \to j, y : i \Vdash (f\ y) : j \qquad \cfrac{}{f : i \to j, y : i :: \cdot \vdash t}\ tR}{\cfrac{f : i \to j, y : i :: \cdot \vdash \exists_j x\, t}{\cfrac{f : i \to j :: \cdot \vdash \forall_i y \exists_j x\, t}{f : i \to j :: \cdot \vdash (\exists_j x\, t) \lor (\forall_i y \exists_j x\, t)}\ \lor R}\ \forall R}\ \exists R}\ \lor R.$$

The following is a **C**-proof of a different formula.

$$\cfrac{\cfrac{\cfrac{f : i \to j, x : i \Vdash (f\ x) : j \qquad \cfrac{}{f : i \to j, x : i :: \cdot \vdash t, f}\ tR}{\cfrac{f : i \to j, x : i :: \cdot \vdash \exists_j x\, t, f}{f : i \to j :: \cdot \vdash \exists_j x\, t, \forall_i x\, f}\ \forall R}\ \exists R}{\cfrac{f : i \to j :: \cdot \vdash (\exists_j x\, t) \lor (\forall_i x\, f), (\exists_j x\, t) \lor (\forall_i x\, f)}{f : i \to j :: \cdot \vdash (\exists_j x\, t) \lor (\forall_i x\, f)}\ cR}\ \lor R \times 2.}$$

There is no **I**-proof of this sequent since contraction on the right is necessary to complete a proof. In both this example and Exercise 4.3(4), completing a proof requires two subformulas separated by a disjunction to "communicate" in the sense that one disjunction puts into the sequent context some item (here, an eigenvariable and in Exercise 4.3(4) an assumption) that the other disjunct uses. This communication can happen in the proof if that disjunction is contracted on the right.

Solution to Exercise 4.11 (page 48). Let p and q be distinct constants of type o. The following is a proof of $p \vdash q$ using the cut rule.

$$\cfrac{\cfrac{\overline{p \vdash p}}{p \vdash p \diamond q} \qquad \cfrac{\overline{q \vdash q}}{p \diamond q \vdash q}}{p \vdash q}\ cut.$$

Clearly, there can be no cut-free proof of the same endsequent. Since it is possible to prove $p \diamond q \vdash p \diamond q$ from $p \vdash p$, it is possible to eliminate non-atomic initial rules in the presence of $\diamond$.

Solution to Exercise 4.8 (page 44). We provide a high-level outline of the proof. For one direction, we show how to transform a **C**-proof with a generalized restart rule to a **C**-proof without restart. Since **I**-proofs are **C**-proofs, this establishes the forward implication. Restarts can be removed one by one via the following transformation.

$$
\cfrac{\cfrac{\Xi}{\Sigma :: \Gamma \vdash B, \Delta}}{\cfrac{\Sigma :: \Gamma \vdash C, \Delta}{\vdots \\ \Sigma' :: \Gamma' \vdash B, \Delta'}} \text{Restart} \quad \Longrightarrow \quad \cfrac{\cfrac{\cfrac{\Xi}{\Sigma :: \Gamma \vdash B, \Delta}}{\Sigma :: \Gamma \vdash C, B, \Delta} wR}{\cfrac{\vdots}{\cfrac{\Sigma' :: \Gamma' \vdash B, B, \Delta'}{\Sigma' :: \Gamma' \vdash B, \Delta'}} cR.}
$$

That is, the restart rule can be implemented using a contraction and a weakening on the right. It is easy to confirm that the formula B can be added to all possible inference rules below this occurrence of the restart rule.

For a sketch of the converse direction, consider a **C**-proof. Mark a formula on the right-hand side of every sequent as follows. The single formula on the right of the endsequent is marked (assuming that the endsequent has a single formula on the right). If the last inference rule of the proof is a left-introduction rule, then the marked occurrence of the formula in the conclusion is also marked in all the premises. If the last inference rule is a right-introduction rule, then we have two cases: If the introduced formula is already marked, then mark its subformulas that appear in the right-hand side of any premise (for example, if the marked formula is $A \Rightarrow B$ then mark B in the premise; if the marked formula is $A \wedge B$ then mark A in one premise and B in the other; and so forth). Otherwise, the right-hand formula introduced is not marked, in which case, we have a *marking break*, and we mark in the premises of the inference rules the subformulas of the right-hand formula introduced and continue. The only other rules that might be applied are: cL, in which case the marked formula on the right persists from conclusion to premise; cR, in which case, if the marked formula is the one contracted then select one of its copies to mark in the premise, otherwise, the marked formula persists in the premise; and *init*, in which case, if the marked formula on the right is not the same as the formula on the left, then this occurrence of the *init* rule is also a marking break.

SOLUTIONS TO SELECTED PROBLEMS 285

$$\frac{\overline{p \vdash p, q^*, p \supset q, p \vee (p \supset q)}\ init^*}{\frac{\vdash p, (p \supset q)^*, p \supset q, p \vee (p \supset q)}{\frac{\vdash p, (p \supset q)^*, p \vee (p \supset q)}{\frac{\vdash p^*, p \vee (p \supset q), p \vee (p \supset q)}{\frac{\vdash p^*, p \vee (p \supset q)}{\frac{\vdash p \vee (p \supset q)^*, p \vee (p \supset q)}{\vdash p \vee (p \supset q)^*}\ cR}\ \vee R}\ cR}\ \vee R^*}\ cR}\ \supset R}$$

Figure 13.13 An annotated C-proof

To illustrate this notion of marking formulas, consider the annotated C-proof in Figure 13.13. Here, an asterisk is used to indicate marked formulas and to indicate which inference rules correspond to marking gaps.

Now the **I**-proof with Restart is built as follows. For sequents that are the conclusion of a rule that is not a marking break, delete all non-marked formulas on the right. For sequents that are the conclusion of a rule that is a marking break, then this one inference rule becomes two: An instance of the Restart rule must be inserted, and then the version of the inference rule corresponding to the marking break is put into the proof with the non-marked right-hand formulas deleted.

For example, performing this transformation on the C-proof yields the following structure.

$$\frac{\overline{p \vdash p}\ init}{\frac{p \vdash q}{\frac{\vdash p \supset q}{\frac{\vdash p \supset q}{\frac{\vdash p \vee (p \supset q)}{\frac{\vdash p}{\frac{\vdash p}{\frac{\vdash p \vee (p \supset q)}{\vdash p \vee (p \supset q)}\ cR.}\ \vee R}\ cR}\ Restart}\ \vee R}\ cR}\ \supset R}\ Restart}$$

This sequence of rules is not yet an **I**-proof: There are three occurrences of cR that are not allowed in **I**-proofs: These can either be deleted or reclassified as

Restart rules. In the example above, all three occurrences of cR can be deleted, yielding an **I**-proof with the restart rule.

Solution to Exercise 4.12 (page 49). Let Π_1 and Π_2 be the following proofs of $p \vdash f$ and $\vdash p$, respectively.

$$\cfrac{\cfrac{\cfrac{\overline{p \vdash p} \; init \quad \overline{f \vdash f} \; init}{p, p \supset f \vdash f} \supset L}{p, p \vdash f} \; defL}{p \vdash f} \; cL \qquad \cfrac{\cfrac{\cfrac{\Pi_1}{p \vdash f}}{\vdash p \supset f} \supset R}{\vdash p} \; defR.$$

Clearly, by defining p as $\neg p$ (hence, the equivalence $p \equiv \neg p$ is provable), one is asking for trouble. (Compare this trouble with Curry's paradox in Exercise 2.5.) It turns out that if the ambient logic does not have the contraction rules (such as in linear logic), then it has been pointed out in Girard [1992] and Schroeder-Heister [1993] that it is not possible for such a problematic definition to yield an inconsistency.

Solution to Exercise 4.15 (page 50). Let $k \geq 1$ and D_k be the formula

$$\forall x.(p\, x \supset p\, (f^{2^k} x)).$$

Give a cut-free proof of D_{k+1} from D_k. Show how these lemmas can be organized into a short proof (with cuts) of, for example,

$$p\, a,\ \forall x.(p\, x \supset p\, (f\, x)) \vdash p(f^{256} a).$$

Solution to Exercise 4.18 (page 53). The following inference rules can prove the invertibility of $\vee L$ and $\forall R$. The remaining two cases can be proved in a similar fashion.

$$\cfrac{\cfrac{\overline{B \vdash B} \; init}{B \vdash B \vee C} \vee R \quad \cfrac{\Xi}{\Gamma, B \vee C \vdash \Delta}}{\Gamma, B \vdash \Delta} \; cut \qquad \cfrac{\cfrac{\cfrac{\overline{C \vdash C} \; init}{C \vdash B \vee C} \vee R \quad \cfrac{\Xi}{\Gamma, B \vee C \vdash \Delta}}{\Gamma, C \vdash \Delta} \; cut}{\Gamma, B \vee C \vdash \Delta} \; \vee L$$

Solutions to Selected Problems 287

$$\frac{\Xi}{\Sigma, c : \tau :: \Gamma \vdash \forall_\tau x.B, \Delta} \quad \frac{\overline{\Sigma, c : \tau :: B[c/x] \vdash B[c/x]}^{\text{init}}}{\Sigma, c : \tau :: \forall_\tau x.B \vdash B[c/x]} \forall L$$
$$\frac{\Sigma, c : \tau :: \Gamma \vdash B[c/x], \Delta}{\Sigma :: \Gamma \vdash \forall_\tau x.B, \Delta} \forall R.$$

Here, c is not declared in Σ. Note that if we start with a proof Ξ of the sequent $\Sigma :: \Gamma \vdash \forall_\tau x.B, \Delta$ then it is a simple matter to view Ξ as a proof of $\Sigma, c : \tau :: \Gamma \vdash \forall_\tau x.B, \Delta$.

Solution to Exercise 4.24 (page 57). The explode inference rules can be derived using the following inference rules.

$$\frac{\Gamma \vdash B \supset \mathsf{f}}{\Gamma \vdash B \supset \mathsf{f}} \quad \frac{\Gamma \vdash B \quad \frac{\overline{B \vdash B}^{\text{init}} \quad \overline{\mathsf{f} \vdash C}^{\mathsf{fL}}}{B, B \supset \mathsf{f} \vdash C} \supset L}{\Gamma, B \supset \mathsf{f} \vdash C} \text{cut}$$
$$\frac{\Gamma, \Gamma \vdash C}{\Gamma \vdash C} cL$$

In a similar fashion, the excluded middle inference rules can be derived using the following inference rules.

$$\frac{\frac{\overline{B \vdash B}^{\text{init}}}{B \vdash B, \mathsf{f}} wR}{\vdash B, B \supset \mathsf{f}} \supset R \quad \Gamma, B \vdash C}{\Gamma \vdash B \supset \mathsf{f}, C} \text{cut} \quad \Gamma, B \supset \mathsf{f} \vdash C}{\Gamma, \Gamma \vdash C, C} \text{cut.}$$
$$\frac{\Gamma, \Gamma \vdash C, C}{\Gamma \vdash C} cL, cR$$

Solution to Exercise 5.6 (page 67). Assume that there is a (cut-free) **C**-proof Ξ of $\Sigma :: \mathcal{P} \vdash \mathsf{f}$ for a multiset of Horn clauses $\mathcal{P}$. Consider the last inference rule of Ξ. It cannot be either *init* or fL since f is not allowed as a Horn clause. Assume that the last rule is $\supset$L, namely,

$$\frac{\Sigma :: \Gamma_1 \vdash \Delta_1, G \quad \Sigma :: D, \Gamma_2 \vdash \Delta_2}{\Sigma :: G \supset D, \Gamma_1, \Gamma_2 \vdash \mathsf{f}} \supset L$$

where the multiset union of Δ_1 and Δ_2 is the multiset containing just one occurrence of f. By Proposition 5.5, Δ_2 must be nonempty so Δ_1 is empty and Δ_2 contains just f. However, the right premise is a shorter proof of f from Horn clauses, which is a contradiction. The only other possible candidates as the last inference rule of Ξ (namely, $\wedge L$, $\forall L$, or a structural rule on the left or right) all would yield a premise that is a sequent with Horn clauses on the left and f on the right. Since that premise has a shorter proof than Ξ, we have again have a contradiction.

Solution to Exercise 5.8 (page 67). Let the Σ-formulas $D_0, \ldots, D_n$ ($n \geq 0$) be Horn clauses using description (5.3). Thus, D_0 is of the form

$$\forall \bar{x}_1.(A_1 \supset \cdots \supset (\forall \bar{x}_m.A_m \supset \forall \bar{x}_0.A_0))$$

where $m \geq 0$ and $\bar{x}_0, \ldots \bar{x}_m$ are lists of variables, all of which are distinct. As was proved in Proposition 4.17, both $\supset R$ and $\forall R$ are invertible rules within **C**-proofs. In particular, the sequent $\Sigma :: D_1, \ldots, D_n \vdash D_0$ has a **C**-proof if and only if

$$\Sigma, \bar{x}_0, \bar{x}_1, \ldots \bar{x}_m :: D_1, \ldots, D_n, A_1, \ldots, A_m \vdash A_0$$

has a **C**-proof. Since all the formulas on the left-hand side of this sequent are Horn clauses, the result follows directly from Proposition 5.5. This result also holds when Horn clauses are defined using description (5.2). The result that the classical entailment among Horn clauses implies their intuitionistic entailment is a special case of a result often referred to as Barr's Theorem (see Negri [2016]).

Solution to Exercise 5.9 (page 67). Exercise 4.3(5) provides a **C**-proof of $((p \supset q) \supset p) \supset p$. It is easy to see that this formula has no **I**-proof (and, hence, no uniform proof). Now assume that there is another formula, say, A, which only contains implications and is strictly smaller while having a **C**-proof but no **I**-proof. Thus B contains 2 or fewer occurrences of implications. Thus, B is of clausal order 2 or less and is of the form $(A_1 \supset (A_2 \supset A_3))$ or $((A_1 \supset A_2) \supset A_3)$ where A_1, A_2, A_3 are atomic formulas. Thus attempting a cut-free proof of B leads to attempting proofs of either $A_1, A_2 \vdash A_3$ or $A_1 \supset A_2 \vdash A_3$. In either case, we have a sequent involving only Horn clauses and, as a result of Proposition 5.5, if it is classically provable, it is also intuitionistically provable. This is a contradiction.

Solution to Exercise 5.14 (page 71). Assume that $\Sigma :: \Gamma \vdash B$ has an **I**-proof, where Γ is a multiset of Harrop formulas, and B is an arbitrary formula.

SOLUTIONS TO SELECTED PROBLEMS   289

By Proposition 4.17, the inference rules $\supset$R, $\wedge$R, and $\forall$R are invertible. Hence, the result follows immediately if B is an implication, a conjunction, or a universal quantifier. Consider the case where B is $B_1 \vee B_2$. We prove by induction on the size of a cut-free **I**-proof Ξ of $\Sigma :: \Gamma \vdash B_1 \vee B_2$ that there is an $i \in \{1, 2\}$ such that $\Sigma :: \Gamma \vdash B_i$ has an **I**-proof. If the last inference rule of Ξ is $\vee$R, the result is immediate. If the last inference rule of Ξ is either $\wedge$L or $\forall$L, the conclusion follows immediately from the inductive assumption. The only remaining case is that the last inference rule of Ξ is $\supset$L, as in the following derivation.

$$\cfrac{\begin{array}{cc} \Xi_0 & \Xi_1 \\ \Gamma \vdash B' & \Gamma, H \vdash B_1 \vee B_2 \end{array}}{\Gamma, B' \supset H \vdash B_1 \vee B_2} \supset\text{L}.$$

Since H is also a Harrop formula, then the inductive assumption applies to the proof Ξ_1: Hence, there is a proof Ξ_2 of $\Gamma, H \vdash B_i$ for some i. Thus, the desired proof is

$$\cfrac{\cfrac{\begin{array}{cc} \Xi_0 & \Xi_2 \\ \Gamma \vdash B' & \Gamma, H \vdash B_i \end{array}}{\Gamma, B' \supset H \vdash B_i} \supset\text{L}}{\Gamma, B' \supset H \vdash B_1 \vee B_2} \vee\text{R}.$$

The case for when B is existentially quantified is similar. Uniform proofs are not complete for sequents that are constrained to contain only Harrop formulas. For example, both sequents

$$\cdot \vdash (p \vee q) \supset (q \vee p) \quad \text{and} \quad ((p \vee q) \supset (q \vee p)) \supset a \vdash a$$

have **I**-proofs but no uniform proofs.

Solution to Exercise 5.16 (page 75). Let $\mathcal{P}$ be the multiset $\{D_0, \ldots, D_n\}$ and let Γ be a multiset that contains $\mathcal{P}$. Applying $\supset$L in a focused manner i times to the assumption D_i in the sequent $\Gamma \vdash A$ yields a derivation of the form

$$\cfrac{\Gamma \vdash a_0 \quad \cdots \quad \Gamma \vdash a_{i-1} \quad \Gamma, a_i \vdash A}{\Gamma \vdash A}.$$

Backchaining, as in $\Downarrow$ *fohh*-proofs, requires that the initial rule proves the right-most premise. In that case, A is a_i, and this derivation justifies the following backchaining inference rule.

$$\frac{\Gamma \vdash a_0 \quad \cdots \quad \Gamma \vdash a_{i-1}}{\Gamma \vdash a_i} \text{BC}_i.$$

As this exercise suggests, forward chaining requires that all the premises except for the right-most premise are the initial rule. In that case, Γ is of the form $\Gamma' \cup \{a_0, \ldots, a_{i-1}\}$, and this derivation justifies the following forward-chaining inference rule.

$$\frac{\Gamma', a_0, \ldots, a_i \vdash A}{\Gamma', a_0, \ldots, a_{i-1} \vdash A} \text{FC}_i.$$

There is one proof using the BC_i inference rules of the sequent $\mathcal{P} \vdash a_n$, and that proof contains 2^n occurrences of backchaining inference rules (and *init*). In contrast, there are many proofs using the FC_i inference rules of the sequent $\mathcal{P} \vdash a_n$ and the shortest one contains n occurrences of the forward-chaining inference rules.

Solution to Exercise 5.43 (page 102). Assume that there is a *fohh* program $\mathcal{P}$ that satisfies the following specification: For every nonempty set $N = \{n_1, \ldots, n_k\}$, we have $\mathcal{A}(N), \mathcal{P} \vdash_I \text{maxa } n$ if and only if n is the maximum of the set $\{n_1, \ldots, n_k\}$. Let N be the set containing the numerals for 0 and 1. Thus, $\mathcal{A}(N)$ is the set of atoms $\{a\ z, a\ (s\ z)\}$. Let $\mathcal{A}'$ be the set of atoms $\{a\ z, a\ (s\ z), a\ (s\ (s\ z))\}$. Thus, it must be the case that $\mathcal{A}(N), \mathcal{P} \vdash_I \text{maxa } (s\ z)$. By the monotonicity property of intuitionistic provability, $\mathcal{A}', \mathcal{P} \vdash_I \text{maxa } (s\ z)$, but this is a contradiction to the choice of $\mathcal{P}$, since $(s\ z)$ is not the maximum of the set of numbers encoded in $\mathcal{A}'$.

Solution to Exercise 5.44 (page 102). Assume that a logic program defines the notconnected predicate. Using the graph described in Figure 5.5, it must be the case that notconnected a e is provable. But if we add adj a e to the logic program, the monotonicity property must force notconnected a e to be provable in that extended program. But this contradicts the assumption about notconnected.

Solution to Exercise 5.46 (page 104). Assume there is a *fohh*-logic specifications P over the signature Σ_P. Also, assume that this signature contains the constants $a : i$ and $f : i \to i \to i$, and that the constants $d : i$ and $e : i$ are not declared in Σ_P. By the specification of *subAll*, it is the case that

$$d : i, e : i, \Sigma_S \vdash_I \text{subAll } d\ a\ (f\ d\ e)\ (f\ a\ e).$$

SOLUTIONS TO SELECTED PROBLEMS 291

By Proposition 5.25 and using the substitution of e for d, we know that

$$e : i, \Sigma_S \vdash_l subAll\ e\ a\ (f\ e\ e)\ (f\ a\ e).$$

But this contradicts the specification for *subAll*.

Solution to Exercise 6.2 (page 116). Assume there is a cut-free proof of

$$\vdash p \otimes q,\ p^\perp \otimes q,\ p \otimes q^\perp,\ p^\perp \otimes q^\perp.$$

Because of the symmetry of replacing p with $p^\perp$ and q with $q^\perp$, we can assume, without loss of generality, that this sequent is proved by the following occurrence of the $\otimes R$ rule.

$$\frac{\vdash p, \Delta \qquad \vdash q, \Delta'}{\vdash p \otimes q,\ p^\perp \otimes q,\ p \otimes q^\perp,\ p^\perp \otimes q^\perp} \otimes R.$$

Here, Δ and Δ' are multisets whose union is the three-element multiset $p^\perp \otimes q,\ p \otimes q^\perp,\ p^\perp \otimes q^\perp$. Note first that neither Δ nor Δ' can be empty. Note also that neither Δ nor Δ' can be a singleton: A simple case analysis shows that if one of these multisets is a singleton, then the corresponding premise is not provable. We have reached a contradiction when we note that every possible partition of three elements must contain either an empty or singleton partition.

Solution to Exercise 6.4 (page 117). Let prefix π be one of the following seven prefixes: empty, !, ?, !?, ?!, !?!, and ?!?. It is easy to show the equivalence $\pi \pi B \equiv \pi B$ for all formulas B. For example, the case for $\pi = ?!$ leads to proving the following two entailments.

$$\frac{\dfrac{\overline{?!B \vdash ?!B}\ init}{\dfrac{!?!B \vdash ?!B}\ !D}}{?!?!B \vdash ?!B}\ ?L \qquad \frac{\dfrac{\dfrac{\overline{!B \vdash !B}\ init}{\dfrac{!B \vdash ?!B}\ ?D}}{\dfrac{!B \vdash !?!B}\ !R}}{\dfrac{!B \vdash ?!?!B}{?!B \vdash ?!?!B}\ ?D}\ ?L.$$

In the case that $\pi = !?!$, similar proofs can be given, although the following chain of equivalences

$$!?\ !!\ ?!\ B \equiv !\ ?!?!\ B \equiv !?!\ B$$

is more convincing (rewriting subformulas by logically equivalent subformulas is justified using the cut-elimination result: See Section 4.3.3) Assuming that the equivalences associated with !, ?, !?, and ?! have already been proved, we can now prove that any prefix π that has length 4 or more must be equivalence to one of shorter length. Thus π can be written as $b_1 b_2 b_3 b_4 \pi'$ where the b_i's are either ! or ?. These first four positions must alternate between these two flavors of exponentials since otherwise they must contain either !! or ?? (which can be shortened). Thus, π must be either $!?!?\pi'$ or $?!?!\pi'$. In the first case, we repeat !?, and in the second case, we repeat ?!. In either case, these repeated patterns can be shortened.

Solution to Exercise 6.20 (page 133). We use the six linear logic connectives $\{\top, \&, \bot, \multimap, \Rightarrow, \forall\}$ to define the remaining connectives.

$$B^\bot \equiv B \multimap \bot \quad 0 \equiv \top \multimap \bot \quad 1 \equiv \bot \multimap \bot \quad B \bindnasrepma C \equiv (B \multimap \bot) \multimap C$$

$$B \oplus C \equiv ((B \multimap \bot) \& (C \multimap \bot)) \multimap \bot \quad B \otimes C \equiv (B \multimap C \multimap \bot) \multimap \bot$$

$$\exists x.B \equiv (\forall x.(B \multimap \bot)) \multimap \bot$$

$$!B \equiv (B \Rightarrow \bot) \multimap \bot \quad ?B \equiv (B \multimap \bot) \Rightarrow \bot.$$

Solution to Exercise 6.26 (page 137). Assume that there is a $\Downarrow \mathcal{L}_2$ proof of a sequent with an empty right side and with only $\mathcal{L}_1$ formulas on the left side. Let Ξ be such a proof of minimal height. Consider the last inference rule of Ξ. This last inference rule cannot be a right-introduction rule since these require a non-empty right side. Similarly, the last rule is not the $decide_l$ or the $decide\,!$ rule since these would yield a premise with an empty right side with a shorter proof. Thus, the endsequent of Ξ must be of the form $\Sigma :: \Psi; \Gamma \Downarrow B \vdash \cdot;\cdot$. However, a check of all possible left-introduction rules ($\bot L$, $\bindnasrepma L$, and $?L$ are not possible) yields at least one premise with an empty right side and shorter proof. This contradicts the choice of Ξ.

Solution to Exercise 6.27 (page 137). We proceed by induction on the structure of the $\Downarrow \mathcal{L}_2$ proof Ξ. By considering all the possible last inference rules of Ξ, we need to show that a single-conclusion sequent in the conclusion will guarantee that all premises are also single conclusion: The inductive hypothesis then completes the proof. The only case that is not immediate is the case for the $\multimap L$ rule, namely,

$$\frac{\Sigma :: \Psi; \Gamma_1 \vdash \mathcal{A}_1, B; \Upsilon \quad \Sigma :: \Psi; \Gamma_2 \Downarrow C \vdash \mathcal{A}_2; \Upsilon}{\Sigma :: \Psi; \Gamma_1, \Gamma_2 \Downarrow B \multimap C \vdash \mathcal{A}_1, \mathcal{A}_2; \Upsilon} \multimap L$$

and where $\mathcal{A}_1 \cup \mathcal{A}_2$ is a singleton multiset. By Exercise 6.26, we know that $\mathcal{A}_2$ is not empty. As a result, $\mathcal{A}_1$ must be empty. Thus, both premises of this inference rule are single-conclusion sequents.

Solution to Exercise 8.1 (page 172). Let Γ be the multiset of atoms $\{A_1, \ldots, A_n\}$ ($n \geq 0$), and let P be $B_1 \;\mathfrak{P}\; \cdots \;\mathfrak{P}\; B_m$ where $B_1, \ldots, B_m$ ($m \geq 0$) are also atomic formulas. We can prove by induction on n that $P \vdash \Gamma$ is provable in linear logic if and only if $n = m$ and the two multisets $\{A_1, \ldots, A_n\}$ and $\{B_1, \ldots, B_m\}$ are equal. If $n = 0$, this case is immediate since P is $\bot$ and the provability of the sequent $\bot \vdash \Gamma$ implies that Γ is empty. If $n = 1$, this case reduces to simply showing that the sequent $B_1 \;\mathfrak{P}\; \cdots \;\mathfrak{P}\; B_m \vdash A_1$ is provable if and only if $m = 1$ and A_1 and B_1 are equal. Now, assume that $n > 1$ and that P is $(A_1 \;\mathfrak{P}\; \cdots \;\mathfrak{P}\; A_i) \;\mathfrak{P}\; (A_{i+1} \;\mathfrak{P}\; \cdots \;\mathfrak{P}\; A_n)$. If $P \vdash \Gamma$ is provable then there is a multiset partition of Γ into Γ_1 and Γ_2 such that both sequents $A_1 \;\mathfrak{P}\; \cdots \;\mathfrak{P}\; A_i \vdash \Gamma_1$ and $A_{i+1} \;\mathfrak{P}\; \cdots \;\mathfrak{P}\; A_n \vdash \Gamma_2$ are provable. By induction, we have that Γ_1 is $\{A_1, \ldots, A_i\}$ and Γ_2 is $\{A_{i+1}, \ldots, A_n\}$ and, hence, Γ is $\{A_1, \ldots, A_n\}$. For the converse, it is easy to construct a proof of $A_1 \;\mathfrak{P}\; \cdots \;\mathfrak{P}\; A_n \vdash A_1, \ldots, A_n$.

Solution to Exercise 8.4 (page 177). Let the program $\mathcal{P}$ be the result of adding the declarations and clauses for leq from Figure 5.3 to the following declarations and clauses.

```
type maxa     nat -> o.

maxa M :- a M.
maxa M :- a N, a P, leq N P, (a P -o maxa M).
```

Solution to Exercise 8.5 (page 177). Let the program $\mathcal{P}$ be the result of adding the declarations and clauses for sum from Figure 5.3 to the following declarations and clauses.

```
type sumall    nat -> o.

sumall M :- a M.
sumall M :- a N, a P, sum N P S, (a S -o sumall M).
```

Solution to Exercise 9.1 (page 190). Below are two $\mathbf{I}^\omega$-proofs that show that $\forall_o p.p$ is logically equivalent to f in intuitionistic logic.

$$\cfrac{\cfrac{\overline{}\;\mathrm{fL}}{f \vdash f}}{\forall_o p.p \vdash f}\;\forall\mathrm{L} \qquad \cfrac{\overline{}}{f \vdash \forall_o p.p}\;\mathrm{fL}.$$

Solution to Exercise 9.3 (page 190). The proofs of cases related to reflectivity and transitivity are straightforward. In the proof related to symmetry, if the ∀R rule introduces the eigenvariable $p : i \to o$, then use the term $\lambda x.px \supset pt$ in the ∀L rule.

Solution to Exercise 9.15 (page 202). The proof of $\Sigma :: E_2; \cdot \vdash E_1; \cdot$ is straightforward since the instantiation needed for the ∀L rule is simple.

$$
\cfrac{
  \cfrac{
    \cfrac{
      \cfrac{
        \cfrac{
          \cfrac{\overline{\Sigma, p :: E_2, pt; \cdot \Downarrow pt \vdash pt; \cdot}\ init}{\Sigma, p :: E_2, pt; \cdot \vdash pt; \cdot}\ decide!
          \quad
          \cfrac{\overline{\Sigma, p :: E_2, pt; \cdot \Downarrow ps \vdash ps; \cdot}\ init}{}
        }{\Sigma, p :: E_2, pt; \cdot \Downarrow pt \multimap ps \vdash ps; \cdot}\ \multimap L
      }{\Sigma, p :: E_2, pt; \cdot \Downarrow \forall P.(Pt \multimap Ps) \vdash ps; \cdot}\ \forall L
    }{\Sigma, p :: E_2, pt; \cdot \vdash ps; \cdot}\ decide!
  }{\Sigma :: E_2; \cdot \vdash \forall P.(Pt \Rightarrow Ps); \cdot}\ \forall L, \Rightarrow R
$$

The proof of the converse requires using the ∀L rule with the slightly more complex term $\lambda w.pt \multimap pw$. Most of this proof is below.

$$
\cfrac{
  \cfrac{
    \cfrac{
      \cfrac{
        \cfrac{\Sigma, p :: E_1; \cdot \vdash pt \multimap pt; \cdot \quad \Sigma, p :: E_1; pt \vdash pt; \cdot \quad \cfrac{\overline{\Sigma, p :: E_1; \cdot \Downarrow ps \vdash ps; \cdot}\ init}{}}{\Sigma, p :: E_1; pt \Downarrow (pt \multimap pt) \Rightarrow pt \multimap ps \vdash ps; \cdot}\ \Rightarrow L, \multimap L
      }{\Sigma, p :: E_1; pt \Downarrow \forall P.(Pt \Rightarrow Ps) \vdash ps; \cdot}\ \forall L
    }{\Sigma, p :: E_1; pt \vdash ps; \cdot}\ decide!
  }{\Sigma :: E_1; \cdot \vdash \forall P.(Pt \multimap Ps); \cdot}\ \forall L, \multimap R
$$

Solution to Exercise 10.1 (page 217). Let $\star : o$ be a non-logical constant, let Γ be the context containing $\forall x.(x \multimap \star \,\mathrm{⅋}\, x)$, and let Γ' be the context containing $\bot \multimap \star$. The required two proofs are below.

$$
\cfrac{
  \cfrac{
    \cfrac{
      \cfrac{
        \cfrac{
          \cfrac{
            \cfrac{\overline{\cdot :: \Gamma; \cdot \Downarrow \bot \vdash \cdot; \cdot}}{\cdot :: \Gamma; \bot \vdash \cdot; \cdot}
          }{\cdot :: \Gamma; \bot \vdash \bot; \cdot}
          \quad
          \cfrac{\cdot :: \Gamma; \cdot \Downarrow \star \vdash \star; \cdot \quad \cdot :: \Gamma; \cdot \Downarrow \bot \vdash \cdot; \cdot}{\cdot :: \Gamma; \cdot \Downarrow \star \,\mathrm{⅋}\, \bot \vdash \star; \cdot}
        }{\cdot :: \Gamma; \bot \Downarrow \bot \multimap \star \,\mathrm{⅋}\, \bot \vdash \star; \cdot}
      }{\cdot :: \Gamma; \bot \Downarrow \forall x.(x \multimap \star \,\mathrm{⅋}\, x) \vdash \star; \cdot}
    }{\cdot :: \Gamma; \bot \vdash \star; \cdot}
  }{\cdot :: \Gamma; \cdot \vdash \bot \multimap \star; \cdot}
$$

$$\frac{\overline{x :: \Gamma'; \cdot \Downarrow x \vdash x; \cdot}}{\frac{x :: \Gamma'; x \vdash x; \cdot}{\frac{x :: \Gamma'; x \vdash \bot, x; \cdot \quad \overline{x :: \Gamma'; \cdot \Downarrow \star \vdash \star; \cdot}}{\frac{x :: \Gamma'; x \Downarrow \bot \multimap \star \vdash \star, x; \cdot}{\frac{x :: \Gamma'; x \vdash \star, x; \cdot}{\cdot :: \Gamma'; \cdot \vdash \forall x.(x \multimap \star \,\mathscr{B}\, x); \cdot}}}}$$

Solution to Exercise 11.2 (page 236). Applying the mapping

$$\begin{aligned}
\text{nil} &\mapsto \bot \\
:: &\mapsto \lambda x \lambda y.\, item\, x \,\mathscr{B}\, y \\
\text{rev} &\mapsto \lambda x \lambda y \lambda z.\, (x \,\mathscr{B}\, y) \multimap z \\
\text{reverse} &\mapsto \lambda x \lambda y.\, x \multimap y
\end{aligned}$$

to the three Horn clauses in this exercise yields the following linear logic formulas, all of which are easily seen as provable in linear logic.

$$\forall L, K\, (L \,\mathscr{B}\, \bot \multimap K) \Rightarrow (L \multimap K)$$
$$\forall L\, (\bot \,\mathscr{B}\, L \multimap L)$$
$$\forall X, L, M, N\, (M \,\mathscr{B}\, (item\, X \,\mathscr{B}\, N) \multimap L) \Rightarrow ((item\, X \,\mathscr{B}\, M) \,\mathscr{B}\, N \multimap L).$$

Solution to Exercise 12.3 (page 256). A proof that the first implies the second contains a subproof of the sequent

$$\forall k.\mathrm{N}\,(k\, m') \vdash \forall k.\mathrm{N}\,(k\, m),$$

and this is proved by introducing an eigenvariable, say c, on the right and the term $\lambda w.(c\, m)$ on the left.

References

Abramsky, Samson. Computational interpretations of linear logic. *Theoretical Computer Science*, 111:3–57, 1993. (Cited on page 3.)

Aiken, Alexander. Set constraints: Results, applications, and future directions. In *PPCP94: Principles and Practice of Constraint Programming*, 874 in LNCS, pages 171–179, 1994. (Cited on page 244.)

Andreoli, Jean-Marc and R. Pareschi. Linear objects: Logical processes with built-in inheritance. *New Generation Computing*, 9(3–4):445–473, 1991a. (Cited on page 185.)

Andreoli, Jean-Marc and R. Pareschi. Communication as fair distribution of knowledge. In Andreas Paepcke, editor, *Proceedings of OOPSLA 91*, pages 212–229, 1991b. (Cited on page 185.)

Andreoli, Jean-Marc. *Proposal for a Synthesis of Logic and Object-Oriented Programming Paradigms*. PhD thesis, University of Paris VI, 1990. (Cited on page 141.)

Andreoli, Jean-Marc. Logic programming with focusing proofs in linear logic. *Journal of Logic and Computation*, 2(3):297–347, 1992. doi: 10.1093/logcom/2.3.297. (Cited on pages 32, 105, 119, 141, 169, and 260.)

Andrews, Peter B. Resolution in type theory. *Journal of Symbolic Logic*, 36:414–432, 1971. (Cited on page 214.)

Andrews, Peter B. General models and extensionality. *Journal of Symbolic Logic*, 37:395–397, 1972. (Cited on page 214.)

Andrews, Peter B. Provability in elementary type theory. *Zeitschrift fur Mathematische Logic und Grundlagen der Mathematik*, 20:411–418, 1974. (Cited on page 9.)

Andrews, Peter B. *An Introduction to Mathematical Logic and Type Theory: To Truth through Proof*. Academic Press, 1986. (Cited on pages 19 and 213.)

Andrews, Peter B., Frank Pfenning, Sunil Issar, and C. P. Klapper. The TPS theorem proving system. In Jörg H. Siekmann, editor, *Eighth International Conference on Automated Deduction*, volume 230 of *LNCS*, pages 663–664. Springer, July 1986. (Cited on page 213.)

Andrews, Peter B., Matthew Bishop, Sunil Issar, Dan Nesmith, Frank Pfenning, and Hongwei Xi. TPS: A theorem proving system for classical type theory. *Journal of Automated Reasoning*, 16(3):321–353, 1996. (Cited on page 213.)

Andrews, Peter B., Matthew Bishop, and Chad E. Brown. TPS: A theorem proving system for type theory. In David McAllester, editor, *Proceedings of the 17th International Conference on Automated Deduction*, number 1831 in LNAI, pages 164–169, Pittsburgh, USA, 2000. Springer. (Cited on page 213.)

Appel, Andrew W. and Amy P. Felty. Polymorphic lemmas and definitions in λProlog and Twelf. *Theory and Practice of Logic Programming*, 4(1–2):1–39, 2004. doi: 10.1017/S1471068403001698. (Cited on page 19.)

Apt, K. R. and M. H. van Emden. Contributions to the theory of logic programming. *Journal of the ACM*, 29(3):841–862, 1982. (Cited on pages 8 and 104.)

Asperti, A., G.-L. Ferrari, and R. Gorrieri. Implicative formulae in the 'proof as computations' analogy. In Frances E. Allen, editor, *Seventeenth ACM Symposium on Principles of Programming Languages*, pages 59–71. ACM, January 1990. (Cited on page 185.)

Baaz, Matthias and Alexander Leitsch. Cut-elimination and redundancy-elimination by resolution. *Journal of Symbolic Computation*, 29(2):149–176, 2000. (Cited on page 214.)

Baelde, David. Least and greatest fixed points in linear logic. *ACM Trans. on Computational Logic*, 13(1):2:1–2:44, April 2012. doi: 10.1145/2071368.2071370. (Cited on page 141.)

Baelde, David and Dale Miller. Least and greatest fixed points in linear logic. In N. Dershowitz and A. Voronkov, editors, *International Conference on Logic for Programming and Automated Reasoning (LPAR)*, volume 4790 of *LNCS*, pages 92–106, 2007. doi: 10.1007/978-3-540-75560-9_9. (Cited on page 141.)

Baelde, David, Dale Miller, and Zachary Snow. Focused inductive theorem proving. In J. Giesl and R. Hähnle, editors, *Fifth International Joint Conference on Automated Reasoning*, number 6173 in LNCS, pages 278–292, 2010. doi: 10.1007/978-3-642-14203-1_24. (Cited on page 60.)

Baelde, David, Kaustuv Chaudhuri, Andrew Gacek, Dale Miller, Gopalan Nadathur, Alwen Tiu, and Yuting Wang. Abella: A system for reasoning about relational specifications. *Journal of Formalized Reasoning*, 7(2):1–89, 2014. doi: 10.6092/issn.1972-5787/4650. (Cited on pages 19 and 278.)

Banâtre, Jean-Pierre and Daniel Le Métayer. Programming by Multiset Transformation. *Communications of the ACM*, 36(1):98–111, January 1993. (Cited on pages 185 and 262.)

Banâtre, Jean-Pierre and Daniel Le Métayer. Gamma and the chemical reaction model: ten years after. In *Coordination Programming: Mechanisms, Models and Semantics*, pages 3–41. World Scientific Publishing, IC Press, 1996. (Cited on page 185.)

Barendregt, Henk. *The Lambda Calculus: Its Syntax and Semantics*, volume 103 of *Studies in Logic and the Foundations of Mathematics*. Elsevier, 1984. (Cited on page 19.)

Barendregt, Henk, Wil Dekkers, and Richard Statman. *Lambda Calculus with Types*. Perspectives in Logic. Cambridge University Press, 2013. (Cited on page 19.)

Benzmüller, Christoph, C. E. Brown, and M. Kohlhase. Cut-simulation and impredicativity. *Logical Methods in Computer Science*, 5(1):1–21, 2009. doi: 10.2168/ LMCS-5(1:6)2009. (Cited on page 214.)

Benzmüller, Christoph and Peter Andrews. Churchs Type Theory. In Edward N. Zalta, editor, *The Stanford Encyclopedia of Philosophy*. Metaphysics Research Lab, Stanford University, summer 2019 edition, 2019. (Cited on page 7.)

Benzmüller, Christoph and Dale Miller. Automation of higher-order logic. In J. Siekmann, editor, *Computational Logic*, volume 9 of *Handbook of the History of Logic*, pages 215–254. North Holland, 2014. ISBN 978-0-444-51624-4. doi: 10.1016/B978-0-444-51624-4.50005-8. (Cited on page 214.)

Benzmüller, Christoph, Chad Brown, and Michael Kohlhase. Higher-order semantics and extensionality. *Journal of Symbolic Logic*, 69(4):1027–1088, 2004. doi: 10. 2178/jsl/1102022211. (Cited on page 214.)

Berry, G. and G. Boudol. The chemical abstract machine. *Theoretical Computer Science*, 96:217–248, 1992. (Cited on pages 185 and 262.)

Bimbó, Katalin. *Proof Theory: Sequent Calculi and Related Formalisms*. CRC Press, 2015. (Cited on pages 36 and 59.)

Bistarelli, Stefano, Iliano Cervesato, Gabriele Lenzini, and Fabio Martinelli. Relating multiset rewriting and process algebras for security protocol analysis. *Journal of Computer Security*, 13(1):3–47, 2005. (Cited on page 262.)

Bledsoe, W. W. A maximal method for set variables in automatic theorem-proving. In J. E. Hayes, Donald Michie, and L. I. Mikulich, editors, *Machine Intelligence 9*, pages 53–100. John Wiley & Sons, 1979. (Cited on page 214.)

Bledsoe, W. W. and Guohui Feng. SET-VAR. *Journal of Automated Reasoning*, 11: 293–314, 1993. (Cited on page 214.)

Bruscoli, Paola and Alessio Guglielmi. On structuring proof search for first order linear logic. *Theoretical Computer Science*, 360(1–3):42–76, 2006. doi: 10.1016/j.tcs. 2005.11.047. (Cited on page 169.)

Bugliesi, M., E. Lamma, and P. Mello. Modularity in logic programming. *Journal of Logic Programming*, 19/20:443–502, 1994. doi: 10.1016/0743-1066(94)90032-9. (Cited on page 106.)

Caires, Luís and Luis Monteiro. Higher-order polymorphic unification for logic programming. In P. Van Hentenryck, editor, *Logic Programming, 11th International Conference, S. Margherita Ligure, Italy*, pages 419–433. MIT Press, 1994. (Cited on page 19.)

Cervesato, Iliano and Mark-Oliver Stehr. Representing the MSR cryptoprotocol specification language in an extension of rewriting logic with dependent types. *Higher-Order Symbolic Computation*, 20:3–35, 2007. doi: 10.1007/s10990-007-9003-3. (Cited on page 260.)

Cervesato, Iliano, Joshua Hodas, and Frank Pfenning. Efficient resource management for linear logic proof search. In Roy Dyckhoff, Heinrich Herre, and Peter Schroeder-Heister, editors, *7th Workshop on Extensions to Logic Programming*, LNAI, pages 28–30, Leipzig, Germany, March 1996. Springer. (Cited on page 141.)

Cervesato, Iliano, Nancy A. Durgin, Patrick D. Lincoln, John C. Mitchell, and Andre Scedrov. A meta-notation for protocol analysis. In R. Gorrieri, editor, *Proceedings of the 12th IEEE Computer Security Foundations Workshop – CSFW'99*, pages 55–69, Mordano, Italy, 28–30 June 1999. IEEE Computer Society Press. (Cited on pages 252, 260, and 262.)

Cervesato, Iliano, Nancy A. Durgin, Patrick D. Lincoln, John C. Mitchell, and Andre Scedrov. Relating strands and multiset rewriting for security protocol analysis. In P. Syverson, editor, *13th IEEE Computer Security Foundations Workshop – CSFW'00*, pages 35–51, Cambridge, UK, 3–5 July 2000a. IEEE Computer Society Press. (Cited on page 260.)

Cervesato, Iliano, Joshua S. Hodas, and Frank Pfenning. Efficient resource management for linear logic proof search. *Theoretical Computer Science*, 232(1–2):133–163, 2000b. (Cited on page 141.)

Chaudhuri, Kaustuv. *The Focused Inverse Method for Linear Logic*. PhD thesis, Carnegie Mellon University, December 2006. Technical report CMU-CS-06-162. (Cited on page 170.)

Chaudhuri, Kaustuv. Encoding additives using multiplicatives and subexponentials. *Math. Structures in Computer Science*, 28(5):651–666, 2018. doi: 10.1017/S0960129516000293. (Cited on page 141.)

Chaudhuri, Kaustuv, Dale Miller, and Alexis Saurin. Canonical sequent proofs via multi-focusing. In G. Ausiello, J. Karhumäki, G. Mauri, and L. Ong, editors, *Fifth International Conference on Theoretical Computer Science*, volume 273 of *IFIP*, pages 383–396. Springer, September 2008a. doi: 10.1007/978-0-387-09680-3_26. (Cited on page 141.)

Chaudhuri, Kaustuv, Frank Pfenning, and Greg Price. A logical characterization of forward and backward chaining in the inverse method. *Journal of Automated Reasoning*, 40(2–3):133–177, 2008b. doi: 10.1007/s10817-007-9091-0. (Cited on page 170.)

Chaudhuri, Kaustuv, Stefan Hetzl, and Dale Miller. A multi-focused proof system isomorphic to expansion proofs. *Journal of Logic and Computation*, 26(2):577–603, 2016. doi: 10.1093/logcom/exu030. (Cited on page 141.)

Chirimar, Jawahar. *Proof Theoretic Approach to Specification Languages*. PhD thesis, University of Pennsylvania, February 1995. URL www.lix.polytechnique.fr/Labo/Dale.Miller/chirimar/phd.pdf. (Cited on pages 276 and 279.)

Church, Alonzo. An unsolvable problem of elementary number theory. *American Journal of Mathematics*, 58:354–363, 1936. (Cited on page 60.)

Church, Alonzo. A formulation of the simple theory of types. *Journal of Symbolic Logic*, 5:56–68, 1940. doi: 10.2307/2266170. (Cited on pages 1, 2, 9, 12, 14, 213, and 214.)

Clark, K. L. Negation as failure. In J. Gallaire and J. Minker, editors, *Logic and Data Bases*, pages 293–322. Plenum Press, New York, 1978. doi: 10.1007/978-1-4684-3384-5_11. (Cited on page 106.)

Clement, D., J. Despeyroux, T. Despeyroux, L. Hascoet, and G. Kahn. Natural semantics on the computer. In *K. Fuchi and M. Nivat, editors, Proceedings of the France-Japan AI and CS Symposium, ICOT, Japan*, pages 49–89, 1986. Also Technical Memorandum PL-86-6 Information Processing Society of Japan and Rapport de recherche #0416, INRIA. (Cited on page 278.)

Cook, Stephen A. and Robert A. Reckhow. The relative efficiency of propositional proof systems. *Journal of Symbolic Logic*, 44(1):36–50, 1979. (Cited on page 60.)

Curien, P.-L. An abstract framework for environment machines. *Theoretical Computer Science*, 82(2):389–402, 1991. doi: https://doi.org/10.1016/0304-3975(91)90230-Y. (Cited on page 271.)

Curry, Haskell. The inconsistency of certain formal logics. *Journal of Symbolic Logic*, 7:115–117, 1942. (Cited on page 12.)

Czerwiński, Wojciech, Sławomir Lasota, Ranko Lazić, Jérôme Leroux, and Filip Mazowiecki. The reachability problem for Petri nets is not elementary. *Journal of the ACM*, 68(1), December 2020. doi: 10.1145/3422822. (Cited on page 242.)

Danos, Vincent, Jean-Baptiste Joinet, and Harold Schellinx. The structure of exponentials: Uncovering the dynamics of linear logic proofs. In Georg Gottlob, Alexander Leitsch, and Daniele Mundici, editors, *Kurt Gödel Colloquium*, volume 713 of *LNCS*, pages 159–171. Springer, 1993. (Cited on page 141.)

Danos, Vincent, Jean-Baptiste Joinet, and Harold Schellinx. A new deconstructive logic: Linear logic. *Journal of Symbolic Logic*, 62(3):755–807, 1997. doi: 10.2307/2275572. (Cited on page 140.)

de Bruijn, Nicolaas Govert. Lambda calculus notation with nameless dummies, a tool for automatic formula manipulation, with an application to the Church-Rosser theorem. *Indagationes Mathematicae*, 34(5):381–392, 1972. doi: 10.1016/1385-7258(72)90034-0. (Cited on page 271.)

Delande, Olivier and Dale Miller. A neutral approach to proof and refutation in MALL. In F. Pfenning, editor, *Twenty-Third Symposium on Logic in Computer Science*, pages 498–508. IEEE Computer Society Press, 2008. doi: 10.1016/j.apal.2009.07.017. (Cited on page 141.)

Delzanno, Giorgio. An overview of MSR(C): A CLP-based framework for the symbolic verification of parameterized concurrent systems. *Electronic Notes in Theoretical Computer Science*, 76:65–82, 2002. doi: 10.1016/S1571-0661(04)80786-2. (Cited on page 185.)

Denecker, Marc, Maurice Bruynooghe, and Victor Marek. Logic programming revisited: Logic programs as inductive definitions. *ACM Transactions on Computational Logic*, 2(4):623–654, October 2001. doi: 10.1145/383779.383789. (Cited on page 106.)

Despeyroux, Jöelle. Proof of translation in natural semantics. In Albert R. Meyer, editor, *First Symposium on Logic in Computer Science*, pages 193–205, Cambridge, MA, June 1986. IEEE. (Cited on page 278.)

Di Cosmo, Roberto and Dale Miller. Linear logic. In Edward N. Zalta, editor, *The Stanford Encyclopedia of Philosophy*. Metaphysics Research Lab, Stanford University, summer 2019 edition, 2019. (Cited on page 7.)

Dunchev, Cvetan, Ferruccio Guidi, Claudio Sacerdoti Coen, and Enrico Tassi. ELPI: Fast, embeddable, λProlog interpreter. In Martin Davis, Ansgar Fehnker,

Annabelle McIver, and Andrei Voronkov, editors, *Logic for Programming, Artificial Intelligence, and Reasoning, LPAR-20*, volume 9450 of *LNCS*, pages 460–468. Springer, 2015. doi: 10.1007/978-3-662-48899-7_32. (Cited on page 105.)

Durgin, Nancy A., Patrick Lincoln, John C. Mitchell, and Andre Scedrov. Multiset rewriting and the complexity of bounded security protocols. *Journal of Computer Security*, 12(2):247–311, 2004. doi: 10.3233/JCS-2004-12203. (Cited on pages 260 and 262.)

Dyckhoff, Roy. Contraction-free sequent calculi for intuitionistic logic. *Journal of Symbolic Logic*, 57(3):795–807, September 1992. doi: 10.2307/2275431. (Cited on page 180.)

van Emden, Maarten H. and Robert A. Kowalski. The semantics of predicate logic as a programming language. *Journal of the ACM*, 23(4):733–742, 1976. (Cited on pages 8 and 104.)

Engburg, U. and G. Winskel. Petri nets and models of linear logic. In A. Arnold, editor, *CAAP'90*, volume 431 of *LNCS*, pages 147–161. Springer, 1990. (Cited on page 185.)

Esparza, Javier and Mogens Nielsen. Decidability issues for Petri Nets: A survey. *Bulletin of the EATCS*, 52:244–262, 1994. (Cited on page 242.)

Farmer, William M. *Simple Type Theory: A Practical Logic for Expressing and Reasoning about Mathematical Ideas*. Springer Nature, 2023. (Cited on pages 19 and 213.)

Felty, Amy. *Specifying and Implementing Theorem Provers in a Higher-Order Logic Programming Language*. PhD thesis, University of Pennsylvania, August 1989. (Cited on page 204.)

Felty, Amy. Implementing tactics and tacticals in a higher-order logic programming language. *Journal of Automated Reasoning*, 11(1):43–81, August 1993. doi: 10.1007/BF00881900. (Cited on pages 204 and 205.)

Felty, Amy. The calculus of constructions as a framework for proof search with set variable instantiation. *Theoretical Computer Science*, 232(1-2):187–229, February 2000. (Cited on page 214.)

Felty, Amy and Dale Miller. Specifying theorem provers in a higher-order logic programming language. In Ewing Lusk and Ross Overbeck, editors, *Ninth International Conference on Automated Deduction*, number 310 in LNCS, pages 61–80, Argonne, IL, May 1988. Springer. doi: 10.1007/BFb0012823. (Cited on page 204.)

Felty, Amy, Carlos Olarte, and Bruno Xavier. A focused linear logical framework and its application to metatheory of object logics. *Mathematical Structures in Computer Science*, 2021. doi: 10.1017/S0960129521000323. (Cited on pages 171 and 186.)

Fitting, Melvin C. *Intuitionistic Logic Model Theory and Forcing*. North-Holland, 1969. (Cited on page 42.)

Gabbay, Dov M. N-Prolog: An extension of Prolog with hypothetical implication II: Logical foundations, and negation as failure. *Journal of Logic Programming*, 2(4): 251–283, December 1985. (Cited on page 44.)

Gabbay, Dov M. and Nicola Olivetti. *Goal-Directed Proof Theory*, volume 21 of *Applied Logic Series*. Kluwer Academic Publishers, August 2000. (Cited on page 105.)

Gallier, Jean H. *Logic for Computer Science: Foundations of Automatic Theorem Proving*. Harper & Row, 1986. (Cited on pages 8, 36, 59, and 105.)

Gallier, Jean H. On Girard's "candidats de reductibilité". In P. Odifreddi, editor, *Logic and Computer Science*, volume 31 of *APIC Studies in Data Processing*, pages 91–122. Academic Press, 1990. (Cited on page 188.)

Gehlot, Vijay and Carl Gunter. Normal process representatives. In John C. Mitchell, editor, *5th Symposium on Logic in Computer Science*, pages 200–207, Philadelphia, Pennsylvania, June 1990. IEEE Computer Society Press. doi: 10.1109/LICS.1990.113746. (Cited on page 185.)

Gentzen, Gerhard. Investigations into logical deduction. In M. E. Szabo, editor, *The Collected Papers of Gerhard Gentzen*, pages 68–131. North-Holland, Amsterdam, 1935. doi: 10.1007/BF01201353. Translation of articles that appeared in 1934-35. Collected papers appeared in 1969. (Cited on pages 2, 17, 19, 26, 36, 38, 42, 49, 59, 108, and 183.)

Girard, Jean-Yves. *Interprétation fonctionnelle et élimination des coupures dans l'arithmétique d'ordre supérieur*. PhD thesis, Universit Paris VII, 1972. (Cited on pages 188 and 200.)

Girard, Jean-Yves. Linear logic. *Theoretical Computer Science*, 50(1):1–102, 1987. doi: 10.1016/0304-3975(87)90045-4. (Cited on pages 2, 32, 127, 140, and 141.)

Girard, Jean-Yves. A fixpoint theorem in linear logic. An email posting to linear@cs.stanford.edu archived at www.seas.upenn.edu/~sweirich/types/archive/1992/msg00030.html, February 1992. (Cited on pages 106, 142, and 286.)

Girard, Jean-Yves. On the unity of logic. *Annals of Pure and Applied Logic*, 59:201–217, 1993. doi: 10.1016/0168-0072(93)90093-S. (Cited on page 141.)

Girard, Jean-Yves, Paul Taylor, and Yves Lafont. *Proofs and Types*. Cambridge University Press, 1989. (Cited on pages 36, 59, 140, and 188.)

Gödel, Kurt. Zur intuitionistischen arithmetik und zahlentheorie. *Ergebnisse eines Mathematischen Kolloquiums*, pages 34–38, 1932. English translation in *The Undecidable* (M. Davis, ed.) 1965, 75–81. (Cited on page 60.)

Gordon, Michael J., Arthur J. Milner, and Christopher P. Wadsworth. *Edinburgh LCF: A Mechanised Logic of Computation*, volume 78 of *LNCS*. Springer, 1979. doi: 10.1007/3-540-09724-4. (Cited on page 204.)

Gordon, Michael J. From LCF to HOL: A short history. In Gordon D. Plotkin, Colin Stirling, and Mads Tofte, editors, *Proof, Language, and Interaction: Essays in Honour of Robin Milner*, pages 169–186. MIT Press, 2000. (Cited on page 18.)

Grishin, Vyacheslav Nikolaevich. Predicate and set-theoretic calculi based on logic without contractions. *Izvestiya Rossiiskoi Akademii Nauk. Seriya Matematicheskaya*, 45(1):47–68, 1981. (Cited on page 142.)

Guglielmi, Alessio. *Abstract Logic Programming in Linear Logic: Independence and Causality in a First Order Calculus*. PhD thesis, Università di Pisa, 1996. (Cited on page 169.)

Guglielmi, Alessio. A system of interaction and structure. *ACM Transactions on Computational Logic*, 8(1):1–64, January 2007. doi: 10.1145/1182613.1182614. (Cited on pages 59 and 120.)

Hallnäs, Lars and Peter Schroeder-Heister. A proof-theoretic approach to logic programming. II. Programs as definitions. *Journal of Logic and Computation*, 1(5): 635–660, October 1991. doi: 10.1093/logcom/1.5.635. (Cited on page 60.)

Hannan, John. Extended natural semantics. *Journal of Functional Programming*, 3(2): 123–152, April 1993. doi: 10.1017/S0956796800000666. (Cited on page 278.)

Hannan, John and Dale Miller. A meta-logic for functional programming. In Harvey Abramson and M. H. Rogers, editors, *Meta-Programming in Logic Programming*, Computer Science and Intelligent Systems, chapter 24, pages 453–476. MIT Press, 1989. ISBN 0-262-51047-2. Proceedings of the 1988 Workshop on Meta-Programming in Logic Programming, Bristol, UK. (Cited on page 278.)

Hannan, John and Dale Miller. From operational semantics to abstract machines. *Mathematical Structures in Computer Science*, 2(4):415–459, 1992. doi: 10.1017/S0960129500001559. (Cited on pages 270 and 279.)

Hannan, John and Frank Pfenning. Compiler verification in LF. In Andre Scedrov, editor, *Seventh Symposium on Logic in Computer Science*, Santa Cruz, California, June 1992. IEEE Computer Society Press. (Cited on page 278.)

Harland, James, David Pym, and Michael Winikoff. Programming in Lygon: An overview. In Martin Wirsing and Maurice Nivat, editors, *Proceedings of the Fifth International Conference on Algebraic Methodology and Software Technology*, number 1101 in LNCS, pages 391–405. Springer, July 1996. (Cited on page 185.)

Harper, Robert, Furio Honsell, and Gordon Plotkin. A framework for defining logics. *Journal of the ACM*, 40(1):143–184, 1993. doi: 10.1145/138027.138060. (Cited on pages 19 and 214.)

Harrop, R. Concerning formulas of the types $A \to B \vee C$, $A \to (Ex)B(x)$ in intuitionistic formal systems. *Journal of Symbolic Logic*, 25:27–32, 1960. (Cited on page 105.)

Heath, Quentin and Dale Miller. A proof theory for model checking. *J. of Automated Reasoning*, 63(4):857–885, 2019. doi: 10.1007/s10817-018-9475-3. (Cited on pages 99, 106, and 141.)

Hermenegildo, Manuel V., Germán Puebla, Francisco Bueno, and Pedro López-García. Integrated program debugging, verification, and optimization using abstract interpretation (and the Ciao system preprocessor). *Science of Computer Programming*, 58(1-2):115–140, 2005. (Cited on page 244.)

Hindley, R. The principal type-scheme of an object in combinatory logic. *Transactions of the American Mathematical Society*, 146:29–60, 1969. (Cited on page 278.)

Hodas, Joshua S. and Dale Miller. Logic programming in a fragment of intuitionistic linear logic: Extended abstract. In G. Kahn, editor, *Sixth Symposium on Logic in Computer Science*, pages 32–42, Amsterdam, July 1991. IEEE. (Cited on page 141.)

Hodas, Joshua S. and Dale Miller. Logic programming in a fragment of intuitionistic linear logic. *Information and Computation*, 110(2):327–365, 1994. doi: 10.1006/inco.1994.1036. (Cited on pages 141, 142, 171, and 185.)

Hodas, Joshua S., Kevin Watkins, Naoyuki Tamura, and Kyoung-Sun Kang. Efficient implementation of a linear logic programming language. In Joxan Jaffar, editor, *Proceedings of the 1998 Joint International Conference and Symposium on Logic Programming*, pages 145–159, 1998. (Cited on page 141.)

Hodas, Joshua S. *Logic Programming in Intuitionistic Linear Logic: Theory, Design, and Implementation*. PhD thesis, University of Pennsylvania, Department of Computer and Information Science, May 1994. (Cited on page 186.)

Hodas, Joshua S. A linear logic treatment of phrase structure grammars for unbounded dependencies. In Alain Lecomte, Françoise Lamarche, and Guy Perrier, editors, *Proceedings of the 2nd International Conference on Logical Aspects of Computational Linguistics (LACL-97)*, volume 1582 of *LNAI*, pages 160–179, Berlin, September 1999. Springer. (Cited on page 186.)

Hodas, Joshua S. and Naoyuki Tamura. lolliCop: A linear logic implementation of a lean connection-method theorem prover for first-order classical logic. In R. Goré, A. Leitsch, and T. Nipkow, editors, *Proceedings of IJCAR: International Joint Conference on Automated Reasoning*, number 2083 in LNCS, pages 670–684. Springer, 2001. (Cited on page 141.)

Hudelmaier, Jörg. Bounds on cut-elimination in intuitionistic propositional logic. *Archive for Mathematical Logic*, 31:331–353, 1992. (Cited on page 180.)

Huet, Gérard P. The undecidability of unification in third order logic. *Information and Control*, 22:257–267, 1973a. (Cited on page 227.)

Huet, Gérard P. A mechanization of type theory. In *Proceedings of the 3rd International Joint Conference on Artificial Intelligence*, pages 139–146. William Kaufmann, 1973b. (Cited on page 213.)

Huet, Gérard P. A unification algorithm for typed λ-calculus. *Theoretical Computer Science*, 1:27–57, 1975. doi: 10.1016/0304-3975(75)90011-0. (Cited on page 213.)

Hughes, Dominic J. D. Proofs without syntax. *Annals of Mathematics*, 143(3):1065–1076, November 2006. (Cited on page 21.)

Kahn, Gilles. Natural semantics. In Franz-Josef Brandenburg, Guy Vidal-Naquet, and Martin Wirsing, editors, *Proceedings of the Symposium on Theoretical Aspects of Computer Science*, volume 247 of *LNCS*, pages 22–39. Springer, March 1987. doi: 10.1007/BFb0039592. (Cited on page 262.)

Kamide, Norihiro. Rules of explosion and excluded middle: Constructing a unified single-succedent gentzen-style framework for classical, paradefinite, paraconsistent, and paracomplete logics. *Journal of Logic, Language and Information*, 2024. doi: 10.1007/s10849-024-09416-6. (Cited on page 57.)

Kanovich, Max I. Petri Nets, Horn programs, Linear Logic and vector games. *Annals of Pure and Applied Logic*, 75(1–2):107–135, 1995. doi: 10.1017/S0960129500001328. (Cited on page 185.)

Kanovich, Max I. Linear logic automata. *Annals of Pure and Applied Logic*, 78:147–188, 1996. doi: 10.1016/0168-0072(95)00035-6. (Cited on page 227.)

Kanovich, Max I. Multiset rewriting over Fibonacci and Tribonacci numbers. *Journal of Computer and System Sciences*, 80:1138–1151, 2014. doi: 10.1016/j.jcss.2014.04.006. (Cited on page 227.)

Ketonen, Oiva. Untersuchungen zum Prädikatenkalkul. *Annales Academiae Scientiarum Fennicae, series A, I. Mathematica-physica 23*, 1944. (Cited on page 60.)

Ketonen, Oiva. *Investigations into the Predicate Calculus*. College Publications, 2022. Ed. by S. Negri and J. von Plato. (Cited on page 60.)

Kleene, Stephen Cole. Permutability of inferences in Gentzen's calculi LK and LJ. *Memoirs of the American Mathematical Society*, 10:1–26, 1952. (Cited on page 36.)

Kobayashi, N., T. Shimizu, and A. Yonezawa. Distributed concurrent linear logic programming. *Theoretical Computer Science*, 227(1–2):185–220, 1999. (Cited on page 185.)

Kobayashi, Naoki and Akinori Yonezawa. Asynchronous communication model based on linear logic. *Formal Aspects of Computing*, 7(2):113–149, 1995. doi: 10.1007/BF01211602. (Cited on page 185.)

Kowalski, R. A. Algorithm = Logic + Control. *Communications of the Association for Computing Machinery*, 22:424–436, 1979. (Cited on page 5.)

Kripke, S. A. A completeness theorem in modal logic. *Journal of Symbolic Logic*, 24(1):1–14, 1959. (Cited on page 105.)

Kripke, S. A. Semantical analysis of intuitionistic logic I. In J. N. Crossley and M. Dummett, editors, *Formal Systems and Recursive Functions*, pages 92–130. (Proc. 8th Logic Colloq. Oxford 1963) North-Holland, 1965. (Cited on pages 37 and 105.)

Krivine, Jean-Louis. *Lambda-Calcul : Types et Modèles*. Etudes et Recherches en Informatique. Masson, 1990. (Cited on page 19.)

Kuzmin, R. Sur une nouvelle classe de nombres transcendants. *Bulletin de l'Acadmie des Sciences de l'URSS*, pages 585–597, 1930. (Cited on page 282.)

Kwon, Keehang, Gopalan Nadathur, and Debra Sue Wilson. Implementing a notion of modules in the logic programming language λProlog. In Evelina Lamma and Paola Mello, editors, *4th Workshop on Extensions to Logic Programming*, volume 660 of *LNAI*, pages 359–393. Springer, 1993. (Cited on page 106.)

Lambek, J. The mathematics of sentence structure. *American Mathematical Monthly*, 65:154–169, 1958. (Cited on page 228.)

Lambek, Joachim. Categorial grammars and natural language structures. In Richard T. Oehrle, Emmon Bach and Deirdre Wheeler, editors, *Categorial and Categorical Grammars*, volume 32, pages 297–317. D. Reidel, Dordrecht, 1988. (Cited on page 228.)

Landin, P. J. The mechanical evaluation of expressions. *Computer Journal*, 6(5):308–320, 1964. (Cited on pages 262 and 271.)

Laurent, Olivier. Around classical and intuitionistic linear logics. In Anuj Dawar and Erich Grädel, editors *LICS '18: Proceedings of the Thirty-Third Annual*

ACM/IEEE Symposium on Logic in Computer Science, pages 629–638, July 2018. doi: 10.1145/3209108.3209132. (Cited on page 142.)

Leroux, Jérôme and Sylvain Schmitz. Reachability in vector addition systems is primitive-recursive in fixed dimension. In Patricia Bouyer, editor, *Thirty-Fourth Annual ACM/IEEE Symposium on Logic in Computer Science, LICS 2019, Vancouver, BC, Canada, June 24-27, 2019*, pages 1–13. IEEE, 2019. doi: 10.1109/LICS.2019.8785796. (Cited on page 242.)

Liang, Chuck and Dale Miller. Focusing and polarization in linear, intuitionistic, and classical logics. *Theoretical Computer Science*, 410(46):4747–4768, 2009. doi: 10.1016/j.tcs.2009.07.041. Abstract Interpretation and Logic Programming: A Special Issue in honor of professor Giorgio Levi. (Cited on page 105.)

Liang, Chuck and Dale Miller. A focused approach to combining logics. *Annals of Pure and Applied Logic*, 162(9):679–697, 2011. doi: 10.1016/j.apal.2011.01.012. (Cited on page 171.)

Liang, Chuck and Dale Miller. On subexponentials, synthetic connectives, and multi-level delimited control. In Martin Davis, Ansgar Fehnker, Annabelle McIver, and Andrei Voronkov, editors, *Logic for Programming, Artificial Intelligence, and Reasoning (LPAR)*, number 9450 in LNCS, November 2015. doi: 10.1007/978-3-662-48899-7_21. (Cited on page 141.)

Liang, Chuck and Dale Miller. Focusing Gentzen's LK proof system. In Thomas Piecha and Kai Wehmeier, editors, *Peter Schroeder-Heister on Proof-Theoretic Semantics*, Outstanding Contributions to Logic, pages 275–313. Springer, February 2024. doi: 10.1007/978-3-031-50981-0_9. (Cited on pages 140 and 171.)

Lincoln, P., J. Mitchell, A. Scedrov, and N. Shankar. Decision problems for propositional linear logic. *Annals of Pure and Applied Logic*, 56:239–311, 1992. (Cited on page 116.)

Lipton, James and Susana Nieva. Kripke semantics for higher-order type theory applied to constraint logic programming languages. *Theoretical Computer Science*, 712: 1–37, 2018. (Cited on page 214.)

Lloyd, John W. *Foundations of Logic Programming, 2nd Edition*. Springer, 2 edition, 1987. ISBN 3-540-18199-7. (Cited on pages 8 and 105.)

López, Pablo and Ernesto Pimentel. The UMA Forum linear logic programming language. An implementation, January 1998. www.lcc.uma.es/~lopez/umaforum/. (Cited on page 141.)

Mackie, Ian. Lilac: A functional programming language based on linear logic. *Journal of Functional Programming*, 4(4):395–433, 1994. doi: 10.1017/S0956796800001131. (Cited on page 141.)

Marin, Sonia, Dale Miller, Elaine Pimentel, and Marco Volpe. From axioms to synthetic inference rules via focusing. *Annals of Pure and Applied Logic*, 173(5):1–32, 2022. doi: 10.1016/j.apal.2022.103091. (Cited on page 105.)

Marti-Oliet, N. and José Meseguer. From Petri nets to linear logic. *Mathematical Structures in Computer Science*, 1(1):69–101, March 1991. (Cited on page 185.)

Martin-Löf, Per. Constructive mathematics and computer programming. In *Sixth International Congress for Logic, Methodology, and Philosophy of Science*, pages 153–175, Amsterdam, 1982. North-Holland. (Cited on page 3.)

McCarthy, John. Artificial intelligence, logic and formalizing common sense. In Richmond Thomason, editor, *Philosophical Logic and Artificial Intelligence*. Kluwer Academic, 1989. URL www-formal.stanford.edu/jmc/ailogic.dvi. (Cited on page 98.)

McDowell, Raymond and Dale Miller. Reasoning with higher-order abstract syntax in a logical framework. *ACM Transactions on Computational Logic*, 3(1):80–136, 2002. doi: 10.1145/504077.504080. (Cited on page 278.)

McDowell, Raymond, Dale Miller, and Catuscia Palamidessi. Encoding transition systems in sequent calculus. *Theoretical Computer Science*, 294(3):411–437, 2003. doi: 10.1016/S0304-3975(01)00168-2. (Cited on page 106.)

Miller, Dale. A theory of modules for logic programming. In Robert M. Keller, editor, *Third Annual IEEE Symposium on Logic Programming*, pages 106–114, Salt Lake City, Utah, September 1986. (Cited on page 105.)

Miller, Dale. Lexical scoping as universal quantification. In G. Levi and M. Martelli, editors, *Sixth International Logic Programming Conference*, pages 268–283, Lisbon, Portugal, June 1989a. MIT Press. URL www.lix.polytechnique.fr/Labo/Dale.Miller/papers/iclp89.pdf. (Cited on page 215.)

Miller, Dale. A logical analysis of modules in logic programming. *Journal of Logic Programming*, 6(1-2):79–108, January 1989b. doi: 10.1016/0743-1066(89)90031-9. (Cited on page 106.)

Miller, Dale. Unification of simply typed lambda-terms as logic programming. In Koichi Furukawa, editor, *Eighth International Logic Programming Conference*, pages 255–269, Paris, France, June 1991a. MIT Press. (Cited on page 106.)

Miller, Dale. A logic programming language with lambda-abstraction, function variables, and simple unification. *Journal of Logic and Computation*, 1(4):497–536, 1991b. doi: 10.1093/logcom/1.4.497. (Cited on page 214.)

Miller, Dale. Abstract syntax and logic programming. In *Logic Programming: Proceedings of the First Russian Conference on Logic Programming, 14-18 September 1990*, number 592 in LNAI, pages 322–337. Springer, 1992. (Cited on page 105.)

Miller, Dale. The π-calculus as a theory in linear logic: Preliminary results. In E. Lamma and P. Mello, editors, *3rd Workshop on Extensions to Logic Programming*, number 660 in LNCS, pages 242–265, Bologna, Italy, 1993. Springer. doi: 10.1007/3-540-56454-3_13. (Cited on pages 185, 260, and 278.)

Miller, Dale. A proposal for modules in λProlog. In R. Dyckhoff, editor, *4th Workshop on Extensions to Logic Programming*, number 798 in LNCS, pages 206–221. Springer, 1994. (Cited on page 106.)

Miller, Dale. Forum: A multiple-conclusion specification logic. *Theoretical Computer Science*, 165(1):201–232, 1996. doi: 10.1016/0304-3975(96)00045-X. (Cited on pages 133, 169, 186, and 276.)

Miller, Dale. Logic programming and meta-logic. In Helmut Schwichtenberg, editor, *Logic of Computation*, volume 157 of *Nato ASI Series*, pages 265–308. Springer, 1997. doi: 10.1007/978-3-642-58622-4_11. (Cited on page 214.)

Miller, Dale. Encryption as an abstract data-type: An extended abstract. In Iliano Cervesato, editor, *Proceedings of FCS'03: Foundations of Computer Security*, volume 84 of *ENTCS*, pages 18–29. Elsevier, 2003. doi: 10.1016/S1571-0661(04) 80841-7. (Cited on page 260.)

Miller, Dale. Overview of linear logic programming. In Thomas Ehrhard, Jean-Yves Girard, Paul Ruet, and Phil Scott, editors, *Linear Logic in Computer Science*, volume 316 of *London Mathematical Society Lecture Note*, pages 119–150. Cambridge University Press, 2004. (Cited on page 185.)

Miller, Dale. Collection analysis for Horn clause programs. In *Proceedings of PPDP 2006: 8th International ACM SIGPLAN Conference on Principles and Practice of Declarative Programming*, pages 179–188, July 2006. doi: 10.1145/1140335. 1140357. (Cited on page 244.)

Miller, Dale. A proof-theoretic approach to the static analysis of logic programs. In Christoph Benzmüller, Chad E. Brown, Jörg Siekmann, and Richard Statman, editors, *Reasoning in Simple Type Theory: Festschrift in Honor of Peter B. Andrews on His 70th Birthday*, number 17 in Studies in Logic, pages 423–442. College Publications, 2008a. (Cited on page 244.)

Miller, Dale. Formalizing operational semantic specifications in logic. *Concurrency Column of the Bulletin of the EATCS*, October 2008b. (Cited on page 279.)

Miller, Dale. Mechanized metatheory revisited. *Journal of Automated Reasoning*, 63 (3):625–665, October 2019. doi: 10.1007/s10817-018-9483-3. (Cited on page 278.)

Miller, Dale. Reciprocal influences between logic programming and proof theory. *Philosophy & Technology*, 34(1):75–104, March 2021. doi: 10.1007/ s13347-019-00370-x. (Cited on page 8.)

Miller, Dale. LK vs LJ: An origin story for linear logic. Proof Theory Blog, July 2022a. URL https://prooftheory.blog/2022/07/06/lk-vs-lj-an-origin-story-for-linear-logic/. (Cited on page 140.)

Miller, Dale. A survey of the proof-theoretic foundations of logic programming. *Theory and Practice of Logic Programming*, 22(6):859–904, October 2022b. doi: 10.1017/S1471068421000533. Published online November 2021. (Cited on page 8.)

Miller, Dale. A system of inference based on proof search: An extended abstract. In Igor Walukiewicz, editor, *Thirty-Eighth Annual ACM/IEEE Symposium on Logic in Computer Science (LICS 2023)*, pages 1–11, 2023. doi: 10.1109/LICS56636. 2023.10175827. (Cited on page 186.)

Miller, Dale and Gopalan Nadathur. Higher-order logic programming. In Ehud Shapiro, editor, *Proceedings of the Third International Logic Programming Conference*, volume 225 of *LNCS*, pages 448–462, London, June 1986. Springer. doi: 10.1007/ 3-540-16492-8_94. (Cited on pages 105 and 212.)

Miller, Dale and Gopalan Nadathur. *Programming with Higher-Order Logic*. Cambridge University Press, June 2012. doi: 10.1017/CBO9781139021326. (Cited on pages 19, 105, 106, 205, 214, and 215.)

Miller, Dale and Catuscia Palamidessi. Foundational aspects of syntax. *ACM Computing Surveys*, 31, September 1999. doi: 10.1145/333580.333590. (Cited on page 278.)

Miller, Dale and Elaine Pimentel. Linear logic as a framework for specifying sequent calculus. In Jan van Eijck, Vincent van Oostrom, and Albert Visser, editors, *Logic Colloquium '99: Proceedings of the Annual European Summer Meeting of the Association for Symbolic Logic*, Lecture Notes in Logic, pages 111–135. A K Peters Ltd, 2004. (Cited on pages 36, 59, and 186.)

Miller, Dale and Elaine Pimentel. A formal framework for specifying sequent calculus proof systems. *Theoretical Computer Science*, 474:98–116, 2013. doi: 10.1016/j.tcs.2012.12.008. (Cited on pages 36, 59, and 186.)

Miller, Dale, Gopalan Nadathur, and Andre Scedrov. Hereditary Harrop formulas and uniform proof systems. In David Gries, editor, *Second Symposium on Logic in Computer Science*, pages 98–105, Ithaca, NY, June 1987. (Cited on page 32.)

Miller, Dale, Gopalan Nadathur, Frank Pfenning, and Andre Scedrov. Uniform proofs as a foundation for logic programming. *Annals of Pure and Applied Logic*, 51 (1–2):125–157, 1991. doi: 10.1016/0168-0072(91)90068-W. (Cited on pages 32 and 213.)

Miller, Dale, Eve Longini Cohen, and Peter B. Andrews. A look at TPS. In Donald W. Loveland, editor, *Sixth Conference on Automated Deduction*, volume 138 of *LNCS*, pages 50–69, New York, 1982. Springer. (Cited on page 213.)

Milner, Robin. A theory of type polymorphism in programming. *Journal of Computer and System Sciences*, 17(3):348–375, 1978. (Cited on page 278.)

Milner, Robin. LCF: A way of doing proofs with a machine. In Jiří Bečvář, editor, *International Symposium on Mathematical Foundations of Computer Science*, pages 146–159. Springer, 1979. (Cited on page 204.)

Milner, Robin. *A Calculus of Communicating Systems*, volume 92 of *LNCS*. Springer, 1980. (Cited on page 262.)

Milner, Robin. *Communication and Concurrency*. Prentice-Hall International, 1989. ISBN 978-0-13-115007-2. (Cited on page 277.)

Milner, Robin, Mads Tofte, and Robert Harper. *The Definition of Standard ML*. MIT Press, 1990. (Cited on page 279.)

Milner, Robin, Joachim Parrow, and David Walker. A calculus of mobile processes, Part I. *Information and Computation*, 100(1):1–40, September 1992a. doi: 10.1016/0890-5401(92)90008-4. (Cited on pages 246 and 278.)

Milner, Robin, Joachim Parrow, and David Walker. A calculus of mobile processes, Part II. *Information and Computation*, 100(1):41–77, 1992b. doi: 10.1016/0890-5401(92)90009-5. (Cited on pages 265 and 266.)

Mints, Grigorii E. Finite investigations of transfinite derivations. In *Selected Papers in Proof Theory*, pages 17–71. Bibliopolis, 1992. (Cited on pages 152 and 212.)

Mitchell, John C. and Eugenio Moggi. Kripke-style models for typed lambda calculus. *Annals of Pure and Applied Logic*, 51(1–2):99–124, 1991. (Cited on page 105.)

Moortgat, Michael. Categorial type logics. In Johan van Benthem and Alice ter Meulen, editors, *Handbook of Logic and Language*, pages 93–177. Elsevier, 1996. (Cited on page 228.)

Moschovakis, Joan. Intuitionistic logic. In Edward N. Zalta and Uri Nodelman, editors, *The Stanford Encyclopedia of Philosophy*. Metaphysics Research Lab, Stanford University, Summer 2024 edition, 2024. (Cited on page 7.)

Nadathur, Gopalan. *A Higher-Order Logic as the Basis for Logic Programming*. PhD thesis, University of Pennsylvania, May 1987. (Cited on page 214.)

Nadathur, Gopalan and Dale Miller. An Overview of λProlog. In Kenneth A. Bowen and Robert A. Kowalski, editors, *Fifth International Logic Programming Conference*, pages 810–827, Seattle, August 1988. MIT Press. URL www.lix.polytechnique.fr/Labo/Dale.Miller/papers/iclp88.pdf. (Cited on pages 214 and 244.)

Nadathur, Gopalan and Dale Miller. Higher-order Horn clauses. *Journal of the ACM*, 37(4):777–814, October 1990. doi: 10.1145/96559.96570. (Cited on pages 212 and 214.)

Nadathur, Gopalan and Dustin J. Mitchell. System description: Teyjus – A compiler and abstract machine based implementation of λProlog. In H. Ganzinger, editor, *16th Conference on Automated Deduction (CADE)*, number 1632 in LNAI, pages 287–291, Trento, 1999. Springer. doi: 10.1007/3-540-48660-7_25. (Cited on page 105.)

Nadathur, Gopalan and Frank Pfenning. The type system of a higher-order logic programming language. In Frank Pfenning, editor, *Types in Logic Programming*, pages 245–283. MIT Press, 1992. (Cited on pages 19 and 244.)

Negri, Sara. Proof analysis beyond geometric theories: From rule systems to systems of rules. *Journal of Logic and Computation*, 26(2):513–537, 2016. doi: 10.1093/LOGCOM/EXU037. (Cited on page 288.)

Negri, Sara and Jan von Plato. *Structural Proof Theory*. Cambridge University Press, 2001. (Cited on pages 36, 59, and 105.)

Nigam, Vivek and Dale Miller. Algorithmic specifications in linear logic with subexponentials. In António Porto and Francisco Javier López-Fraguas, editors, *ACM SIGPLAN Conference on Principles and Practice of Declarative Programming (PPDP)*, pages 129–140. ACM, 2009. doi: 10.1145/1599410.1599427. (Cited on page 141.)

Nigam, Vivek, Elaine Pimentel, and Giselle Reis. An extended framework for specifying and reasoning about proof systems. *J. of Logic and Computation*, 2014. doi: 10.1093/logcom/exu029. (Cited on page 186.)

Nipkow, Tobias, Lawrence C. Paulson, and Markus Wenzel. *Isabelle/HOL: A Proof Assistant for Higher-Order Logic*. Number 2283 in LNCS. Springer, 2002. doi: 10.1007/3-540-45949-9. (Cited on page 214.)

Okada, Mitsuhiro. An introduction to linear logic: Expressiveness and phase semantics. *Mathematical Society of Japan Memoirs*, 2:255–295, 1998. doi: 10.2969/msjmemoirs/00201C070. (Cited on page 140.)

REFERENCES   311

Olarte, Carlos, Vivek Nigam, and Elaine Pimentel. Subexponential concurrent constraint programming. *Theoretical Computer Science*, 606:98–120, November 2015. doi: 10.1016/j.tcs.2015.06.031. (Cited on page 141.)

Pacholski, Leszek and Andreas Podelski. Set constraints: A pearl in research on constraints. In Gert Smolka, editor, *Principles and Practice of Constraint Programming - CP97*, number 1330 in LNCS, pages 549–562. Springer, 1997. (Cited on page 244.)

Pareschi, Remo and Dale Miller. Extending definite clause grammars with scoping constructs. In David H. D. Warren and Peter Szeredi, editors, *1990 International Conference in Logic Programming*, pages 373–389. MIT Press, June 1990. (Cited on page 186.)

Paulson, Lawrence C. *Isabelle: A Generic Theorem Prover*. Number 828 in LNCS. Springer, 1994. doi: 10.1007/BFb0030541. (Cited on page 18.)

Pfenning, Frank. Elf: A language for logic definition and verified metaprogramming. In Rohit Parikh, editor, *Fourth Symposium on Logic in Computer Science*, pages 313–321, Monterey, CA, June 1989. IEEE. (Cited on page 19.)

Pfenning, Frank. Logic programming in the LF logical framework. In Gérard Huet and Gordon Plotkin, editors, *Logical Frameworks*, pages 149–181. Cambridge University Press, 1991. (Cited on page 214.)

Pfenning, Frank, editor. *Types in Logic Programming*. MIT Press, 1992. (Cited on page 244.)

Pfenning, Frank. Structural cut elimination I: Intuitionistic and classical logic. *Information and Computation*, 157(1/2):84–141, March 2000. (Cited on page 36.)

Pfenning, Frank. Church and Curry: Combining intrinsic and extrinsic typing. In Christoph Benzmüller, Chad E. Brown, Jörg Siekmann, and Richard Statman, editors, *Reasoning in Simple Type Theory: Festschrift in Honor of Peter B. Andrews on His 70th Birthday*, number 17 in Studies in Logic, pages 303–338. College Publications, 2008. (Cited on page 19.)

Pfenning, Frank and Carsten Schürmann. System description: Twelf – A meta-logical framework for deductive systems. In H. Ganzinger, editor, *16th Conference on Automated Deduction (CADE)*, number 1632 in LNAI, pages 202–206, Trento, 1999. Springer. doi: 10.1007/3-540-48660-7_14. (Cited on pages 19 and 278.)

von Plato, Jan Gentzen's proof of normalization for natural deduction. *Bulletin of Symbolic Logic*, 14(2):240–257, June 2008. doi: 10.2178/bsl/1208442829. (Cited on page 59.)

von Plato, Jan. The development of proof theory. In Edward N. Zalta, editor, *The Stanford Encyclopedia of Philosophy*. Metaphysics Research Lab, Stanford University, winter 2018 edition, 2018. (Cited on page 7.)

Plotkin, Gordon D. A structural approach to operational semantics. DAIMI FN-19, Aarhus University, Aarhus, Denmark, September 1981. (Cited on page 262.)

Plotkin, Gordon D. A structural approach to operational semantics. *Journal of Logic and Algebraic Programming*, 60-61:17–139, 2004. (Cited on page 262.)

Prawitz, Dag. *Natural Deduction*. Almqvist & Wiksell, 1965. (Cited on page 42.)

Prior, A. N. The runabout inference-ticket. *Analysis*, 21(2):38–39, December 1960. (Cited on page 48.)

Pym, David and James Harland. The uniform proof-theoretic foundation of linear logic programming. *Journal of Logic and Computation*, 4(2):175–207, 1994. doi: 10.1093/logcom/4.2.175. (Cited on page 185.)

Rathjen, Michael and Wilfried Sieg. Proof theory. In Edward N. Zalta, editor, *The Stanford Encyclopedia of Philosophy*. Metaphysics Research Lab, Stanford University, fall 2020 edition, 2020. (Cited on page 7.)

Reppy, John H. CML: A higher-order concurrent language. In *ACM SIGPLAN Conference on Programming Language Design and Implementation*, pages 293–305, June 1991. (Cited on page 276.)

Robinson, J. A. A machine-oriented logic based on the resolution principle. *Journal of the ACM*, 12:23–41, January 1965. (Cited on pages 4 and 63.)

Schroeder-Heister, Peter. Rules of definitional reflection. In M. Vardi, editor, *Eighth Symposium on Logic in Computer Science*, pages 222–232. IEEE Computer Society Press, IEEE, June 1993. doi: 10.1109/LICS.1993.287585. (Cited on pages 106, 142, and 286.)

Simmons, Robert J. Structural focalization. *ACM Transactions on Computational Logic*, 15(3):21, 2014. doi: 10.1145/2629678. (Cited on page 171.)

Sørensen, Morten Heine and Pawel Urzyczyn. *Lectures on the Curry-Howard Isomorphism*, volume 149 of *Studies in Logic*. Elsevier, 2006. (Cited on page 19.)

Statman, Richard. Bounds for proof-search and speed-up in the predicate calculus. *Annals of Mathematical Logic*, 15:225–287, 1978. (Cited on page 36.)

Statman, Richard. Intuitionistic propositional logic is polynomial-space complete. *Theoretical Computer Science*, 9:67–72, 1979. (Cited on page 60.)

Tarau, Paul. Program transformations and WAM-support for the compilation of definite metaprograms. In *Proceedings of the First and Second Russian Conference on Logic Programming*, number 592 in LNAI, pages 462–473. Springer, 1992. (Cited on page 268.)

Tärnlund, Sten-Ake. Horn clause computability. *BIT*, 17:215–226, 1977. doi: 10.1007/BF01932293. (Cited on page 106.)

Tassi, Enrico. Elpi: Rule-based meta-languge for Rocq. In *Proceedings of CoqPL 2025*. ACM, January 2025. (Cited on page 105.)

Tiu, Alwen. *A Logical Framework for Reasoning about Logical Specifications*. PhD thesis, Pennsylvania State University, May 2004. URL https://etda.libraries.psu.edu/files/final_submissions/119. (Cited on page 268.)

Tiu, Alwen and Dale Miller. Proof search specifications of bisimulation and modal logics for the π-calculus. *ACM Transactions on Computational Logic*, 11(2):13:1–13:35, 2010. doi: 10.1145/1656242.1656248. (Cited on page 268.)

Tiu, Alwen, Gopalan Nadathur, and Dale Miller. Mixing finite success and finite failure in an automated prover. In Christoph Benzmüller, John Harrison, and Carsten Schürmann, editors, *Empirically Successful Automated Reasoning in Higher-Order Logics (ESHOL'05)*, pages 79–98, December 2005. (Cited on page 106.)

Troelstra, Anne Sjerp and Helmut Schwichtenberg. *Basic Proof Theory*. Cambridge University Press, 1996. (Cited on page 186.)

Troelstra, Anne Sjerp, editor. *Metamathematical Investigation of Intuitionistic Arithmetic and Analysis*, volume 344 of *Lecture Notes in Mathematics*. Springer, 1973. (Cited on page 42.)

Troelstra, Anne Sjerp and Dirk van Dalen. *Constructivism in Mathematics*, volume 1. North-Holland, 1988. (Cited on page 37.)

Urban, Christian. Forum and Its Implementations. Master's thesis, University of St. Andrews, December 1997. (Cited on page 141.)

Index

!, bang exponential, 111
?, question mark exponential, 111
∥, symbol denoting $\invamp$, 140
∷ signature declaration for sequents, 18
: : nonempty list constructor, 96
⊸, linear equivalence, 121, 173
(‡), xii

Abella, proof assistant, 19, 278
absorb inference rule, 124, 153
abstract data types, 98, 215, 253
abstract evaluation system (AES), 270
abstract logic programming language, 63, 134
abstract machines, 262, 270
additive connective, 109
additive inference rule, 27
admissible rule, 53
agents
  formulas, 258
  identifier, 254
  state atom, 254
  state predicate, 254
  theory, 254
α-conversion, 10
alphabet, 218
alternating finite automata, 226
Andreoli, Jean-Marc, 32, 169, 260
answer-set programming, xii
append, appending two lists, 97
application of substitution θ to t, 10
argument types, 13
associated sequent, 77, 145
asynchronous phase, 169

atomic cut_k rule, 152
atomic formula, 16
atomic initial rule, 44, 193
atomic key cut, 152
atomically closed proof, 44, 62
axioms, 20, 25

backchaining, 73, 90, 105, 290
backchaining inference rule, 290
backchaining phase, 32
bang !, 111
Barr's Theorem, 288
β-conversion, 10
β-normal form, 10, 188
$\beta\eta$-long normal form, 14
big-step semantic specification, 262, 265
binary clauses, 223, 263, 268
binder mobility, 26
border cut, 150
border sequent, 138
  for $\mathcal{L}_0$ proofs, 92
  for $\Downarrow \mathcal{L}_2$-proofs, 138

C-proof, 40
call-by-name evaluation, 4
call-by-value evaluation, 4, 265
candidats de réductibilité, 188, 200
chemical abstract machine, 262
Church, Alonzo, 2, 9, 214, 263
Church numerals, 11
classical linear logic, 142
classical logic, 2
classical provability, $\Sigma :: \Delta \vdash_C B$, 40

314

INDEX

clausal order, order(·), 16
clause, 69
collection analysis, 229
    list approximations, 243
    multiset approximations, 233
    set approximations, 238
completeness, 43, 87, 188
computation-as-deduction, 3
computation-as-model, 3
concurrency primitives, 276
Concurrent ML (CML), 276
conjunction $\wedge$, 2
conjunctive normal form, 4
conservativity of $\Downarrow \mathcal{L}_2$ over $\Downarrow \mathcal{L}_1$ and $\Downarrow \mathcal{L}_0$, 138
consistency, 33
constraint programming, xii
context occurrence of a formula, 27
continuation-passing style (CPS), 268
contraction, structural rule, 24
contrapositive of $\multimap$, 137
CPS transformation, 268
Curry, Haskell, 12
Curry–Howard correspondence, xii, 19
curry/uncurry equivalences, 65, 121
Curry's paradox, 12, 142, 281, 286
cut rule, 24
    atomic cut_k, 152
    exponential cuts, $cut\,!$, $cut\,?$, 150
    for $\Downarrow^+\mathcal{L}_0$, 81
    for $\Downarrow^+\mathcal{L}_2$, 150
    key cut, cut_k, 150
    linear cut, cut_l, 150
cut-admissibility theorem for $\Downarrow \mathcal{L}_1$, 143
cut-elimination procedure, 59
cut-elimination theorem, 33
    for $\Downarrow^+\mathcal{L}_0$, 84
    for $\Downarrow^+\mathcal{L}_2$, 159
    for $\Downarrow \mathcal{N}^+$, 200
cut-free proof, 33, 49
cut-simulation, 190, 214

$\mathcal{D}_1$, fohc clauses, 64
$\mathcal{D}_2$, fohh clauses, 68
De Bruijn notation, 271
definite clauses, 64
degree of a formula, 151
dependently type λ-terms, 19
dereliction rules, 116

derivable rule, 53
derivation, as partial proof, 29
diamond translation
    $(\cdot)^\diamond$, removing implications, 124
disjunction $\vee$, 2
disjunction property, 63, 105
don't-care nondeterminism, 58
don't-know nondeterminism, 58
dynamic semantics, 278
dynamics of proof search
    $\Downarrow \mathcal{L}_1$, 126
    $\Downarrow \mathcal{L}_2$, 137
    fohc, 98
    fohh, 101

eigenvariables, 18, 19, 26
Elementary Theory of Types, 9
Elf, logic programming language, 19
Elpi, implementation of λProlog, 105
embedding fohh into linear logic, 127
endsequent, 29
ϵ, empty word, 219
ϵ-transition, 219
equivalence $\equiv$, 51
equivalent in linear logic, $\dashv\vdash$, 116
η-conversion, 10
ex falso quodlibet, 21, 55, 57
exchange, structural rule, 24
excluded middle, 37, 41
excluded middle inference rule, 57
existence property, 63, 105
existential quantifier, $\exists_\tau$, 15
explode inference rule, 57
exponential prefixes, 117, 292
exponentials $!$, $?$, 41, 116

Fibonacci numbers, 5, 218, 227
finite automata, 219
first-order Horn clauses, xi, 64
first-order logic, 2, 16
flexible atomic formula, 211
focused proofs, 31, 53, 124
fohc, first-order Horn clauses, 64
fohh, first-order hereditary Harrop formulas, 68
$\Downarrow$fohh-proof, 73, 93
Forum presentation of linear logic, xi, 133, 246
forward chaining, 75, 105, 290

forward-chaining inference rule, 290
Frege proofs, 20, 25, 34
function symbol of arity n, 15

$\mathcal{G}_1$, fohc goals, 64
$\mathcal{G}_2$, fohh goals, 68
G-proof, 56
G3ip and G4ip proof systems, 186
Gamma programming language, 262
Gentzen, Gerhard, xi, 2, 17, 36, 38, 55, 109
Girard, Jean-Yves, 2, 32, 59, 127, 141
goal reduction, 73
goal-directed proof search, 62, 105
goal-reduction phase, 32

Harrop formulas, 71, 105, 289
hereditary Harrop formulas, 68
higher-order hereditary Harrop formulas, xi, 213
higher-order Horn clauses, 93, 212
higher-order logic, 16
higher-order pattern unification, 214
higher-order programming, 189, 202
Hindley–Milner type inference, 278
HOL proof assistant, 19
Horn clauses, 63
hyperexponential function, 36

I-proof, 40
identity rules, 23
implication
 classical and intuitionistic $\supset$, 2, 16
 intuitionistic in linear logic $\Rightarrow$, 120
 linear $\multimap$, 120
incompleteness theorems, 188
inductive definitions, 106
inference rule permutabilities, 134
inference rules
 identity, 23
 introduction, 23
 structural, 23
`infixr`, λProlog infix declaration, 96, 180
initial rule, 24
instan inference rule, 54, 87
interpretation, 87
introduction rules, 23
intuitionistic implication in linear logic $\Rightarrow$, 120
intuitionistic linear logic, 142

intuitionistic logic, 2
intuitionistic provability, $\Sigma :: \Delta \vdash B$, 40
invertible inference rule, 31, 32, 52, 59, 108, 118
IO-proof system, 129
Isabelle proof assistant, 19

Ketonen, Oiva, 60
key-cut rule, 81, 150
 for $\Downarrow^+\mathcal{L}_0$, 81
 for $\Downarrow^+\mathcal{L}_2$, 150
Kowalski, Robert, 5
Kripke models, 37, 87, 171
 canonical model, 87
Krivine machine, 271

L, proof system for linear logic, 112
L-formulas, 112
$\mathcal{L}_0 = \{\mathsf{t}, \wedge, \supset, \forall\}$, 68, 76
$\mathcal{L}_0$-formula, 76
$\Downarrow \mathcal{L}_0$-proof system, 68, 76
$\Downarrow \mathcal{L}_0'$ system, 90
$\mathcal{L}_0$-sequent, 138
$\mathcal{L}_1 = \{\top, \&, \multimap, \Rightarrow, \forall\}$, 122
$\mathcal{L}_1$-formula, 122
$\Downarrow \mathcal{L}_1$-proof system, 125
$\mathcal{L}_1$-sequent, 137
$\mathcal{L}_2 = \{\top, \&, \multimap, \Rightarrow, \forall, \bot, \invamp, ?\}$, 133
$\mathcal{L}_2$-formula, 133
$\mathcal{L}_2$-proof system, 134, 136
$\Downarrow^q \mathcal{L}_2$-proof system, 153
$\Downarrow^+ \mathcal{L}_2$-proof system, 150
λProlog, xi, xii, 19, 95
λProlog implementations
 Elpi, 105
 Teyjus, 105
λ-calculus, 9, 261
λ-term, untyped, 263
λ-term, simply typed, 13
λ-term, untyped, 9
Lambek, Joachim, 228
least fixed points, 106
left-bounded zone, 122, 134
left-introduction phase, 73
left-unbounded zone, 122, 134
Leibniz equality, 190, 202, 212
LF, logical framework, 19
linear equivalence $\circ\!\!-\!\!\circ$, 121, 173
linear implication $\multimap$, 112, 120

INDEX 317

linear logic, 2, 41, 111
linear logic negation, $B^\perp$, 121
linear logic programming, 172
list constructors, 96
    :: nonempty list constructor, 96
    nil empty list constructor, 96
literals, 63
LJ proof system, 38, 55, 109
LJF proof system, 105
LK proof system, 38, 55, 109
logic variables, 58
logical constants, 15
Lolli, xi, 127, 173

M-proof, 55, 67
MALL, multiplicative additive linear logic, 115, 141
measure $|\Xi|$, 151
medial entailment, 120
memb, membership in list, 97, 206
metalogic, 178
minimal logic provability, 55
mix entailment, 120
mobility of binders, 26
modus ponens, 21
monotonicity property, 101
most general unifiers, 4
multifocusing proof system, 141
multiple-conclusion proof system, 40
multiple-conclusion sequent, 23
multiple-conclusion uniform proofs, 134
multiplicative connective, 109
multiplicative inference rule, 27
multiset expression, 233
multiset rewriting, 216, 262
    on the left, 176
    on the right, 181
multiset rewriting system, 176

n-way synchronization, 256
natural deduction, 59, 178
near-focused proof system, 191, 192
Needham–Schroeder Shared Key Protocol, 249
negation ¬, 2, 16
negation defined using ⊃ and f, 41
negation in sequent calculus, 55
negation normal form, 117
negation-as-failure, xii, 5, 106

negative subformula occurrence, 17
nil empty list constructor, 96
non-atomic formula, 16
non-invertible inference rule, 32
nondeterminism, don't know vs don't care, 58

o, the Greek letter omicron, 2, 15
    the type of formulas, 15
object logic, 178
oplus, ⊕, 115
ord(τ), order of type τ, 13
order(B), clausal order of formula B, 16

P-proof system, 122, 123
par, ⅋, 115
paths in a formula, $B \uparrow P$, 76, 144
permutation of inference rules, 30
π-calculus, 246, 261, 264, 266
polarity, 118, 141
polymorphic typing, 13, 19, 96, 131, 244
positive subformula occurrence, 17
possible world semantics, 37
Post correspondence problem, 227
predicate symbol of arity n, 15
primitive types, 12
Prior, A. N., 48
Prolog, xi
Prolog's cut (!), 5
promotion rule, 114, 116
proof search, xi
proof system, 29
proof systems, focused, 31
    IO, variant of $\Downarrow \mathcal{L}_1$, 129
    $\Downarrow \mathcal{L}_0$, 68
    $\Downarrow^+ \mathcal{L}_0$, 81
    $\Downarrow \mathcal{L}_0'$, 90
    $\Downarrow \mathcal{L}_1$, 125
    $\mathcal{L}_2$, 134
    $\Downarrow^+ \mathcal{L}_2$, 150
    $\Downarrow \mathcal{L}_2^\omega$, 191
proof systems, near focused
    $\Downarrow \mathcal{N}$, 191
    $\Downarrow \mathcal{N}^+$, 199
proof systems, unfocused, 31
    C (classical), 40
    I (intuitionistic), 40
    L (linear), 112
    M (minimal), 67
    P (for $\mathcal{L}_1$), 122, 123

proof nets, 141
proof-normalization, 3
proof-search, 3
propositional constants, 15
propositional logic, 2, 16
pumping lemmas, 101
pushdown automaton, 226

quantificational logic, 2
question mark ?, 111

rank, 151
redex, in cut-elimination proof, 153
relational composition, 205
Rep, repetition rule, 153
replacing subformulas, $\Sigma :: C \bowtie D$, 51
resolution refutations, 4, 8, 105
resource-indexed model, 171
restart rule, 44
restaurant semantics, 140
reverse a list
  in *fohc* and *fohh*, 99, 236
  in linear logic, 207, 209
  proof of symmetry, 207, 214
right-bounded zone, 122, 134
right-introduction phase, 73
right-unbounded zone, 134
rigid atomic formula, 211
Robinson, J. A., 63

S, the set of sorts, 12
scope extrusion, 100, 246, 253
scoped constant, 231
search semantics, 61
SECD machine, 271
security protocol, 245
sequent calculus, xi, 2
sequent calculus proofs, 29
sequents, 17
  left-hand side, 17
  one-sided, $\vdash \Delta$, 17
  right-hand side, 17
  with signature, $\Sigma :: \Gamma \vdash \Delta$, 29
  two-sided, $\Gamma \vdash \Delta$, 17
  ᴢᴏɴᴇs, 17
Σ inhabits primitive type, 43
Σ_0, signature of non-logical constants, 15

Σ_{-1}, signature of logical connectives, 15, 18, 231
Σ-formula, 15
Σ-term of type τ, 14
signature over S, 13
Simple Theory of Types, 2, 9, 19
simple types, 12
simultaneous rule application, 134
single-conclusion proof system, 39
single-conclusion sequents, 39, 137
size of a formula, $|B|$, 83
Skolem functions, 5
Skolem normal form, 4
SLD resolution, 4, 8, 104
small-step semantic specification, 262
sorts, a.k.a. primitive types, 12
soundness, 43, 87, 188
stable models, xii
static semantics, 278
sterile jar specification, 99, 102
strengthening, 54, 80, 151
structural operational semantics, 262
structural rules, 23
subexponentials, 141
subformula property, 34, 189
subject occurrence of a formula, 27
substitution, $M[N/x]$, 10
substitution, $t\theta$, 10
switch entailment, 120
synchronous phase, 169
syntactic categories, 13, 263
syntactic types, 13
synthetic inference rules, 53, 92, 105, 138, 211

tacticals, 204
tactics, 204
target type, 13
tensor, $\otimes$, 114
term rewriting system, 270
Teyjus, implementation of λProlog, 105
third-order unification, 227
thread in a $\Downarrow \mathcal{L}_2$-proof, 151
tonk, 48, 284
typing judgment, $\Sigma \Vdash t : \tau$, 13, 26

unfocused proofs, 31
unification, 4, 58, 227
unification of simply typed λ-terms, 213

uniform proofs, 32, 62
    multiple-conclusion version, 134
    single-conclusion version, 63
universal quantifier, $\forall_\tau$, 15
untyped λ-terms, 263

weakening, structural rule, 24
with, &, 114
word, 219
world, in a Kripke model, 87

For EU product safety concerns, contact us at Calle de José Abascal, 56–1°, 28003 Madrid, Spain or eugpsr@cambridge.org.

www.ingramcontent.com/pod-product-compliance
Ingram Content Group UK Ltd.
Pitfield, Milton Keynes, MK11 3LW, UK
UKHW022128020426
469639UK00006B/43